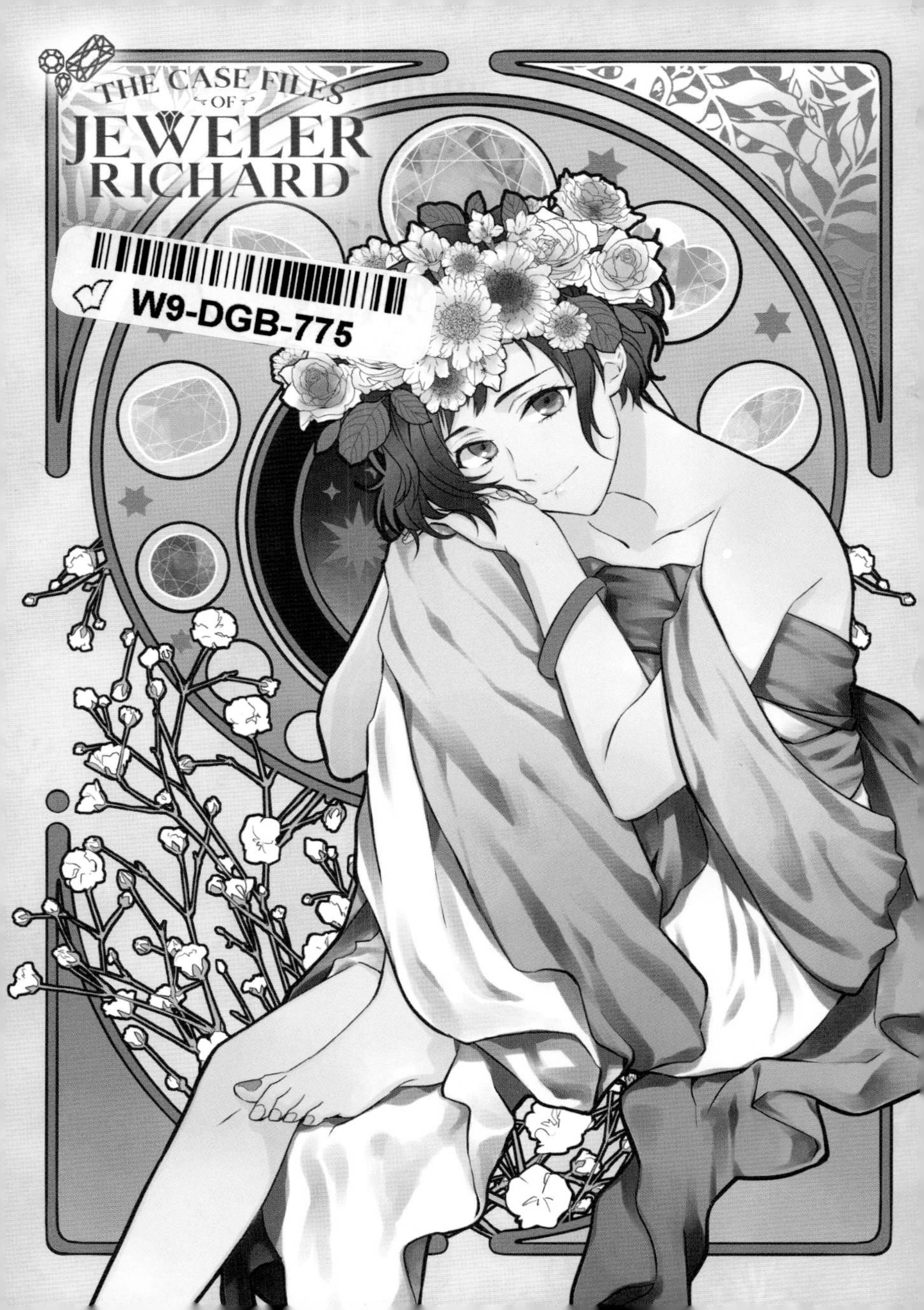
THE CASE FILES
OF
JEWELER
RICHARD

Contents

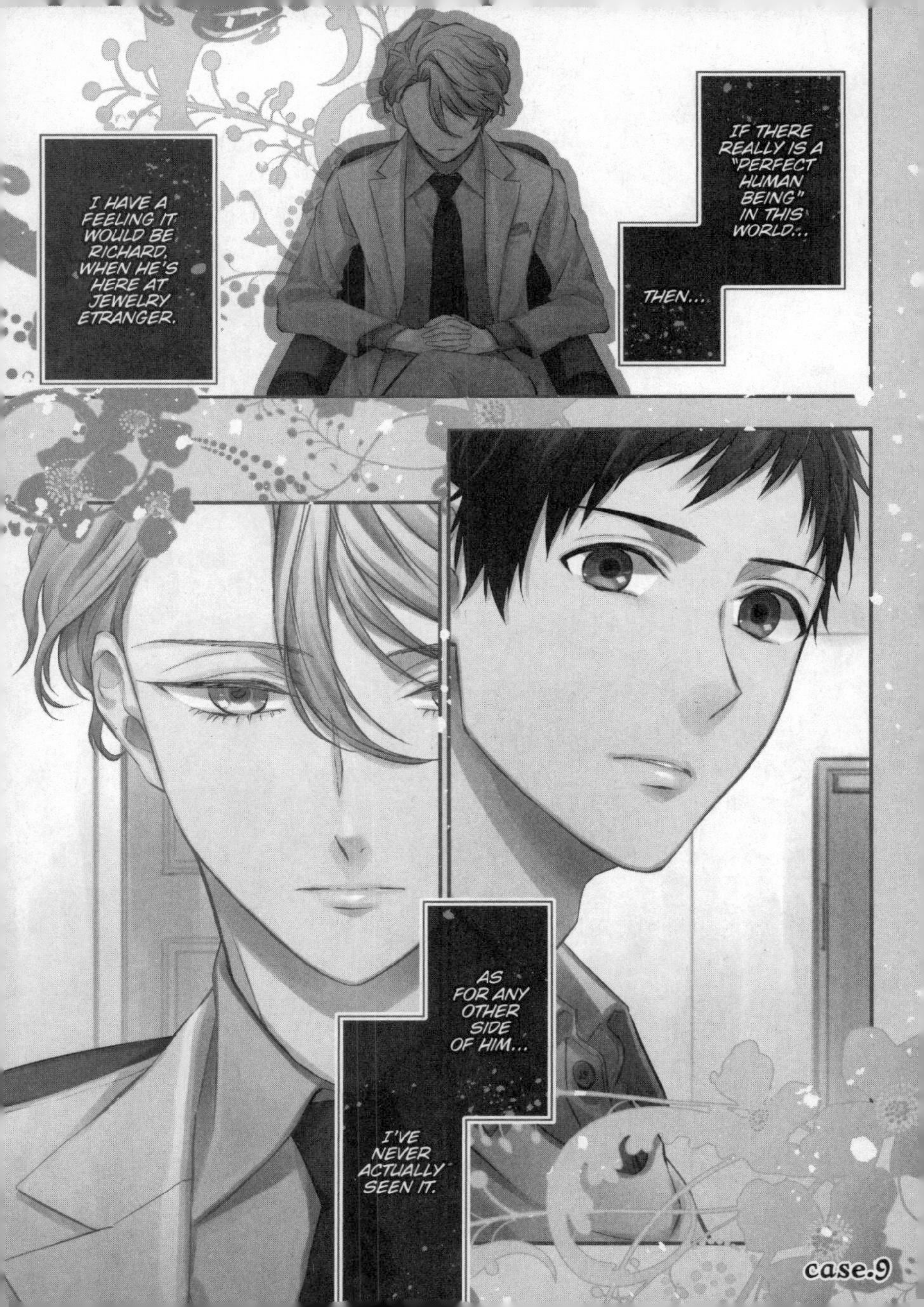
IF THERE REALLY IS A "PERFECT HUMAN BEING" IN THIS WORLD...
THEN...
I HAVE A FEELING IT WOULD BE RICHARD, WHEN HE'S HERE AT JEWELRY ETRANGER.
AS FOR ANY OTHER SIDE OF HIM...
I'VE NEVER ACTUALLY SEEN IT.
case.9

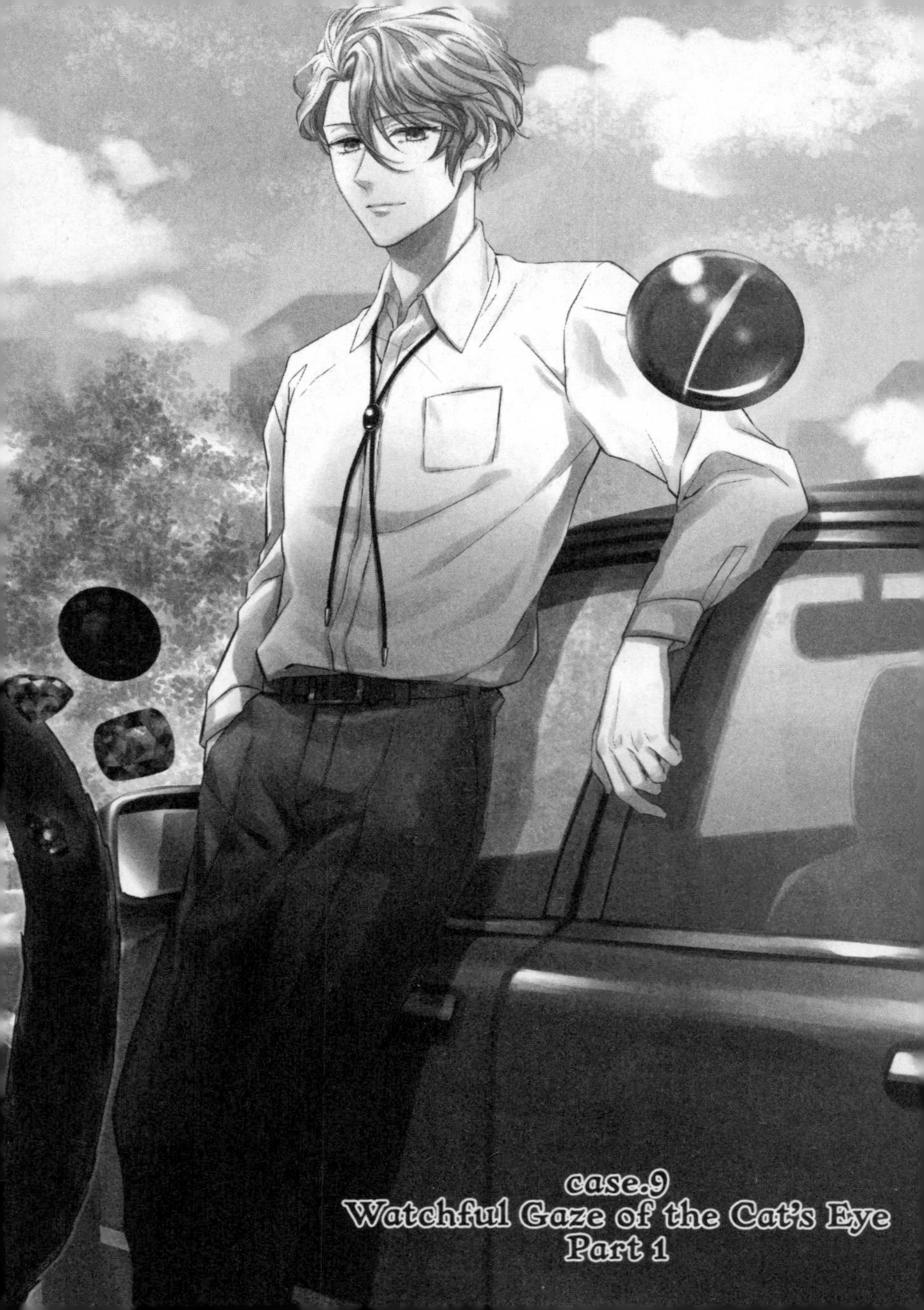

case.9
Watchful Gaze of the Cat's Eye
Part 1

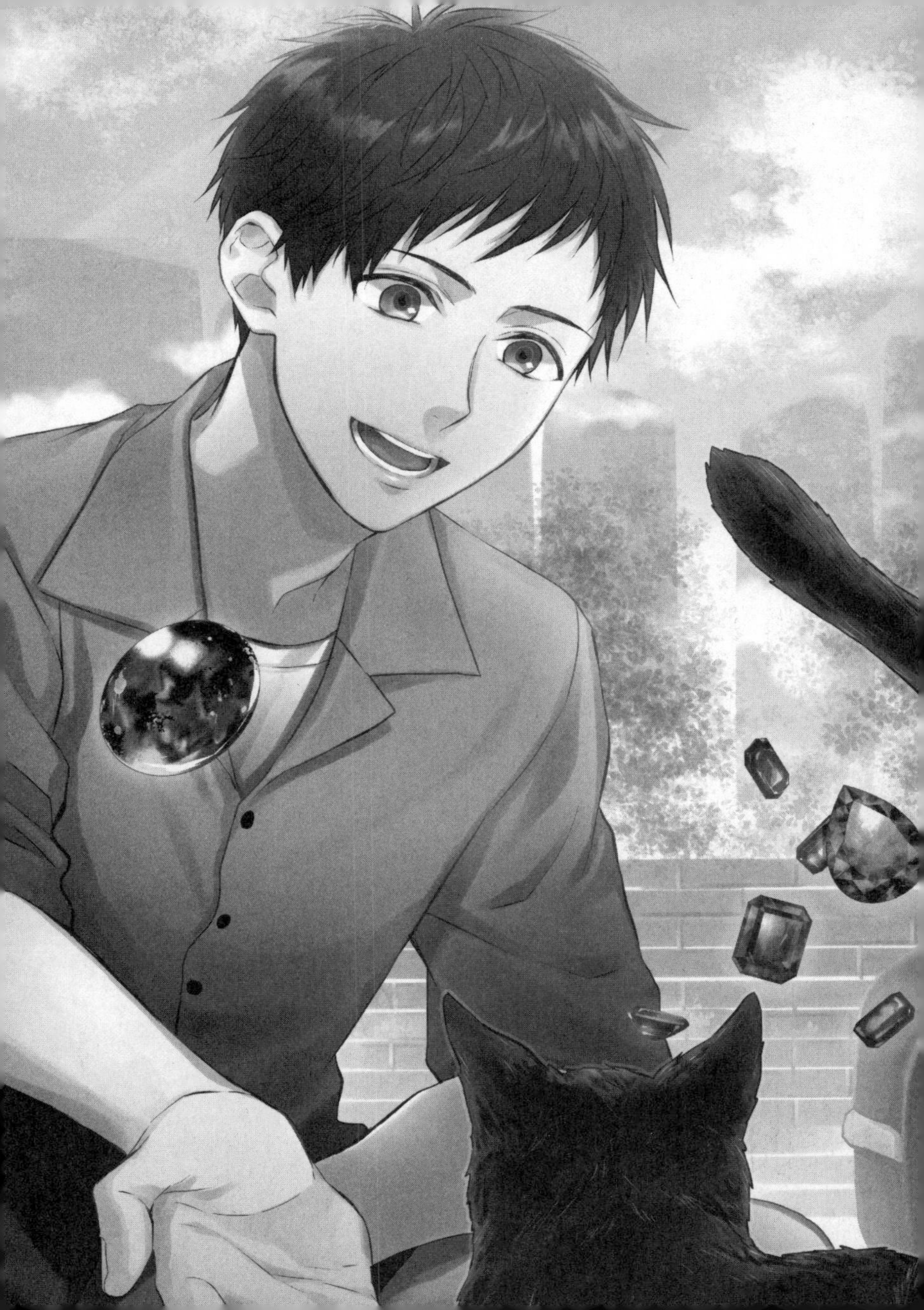

THE CASE FILES
OF
JEWELER
RICHARD

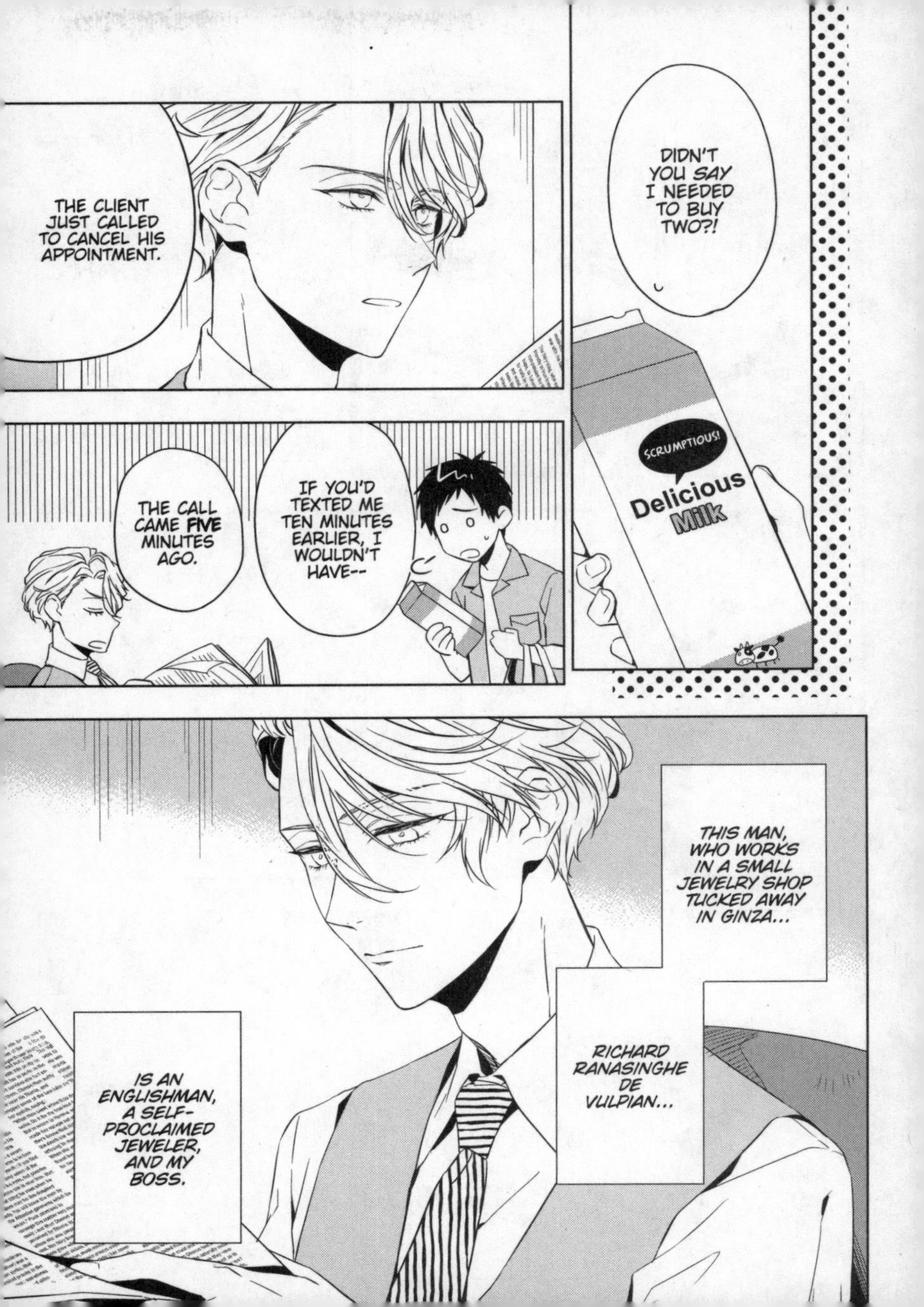
DIDN'T YOU SAY I NEEDED TO BUY TWO?!
SCRUMPTIOUS!
Delicious Milk
THE CLIENT JUST CALLED TO CANCEL HIS APPOINTMENT.
IF YOU'D TEXTED ME TEN MINUTES EARLIER, I WOULDN'T HAVE--
THE CALL CAME FIVE MINUTES AGO.
THIS MAN, WHO WORKS IN A SMALL JEWELRY SHOP TUCKED AWAY IN GINZA...
RICHARD RANASINGHE DE VULPIAN...
IS AN ENGLISHMAN, A SELF-PROCLAIMED JEWELER, AND MY BOSS.

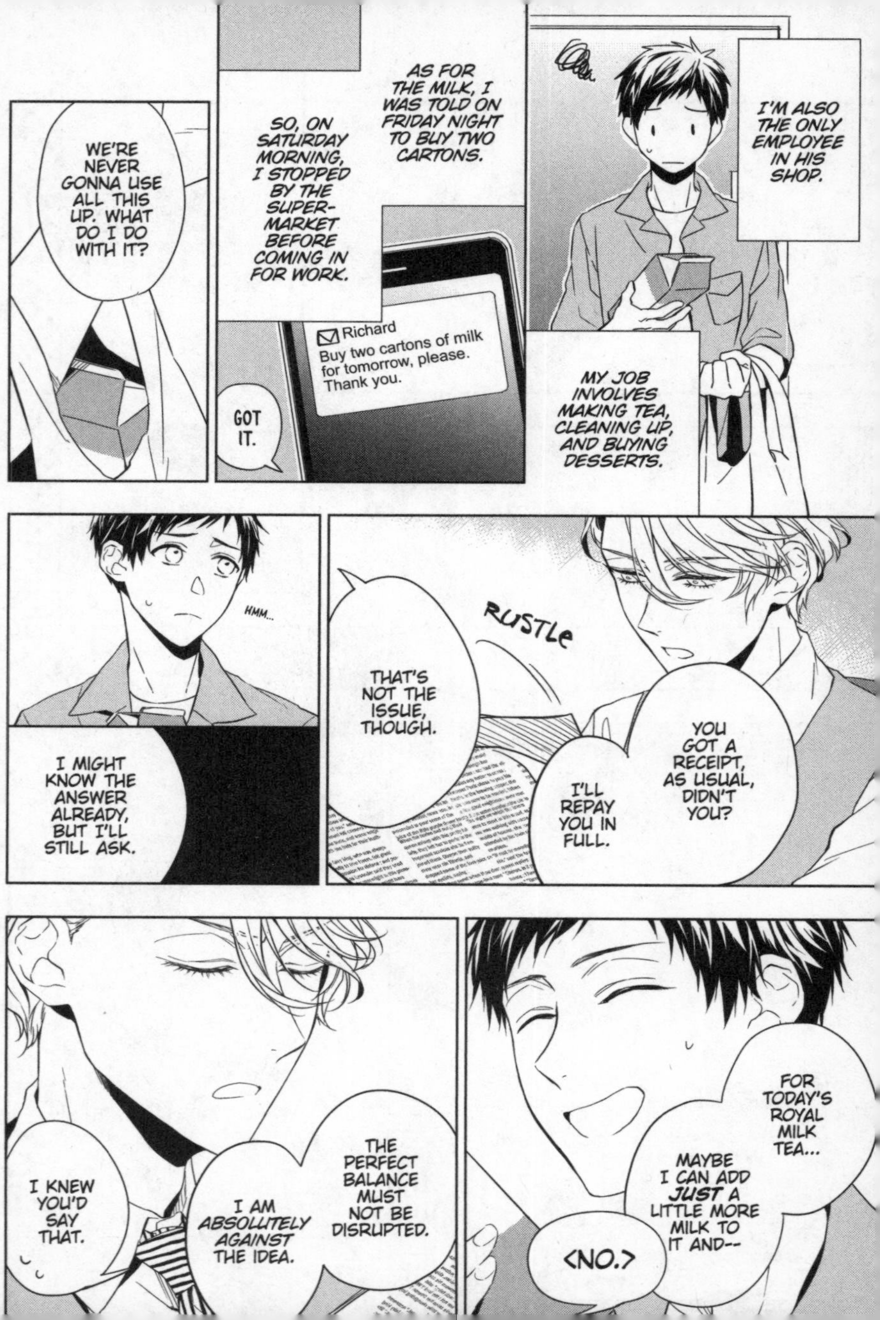
I'M ALSO THE ONLY EMPLOYEE IN HIS SHOP.
MY JOB INVOLVES MAKING TEA, CLEANING UP, AND BUYING DESSERTS.
AS FOR THE MILK, I WAS TOLD ON FRIDAY NIGHT TO BUY TWO CARTONS.
Richard
Buy two cartons of milk for tomorrow, please. Thank you.
GOT IT.
SO, ON SATURDAY MORNING, I STOPPED BY THE SUPER-MARKET BEFORE COMING IN FOR WORK.
WE'RE NEVER GONNA USE ALL THIS UP. WHAT DO I DO WITH IT?
RUSTLE
YOU GOT A RECEIPT, AS USUAL, DIDN'T YOU?
I'LL REPAY YOU IN FULL.
THAT'S NOT THE ISSUE, THOUGH.
HMM...
I MIGHT KNOW THE ANSWER ALREADY, BUT I'LL STILL ASK.
FOR TODAY'S ROYAL MILK TEA...
MAYBE I CAN ADD *JUST* A LITTLE MORE MILK TO IT AND--
<NO.>
THE PERFECT BALANCE MUST NOT BE DISRUPTED.
I AM *ABSOLUTELY* AGAINST THE IDEA.
I KNEW YOU'D SAY THAT.

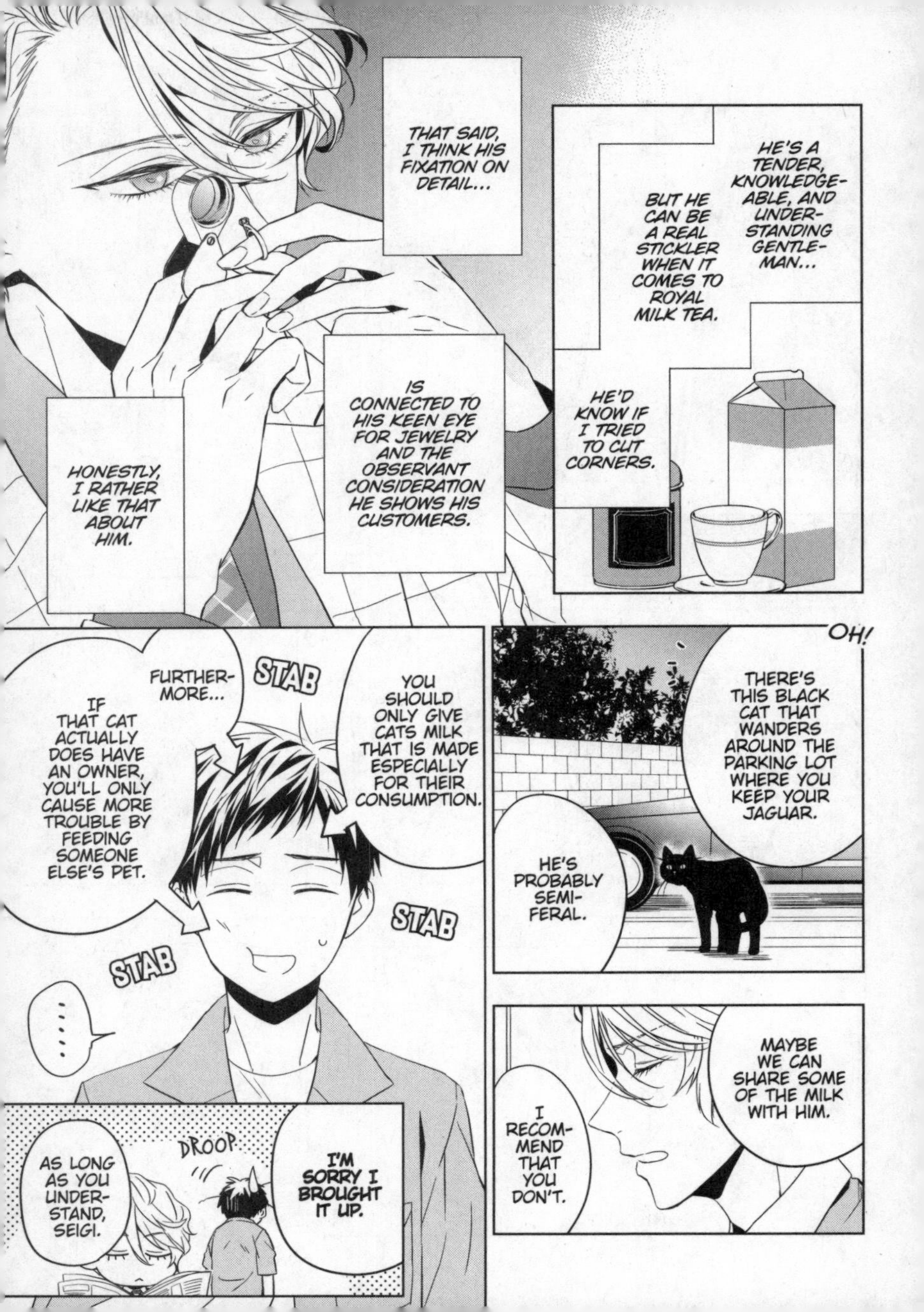
HE'S A TENDER, KNOWLEDGE-ABLE, AND UNDER-STANDING GENTLE-MAN...
BUT HE CAN BE A REAL STICKLER WHEN IT COMES TO ROYAL MILK TEA.
HE'D KNOW IF I TRIED TO CUT CORNERS.
THAT SAID, I THINK HIS FIXATION ON DETAIL...
IS CONNECTED TO HIS KEEN EYE FOR JEWELRY AND THE OBSERVANT CONSIDERATION HE SHOWS HIS CUSTOMERS.
HONESTLY, I RATHER LIKE THAT ABOUT HIM.
OH!
THERE'S THIS BLACK CAT THAT WANDERS AROUND THE PARKING LOT WHERE YOU KEEP YOUR JAGUAR.
HE'S PROBABLY SEMI-FERAL.
MAYBE WE CAN SHARE SOME OF THE MILK WITH HIM.
I RECOM-MEND THAT YOU DON'T.
YOU SHOULD ONLY GIVE CATS MILK THAT IS MADE ESPECIALLY FOR THEIR CONSUMPTION.
STAB
FURTHER-MORE...
IF THAT CAT ACTUALLY DOES HAVE AN OWNER, YOU'LL ONLY CAUSE MORE TROUBLE BY FEEDING SOMEONE ELSE'S PET.
STAB
STAB
......
I'M SORRY I BROUGHT IT UP.
DROOP
AS LONG AS YOU UNDER-STAND, SEIGI.

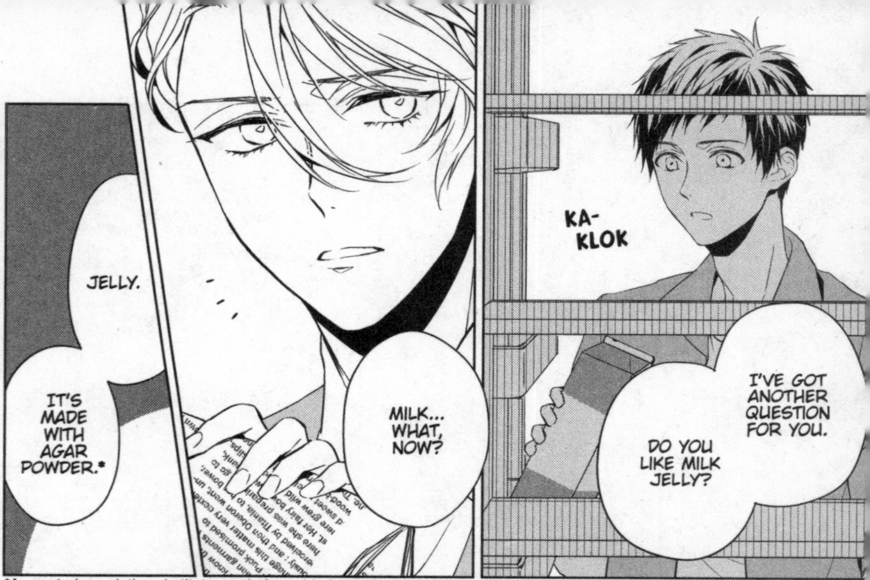
KA-KLOK
I'VE GOT ANOTHER QUESTION FOR YOU.
DO YOU LIKE MILK JELLY?
MILK... WHAT, NOW?
JELLY.
IT'S MADE WITH AGAR POWDER.*

*A vegetarian gelatin substitute, made from dried red algae. It's frequently used as a thickening or gelling agent in Asian cuisine, especially sweets.

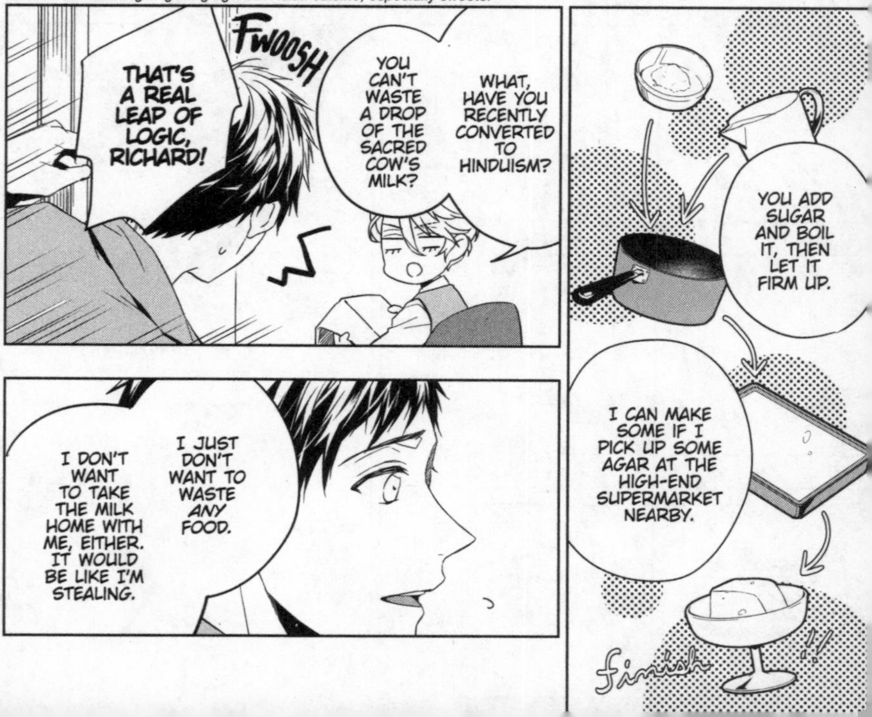
YOU ADD SUGAR AND BOIL IT, THEN LET IT FIRM UP.
I CAN MAKE SOME IF I PICK UP SOME AGAR AT THE HIGH-END SUPERMARKET NEARBY.
finish!!
WHAT, HAVE YOU RECENTLY CONVERTED TO HINDUISM?
YOU CAN'T WASTE A DROP OF THE SACRED COW'S MILK?
FWOOSH
THAT'S A REAL LEAP OF LOGIC, RICHARD!
I JUST DON'T WANT TO WASTE *ANY* FOOD.
I DON'T WANT TO TAKE THE MILK HOME WITH ME, EITHER. IT WOULD BE LIKE I'M STEALING.

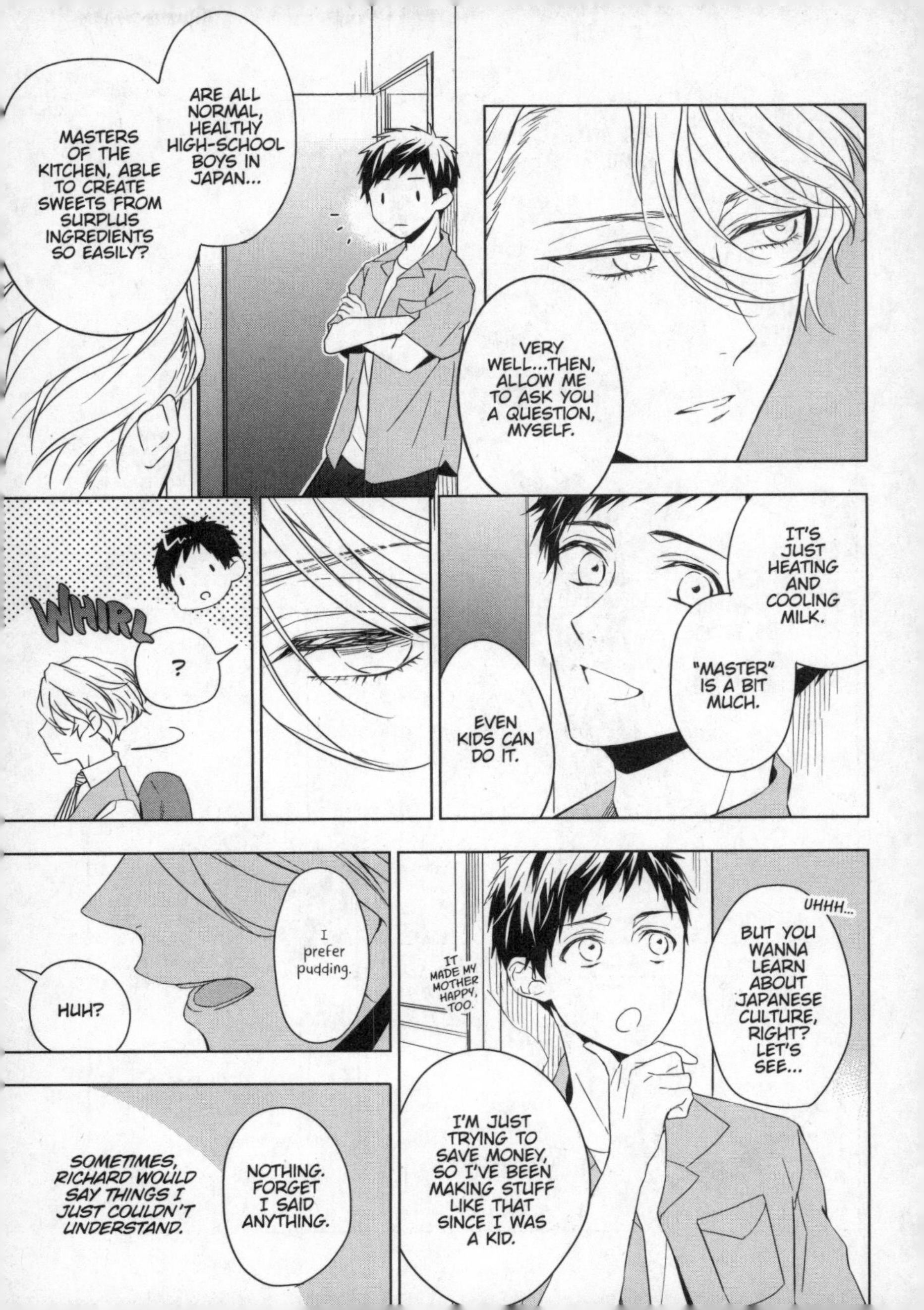
VERY WELL...THEN, ALLOW ME TO ASK YOU A QUESTION, MYSELF.
ARE ALL NORMAL, HEALTHY HIGH-SCHOOL BOYS IN JAPAN...
MASTERS OF THE KITCHEN, ABLE TO CREATE SWEETS FROM SURPLUS INGREDIENTS SO EASILY?
IT'S JUST HEATING AND COOLING MILK.
"MASTER" IS A BIT MUCH.
EVEN KIDS CAN DO IT.
WHIRL
?
UHHH...
BUT YOU WANNA LEARN ABOUT JAPANESE CULTURE, RIGHT? LET'S SEE...
I'M JUST TRYING TO SAVE MONEY, SO I'VE BEEN MAKING STUFF LIKE THAT SINCE I WAS A KID.
IT MADE MY MOTHER HAPPY, TOO.
I prefer pudding.
HUH?
NOTHING. FORGET I SAID ANYTHING.
SOMETIMES, RICHARD WOULD SAY THINGS I JUST COULDN'T UNDERSTAND.

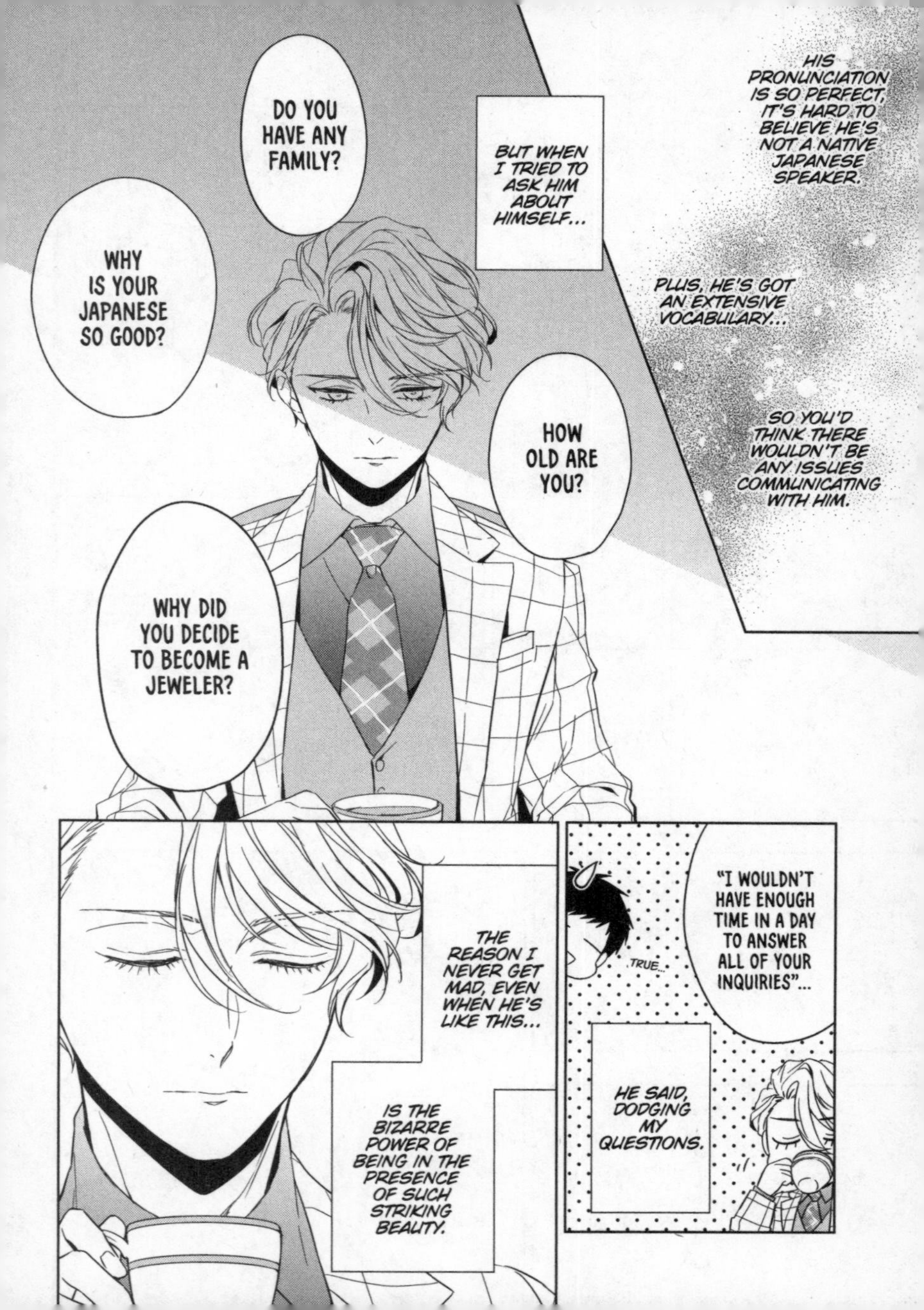
HIS PRONUNCIATION IS SO PERFECT, IT'S HARD TO BELIEVE HE'S NOT A NATIVE JAPANESE SPEAKER.
PLUS, HE'S GOT AN EXTENSIVE VOCABULARY...
SO YOU'D THINK THERE WOULDN'T BE ANY ISSUES COMMUNICATING WITH HIM.
BUT WHEN I TRIED TO ASK HIM ABOUT HIMSELF...
DO YOU HAVE ANY FAMILY?
WHY IS YOUR JAPANESE SO GOOD?
HOW OLD ARE YOU?
WHY DID YOU DECIDE TO BECOME A JEWELER?
"I WOULDN'T HAVE ENOUGH TIME IN A DAY TO ANSWER ALL OF YOUR INQUIRIES"...
TRUE...
HE SAID, DODGING MY QUESTIONS.
THE REASON I NEVER GET MAD, EVEN WHEN HE'S LIKE THIS...
IS THE BIZARRE POWER OF BEING IN THE PRESENCE OF SUCH STRIKING BEAUTY.

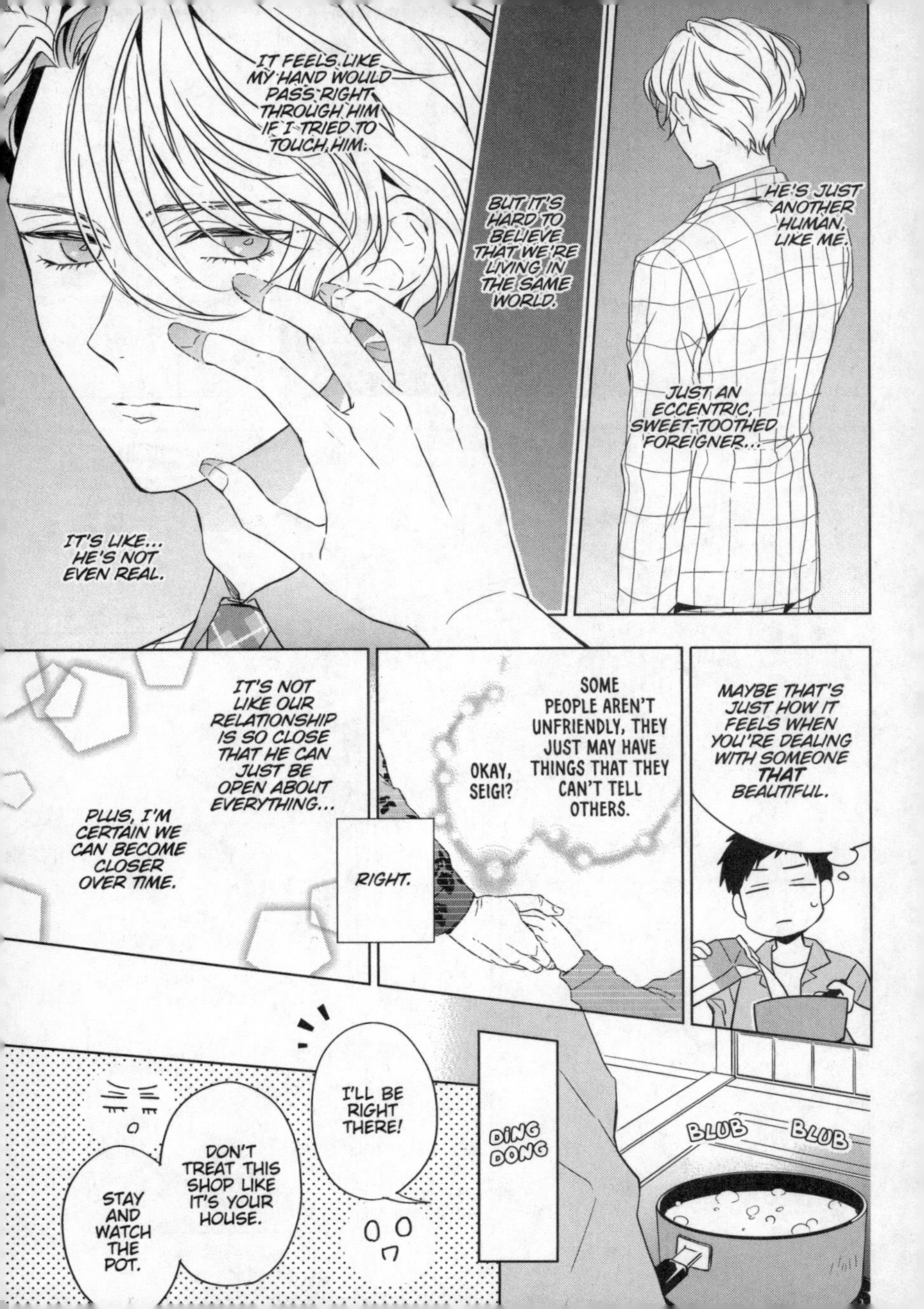
HE'S JUST ANOTHER HUMAN, LIKE ME.
JUST AN ECCENTRIC, SWEET-TOOTHED FOREIGNER...
BUT IT'S HARD TO BELIEVE THAT WE'RE LIVING IN THE SAME WORLD.
IT FEELS LIKE MY HAND WOULD PASS RIGHT THROUGH HIM IF I TRIED TO TOUCH HIM.
IT'S LIKE... HE'S NOT EVEN REAL.
MAYBE THAT'S JUST HOW IT FEELS WHEN YOU'RE DEALING WITH SOMEONE THAT BEAUTIFUL.
SOME PEOPLE AREN'T UNFRIENDLY, THEY JUST MAY HAVE THINGS THAT THEY CAN'T TELL OTHERS.
OKAY, SEIGI?
RIGHT.
IT'S NOT LIKE OUR RELATIONSHIP IS SO CLOSE THAT HE CAN JUST BE OPEN ABOUT EVERYTHING...
PLUS, I'M CERTAIN WE CAN BECOME CLOSER OVER TIME.
BLUB BLUB
DING DONG
I'LL BE RIGHT THERE!
DON'T TREAT THIS SHOP LIKE IT'S YOUR HOUSE.
STAY AND WATCH THE POT.

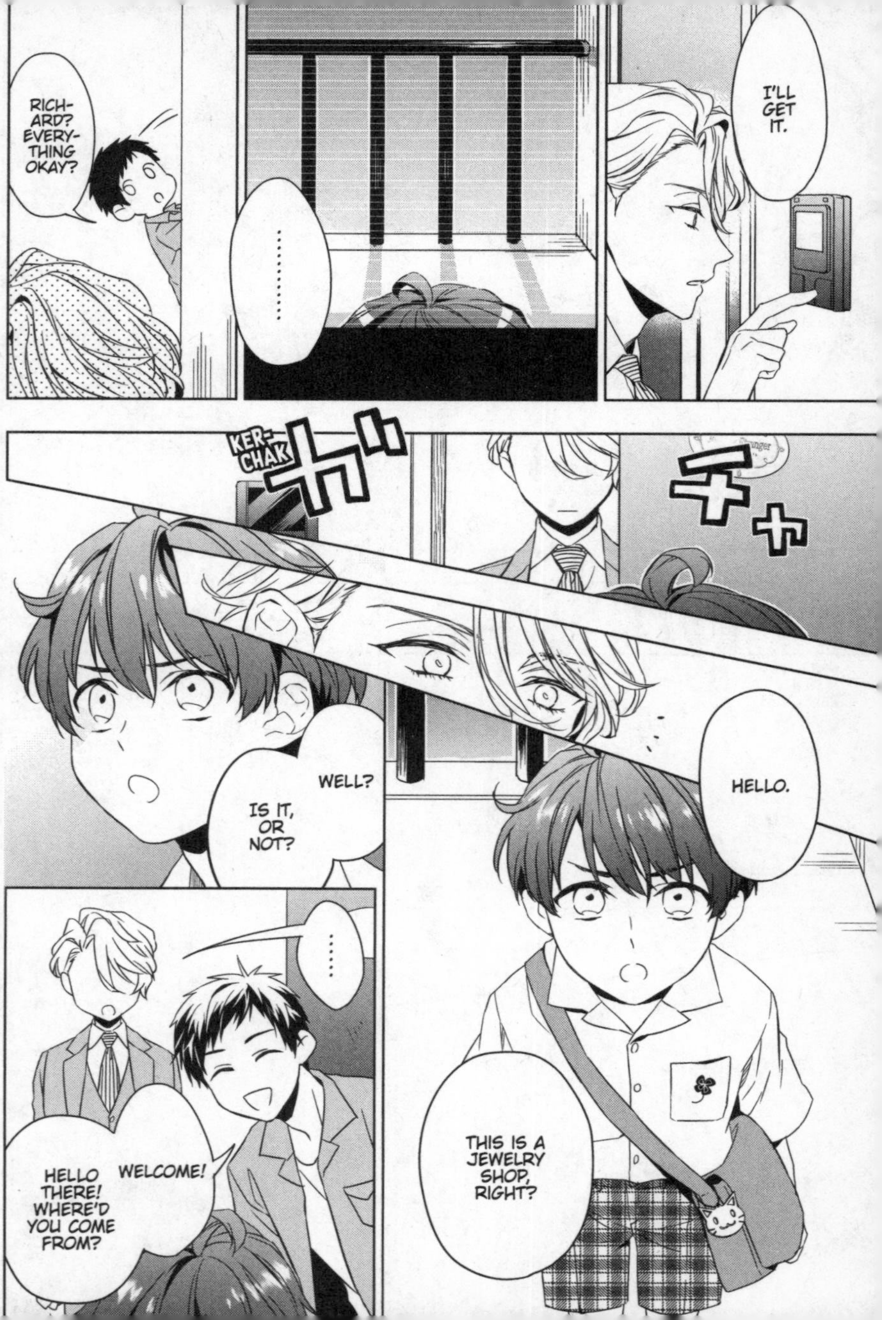
I'LL GET IT.
......
RICH-ARD? EVERY-THING OKAY?
KER-CHAK
HELLO.
THIS IS A JEWELRY SHOP, RIGHT?
WELL?
IS IT, OR NOT?
......
WELCOME!
HELLO THERE! WHERE'D YOU COME FROM?

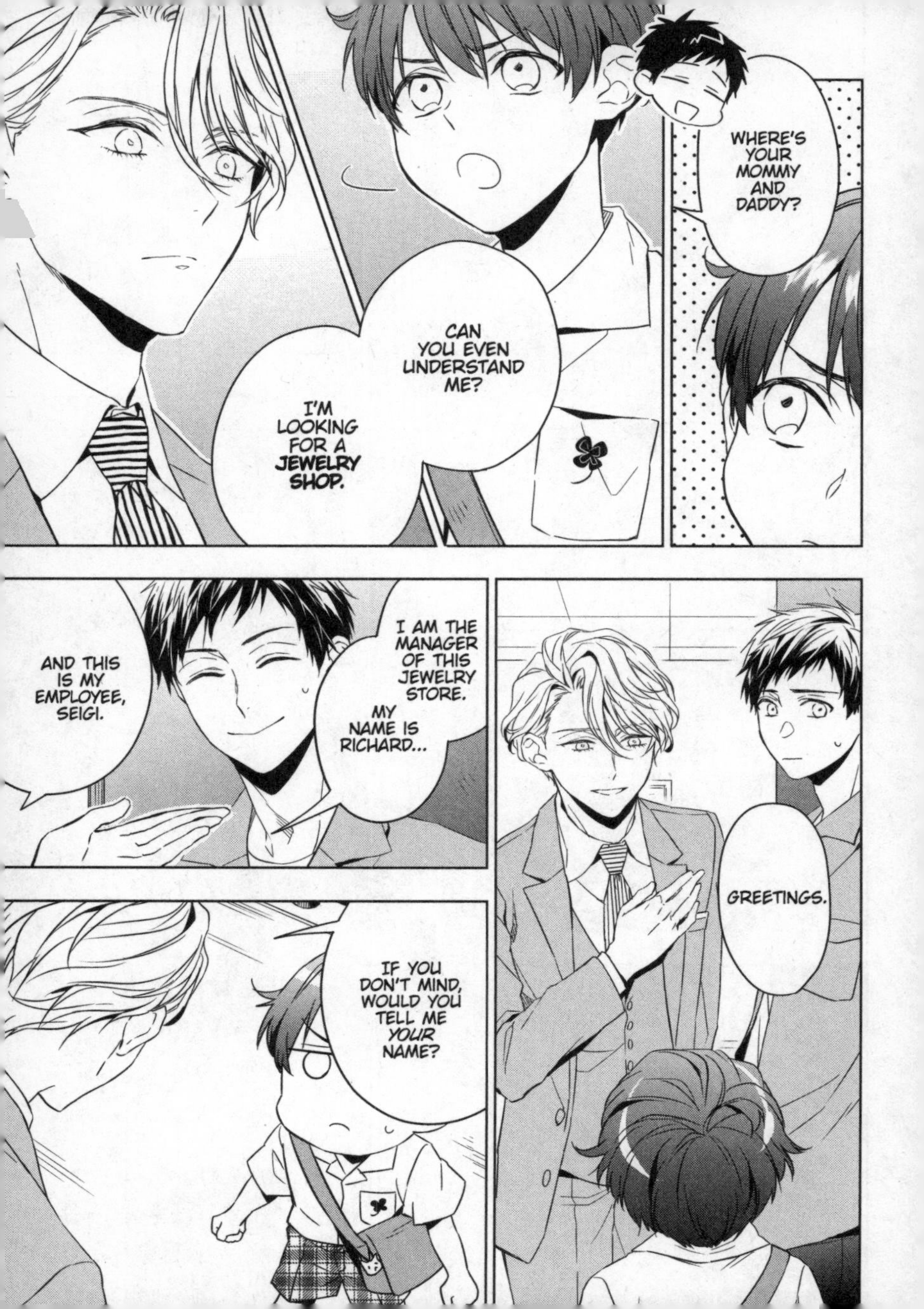
WHERE'S YOUR MOMMY AND DADDY?
CAN YOU EVEN UNDERSTAND ME?
I'M LOOKING FOR A JEWELRY SHOP.
GREETINGS.
I AM THE MANAGER OF THIS JEWELRY STORE.
MY NAME IS RICHARD...
AND THIS IS MY EMPLOYEE, SEIGI.
IF YOU DON'T MIND, WOULD YOU TELL ME *YOUR* NAME?

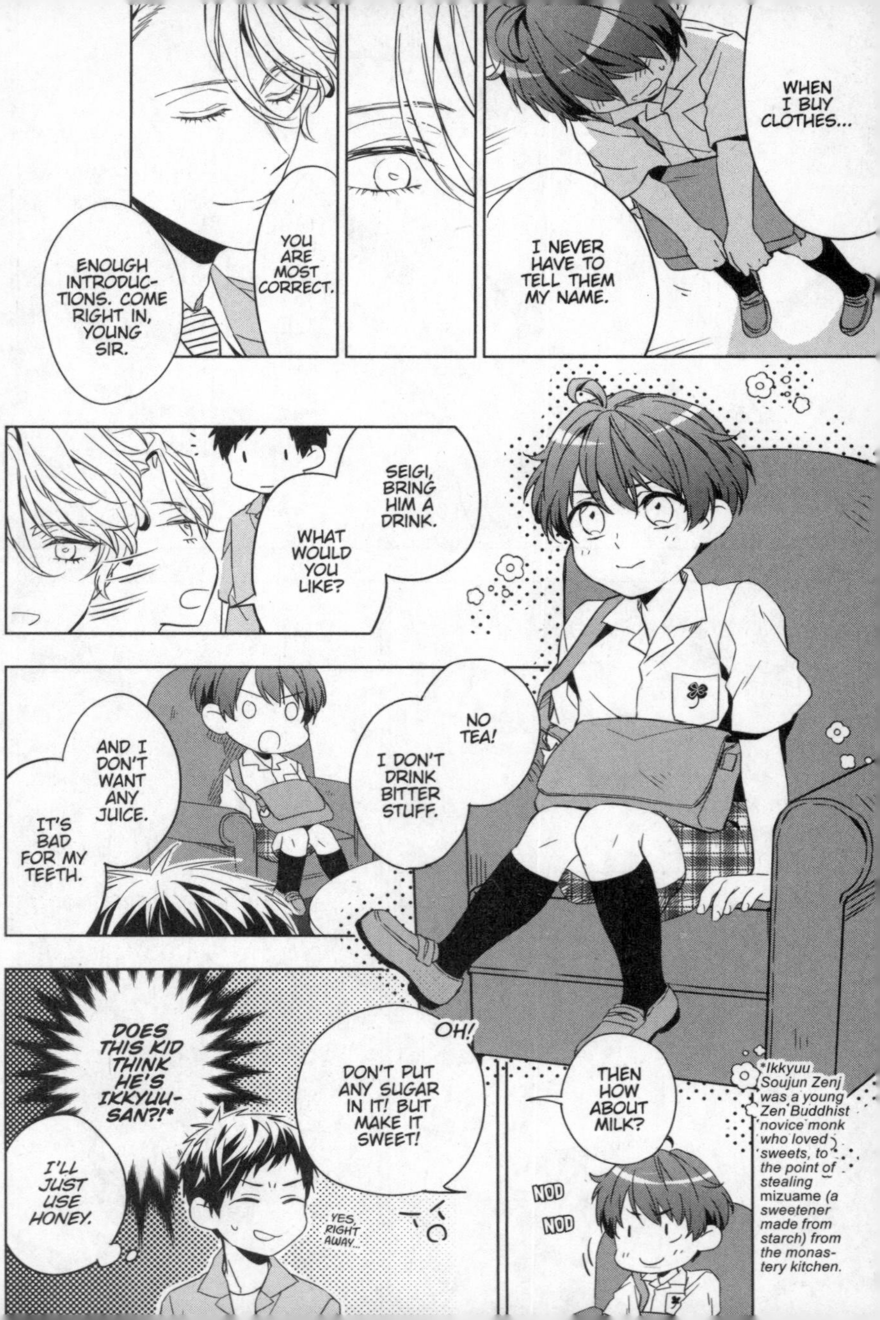
WHEN I BUY CLOTHES...
I NEVER HAVE TO TELL THEM MY NAME.
YOU ARE MOST CORRECT.
ENOUGH INTRODUCTIONS. COME RIGHT IN, YOUNG SIR.
SEIGI, BRING HIM A DRINK.
WHAT WOULD YOU LIKE?
NO TEA!
I DON'T DRINK BITTER STUFF.
AND I DON'T WANT ANY JUICE.
IT'S BAD FOR MY TEETH.
THEN HOW ABOUT MILK?
NOD
NOD
*Ikkyuu Soujun Zenj was a young Zen Buddhist novice monk who loved sweets, to the point of stealing mizuame (a sweetener made from starch) from the monastery kitchen.
OH!
DON'T PUT ANY SUGAR IN IT! BUT MAKE IT SWEET!
DOES THIS KID THINK HE'S IKKYUU-SAN?!*
YES, RIGHT AWAY...
I'LL JUST USE HONEY.

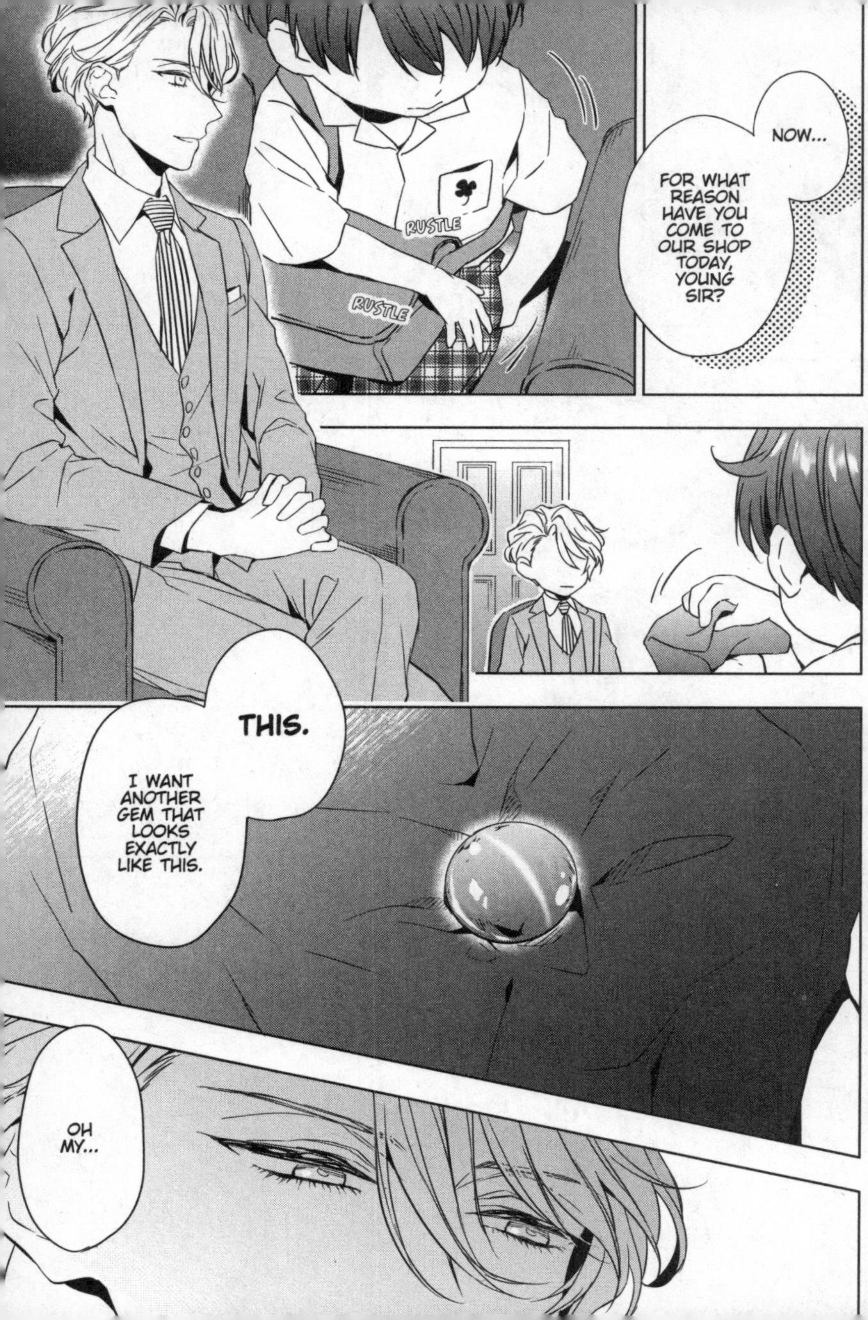
NOW...
FOR WHAT REASON HAVE YOU COME TO OUR SHOP TODAY, YOUNG SIR?
RUSTLE
RUSTLE
THIS.
I WANT ANOTHER GEM THAT LOOKS EXACTLY LIKE THIS.
OH MY...

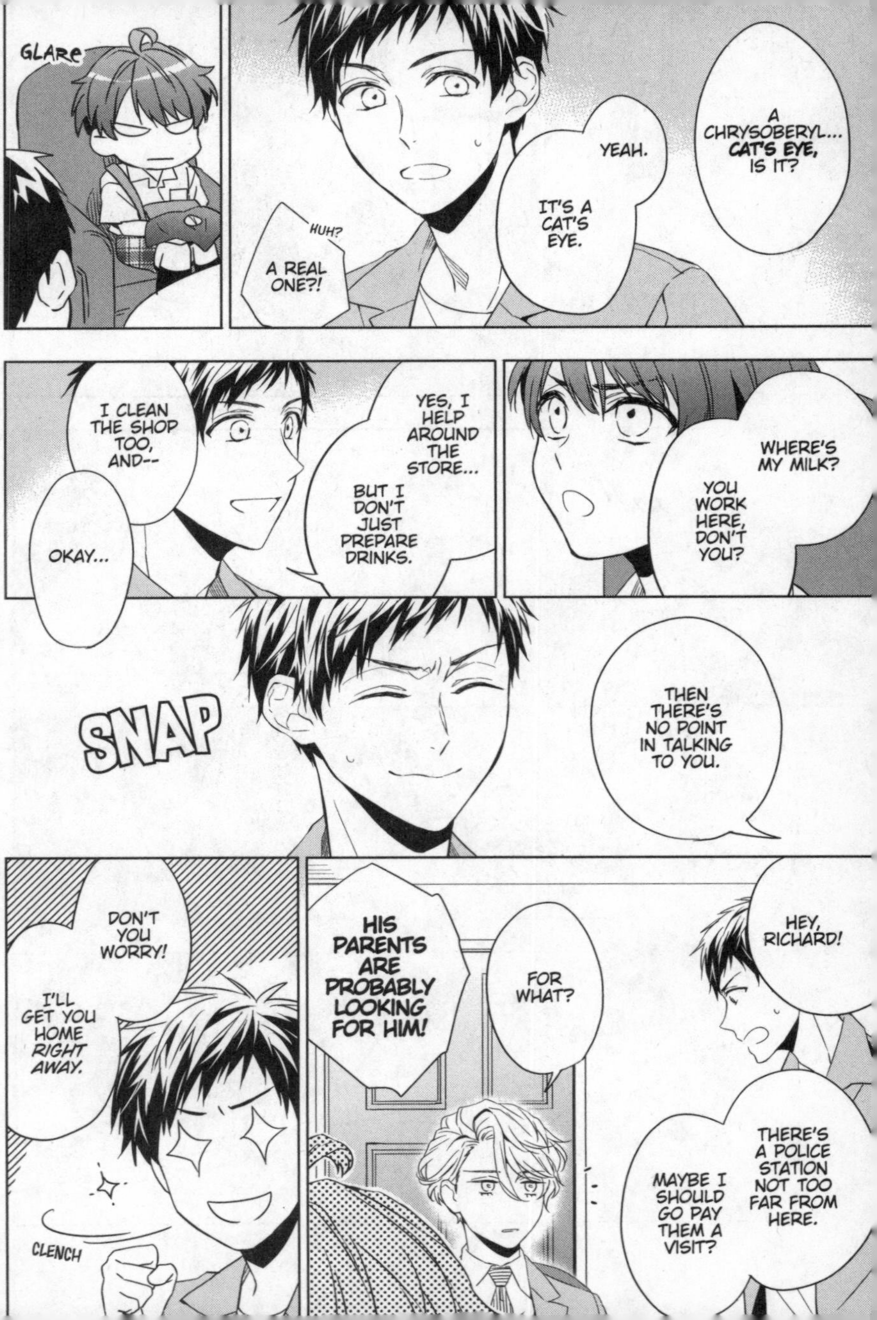
A CHRYSOBERYL... CAT'S EYE, IS IT?
YEAH.
IT'S A CAT'S EYE.
HUH?
A REAL ONE?!
GLARE
WHERE'S MY MILK?
YOU WORK HERE, DON'T YOU?
YES, I HELP AROUND THE STORE...
BUT I DON'T JUST PREPARE DRINKS.
I CLEAN THE SHOP TOO, AND--
OKAY...
THEN THERE'S NO POINT IN TALKING TO YOU.
SNAP
HEY, RICHARD!
THERE'S A POLICE STATION NOT TOO FAR FROM HERE.
MAYBE I SHOULD GO PAY THEM A VISIT?
FOR WHAT?
HIS PARENTS ARE PROBABLY LOOKING FOR HIM!
DON'T YOU WORRY!
I'LL GET YOU HOME RIGHT AWAY.
CLENCH

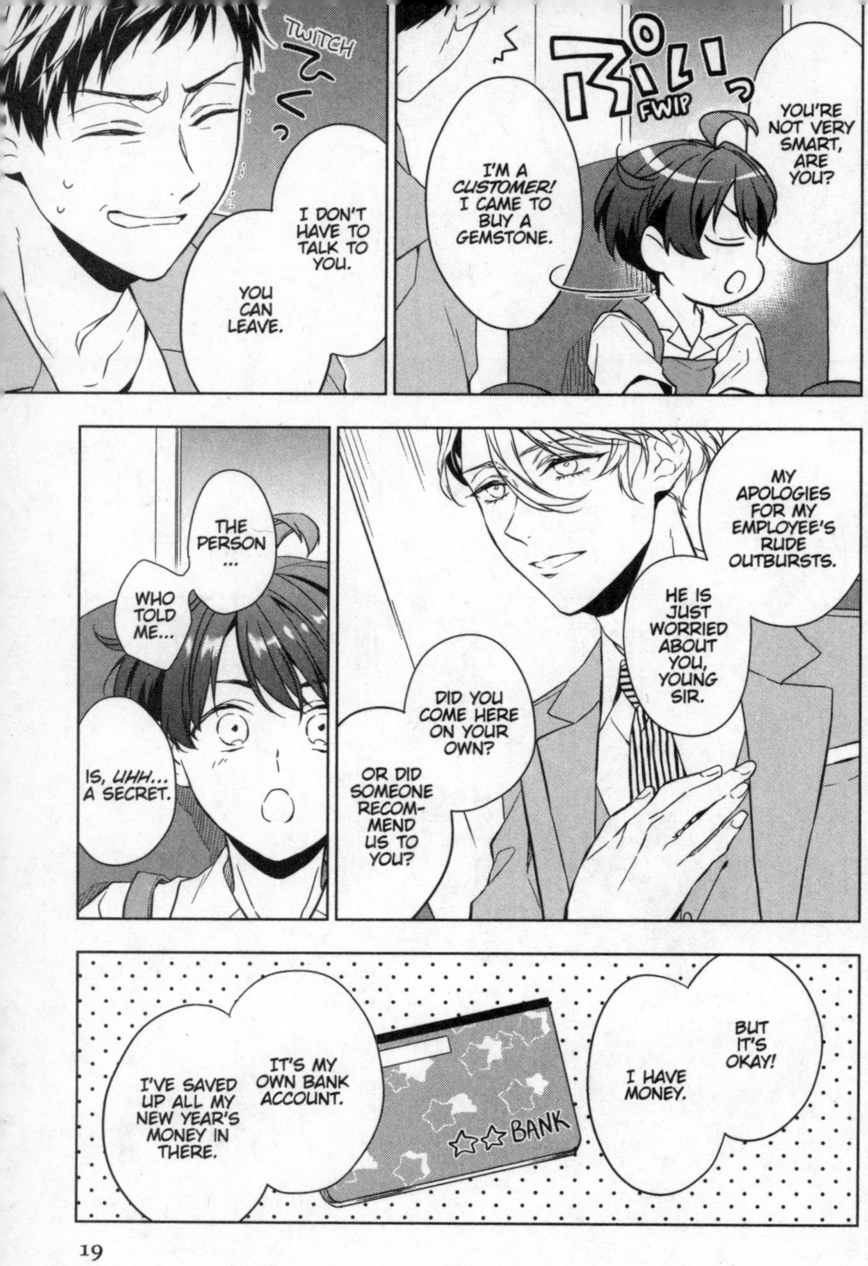
ぷいっ
FWIP
YOU'RE NOT VERY SMART, ARE YOU?
I'M A CUSTOMER! I CAME TO BUY A GEMSTONE.
TWITCH
I DON'T HAVE TO TALK TO YOU.
YOU CAN LEAVE.
MY APOLOGIES FOR MY EMPLOYEE'S RUDE OUTBURSTS.
HE IS JUST WORRIED ABOUT YOU, YOUNG SIR.
DID YOU COME HERE ON YOUR OWN?
OR DID SOMEONE RECOM-MEND US TO YOU?
THE PERSON ...
WHO TOLD ME...
IS, UHH... A SECRET.
BUT IT'S OKAY!
I HAVE MONEY.
IT'S MY OWN BANK ACCOUNT.
☆☆BANK
I'VE SAVED UP ALL MY NEW YEAR'S MONEY IN THERE.

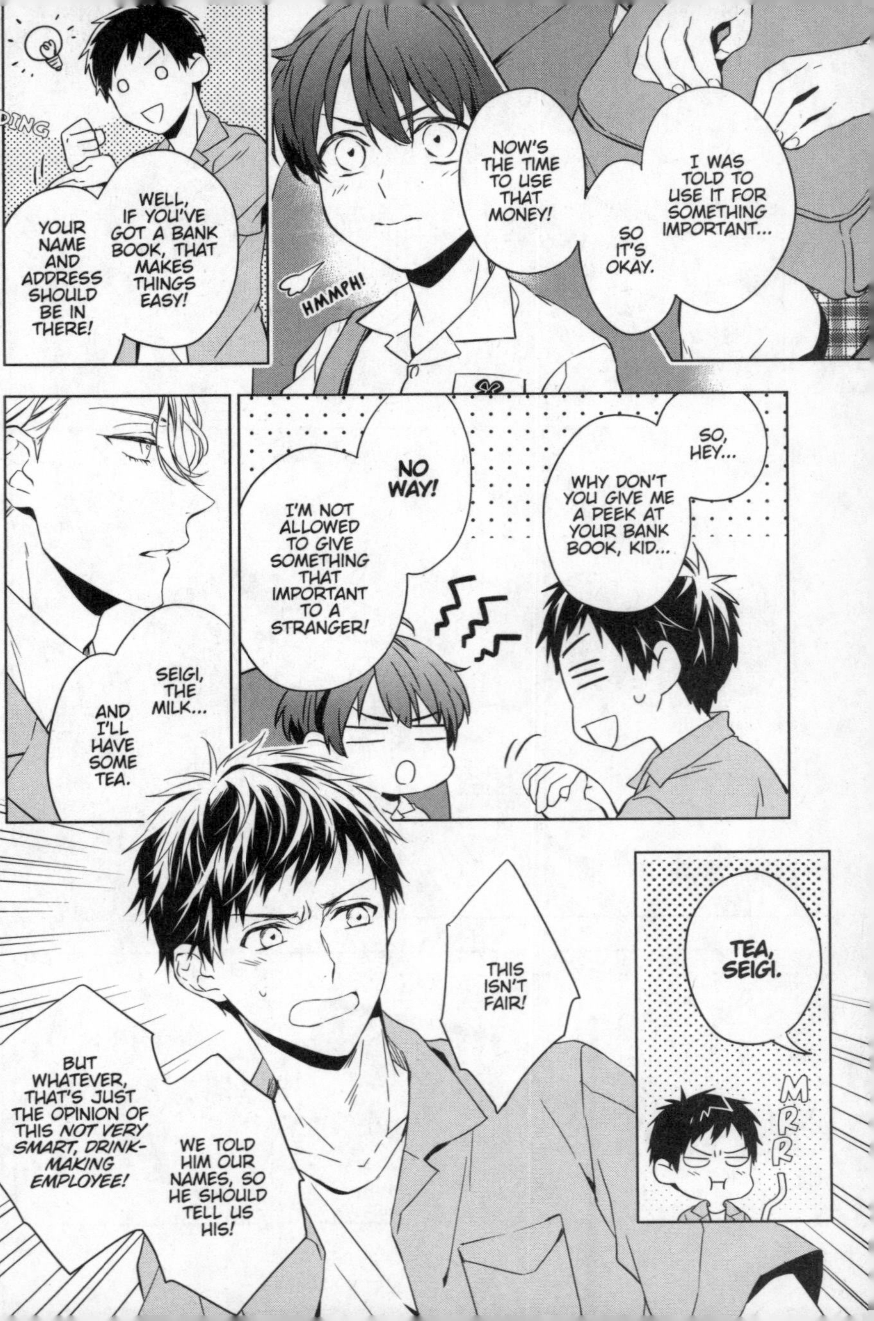
I WAS TOLD TO USE IT FOR SOMETHING IMPORTANT...
SO IT'S OKAY.
NOW'S THE TIME TO USE THAT MONEY!
HMMPH!
DING
WELL, IF YOU'VE GOT A BANK BOOK, THAT MAKES THINGS EASY!
YOUR NAME AND ADDRESS SHOULD BE IN THERE!
SO, HEY...
WHY DON'T YOU GIVE ME A PEEK AT YOUR BANK BOOK, KID...
NO WAY!
I'M NOT ALLOWED TO GIVE SOMETHING THAT IMPORTANT TO A STRANGER!
SEIGI, THE MILK...
AND I'LL HAVE SOME TEA.
TEA, SEIGI.
MRR!
THIS ISN'T FAIR!
WE TOLD HIM OUR NAMES, SO HE SHOULD TELL US HIS!
BUT WHATEVER, THAT'S JUST THE OPINION OF THIS *NOT VERY SMART, DRINK-MAKING EMPLOYEE!*

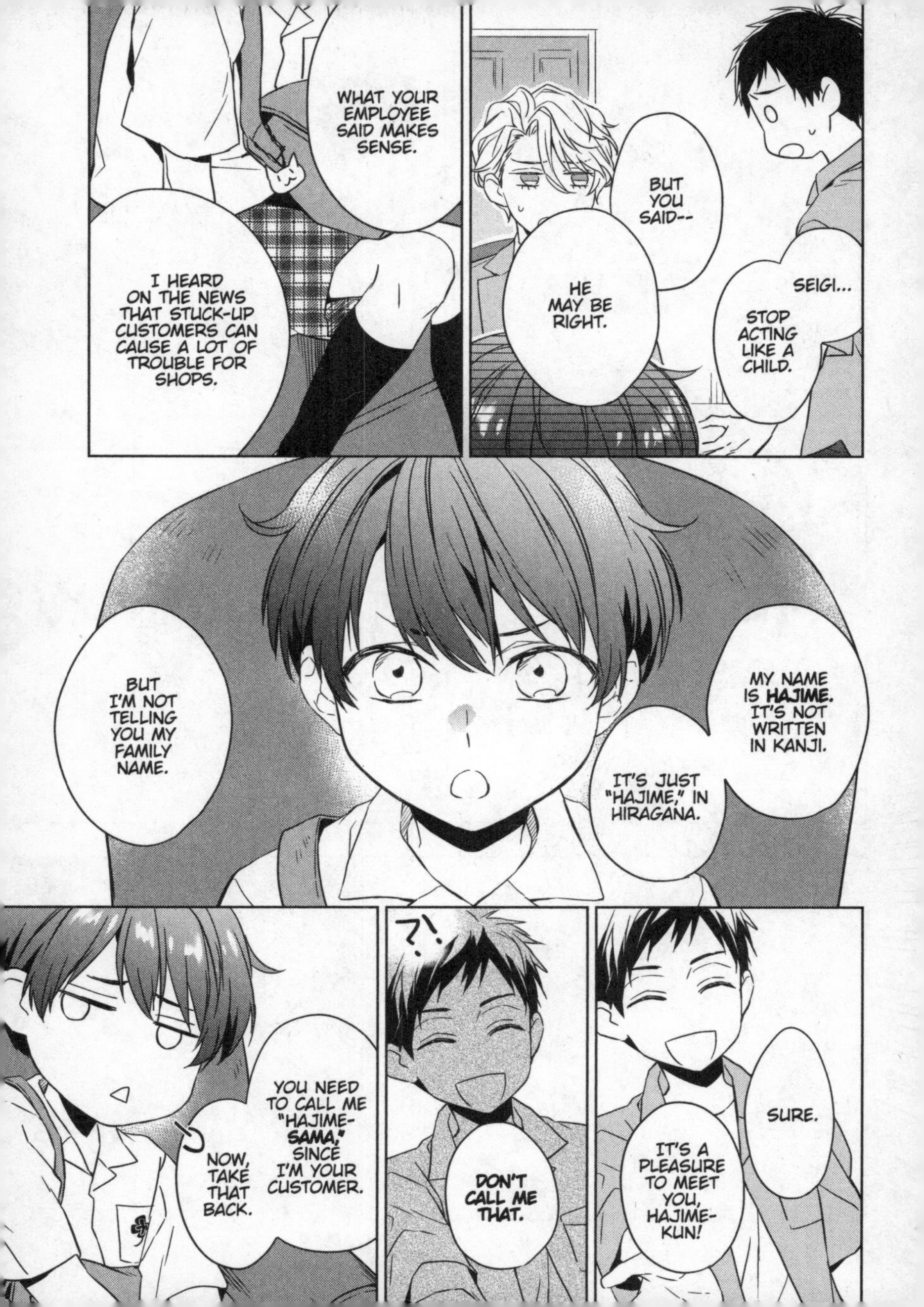
BUT YOU SAID--
SEIGI...
STOP ACTING LIKE A CHILD.
HE MAY BE RIGHT.
WHAT YOUR EMPLOYEE SAID MAKES SENSE.
I HEARD ON THE NEWS THAT STUCK-UP CUSTOMERS CAN CAUSE A LOT OF TROUBLE FOR SHOPS.
MY NAME IS **HAJIME.** IT'S NOT WRITTEN IN KANJI.
IT'S JUST "HAJIME," IN HIRAGANA.
BUT I'M NOT TELLING YOU MY FAMILY NAME.
SURE.
IT'S A PLEASURE TO MEET YOU, HAJIME-KUN!
?!
DON'T CALL ME THAT.
YOU NEED TO CALL ME "HAJIME-**SAMA,**" SINCE I'M YOUR CUSTOMER.
NOW, TAKE THAT BACK.

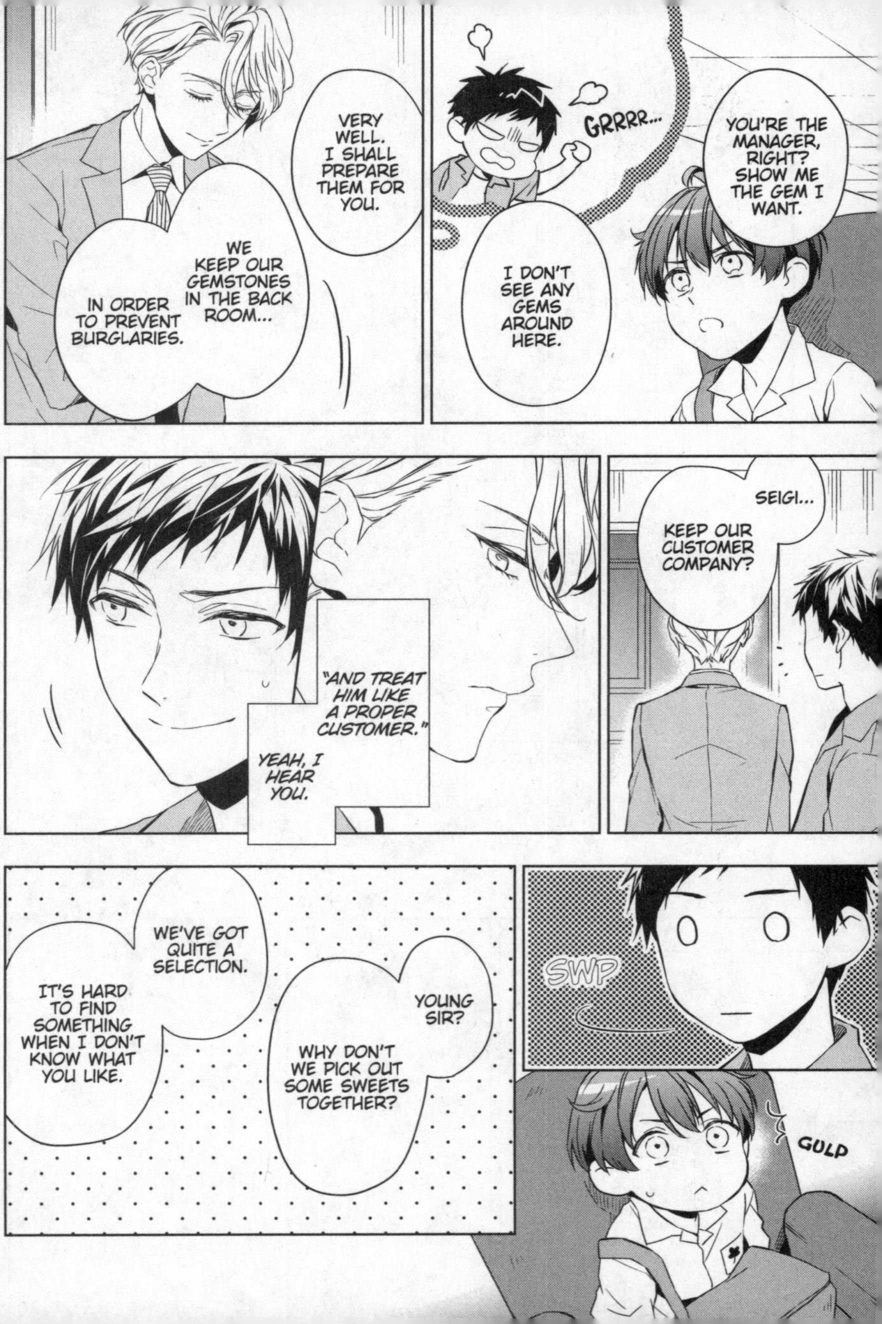
YOU'RE THE MANAGER, RIGHT? SHOW ME THE GEM I WANT.
I DON'T SEE ANY GEMS AROUND HERE.
GRRRR...
VERY WELL. I SHALL PREPARE THEM FOR YOU.
WE KEEP OUR GEMSTONES IN THE BACK ROOM...
IN ORDER TO PREVENT BURGLARIES.
SEIGI...
KEEP OUR CUSTOMER COMPANY?
"AND TREAT HIM LIKE A PROPER CUSTOMER."
YEAH, I HEAR YOU.
SWP
GULP
YOUNG SIR?
WHY DON'T WE PICK OUT SOME SWEETS TOGETHER?
WE'VE GOT QUITE A SELECTION.
IT'S HARD TO FIND SOMETHING WHEN I DON'T KNOW WHAT YOU LIKE.

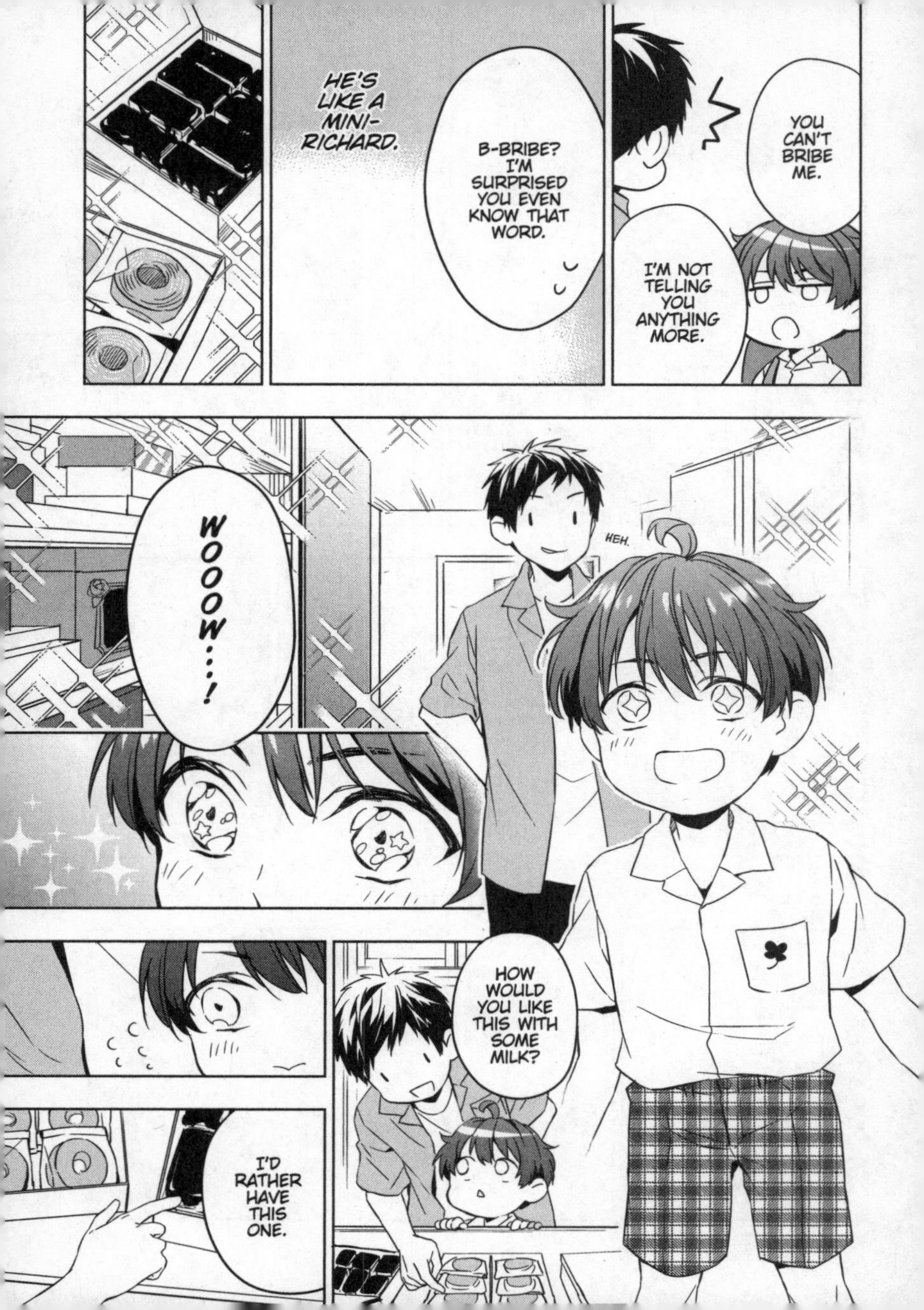
YOU CAN'T BRIBE ME.
I'M NOT TELLING YOU ANYTHING MORE.
B-BRIBE? I'M SURPRISED YOU EVEN KNOW THAT WORD.
HE'S LIKE A MINI-RICHARD.
HEH.
WOOOOW...!
HOW WOULD YOU LIKE THIS WITH SOME MILK?
I'D RATHER HAVE THIS ONE.

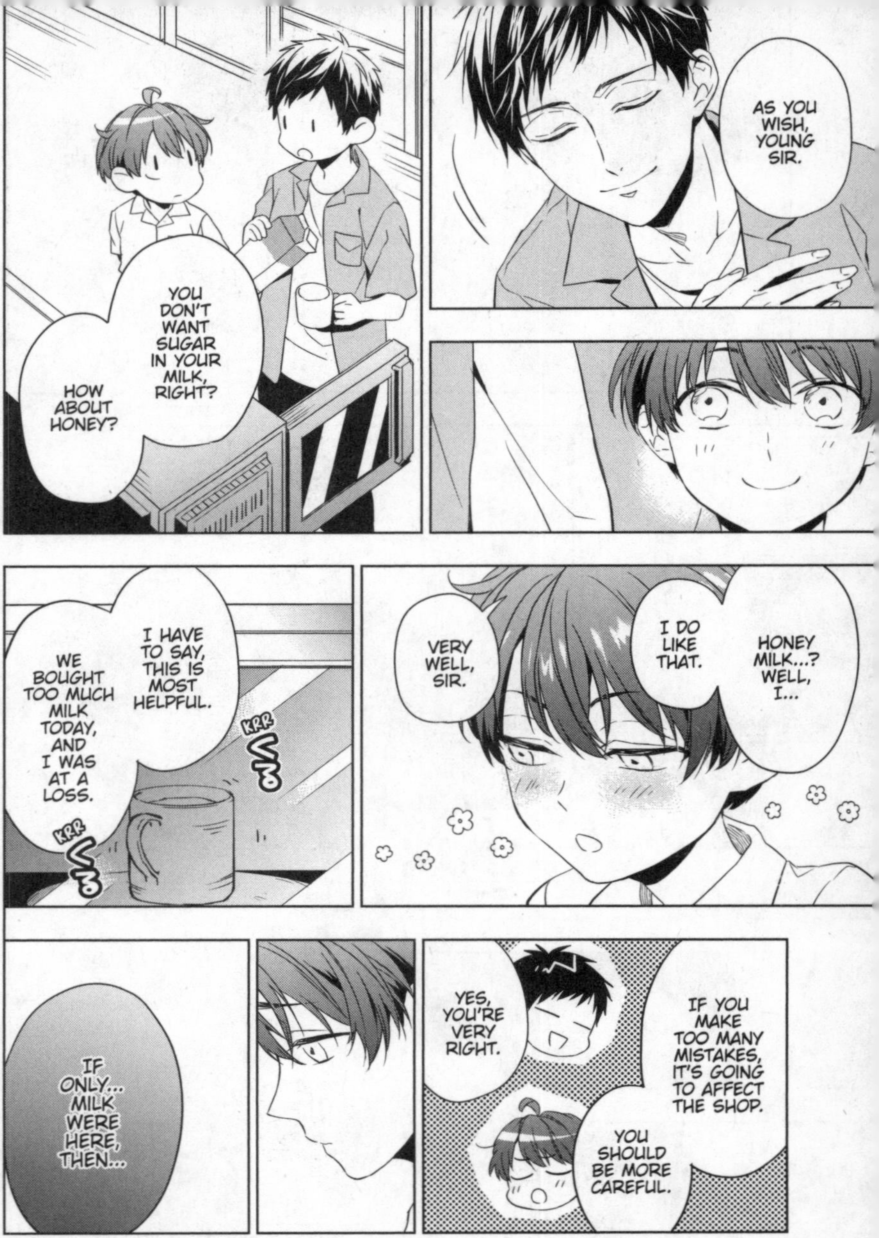
AS YOU WISH, YOUNG SIR.
YOU DON'T WANT SUGAR IN YOUR MILK, RIGHT?
HOW ABOUT HONEY?
HONEY MILK...? WELL, I...
I DO LIKE THAT.
VERY WELL, SIR.
I HAVE TO SAY, THIS IS MOST HELPFUL.
WE BOUGHT TOO MUCH MILK TODAY, AND I WAS AT A LOSS.
KRR
KRR
IF YOU MAKE TOO MANY MISTAKES, IT'S GOING TO AFFECT THE SHOP.
YOU SHOULD BE MORE CAREFUL.
YES, YOU'RE VERY RIGHT.
IF ONLY... MILK WERE HERE, THEN...

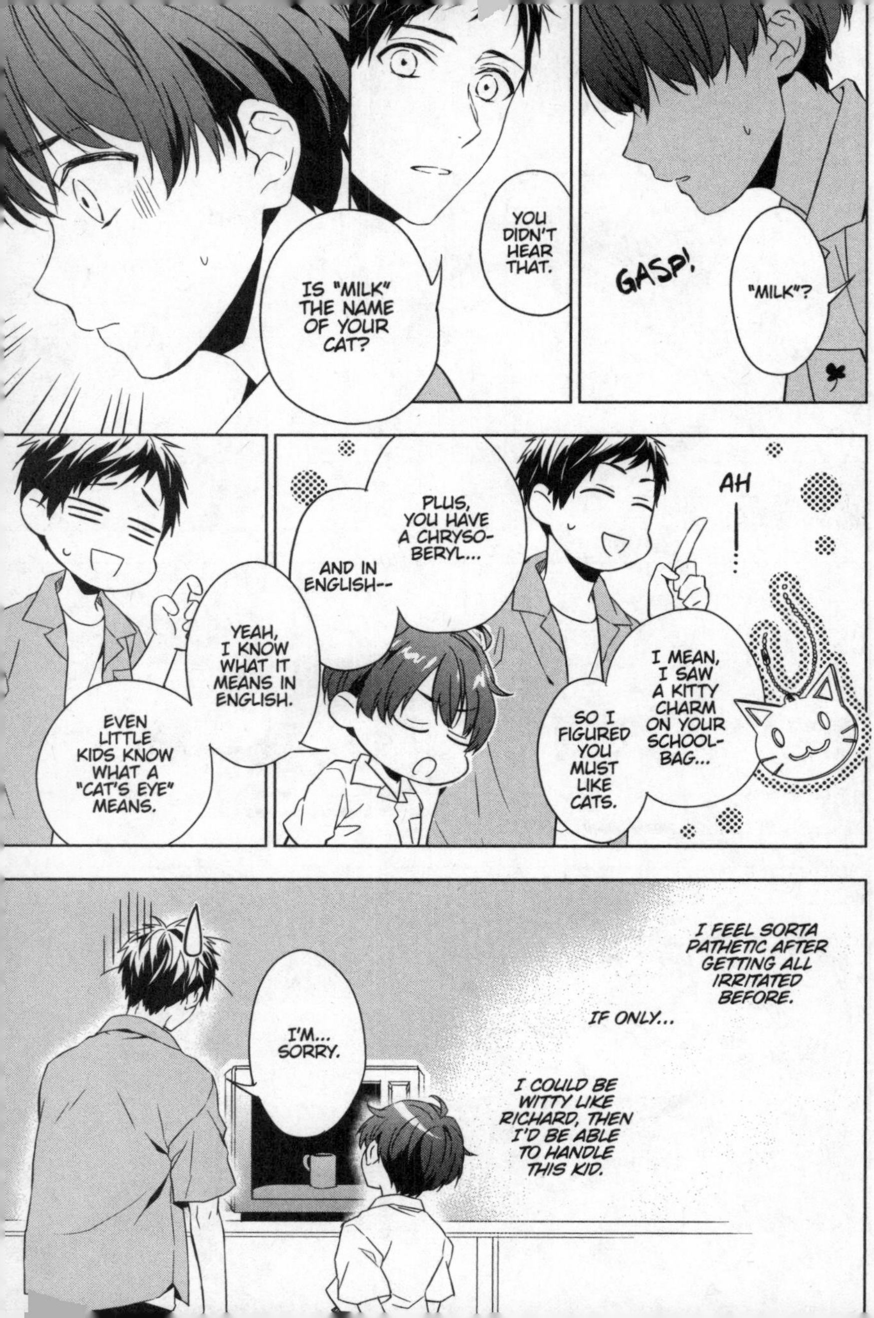
"MILK"?
GASP!
YOU DIDN'T HEAR THAT.
IS "MILK" THE NAME OF YOUR CAT?
AH—!
I MEAN, I SAW A KITTY CHARM ON YOUR SCHOOL-BAG...
SO I FIGURED YOU MUST LIKE CATS.
PLUS, YOU HAVE A CHRYSO-BERYL...
AND IN ENGLISH--
YEAH, I KNOW WHAT IT MEANS IN ENGLISH.
EVEN LITTLE KIDS KNOW WHAT A "CAT'S EYE" MEANS.
I FEEL SORTA PATHETIC AFTER GETTING ALL IRRITATED BEFORE.
IF ONLY...
I COULD BE WITTY LIKE RICHARD, THEN I'D BE ABLE TO HANDLE THIS KID.
I'M... SORRY.

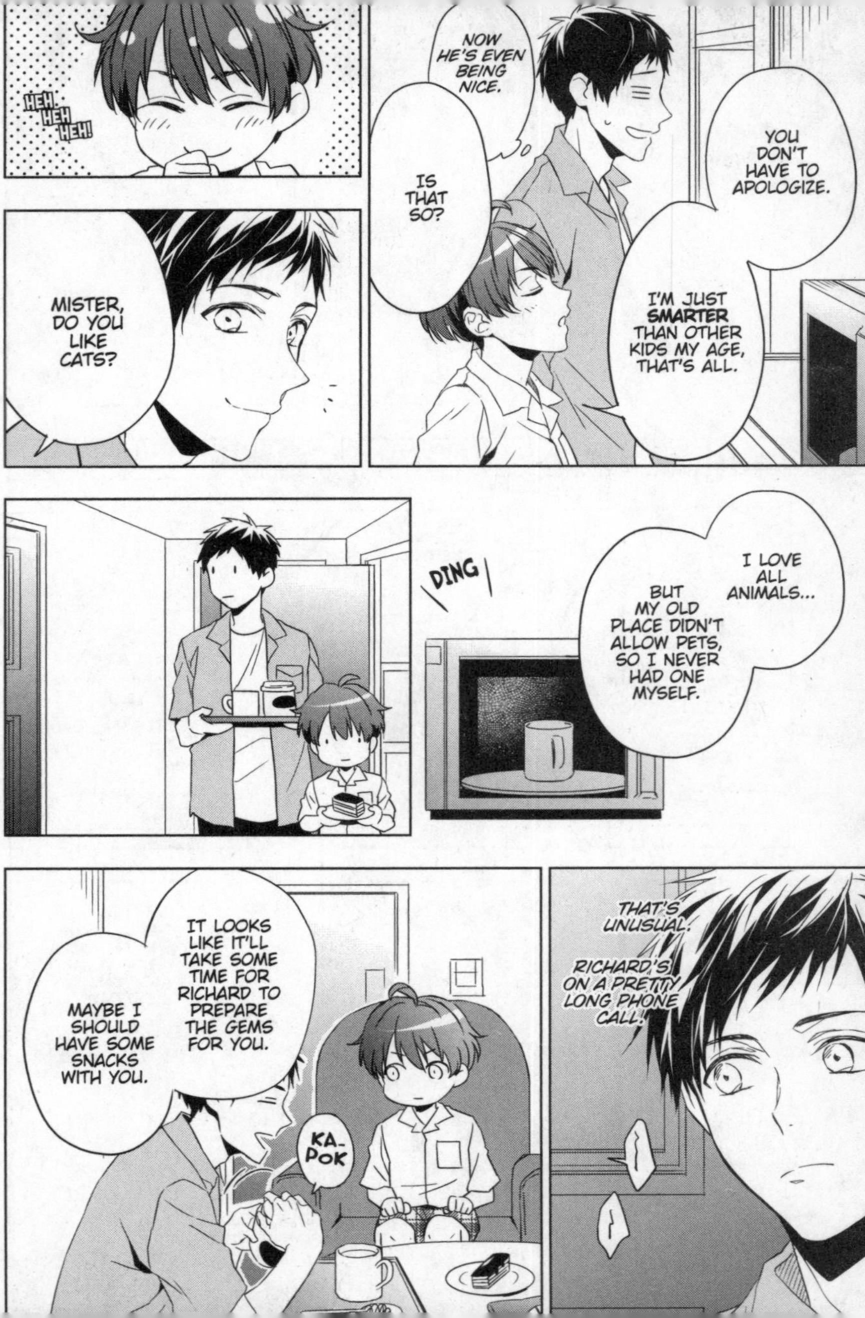
YOU DON'T HAVE TO APOLOGIZE.
NOW HE'S EVEN BEING NICE.
IS THAT SO?
I'M JUST **SMARTER** THAN OTHER KIDS MY AGE, THAT'S ALL.
HEH HEH HEH!
MISTER, DO YOU LIKE CATS?
I LOVE ALL ANIMALS...
BUT MY OLD PLACE DIDN'T ALLOW PETS, SO I NEVER HAD ONE MYSELF.
DING
THAT'S UNUSUAL.
RICHARD'S ON A PRETTY LONG PHONE CALL.
IT LOOKS LIKE IT'LL TAKE SOME TIME FOR RICHARD TO PREPARE THE GEMS FOR YOU.
MAYBE I SHOULD HAVE SOME SNACKS WITH YOU.
KA-POK

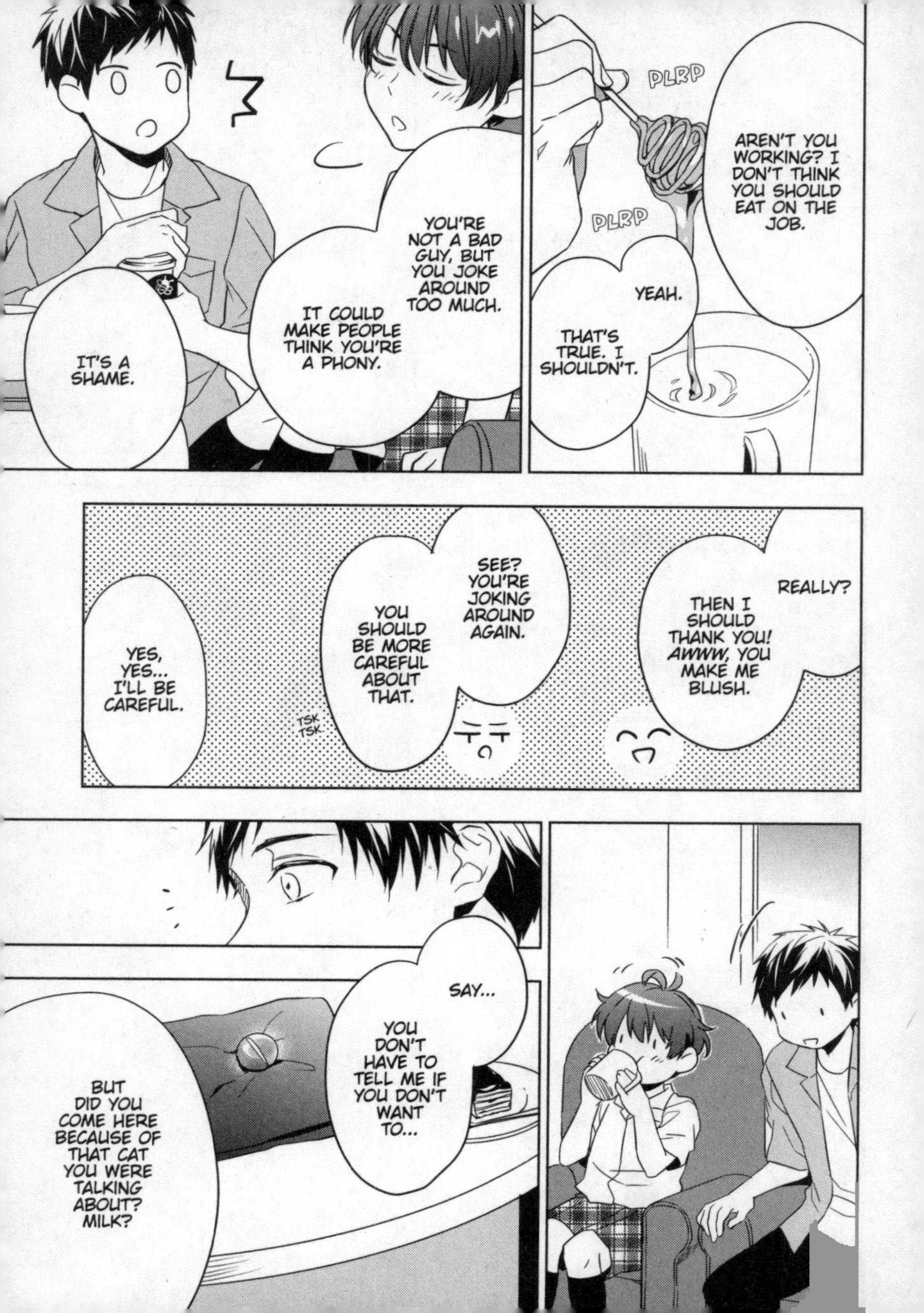
AREN'T YOU WORKING? I DON'T THINK YOU SHOULD EAT ON THE JOB.
PLRP
PLRP
YEAH.
THAT'S TRUE. I SHOULDN'T.
YOU'RE NOT A BAD GUY, BUT YOU JOKE AROUND TOO MUCH.
IT COULD MAKE PEOPLE THINK YOU'RE A PHONY.
IT'S A SHAME.
REALLY?
THEN I SHOULD THANK YOU! *AWWW*, YOU MAKE ME BLUSH.
SEE? YOU'RE JOKING AROUND AGAIN.
YOU SHOULD BE MORE CAREFUL ABOUT THAT.
TSK TSK
YES, YES... I'LL BE CAREFUL.
SAY...
YOU DON'T HAVE TO TELL ME IF YOU DON'T WANT TO...
BUT DID YOU COME HERE BECAUSE OF THAT CAT YOU WERE TALKING ABOUT? MILK?

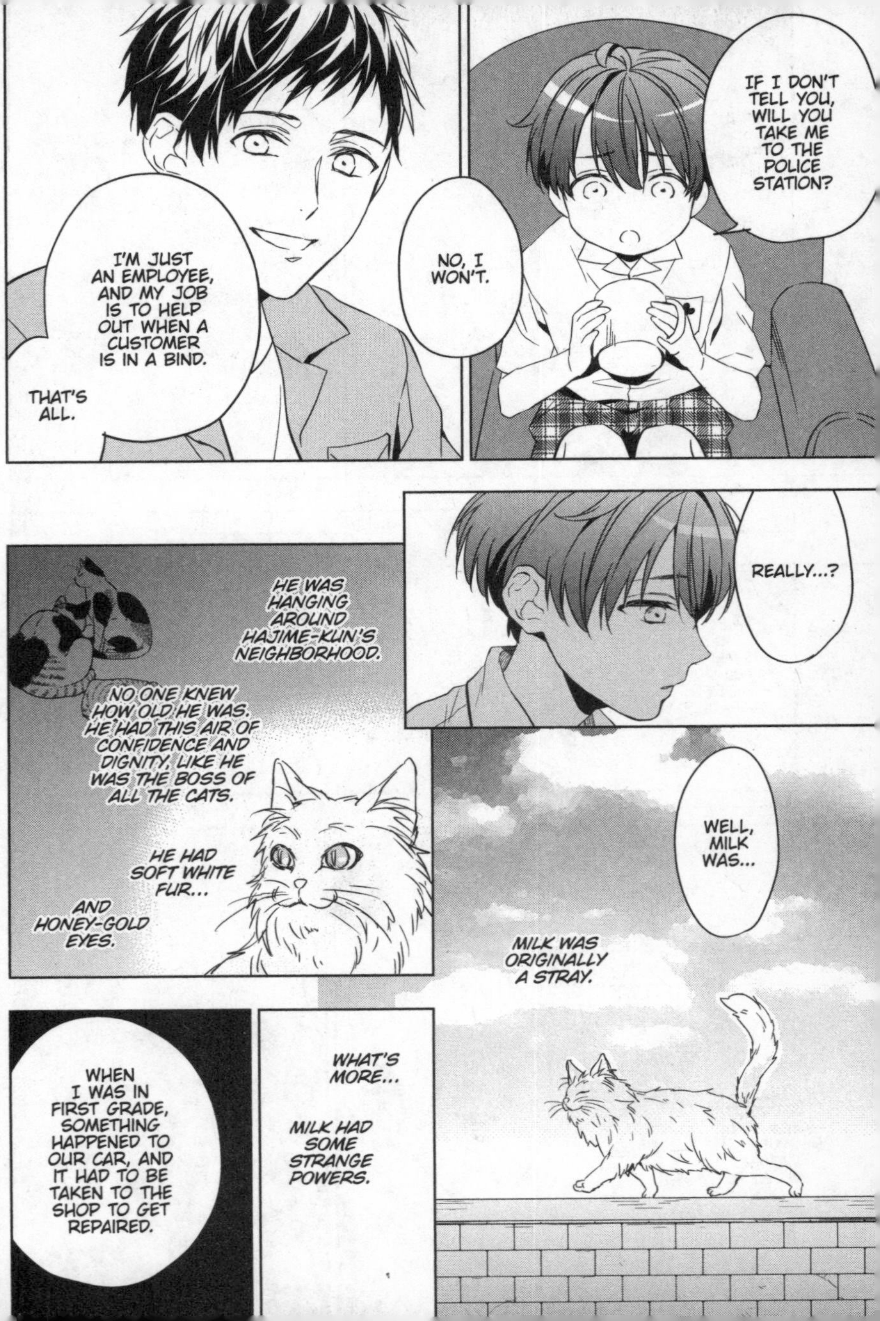
IF I DON'T TELL YOU, WILL YOU TAKE ME TO THE POLICE STATION?
NO, I WON'T.
I'M JUST AN EMPLOYEE, AND MY JOB IS TO HELP OUT WHEN A CUSTOMER IS IN A BIND.
THAT'S ALL.
REALLY...?
WELL, MILK WAS...
MILK WAS ORIGINALLY A STRAY.
HE WAS HANGING AROUND HAJIME-KUN'S NEIGHBORHOOD.
NO ONE KNEW HOW OLD HE WAS. HE HAD THIS AIR OF CONFIDENCE AND DIGNITY, LIKE HE WAS THE BOSS OF ALL THE CATS.
HE HAD SOFT WHITE FUR...
AND HONEY-GOLD EYES.
WHAT'S MORE...
MILK HAD SOME STRANGE POWERS.
WHEN I WAS IN FIRST GRADE, SOMETHING HAPPENED TO OUR CAR, AND IT HAD TO BE TAKEN TO THE SHOP TO GET REPAIRED.

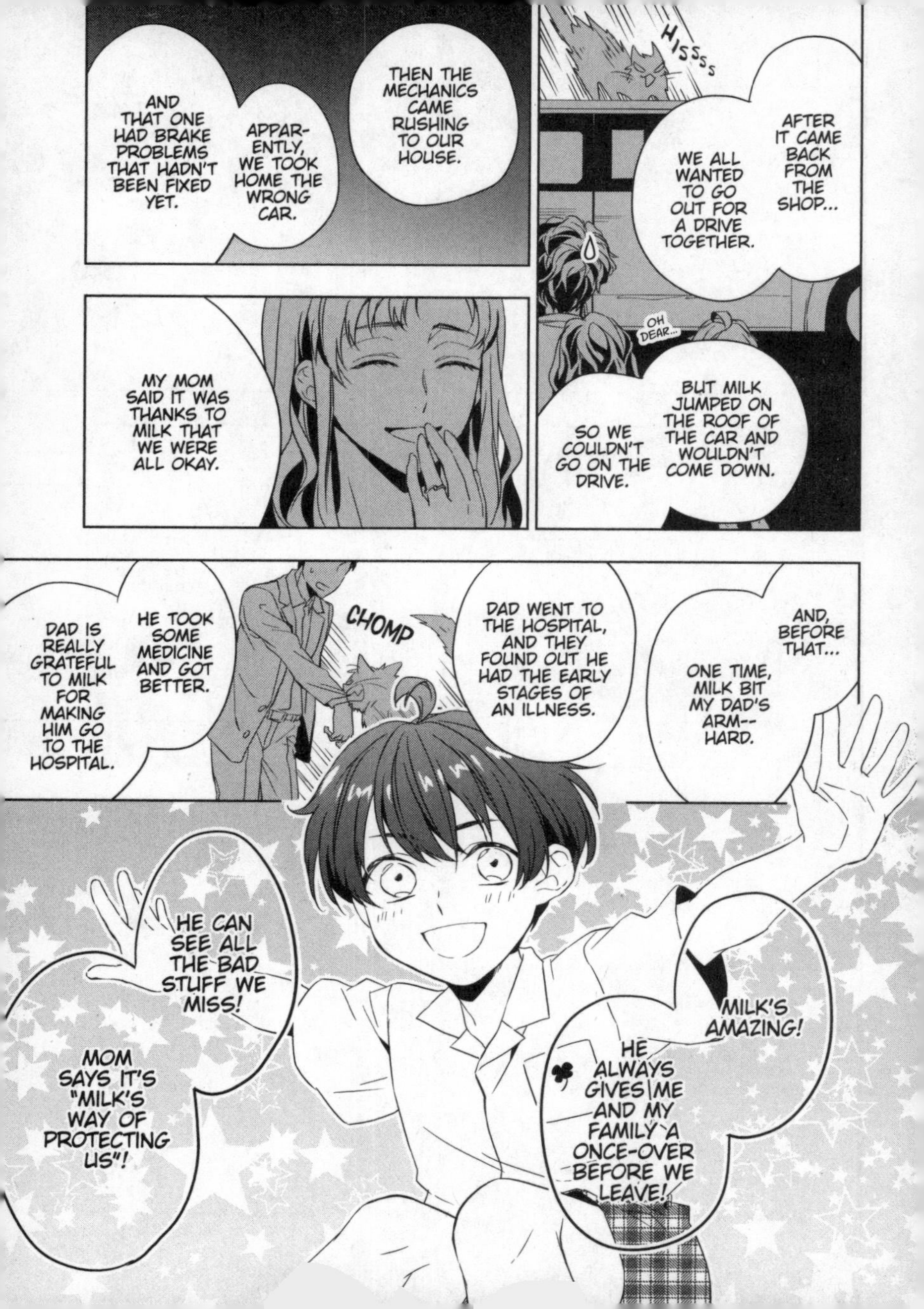
HISSSSS
AFTER IT CAME BACK FROM THE SHOP...
WE ALL WANTED TO GO OUT FOR A DRIVE TOGETHER.
OH DEAR...
BUT MILK JUMPED ON THE ROOF OF THE CAR AND WOULDN'T COME DOWN.
SO WE COULDN'T GO ON THE DRIVE.
THEN THE MECHANICS CAME RUSHING TO OUR HOUSE.
APPARENTLY, WE TOOK HOME THE WRONG CAR.
AND THAT ONE HAD BRAKE PROBLEMS THAT HADN'T BEEN FIXED YET.
MY MOM SAID IT WAS THANKS TO MILK THAT WE WERE ALL OKAY.
AND, BEFORE THAT...
ONE TIME, MILK BIT MY DAD'S ARM--HARD.
CHOMP
DAD WENT TO THE HOSPITAL, AND THEY FOUND OUT HE HAD THE EARLY STAGES OF AN ILLNESS.
HE TOOK SOME MEDICINE AND GOT BETTER.
DAD IS REALLY GRATEFUL TO MILK FOR MAKING HIM GO TO THE HOSPITAL.
MILK'S AMAZING!
HE ALWAYS GIVES ME AND MY FAMILY A ONCE-OVER BEFORE WE LEAVE!
HE CAN SEE ALL THE BAD STUFF WE MISS!
MOM SAYS IT'S "MILK'S WAY OF PROTECTING US"!

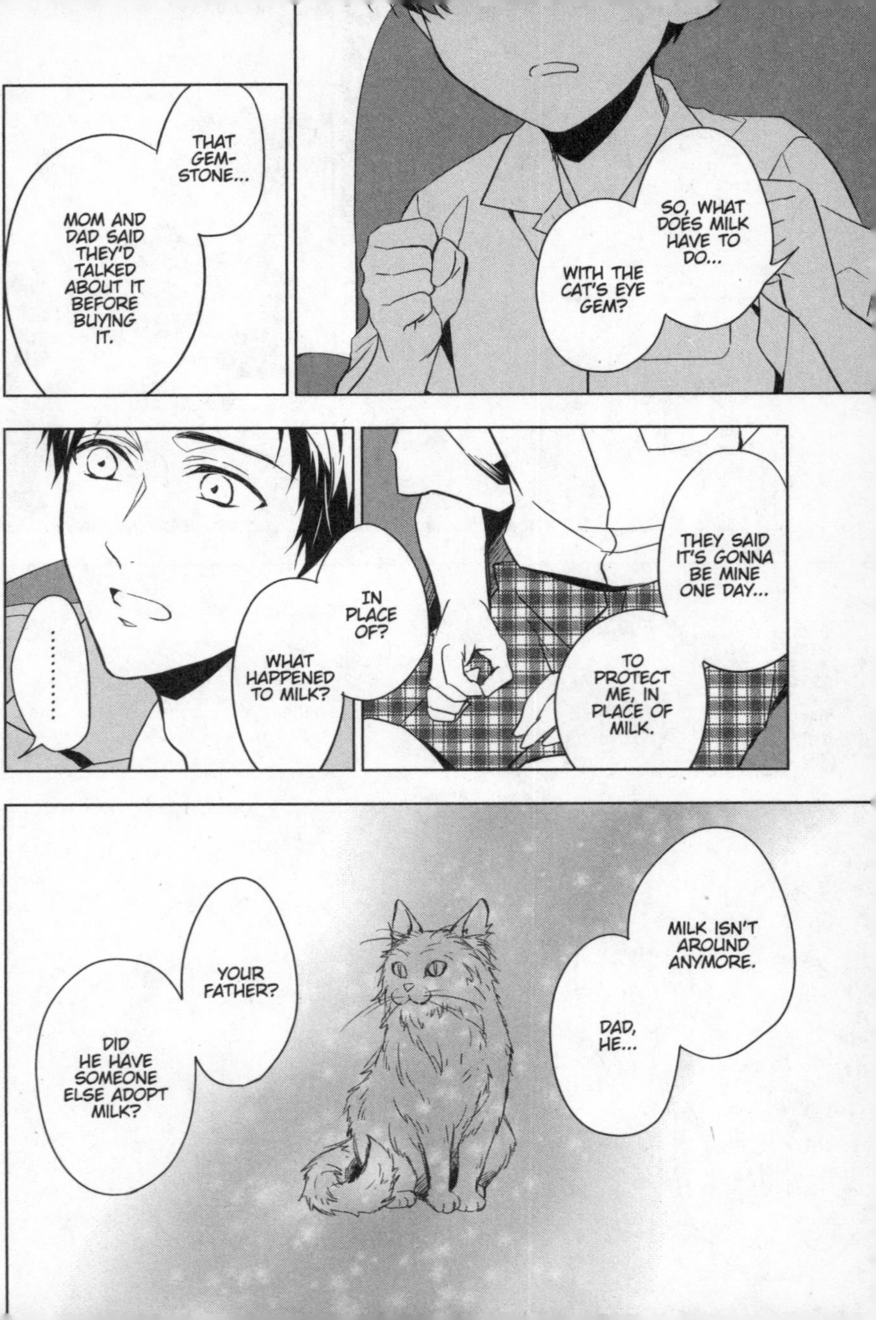
SO, WHAT DOES MILK HAVE TO DO...
WITH THE CAT'S EYE GEM?
THAT GEM-STONE...
MOM AND DAD SAID THEY'D TALKED ABOUT IT BEFORE BUYING IT.
THEY SAID IT'S GONNA BE MINE ONE DAY...
TO PROTECT ME, IN PLACE OF MILK.
IN PLACE OF?
WHAT HAPPENED TO MILK?
......
MILK ISN'T AROUND ANYMORE.
DAD, HE...
YOUR FATHER?
DID HE HAVE SOMEONE ELSE ADOPT MILK?

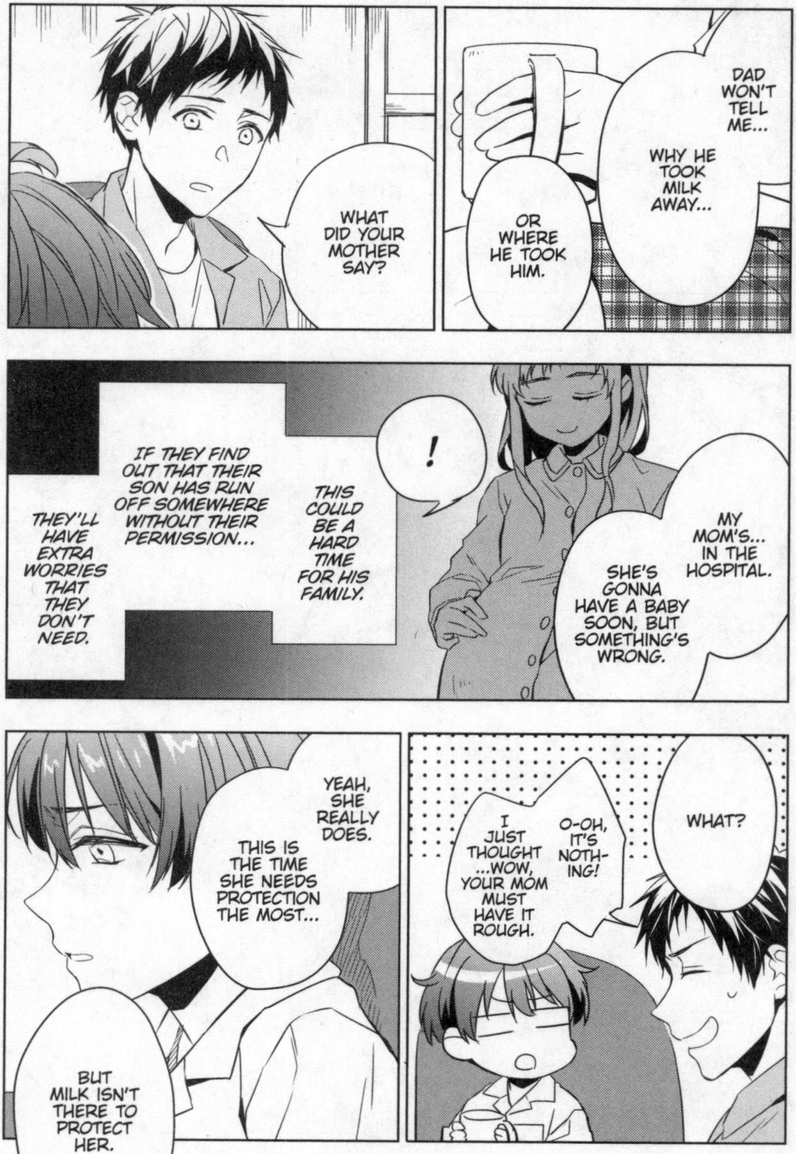
DAD WON'T TELL ME... WHY HE TOOK MILK AWAY...
OR WHERE HE TOOK HIM.
WHAT DID YOUR MOTHER SAY?
MY MOM'S... IN THE HOSPITAL.
SHE'S GONNA HAVE A BABY SOON, BUT SOMETHING'S WRONG.
!
THIS COULD BE A HARD TIME FOR HIS FAMILY.
IF THEY FIND OUT THAT THEIR SON HAS RUN OFF SOMEWHERE WITHOUT THEIR PERMISSION...
THEY'LL HAVE EXTRA WORRIES THAT THEY DON'T NEED.
WHAT?
O-OH, IT'S NOTH-ING!
I JUST THOUGHT ...WOW, YOUR MOM MUST HAVE IT ROUGH.
YEAH, SHE REALLY DOES.
THIS IS THE TIME SHE NEEDS PROTECTION THE MOST...
BUT MILK ISN'T THERE TO PROTECT HER.

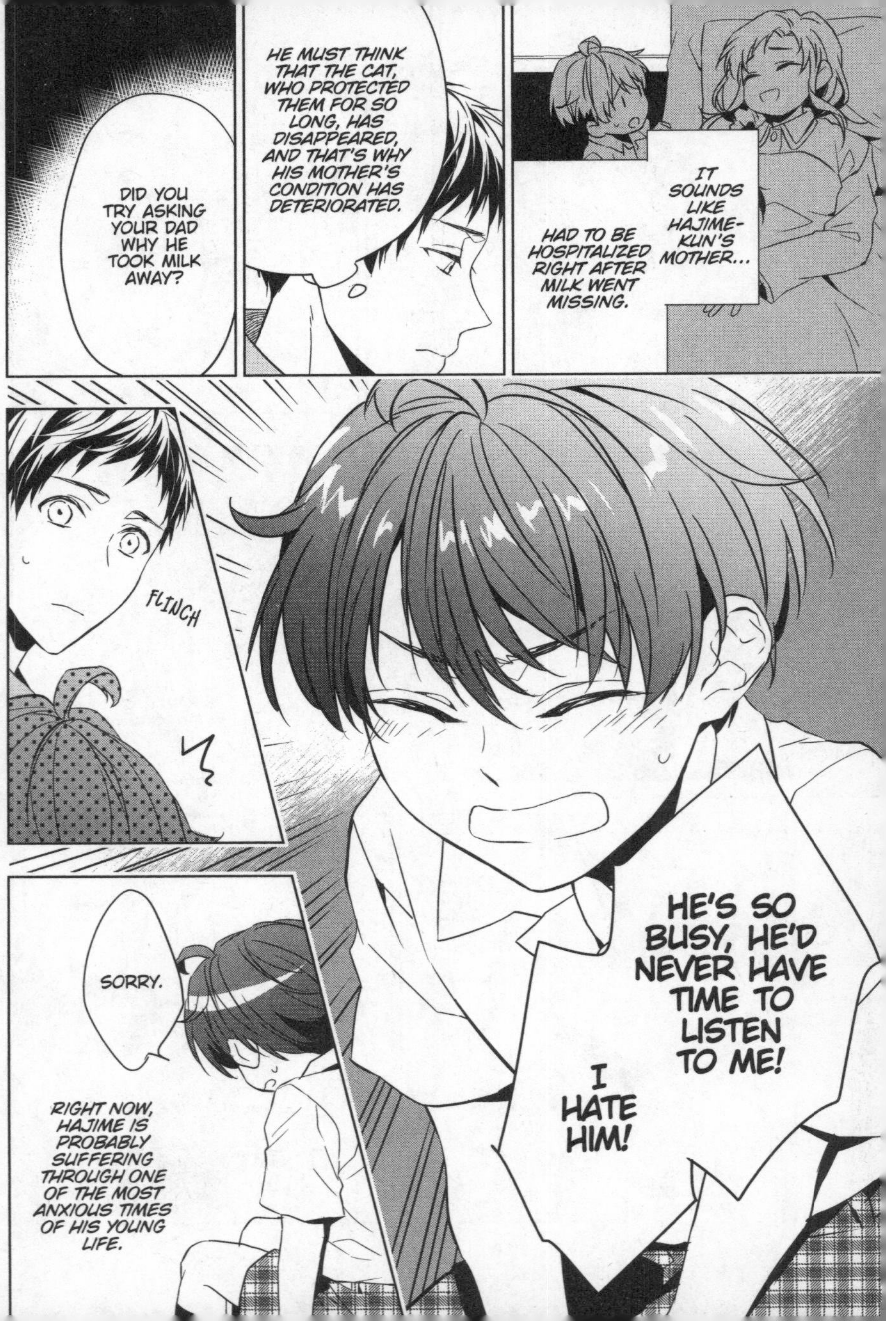
IT SOUNDS LIKE HAJIME-KUN'S MOTHER...
HAD TO BE HOSPITALIZED RIGHT AFTER MILK WENT MISSING.
HE MUST THINK THAT THE CAT, WHO PROTECTED THEM FOR SO LONG, HAS DISAPPEARED, AND THAT'S WHY HIS MOTHER'S CONDITION HAS DETERIORATED.
DID YOU TRY ASKING YOUR DAD WHY HE TOOK MILK AWAY?
HE'S SO BUSY, HE'D NEVER HAVE TIME TO LISTEN TO ME!
I HATE HIM!
FLINCH
SORRY.
RIGHT NOW, HAJIME IS PROBABLY SUFFERING THROUGH ONE OF THE MOST ANXIOUS TIMES OF HIS YOUNG LIFE.

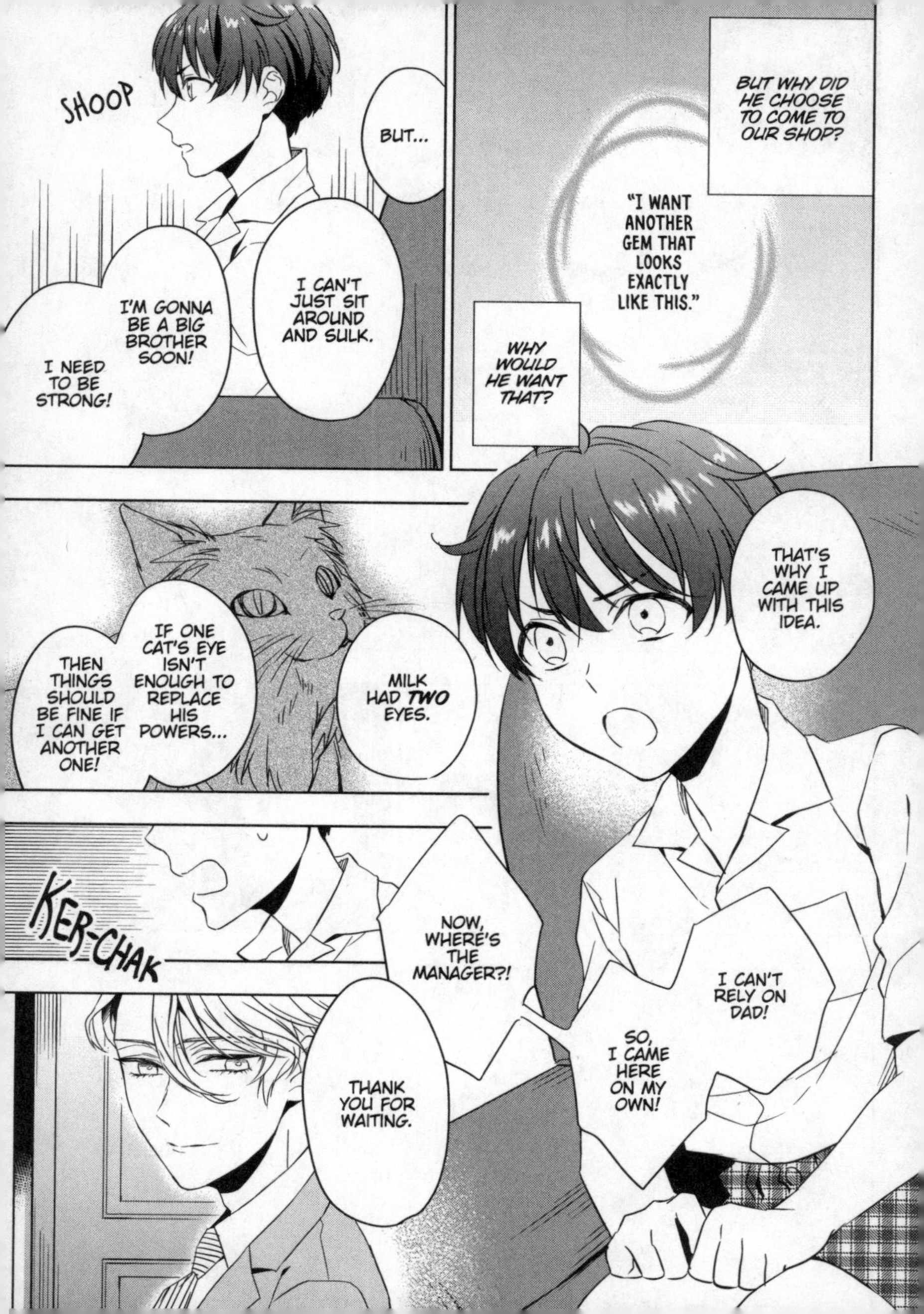
BUT WHY DID HE CHOOSE TO COME TO OUR SHOP?
"I WANT ANOTHER GEM THAT LOOKS EXACTLY LIKE THIS."
WHY WOULD HE WANT THAT?
SHOOP
BUT...
I CAN'T JUST SIT AROUND AND SULK.
I'M GONNA BE A BIG BROTHER SOON!
I NEED TO BE STRONG!
THAT'S WHY I CAME UP WITH THIS IDEA.
I CAN'T RELY ON DAD!
SO, I CAME HERE ON MY OWN!
MILK HAD ***TWO*** EYES.
IF ONE CAT'S EYE ISN'T ENOUGH TO REPLACE HIS POWERS...
THEN THINGS SHOULD BE FINE IF I CAN GET ANOTHER ONE!
KER-CHAK
NOW, WHERE'S THE MANAGER?!
THANK YOU FOR WAITING.

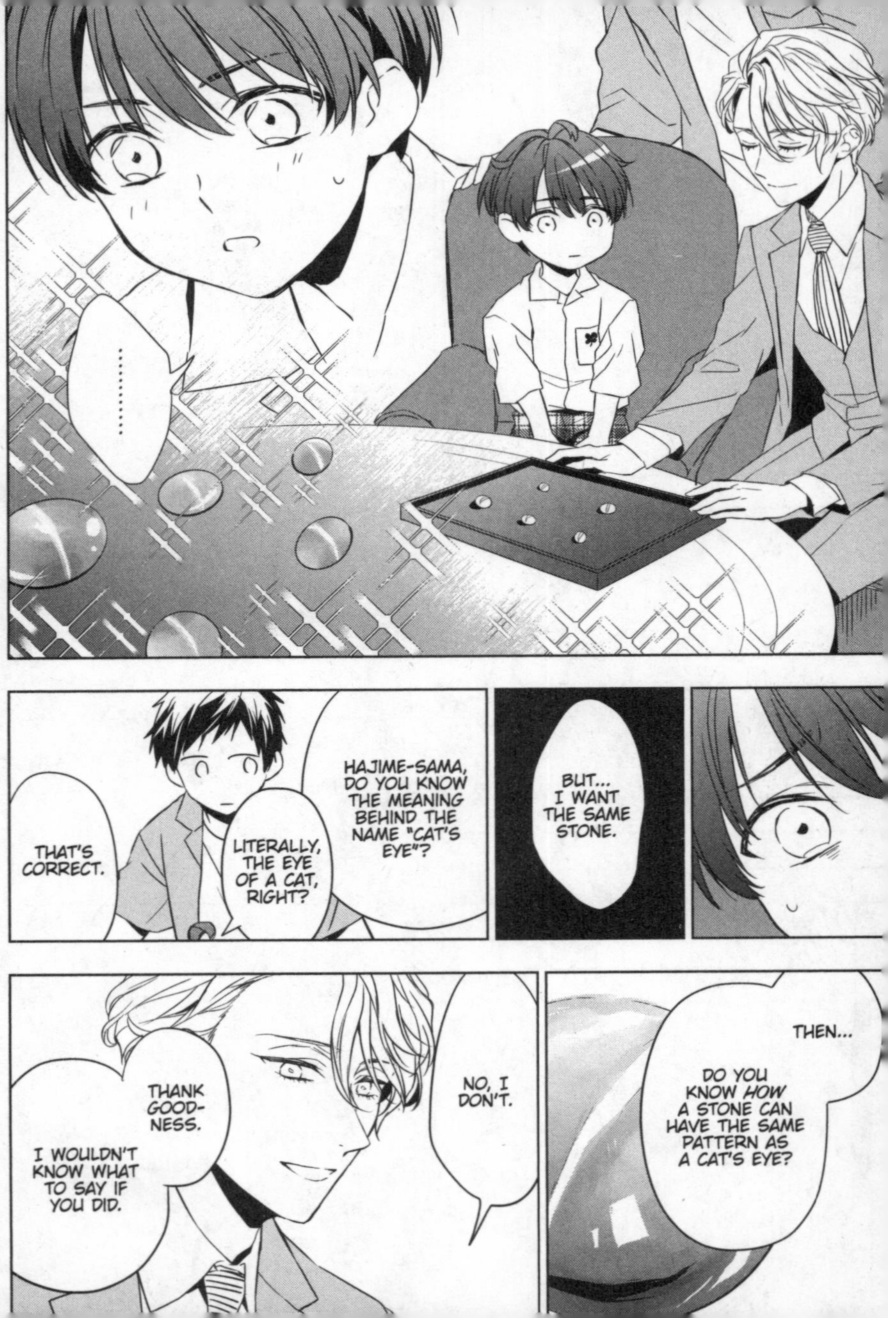
......
BUT... I WANT THE SAME STONE.
HAJIME-SAMA, DO YOU KNOW THE MEANING BEHIND THE NAME "CAT'S EYE"?
LITERALLY, THE EYE OF A CAT, RIGHT?
THAT'S CORRECT.
THEN...
DO YOU KNOW *HOW* A STONE CAN HAVE THE SAME PATTERN AS A CAT'S EYE?
NO, I DON'T.
THANK GOOD-NESS.
I WOULDN'T KNOW WHAT TO SAY IF YOU DID.

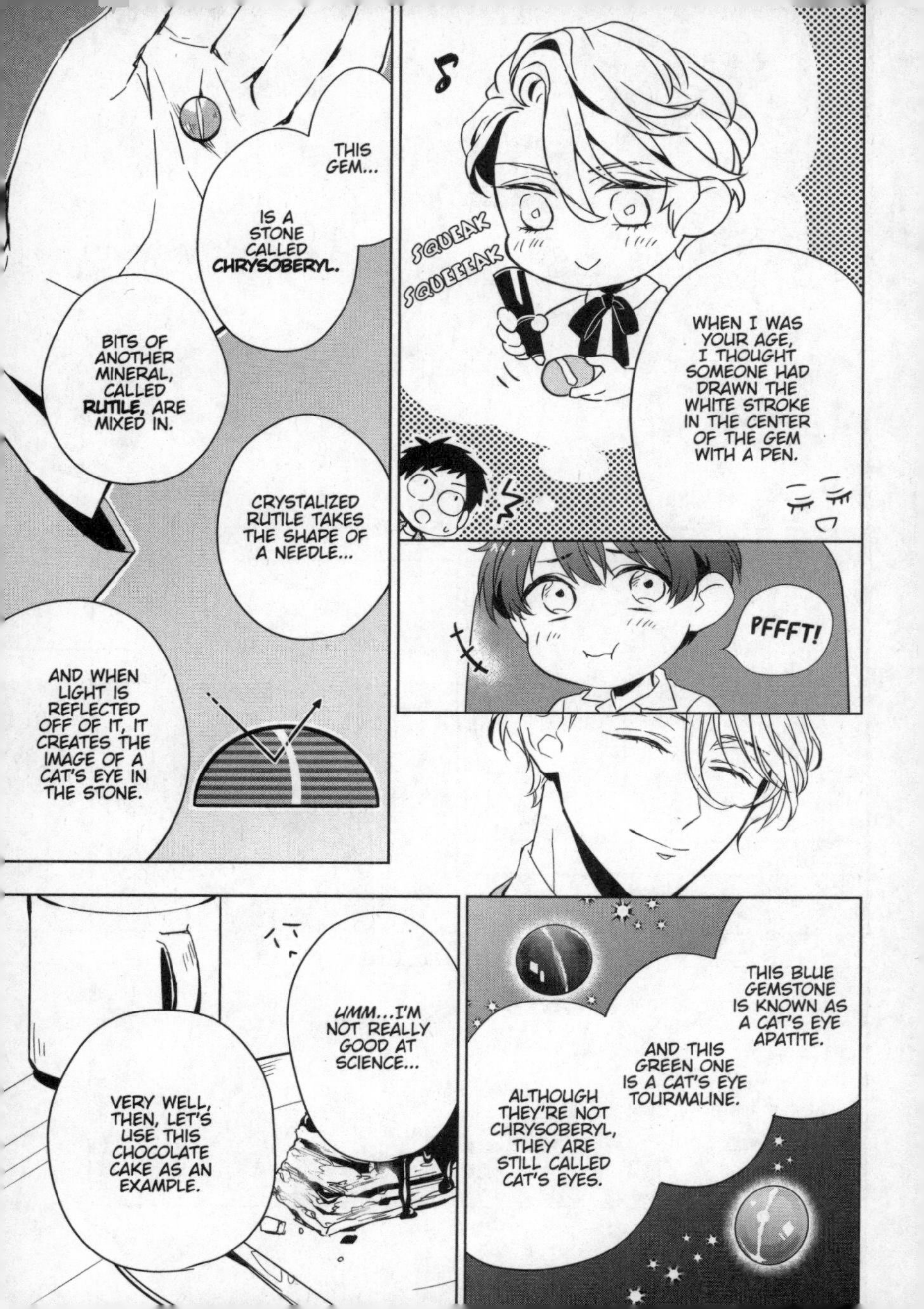
SQUEAK
SQUEEEAK
WHEN I WAS YOUR AGE, I THOUGHT SOMEONE HAD DRAWN THE WHITE STROKE IN THE CENTER OF THE GEM WITH A PEN.
PFFFT!
THIS GEM...
IS A STONE CALLED CHRYSOBERYL.
BITS OF ANOTHER MINERAL, CALLED RUTILE, ARE MIXED IN.
CRYSTALIZED RUTILE TAKES THE SHAPE OF A NEEDLE...
AND WHEN LIGHT IS REFLECTED OFF OF IT, IT CREATES THE IMAGE OF A CAT'S EYE IN THE STONE.
THIS BLUE GEMSTONE IS KNOWN AS A CAT'S EYE APATITE.
AND THIS GREEN ONE IS A CAT'S EYE TOURMALINE.
ALTHOUGH THEY'RE NOT CHRYSOBERYL, THEY ARE STILL CALLED CAT'S EYES.
UMM...I'M NOT REALLY GOOD AT SCIENCE...
VERY WELL, THEN, LET'S USE THIS CHOCOLATE CAKE AS AN EXAMPLE.

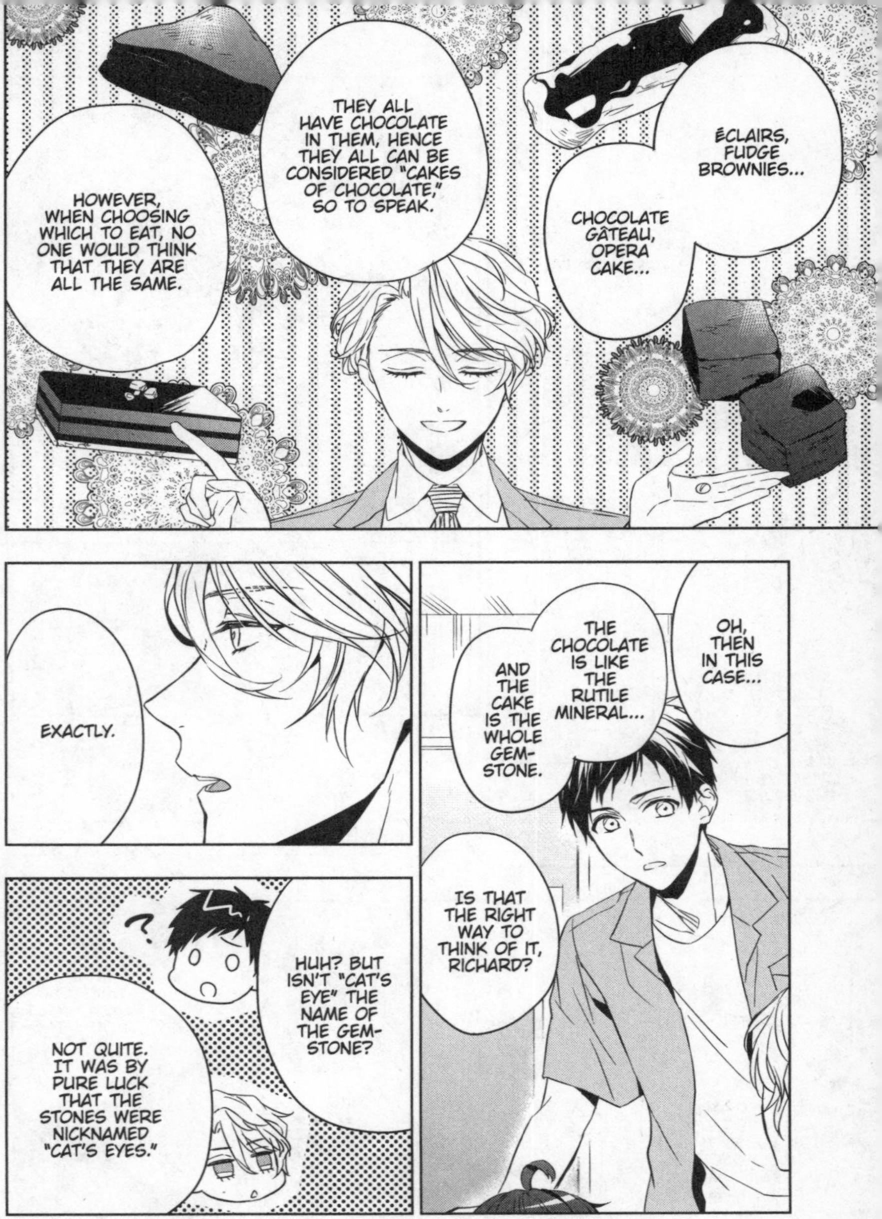
ÉCLAIRS, FUDGE BROWNIES...
CHOCOLATE GÂTEAU, OPERA CAKE...
THEY ALL HAVE CHOCOLATE IN THEM, HENCE THEY ALL CAN BE CONSIDERED "CAKES OF CHOCOLATE," SO TO SPEAK.
HOWEVER, WHEN CHOOSING WHICH TO EAT, NO ONE WOULD THINK THAT THEY ARE ALL THE SAME.
OH, THEN IN THIS CASE...
THE CHOCOLATE IS LIKE THE RUTILE MINERAL...
AND THE CAKE IS THE WHOLE GEM-STONE.
IS THAT THE RIGHT WAY TO THINK OF IT, RICHARD?
EXACTLY.
?
HUH? BUT ISN'T "CAT'S EYE" THE NAME OF THE GEM-STONE?
NOT QUITE. IT WAS BY PURE LUCK THAT THE STONES WERE NICKNAMED "CAT'S EYES."

※The optical reflection effect that makes the gems look like a cat's eye.

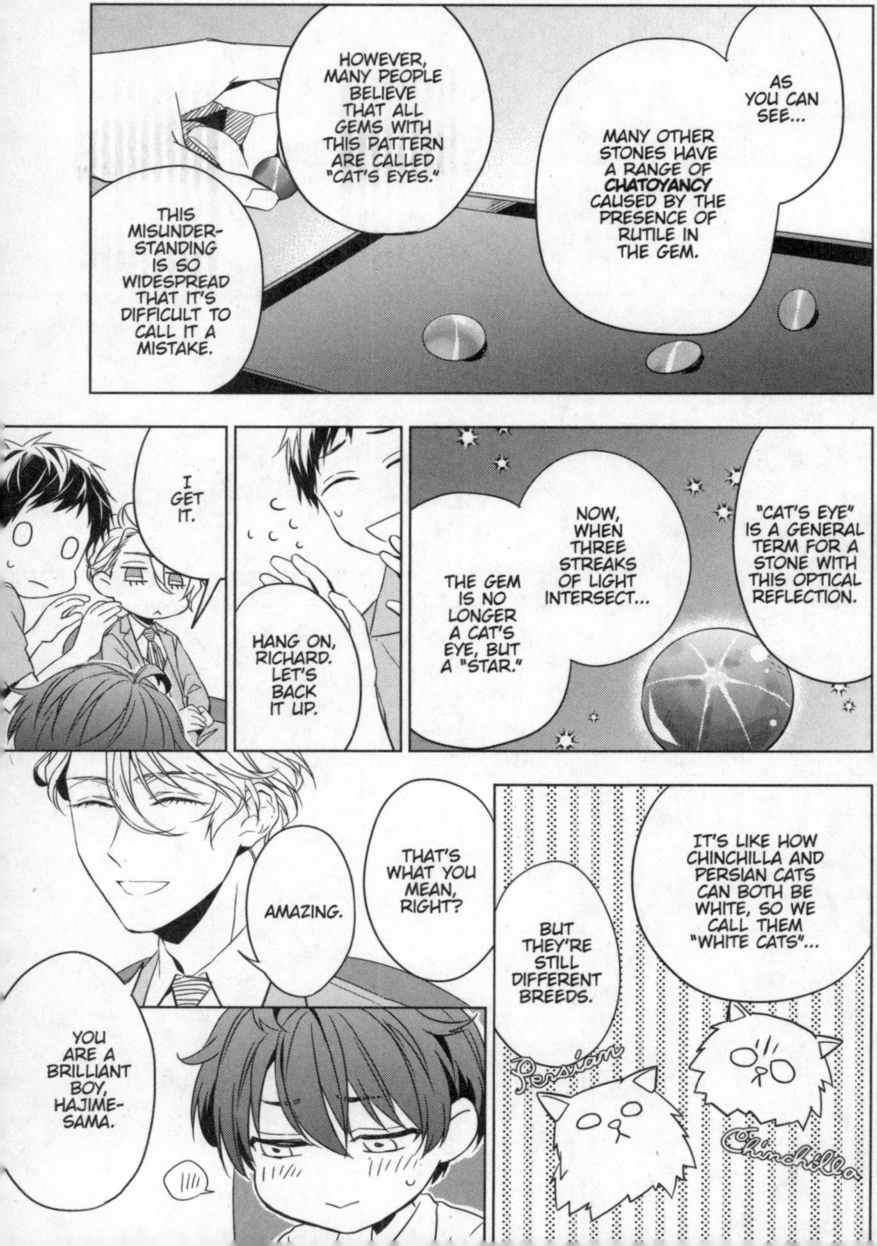
AS YOU CAN SEE...
MANY OTHER STONES HAVE A RANGE OF **CHATOYANCY** CAUSED BY THE PRESENCE OF RUTILE IN THE GEM.
HOWEVER, MANY PEOPLE BELIEVE THAT ALL GEMS WITH THIS PATTERN ARE CALLED "CAT'S EYES."
THIS MISUNDERSTANDING IS SO WIDESPREAD THAT IT'S DIFFICULT TO CALL IT A MISTAKE.
"CAT'S EYE" IS A GENERAL TERM FOR A STONE WITH THIS OPTICAL REFLECTION.
NOW, WHEN THREE STREAKS OF LIGHT INTERSECT...
THE GEM IS NO LONGER A CAT'S EYE, BUT A "STAR."
HANG ON, RICHARD. LET'S BACK IT UP.
I GET IT.
IT'S LIKE HOW CHINCHILLA AND PERSIAN CATS CAN BOTH BE WHITE, SO WE CALL THEM "WHITE CATS"...
BUT THEY'RE STILL DIFFERENT BREEDS.
Persian
Chinchilla
THAT'S WHAT YOU MEAN, RIGHT?
AMAZING.
YOU ARE A BRILLIANT BOY, HAJIME-SAMA.

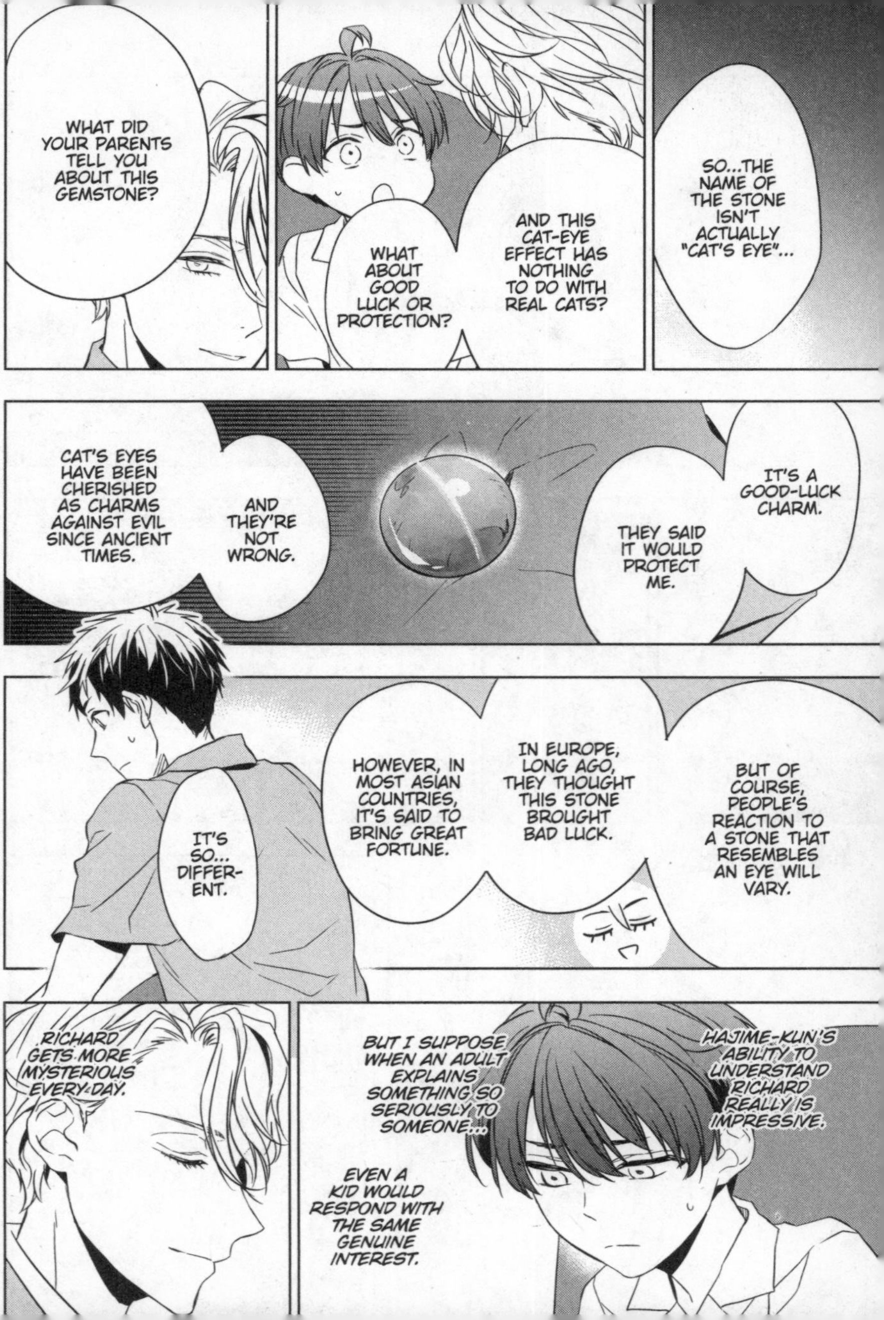

SO...THE NAME OF THE STONE ISN'T ACTUALLY "CAT'S EYE"...
AND THIS CAT-EYE EFFECT HAS NOTHING TO DO WITH REAL CATS?
WHAT ABOUT GOOD LUCK OR PROTECTION?
WHAT DID YOUR PARENTS TELL YOU ABOUT THIS GEMSTONE?
IT'S A GOOD-LUCK CHARM.
THEY SAID IT WOULD PROTECT ME.
AND THEY'RE NOT WRONG.
CAT'S EYES HAVE BEEN CHERISHED AS CHARMS AGAINST EVIL SINCE ANCIENT TIMES.
BUT OF COURSE, PEOPLE'S REACTION TO A STONE THAT RESEMBLES AN EYE WILL VARY.
IN EUROPE, LONG AGO, THEY THOUGHT THIS STONE BROUGHT BAD LUCK.
HOWEVER, IN MOST ASIAN COUNTRIES, IT'S SAID TO BRING GREAT FORTUNE.
IT'S SO... DIFFER-ENT.
HAJIME-KUN'S ABILITY TO UNDERSTAND RICHARD REALLY IS IMPRESSIVE.
BUT I SUPPOSE WHEN AN ADULT EXPLAINS SOMETHING SO SERIOUSLY TO SOMEONE...
EVEN A KID WOULD RESPOND WITH THE SAME GENUINE INTEREST.
RICHARD GETS MORE MYSTERIOUS EVERY DAY.

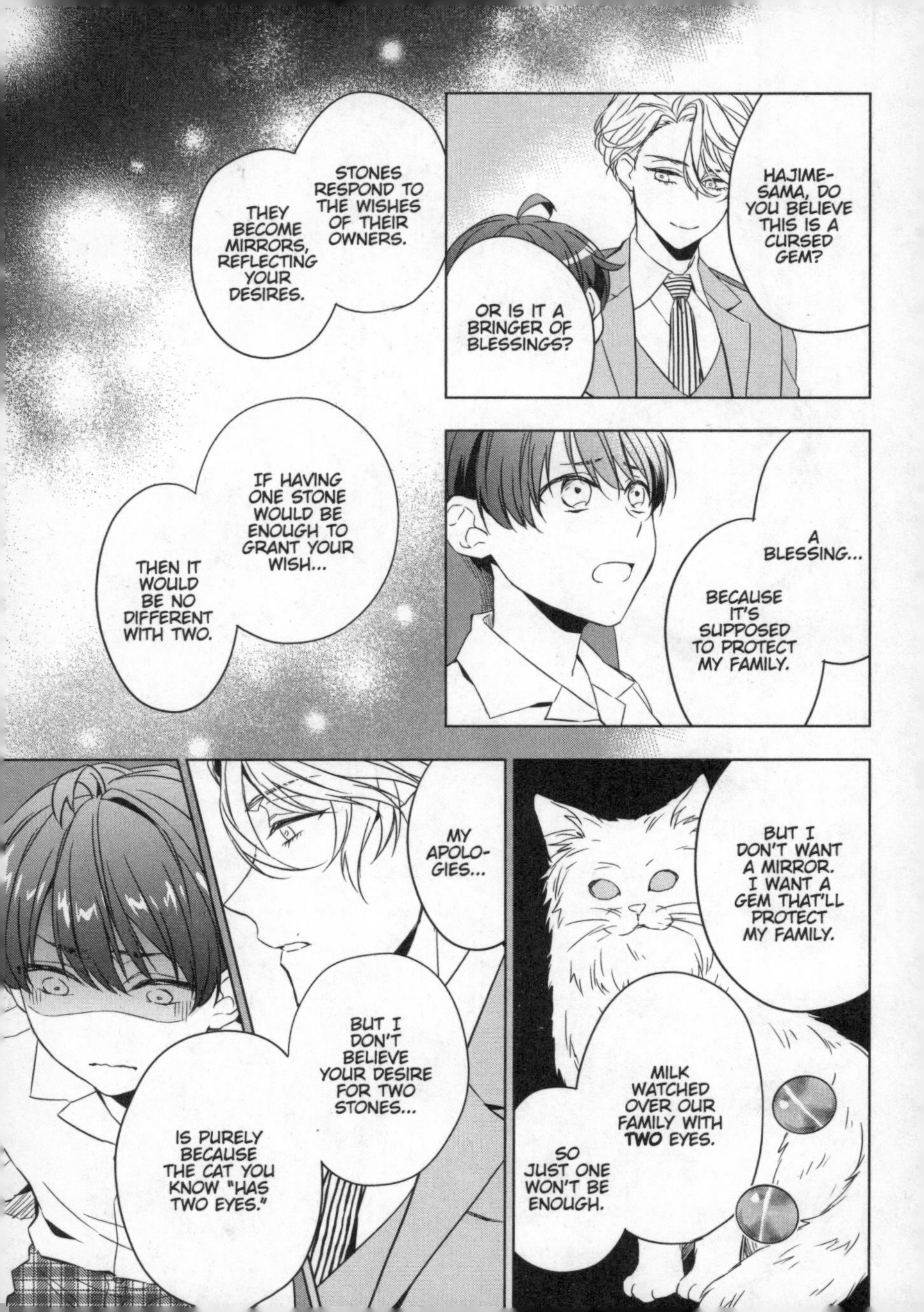
HAJIME-SAMA, DO YOU BELIEVE THIS IS A CURSED GEM?
OR IS IT A BRINGER OF BLESSINGS?
STONES RESPOND TO THE WISHES OF THEIR OWNERS.
THEY BECOME MIRRORS, REFLECTING YOUR DESIRES.
A BLESSING...
BECAUSE IT'S SUPPOSED TO PROTECT MY FAMILY.
IF HAVING ONE STONE WOULD BE ENOUGH TO GRANT YOUR WISH...
THEN IT WOULD BE NO DIFFERENT WITH TWO.
BUT I DON'T WANT A MIRROR. I WANT A GEM THAT'LL PROTECT MY FAMILY.
MILK WATCHED OVER OUR FAMILY WITH TWO EYES.
SO JUST ONE WON'T BE ENOUGH.
MY APOLOGIES...
BUT I DON'T BELIEVE YOUR DESIRE FOR TWO STONES...
IS PURELY BECAUSE THE CAT YOU KNOW "HAS TWO EYES."

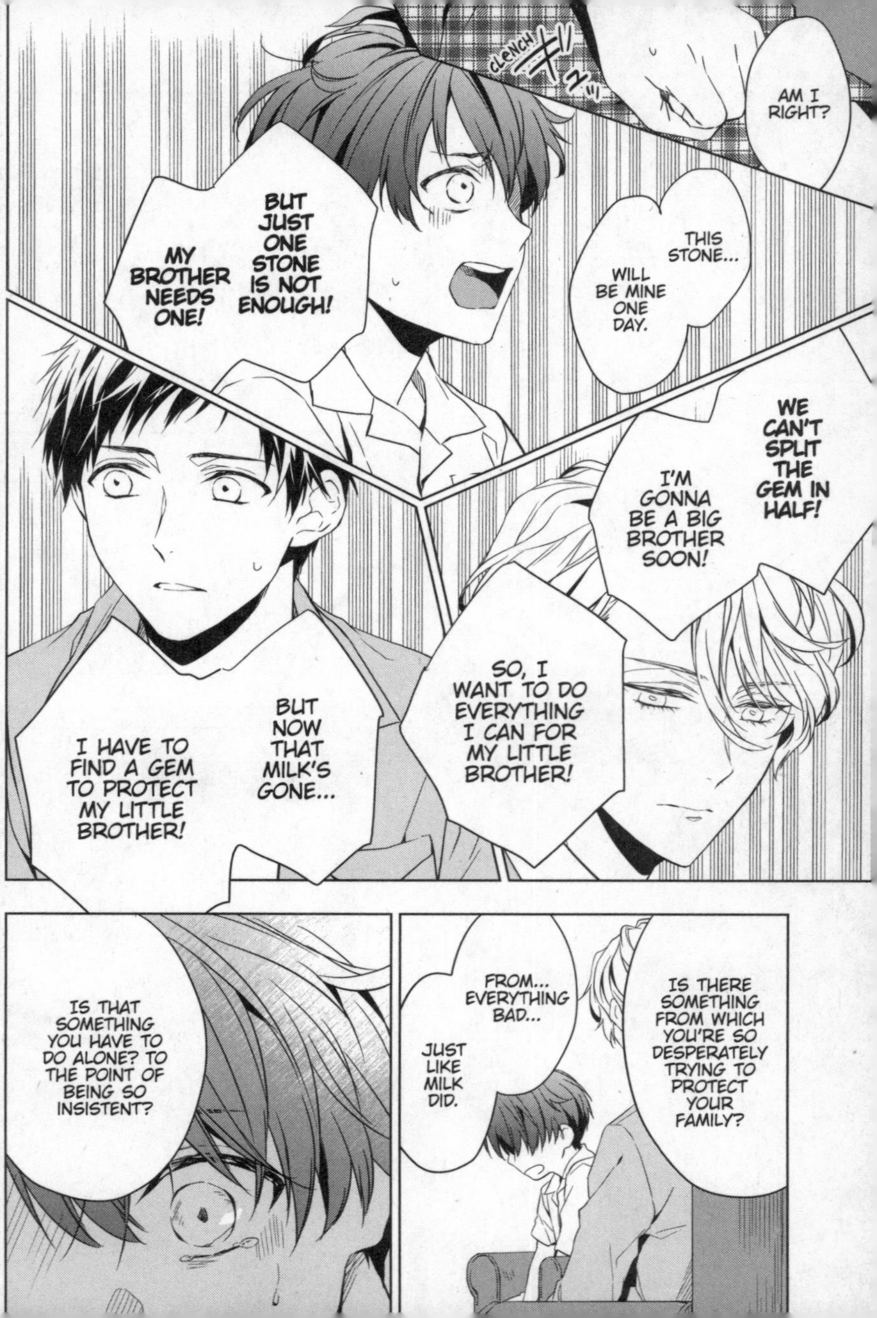
CLENCH
AM I RIGHT?
THIS STONE... WILL BE MINE ONE DAY.
BUT JUST ONE STONE IS NOT ENOUGH! MY BROTHER NEEDS ONE!
WE CAN'T SPLIT THE GEM IN HALF! I'M GONNA BE A BIG BROTHER SOON!
SO, I WANT TO DO EVERYTHING I CAN FOR MY LITTLE BROTHER!
BUT NOW THAT MILK'S GONE... I HAVE TO FIND A GEM TO PROTECT MY LITTLE BROTHER!
IS THERE SOMETHING FROM WHICH YOU'RE SO DESPERATELY TRYING TO PROTECT YOUR FAMILY?
FROM... EVERYTHING BAD... JUST LIKE MILK DID.
IS THAT SOMETHING YOU HAVE TO DO ALONE? TO THE POINT OF BEING SO INSISTENT?

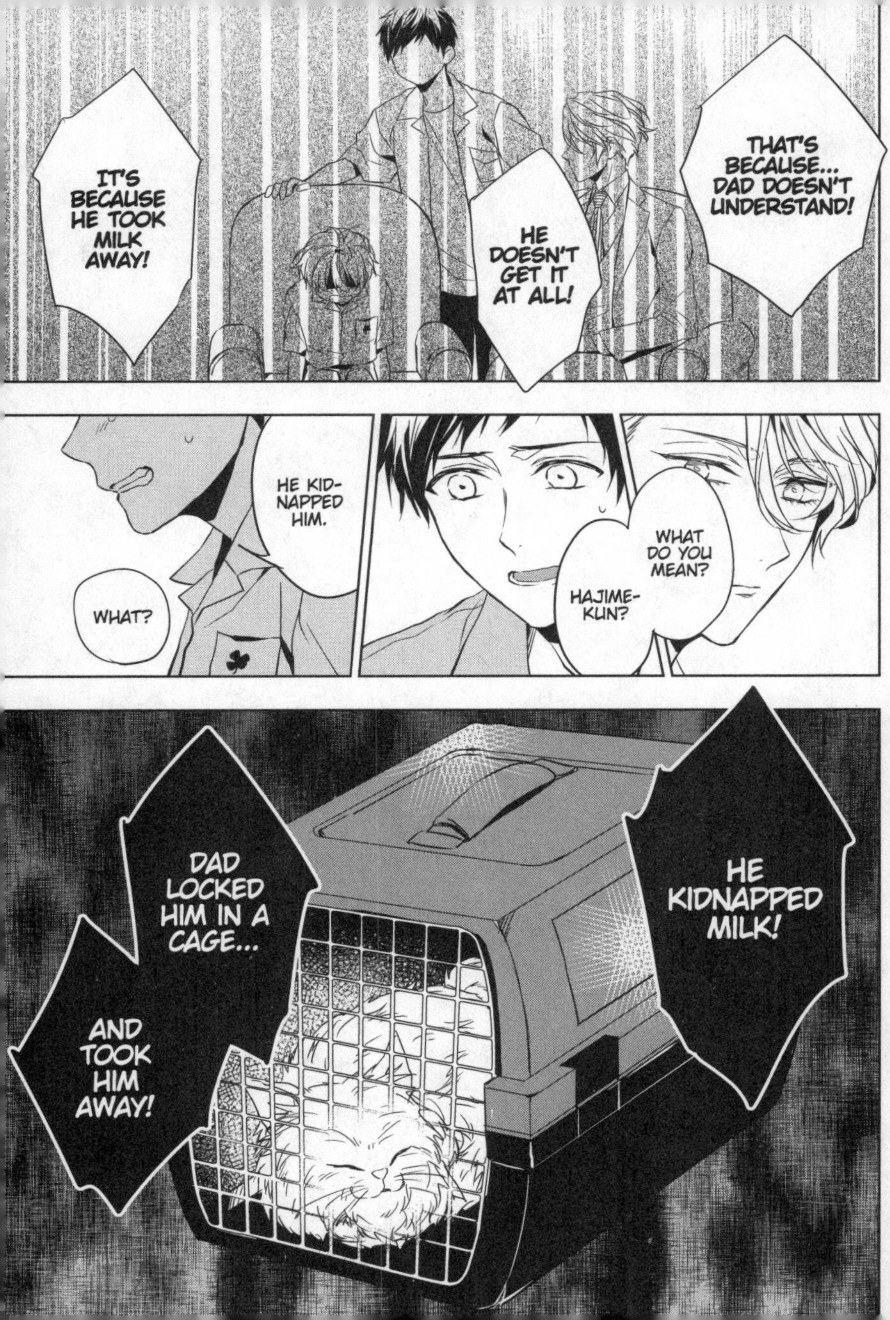
THAT'S BECAUSE... DAD DOESN'T UNDERSTAND!
HE DOESN'T GET IT AT ALL!
IT'S BECAUSE HE TOOK MILK AWAY!
WHAT DO YOU MEAN?
HAJIME-KUN?
HE KID-NAPPED HIM.
WHAT?
HE KIDNAPPED MILK!
DAD LOCKED HIM IN A CAGE...
AND TOOK HIM AWAY!

THE CASE FILES OF JEWELER RICHARD

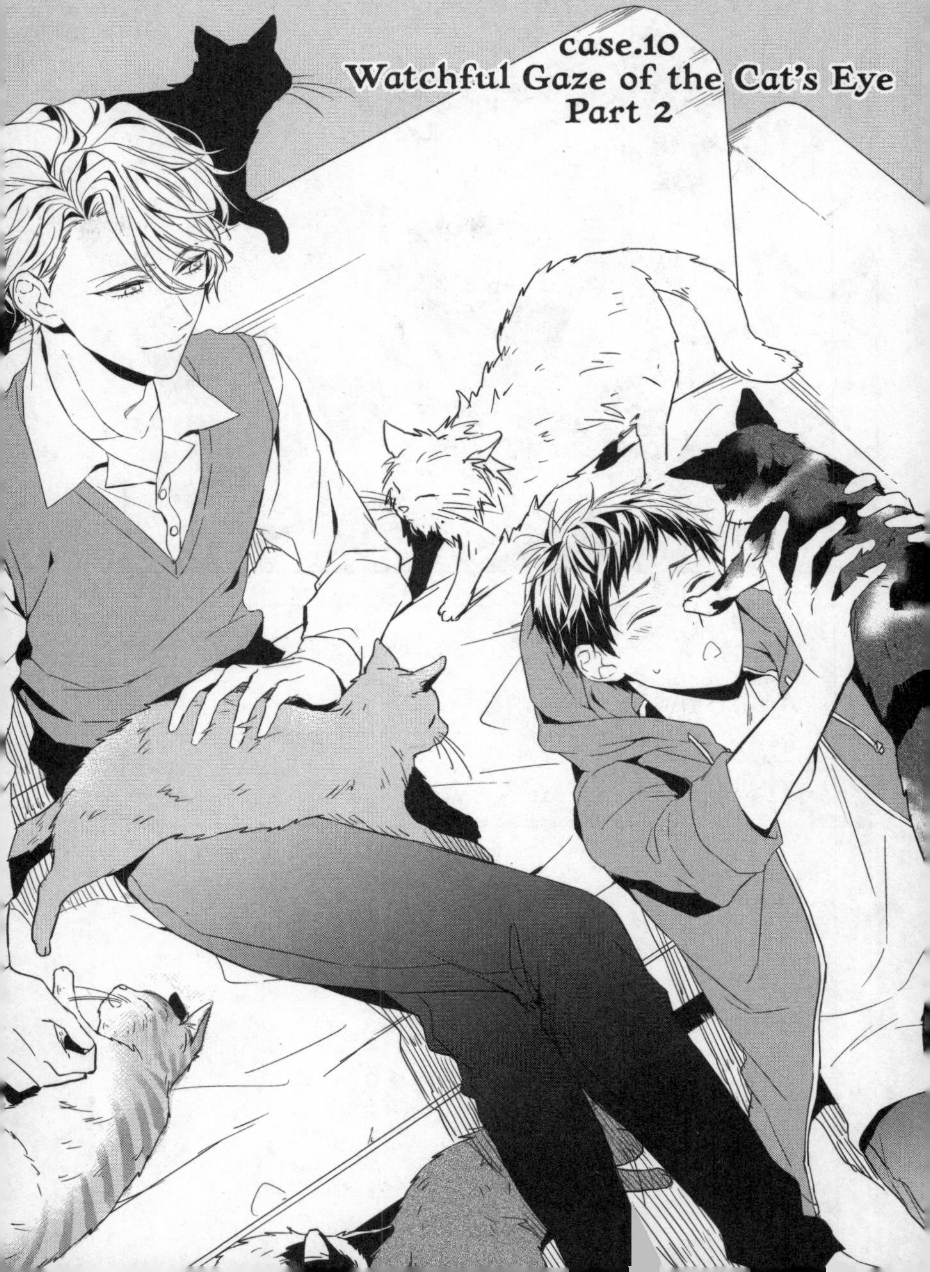
case.10
Watchful Gaze of the Cat's Eye
Part 2

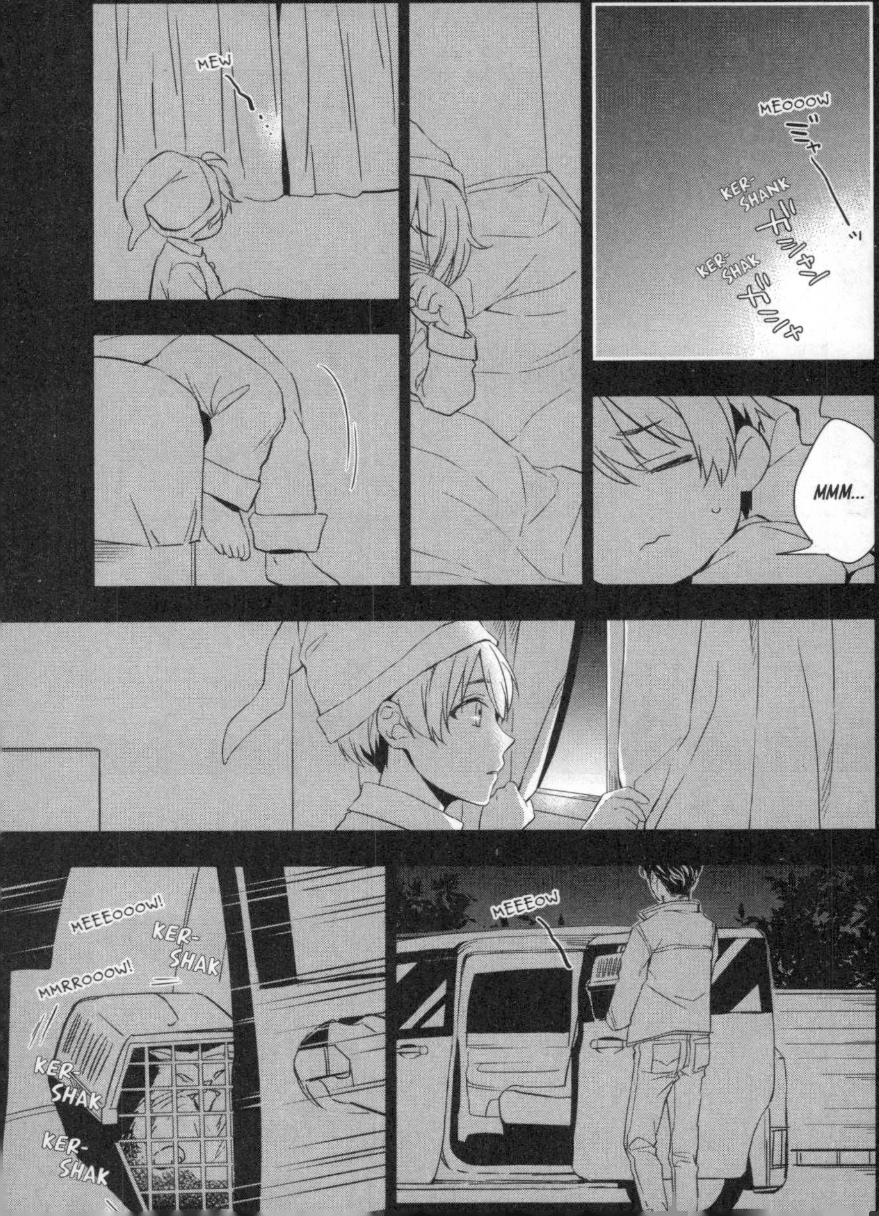
MEOOOW
KER-SHANK
KER-SHAK
MMM...
MEW
MEEEOW
MEEEOOOW!
KER-SHAK
MMRROOOW!
KER-SHAK
KER-SHAK

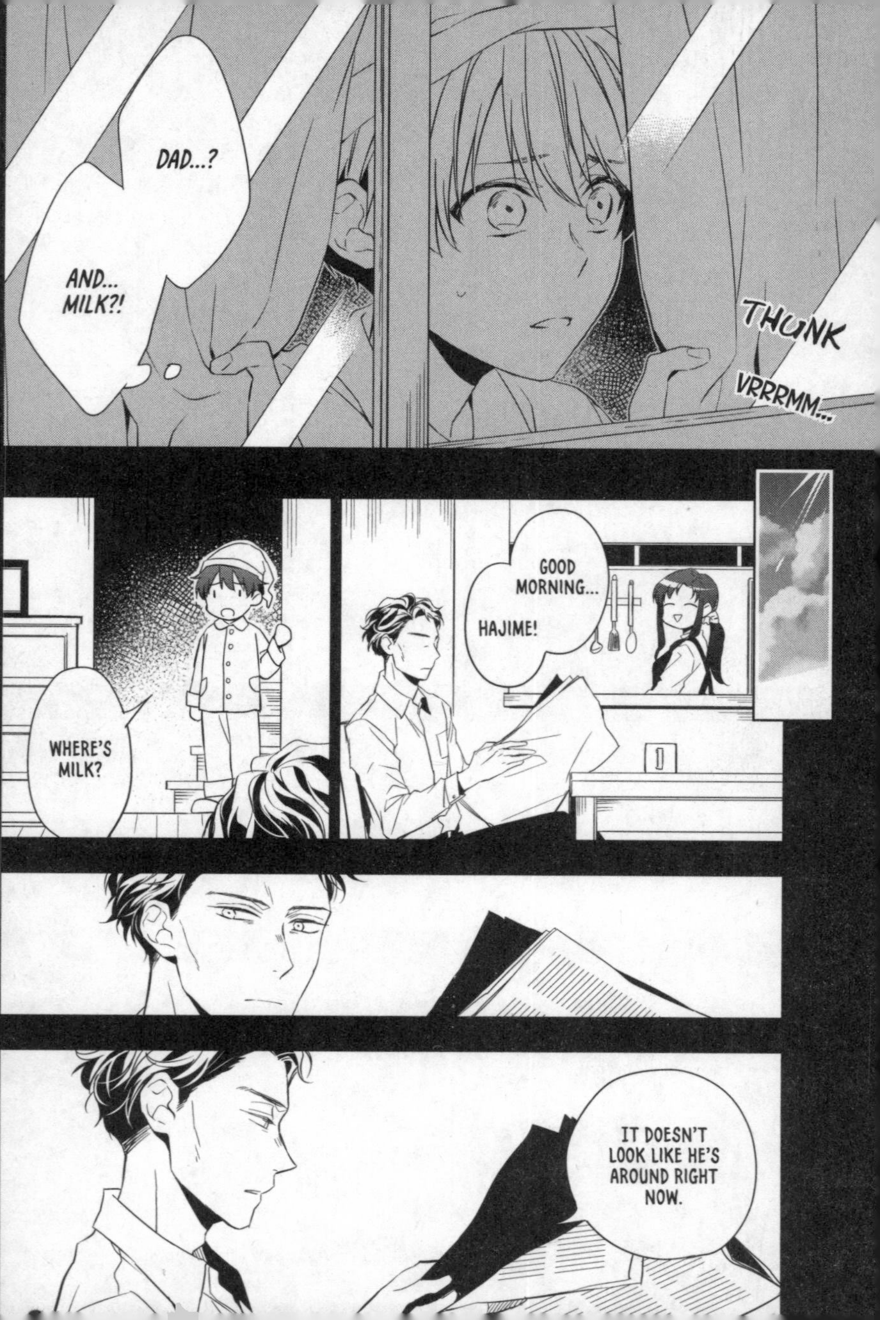
THUNK
VRRRMM...
DAD...?
AND... MILK?!
GOOD MORNING... HAJIME!
WHERE'S MILK?
IT DOESN'T LOOK LIKE HE'S AROUND RIGHT NOW.

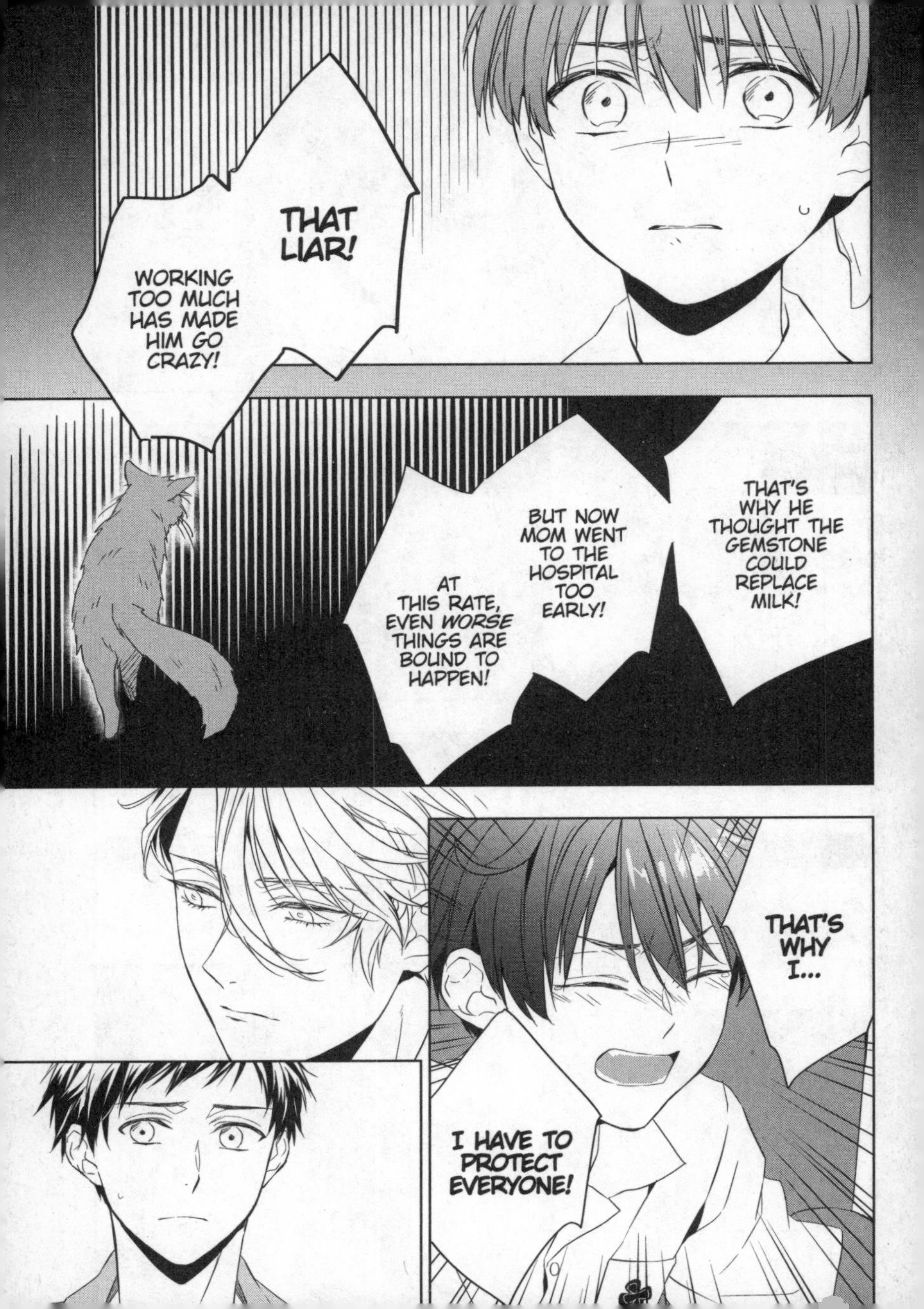
THAT LIAR!
WORKING TOO MUCH HAS MADE HIM GO CRAZY!
THAT'S WHY HE THOUGHT THE GEMSTONE COULD REPLACE MILK!
BUT NOW MOM WENT TO THE HOSPITAL TOO EARLY!
AT THIS RATE, EVEN *WORSE* THINGS ARE BOUND TO HAPPEN!
THAT'S WHY I...
I HAVE TO PROTECT EVERYONE!

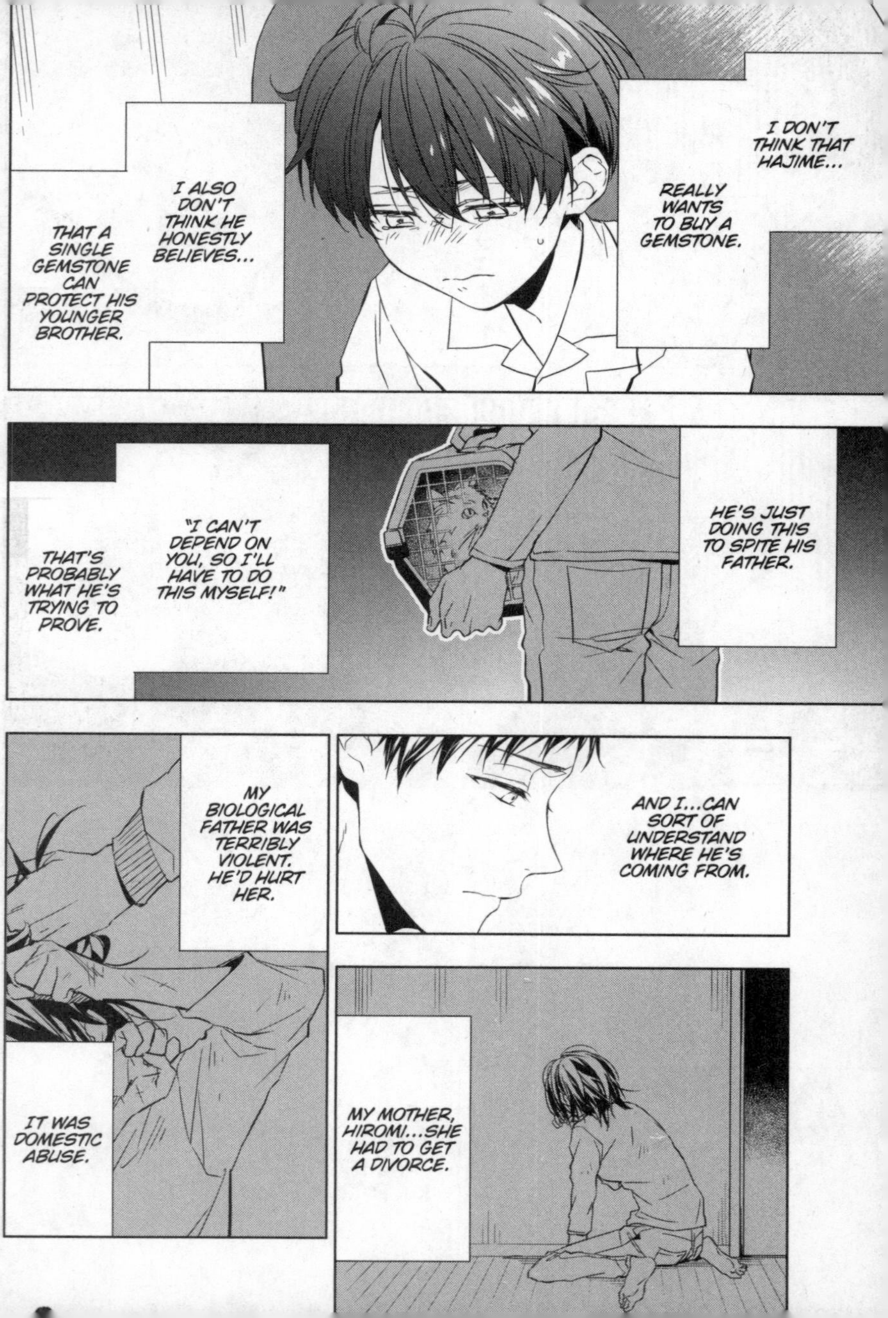
I DON'T THINK THAT HAJIME...
REALLY WANTS TO BUY A GEMSTONE.
I ALSO DON'T THINK HE HONESTLY BELIEVES...
THAT A SINGLE GEMSTONE CAN PROTECT HIS YOUNGER BROTHER.
HE'S JUST DOING THIS TO SPITE HIS FATHER.
"I CAN'T DEPEND ON YOU, SO I'LL HAVE TO DO THIS MYSELF!"
THAT'S PROBABLY WHAT HE'S TRYING TO PROVE.
AND I...CAN SORT OF UNDERSTAND WHERE HE'S COMING FROM.
MY MOTHER, HIROMI...SHE HAD TO GET A DIVORCE.
MY BIOLOGICAL FATHER WAS TERRIBLY VIOLENT. HE'D HURT HER.
IT WAS DOMESTIC ABUSE.

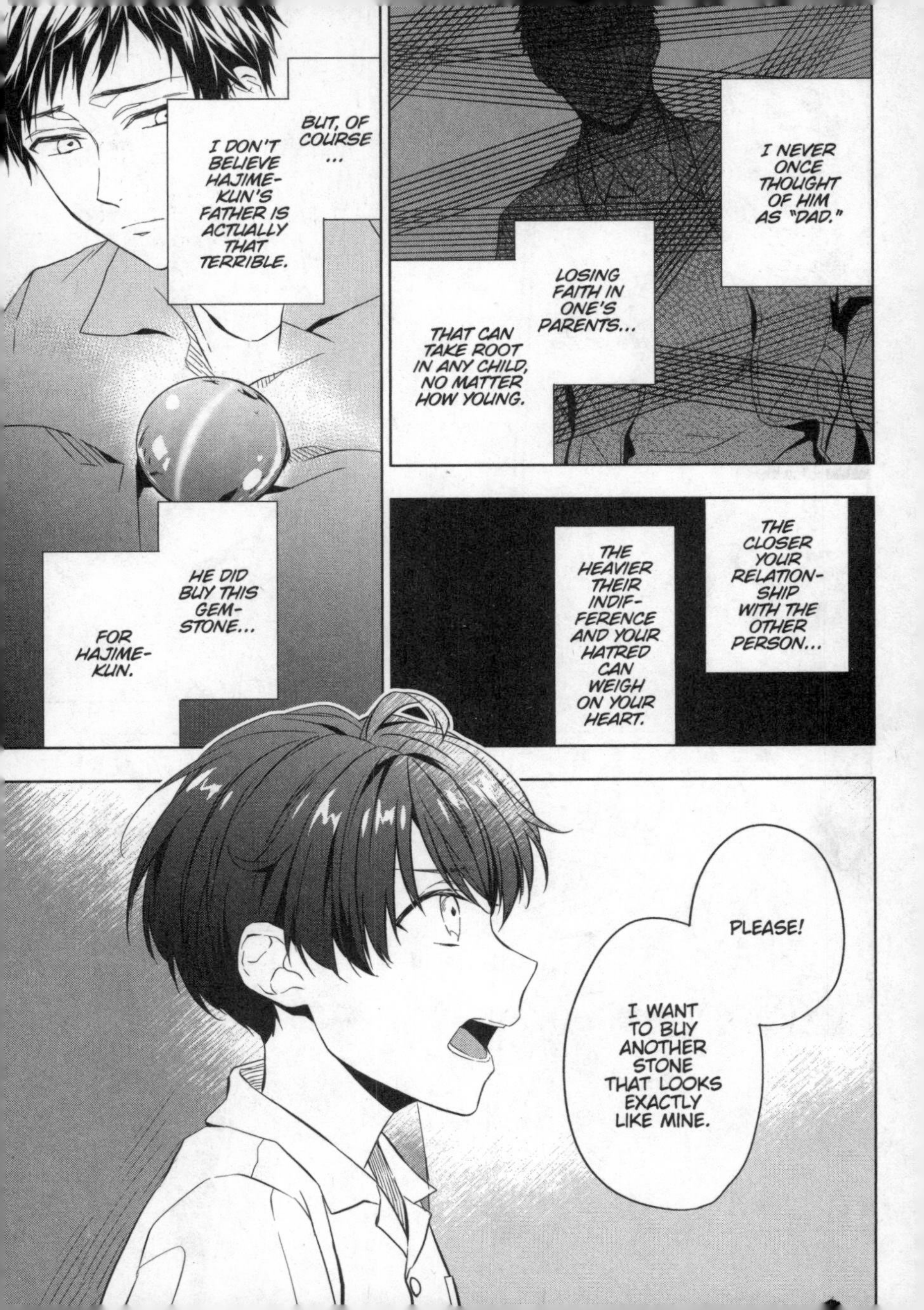

I NEVER ONCE THOUGHT OF HIM AS "DAD."
LOSING FAITH IN ONE'S PARENTS...
THAT CAN TAKE ROOT IN ANY CHILD, NO MATTER HOW YOUNG.
THE CLOSER YOUR RELATIONSHIP WITH THE OTHER PERSON...
THE HEAVIER THEIR INDIFFERENCE AND YOUR HATRED CAN WEIGH ON YOUR HEART.
BUT, OF COURSE...
I DON'T BELIEVE HAJIME-KUN'S FATHER IS ACTUALLY THAT TERRIBLE.
HE DID BUY THIS GEMSTONE...
FOR HAJIME-KUN.
PLEASE!
I WANT TO BUY ANOTHER STONE THAT LOOKS EXACTLY LIKE MINE.

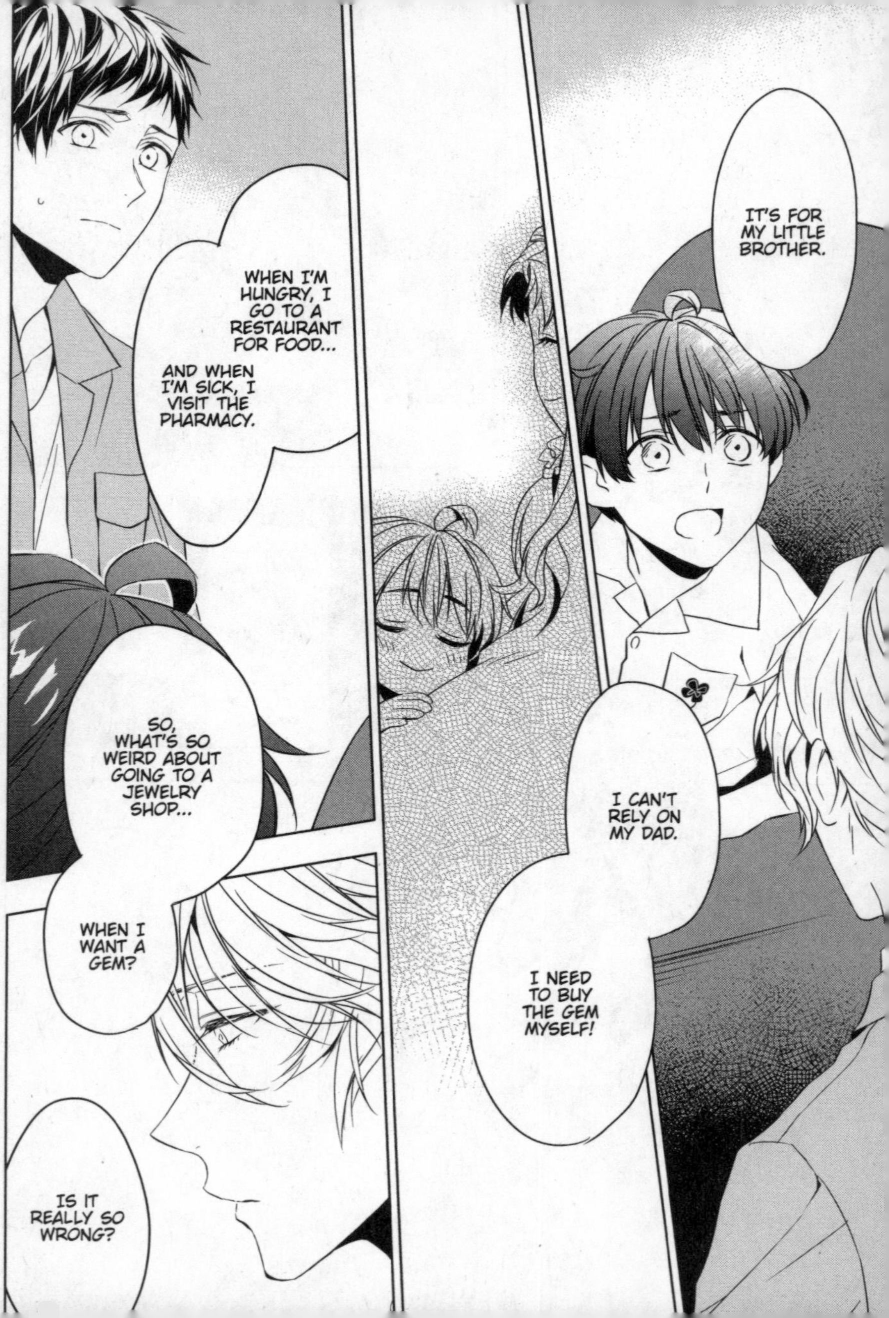
IT'S FOR MY LITTLE BROTHER.
I CAN'T RELY ON MY DAD.
I NEED TO BUY THE GEM MYSELF!
WHEN I'M HUNGRY, I GO TO A RESTAURANT FOR FOOD...
AND WHEN I'M SICK, I VISIT THE PHARMACY.
SO, WHAT'S SO WEIRD ABOUT GOING TO A JEWELRY SHOP...
WHEN I WANT A GEM?
IS IT REALLY SO WRONG?

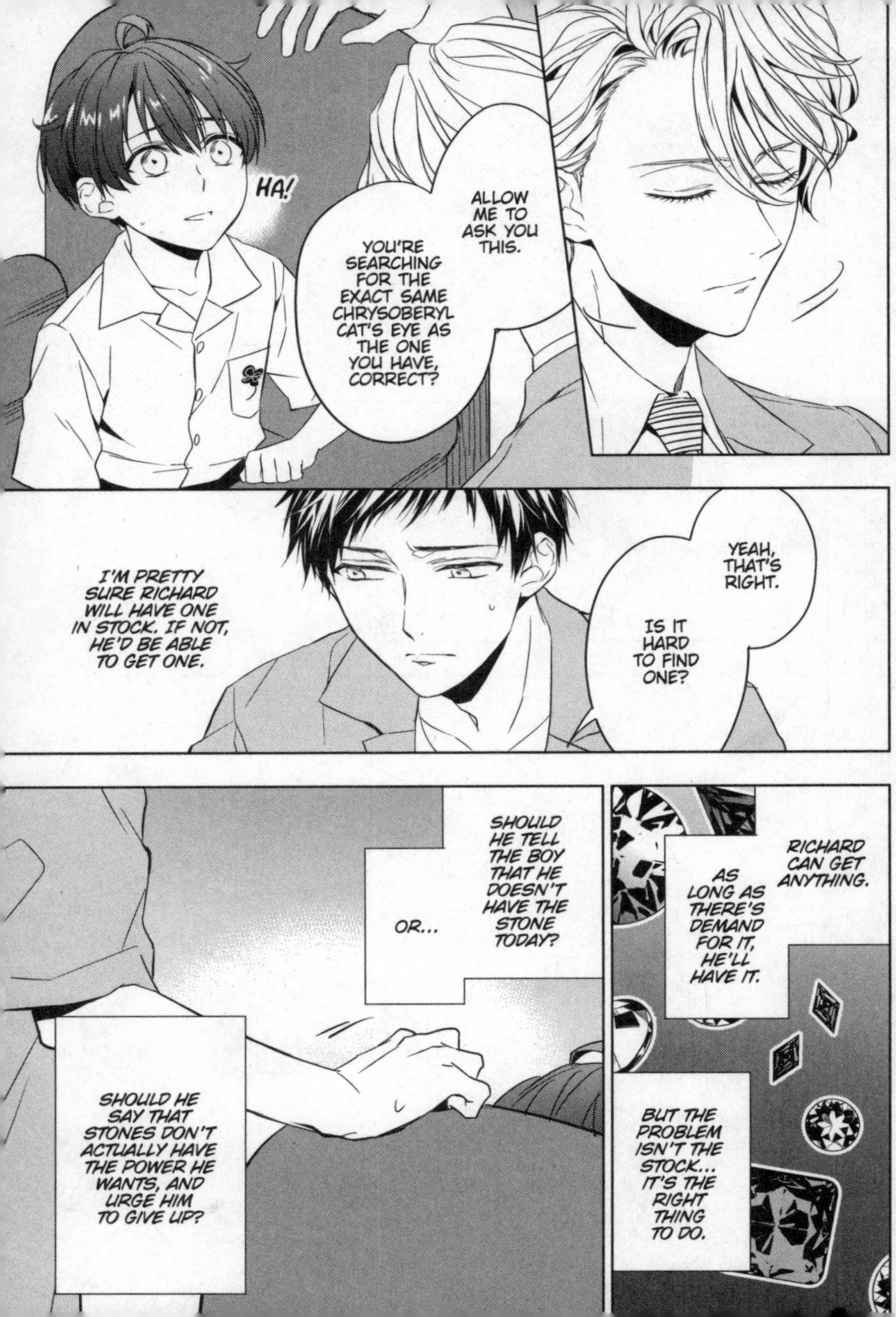
ALLOW ME TO ASK YOU THIS.
YOU'RE SEARCHING FOR THE EXACT SAME CHRYSOBERYL CAT'S EYE AS THE ONE YOU HAVE, CORRECT?
HA!
YEAH, THAT'S RIGHT.
IS IT HARD TO FIND ONE?
I'M PRETTY SURE RICHARD WILL HAVE ONE IN STOCK. IF NOT, HE'D BE ABLE TO GET ONE.
RICHARD CAN GET ANYTHING.
AS LONG AS THERE'S DEMAND FOR IT, HE'LL HAVE IT.
BUT THE PROBLEM ISN'T THE STOCK... IT'S THE RIGHT THING TO DO.
SHOULD HE TELL THE BOY THAT HE DOESN'T HAVE THE STONE TODAY?
OR...
SHOULD HE SAY THAT STONES DON'T ACTUALLY HAVE THE POWER HE WANTS, AND URGE HIM TO GIVE UP?

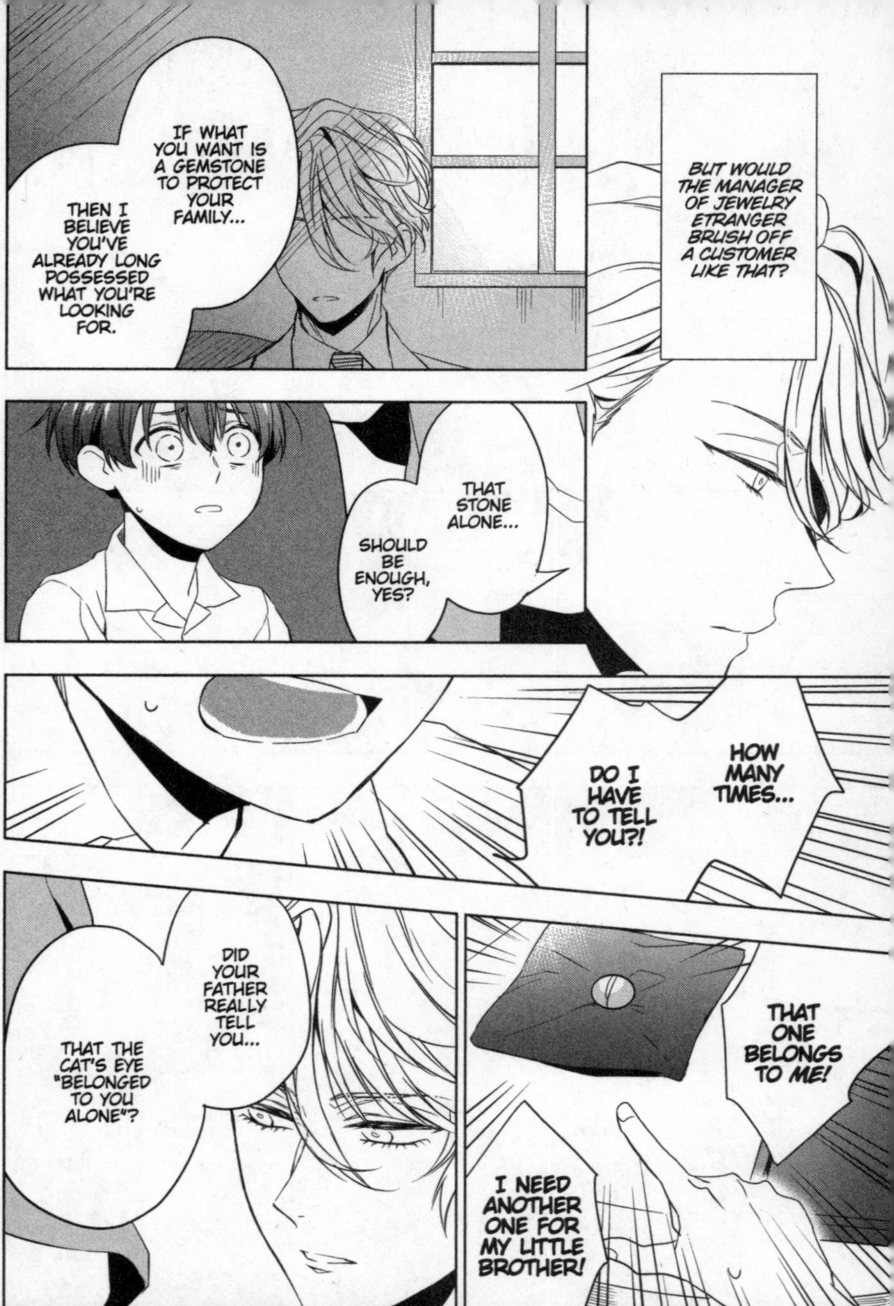
BUT WOULD THE MANAGER OF JEWELRY ETRANGER BRUSH OFF A CUSTOMER LIKE THAT?
IF WHAT YOU WANT IS A GEMSTONE TO PROTECT YOUR FAMILY...
THEN I BELIEVE YOU'VE ALREADY LONG POSSESSED WHAT YOU'RE LOOKING FOR.
THAT STONE ALONE...
SHOULD BE ENOUGH, YES?
HOW MANY TIMES...
DO I HAVE TO TELL YOU?!
THAT ONE BELONGS TO ME!
I NEED ANOTHER ONE FOR MY LITTLE BROTHER!
DID YOUR FATHER REALLY TELL YOU...
THAT THE CAT'S EYE "BELONGED TO YOU ALONE"?

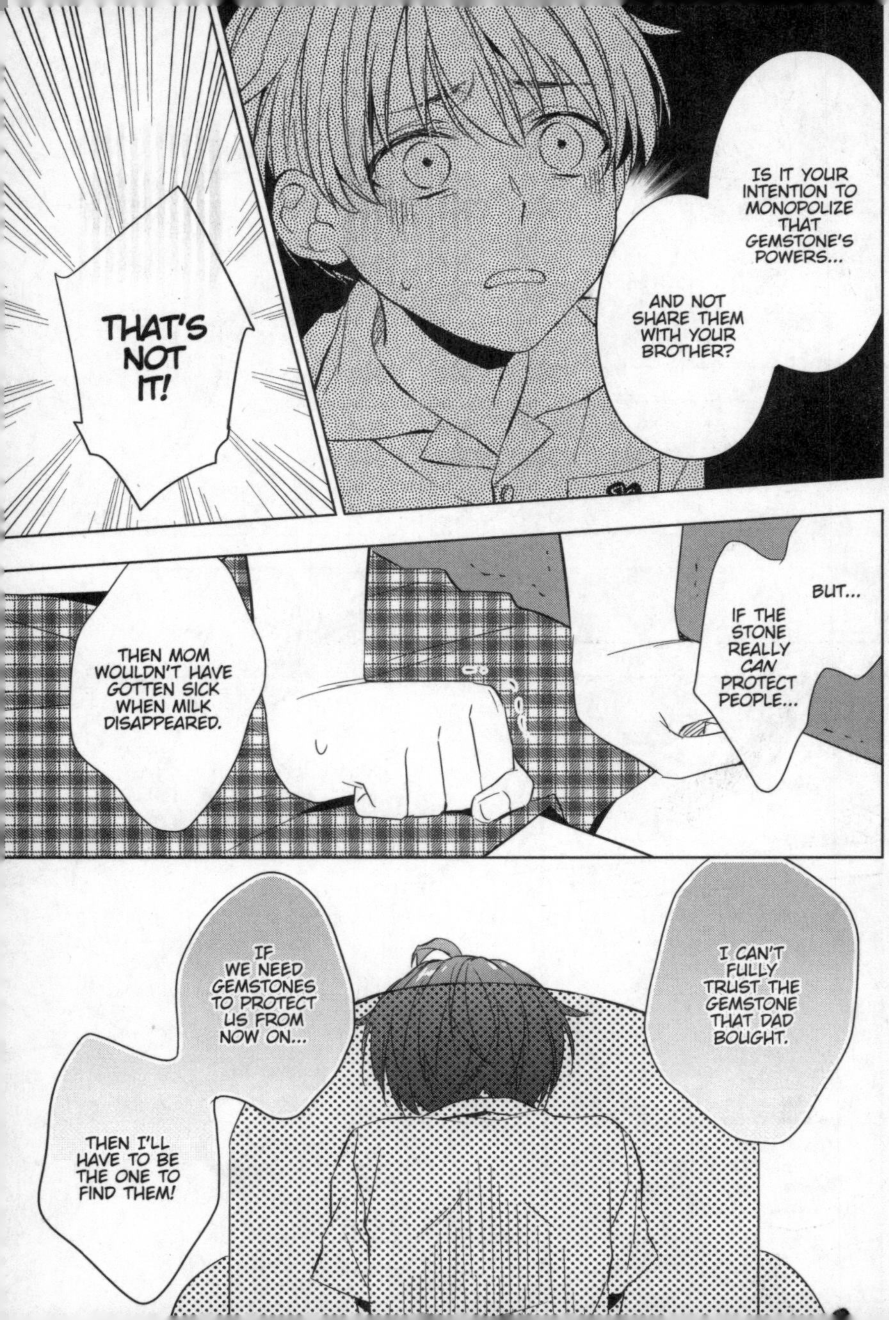
IS IT YOUR INTENTION TO MONOPOLIZE THAT GEMSTONE'S POWERS...
AND NOT SHARE THEM WITH YOUR BROTHER?
THAT'S NOT IT!
BUT...
IF THE STONE REALLY CAN PROTECT PEOPLE...
THEN MOM WOULDN'T HAVE GOTTEN SICK WHEN MILK DISAPPEARED.
I CAN'T FULLY TRUST THE GEMSTONE THAT DAD BOUGHT.
IF WE NEED GEMSTONES TO PROTECT US FROM NOW ON...
THEN I'LL HAVE TO BE THE ONE TO FIND THEM!

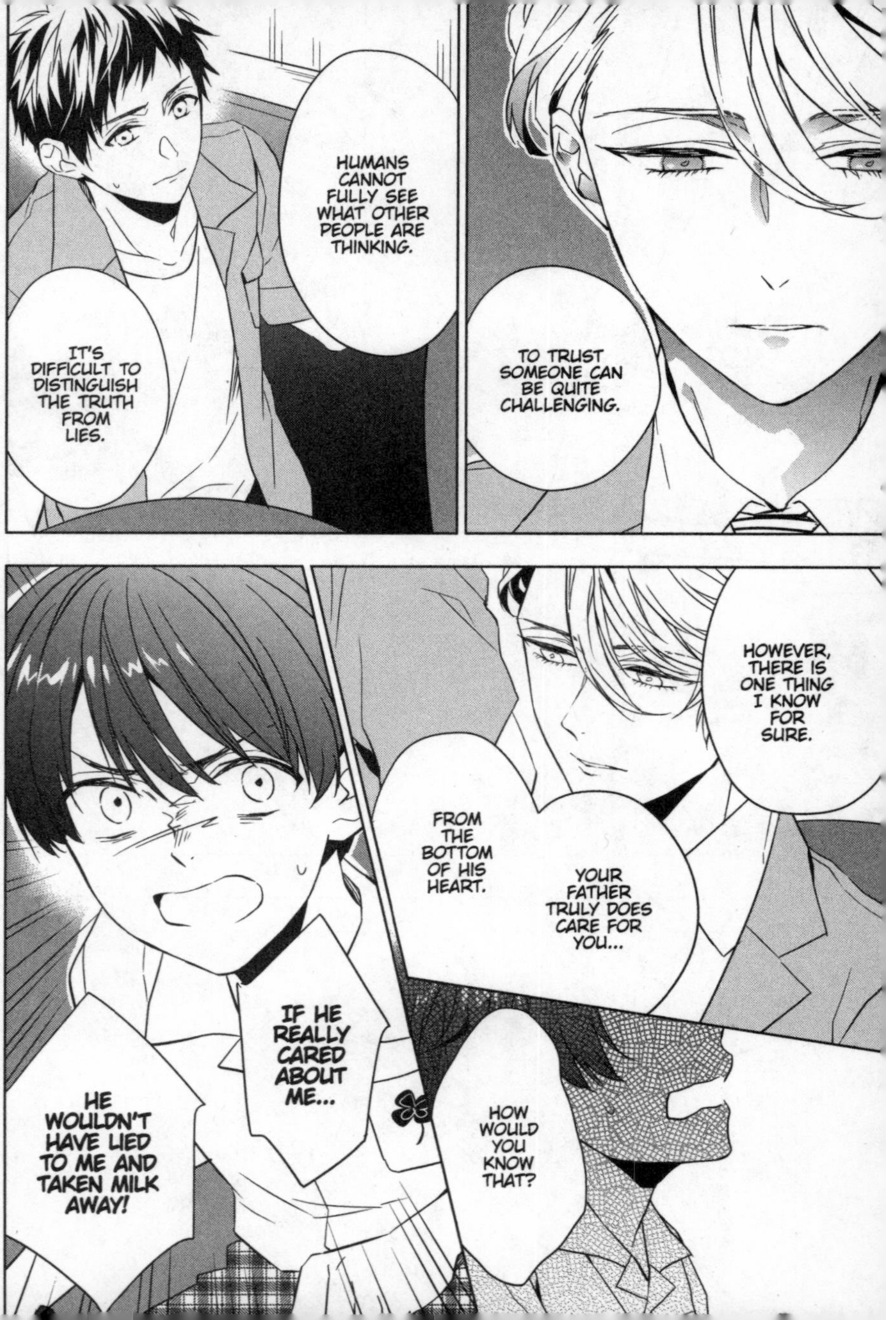
TO TRUST SOMEONE CAN BE QUITE CHALLENGING.
HUMANS CANNOT FULLY SEE WHAT OTHER PEOPLE ARE THINKING.
IT'S DIFFICULT TO DISTINGUISH THE TRUTH FROM LIES.
HOWEVER, THERE IS ONE THING I KNOW FOR SURE.
YOUR FATHER TRULY DOES CARE FOR YOU...
FROM THE BOTTOM OF HIS HEART.
HOW WOULD YOU KNOW THAT?
IF HE REALLY CARED ABOUT ME...
HE WOULDN'T HAVE LIED TO ME AND TAKEN MILK AWAY!

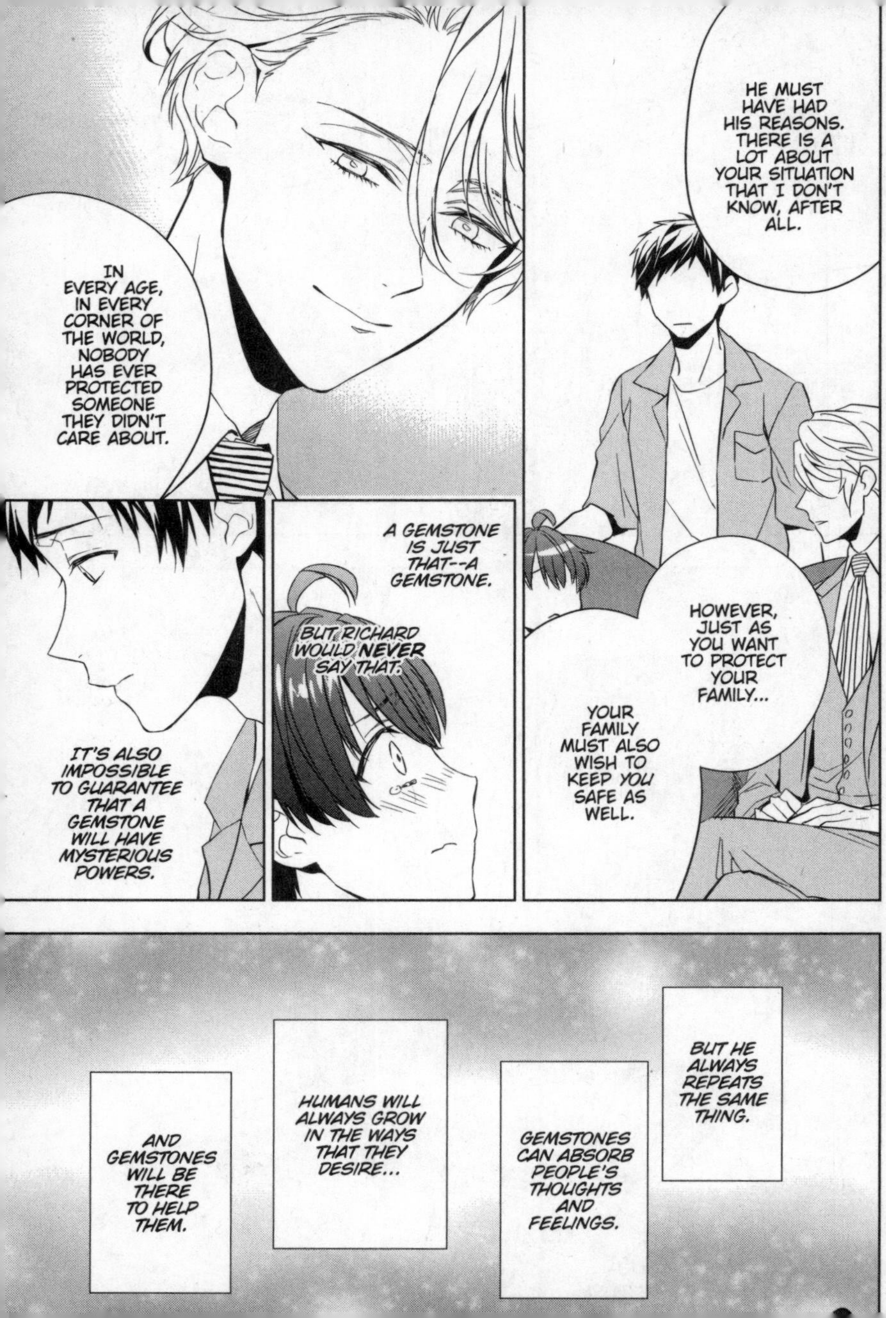
HE MUST HAVE HAD HIS REASONS. THERE IS A LOT ABOUT YOUR SITUATION THAT I DON'T KNOW, AFTER ALL.
HOWEVER, JUST AS YOU WANT TO PROTECT YOUR FAMILY...
YOUR FAMILY MUST ALSO WISH TO KEEP YOU SAFE AS WELL.
IN EVERY AGE, IN EVERY CORNER OF THE WORLD, NOBODY HAS EVER PROTECTED SOMEONE THEY DIDN'T CARE ABOUT.
A GEMSTONE IS JUST THAT--A GEMSTONE.
BUT RICHARD WOULD **NEVER** SAY THAT.
IT'S ALSO IMPOSSIBLE TO GUARANTEE THAT A GEMSTONE WILL HAVE MYSTERIOUS POWERS.
BUT HE ALWAYS REPEATS THE SAME THING.
GEMSTONES CAN ABSORB PEOPLE'S THOUGHTS AND FEELINGS.
HUMANS WILL ALWAYS GROW IN THE WAYS THAT THEY DESIRE...
AND GEMSTONES WILL BE THERE TO HELP THEM.

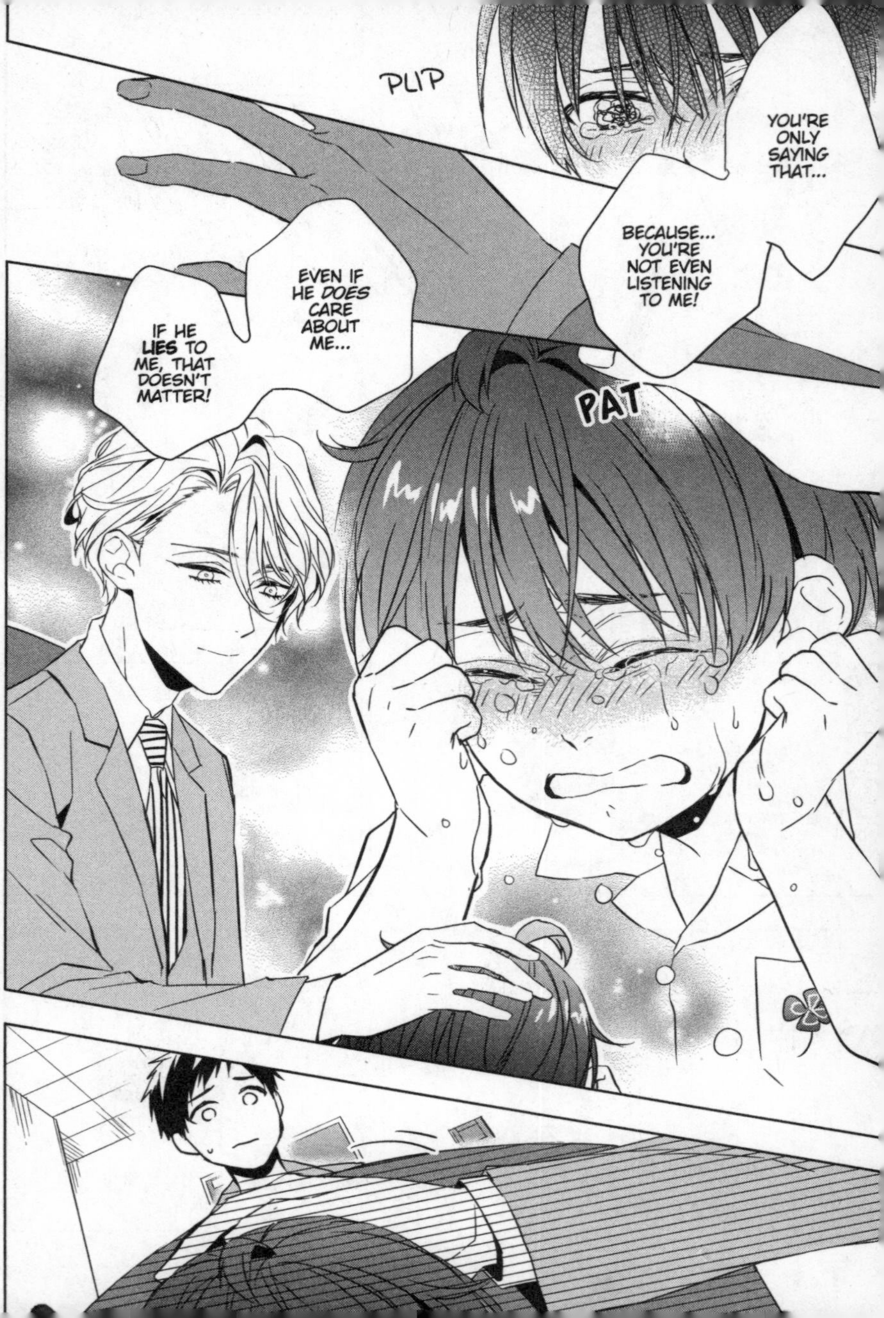
YOU'RE ONLY SAYING THAT...
BECAUSE... YOU'RE NOT EVEN LISTENING TO ME!
PLIP
EVEN IF HE *DOES* CARE ABOUT ME...
IF HE **LIES** TO ME, THAT DOESN'T MATTER!
PAT

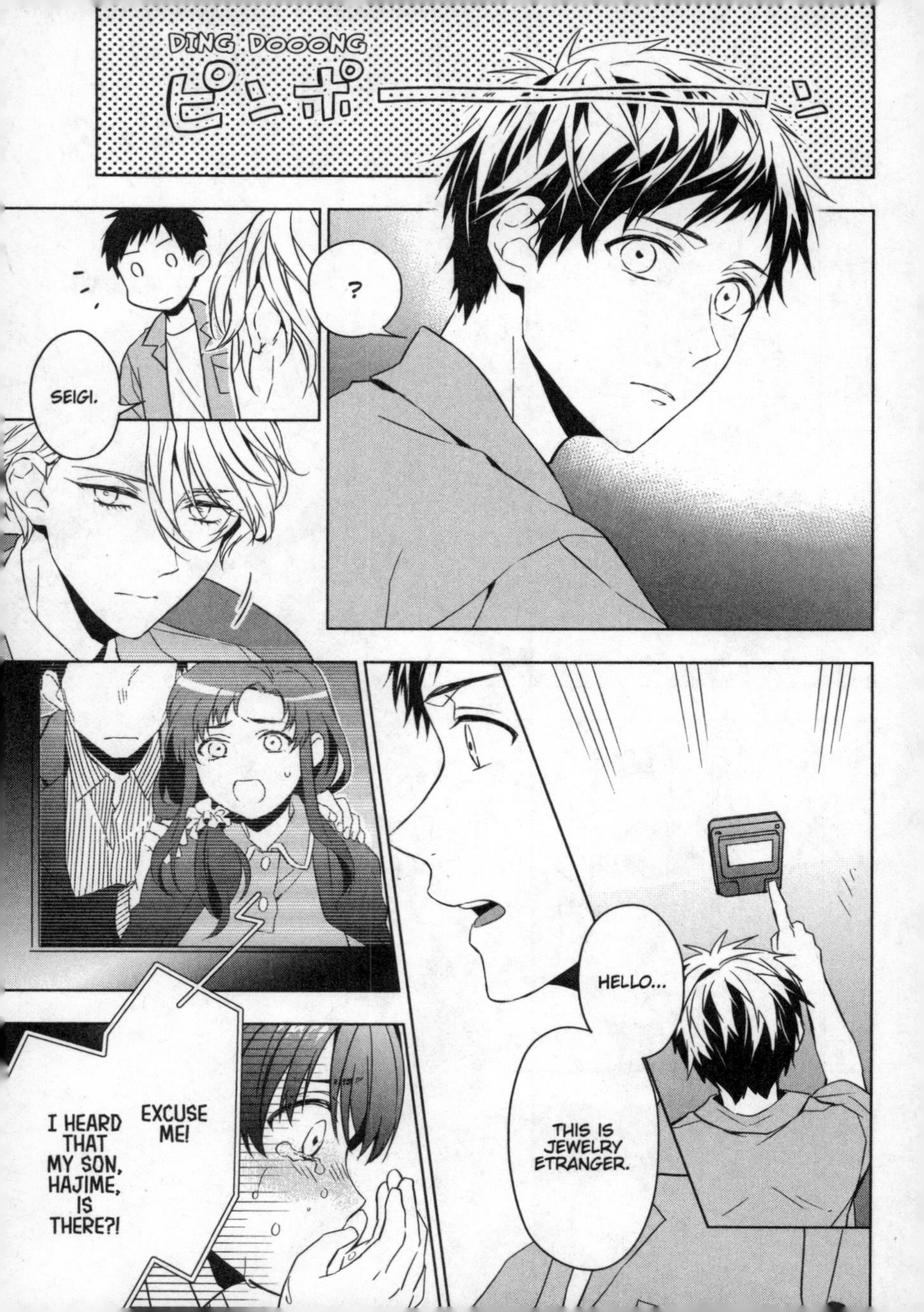
DING DOOONG
ピンポ——ン
?
SEIGI.
HELLO...
THIS IS JEWELRY ETRANGER.
EXCUSE ME!
I HEARD THAT MY SON, HAJIME, IS THERE?!

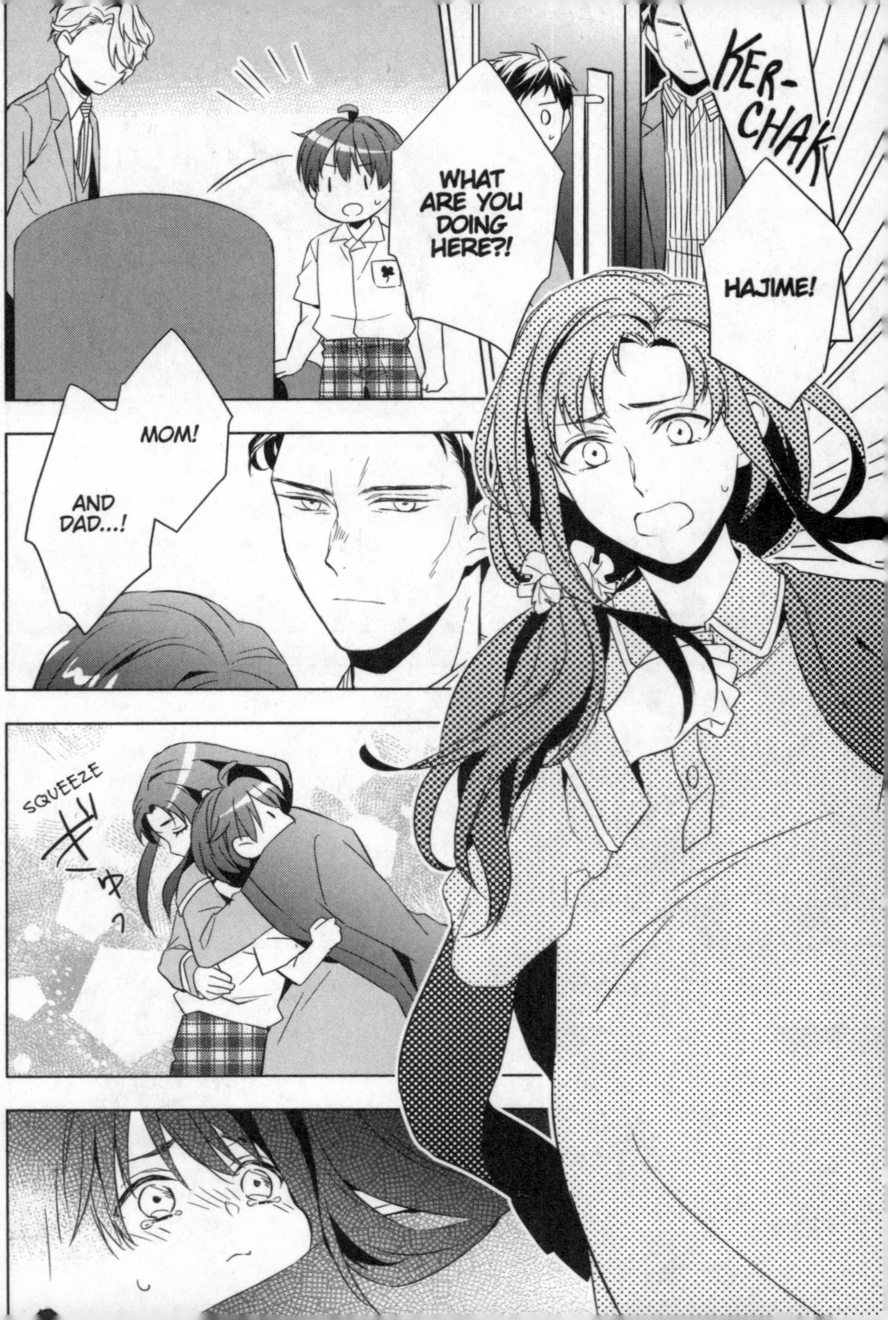
KER-CHAK
HAJIME!
WHAT ARE YOU DOING HERE?!
MOM!
AND DAD...!
SQUEEZE

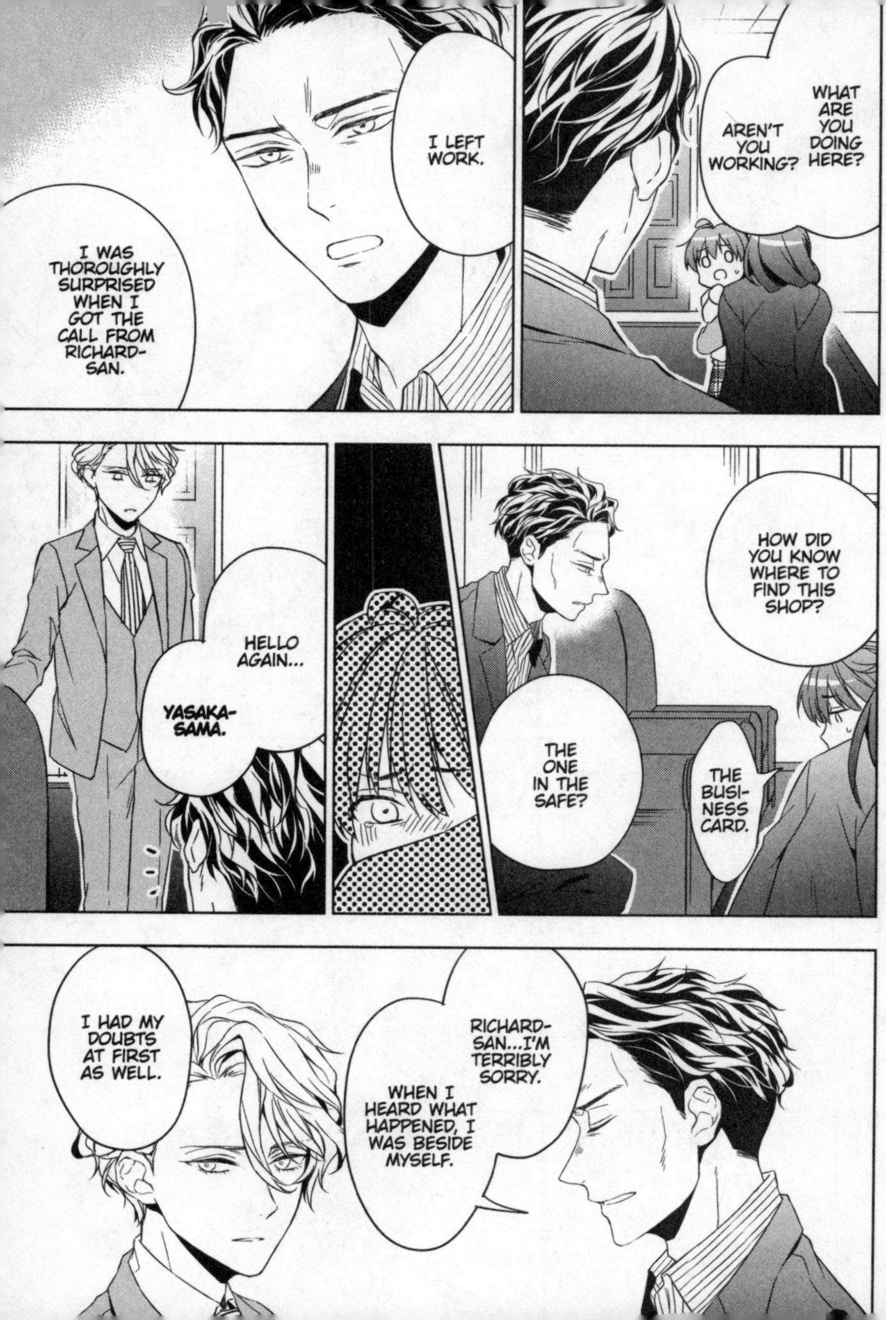
WHAT ARE YOU DOING HERE?
AREN'T YOU WORKING?
I LEFT WORK.
I WAS THOROUGHLY SURPRISED WHEN I GOT THE CALL FROM RICHARD-SAN.
HOW DID YOU KNOW WHERE TO FIND THIS SHOP?
THE BUSI-NESS CARD.
THE ONE IN THE SAFE?
HELLO AGAIN...
YASAKA-SAMA.
RICHARD-SAN...I'M TERRIBLY SORRY.
WHEN I HEARD WHAT HAPPENED, I WAS BESIDE MYSELF.
I HAD MY DOUBTS AT FIRST AS WELL.

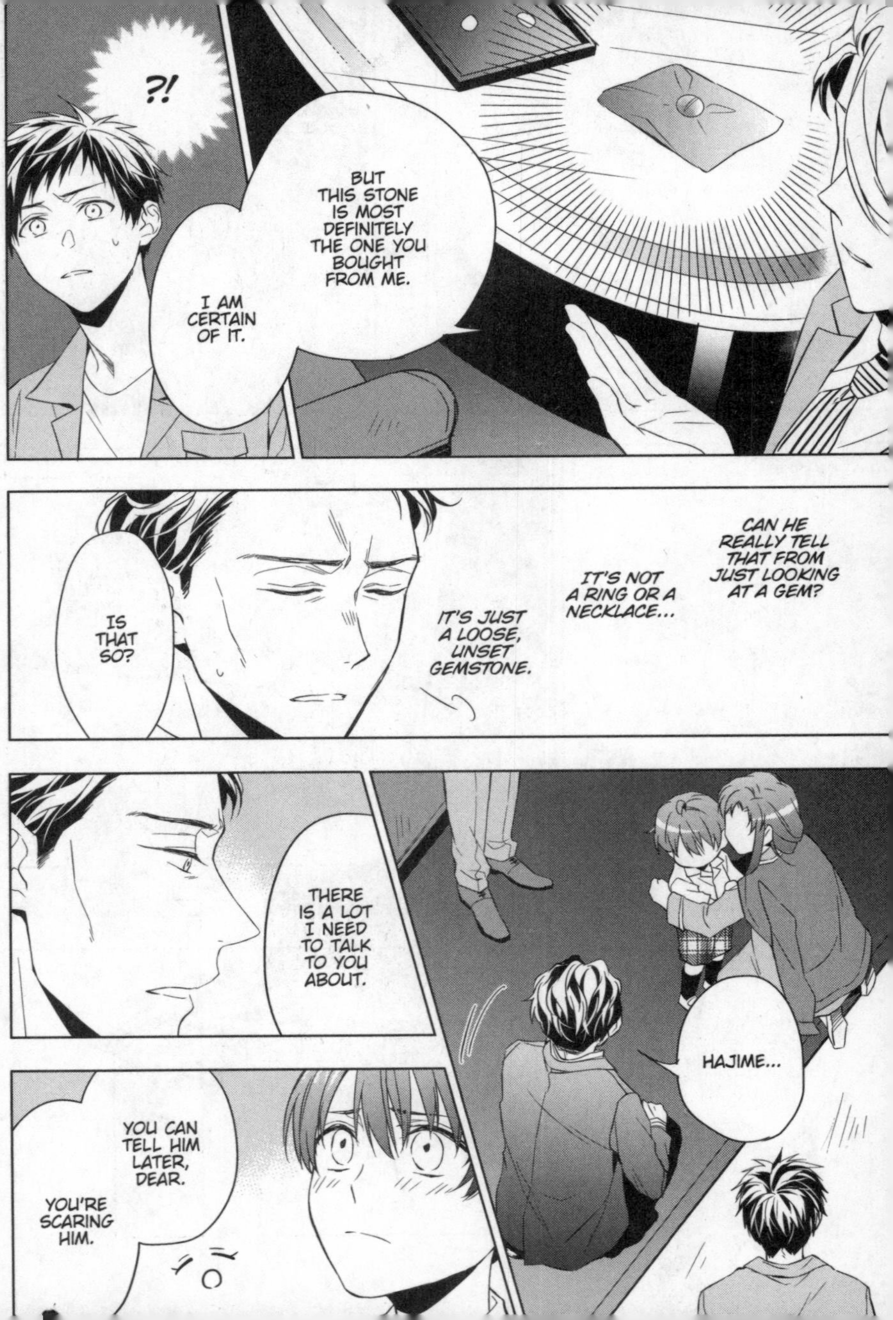
BUT THIS STONE IS MOST DEFINITELY THE ONE YOU BOUGHT FROM ME.
I AM CERTAIN OF IT.
?!
CAN HE REALLY TELL THAT FROM JUST LOOKING AT A GEM?
IT'S NOT A RING OR A NECKLACE...
IT'S JUST A LOOSE, UNSET GEMSTONE.
IS THAT SO?
HAJIME...
THERE IS A LOT I NEED TO TALK TO YOU ABOUT.
YOU CAN TELL HIM LATER, DEAR.
YOU'RE SCARING HIM.

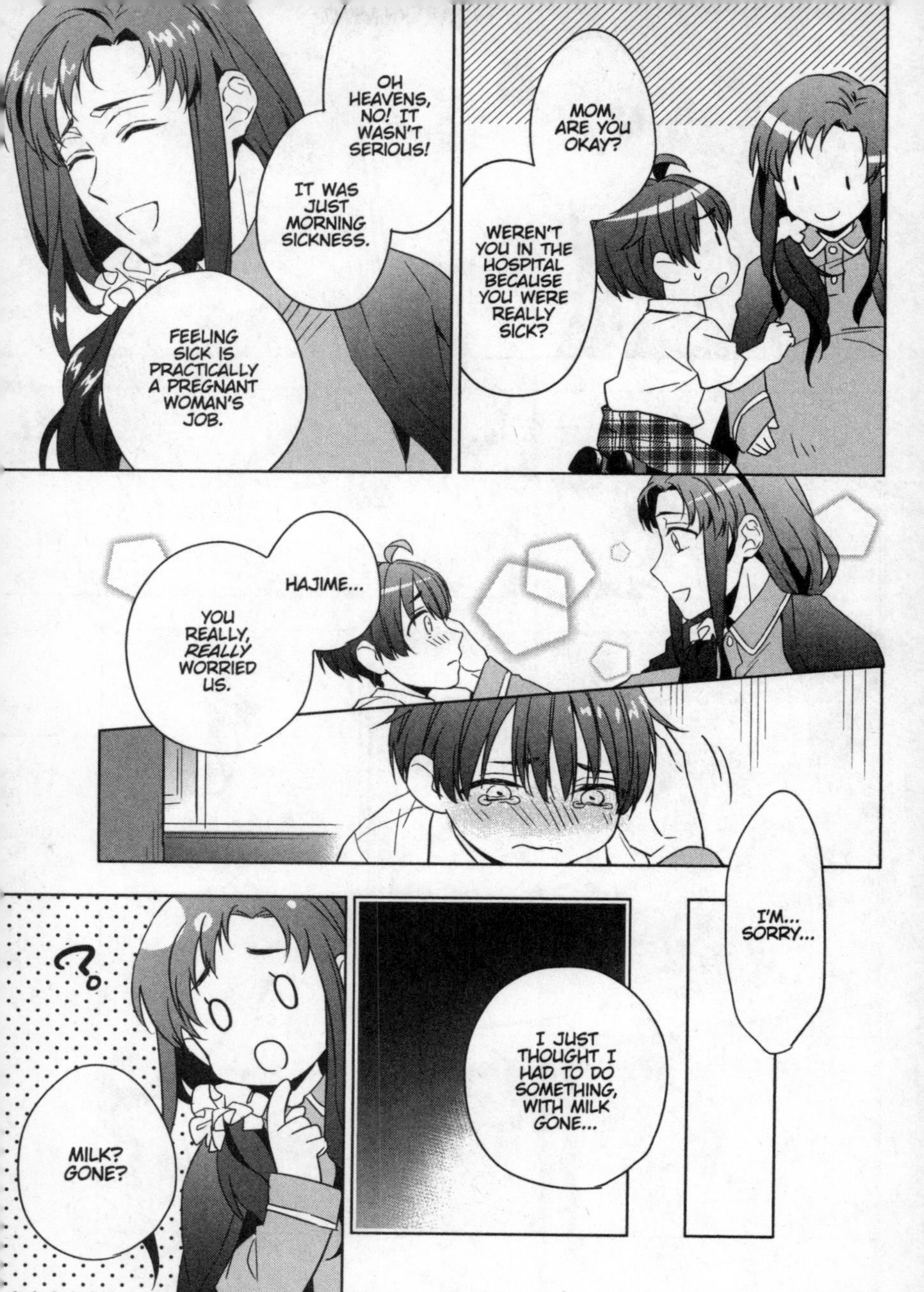
MOM, ARE YOU OKAY?
WEREN'T YOU IN THE HOSPITAL BECAUSE YOU WERE REALLY SICK?
OH HEAVENS, NO! IT WASN'T SERIOUS!
IT WAS JUST MORNING SICKNESS.
FEELING SICK IS PRACTICALLY A PREGNANT WOMAN'S JOB.
HAJIME...
YOU REALLY, *REALLY* WORRIED US.
I'M... SORRY...
I JUST THOUGHT I HAD TO DO SOMETHING, WITH MILK GONE...
?
MILK? GONE?

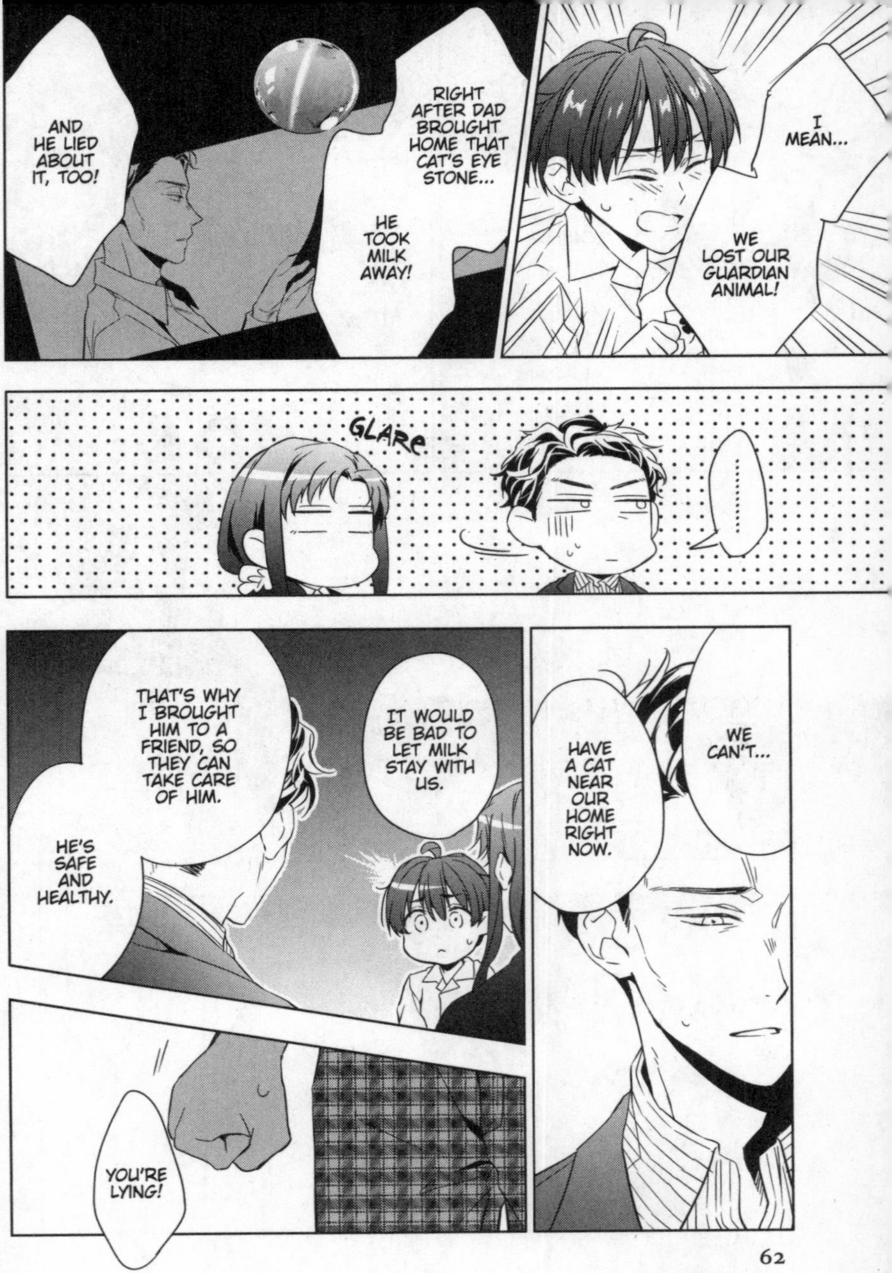
I MEAN...
WE LOST OUR GUARDIAN ANIMAL!
RIGHT AFTER DAD BROUGHT HOME THAT CAT'S EYE STONE...
HE TOOK MILK AWAY!
AND HE LIED ABOUT IT, TOO!
GLARE
WE CAN'T...
HAVE A CAT NEAR OUR HOME RIGHT NOW.
IT WOULD BE BAD TO LET MILK STAY WITH US.
THAT'S WHY I BROUGHT HIM TO A FRIEND, SO THEY CAN TAKE CARE OF HIM.
HE'S SAFE AND HEALTHY.
YOU'RE LYING!

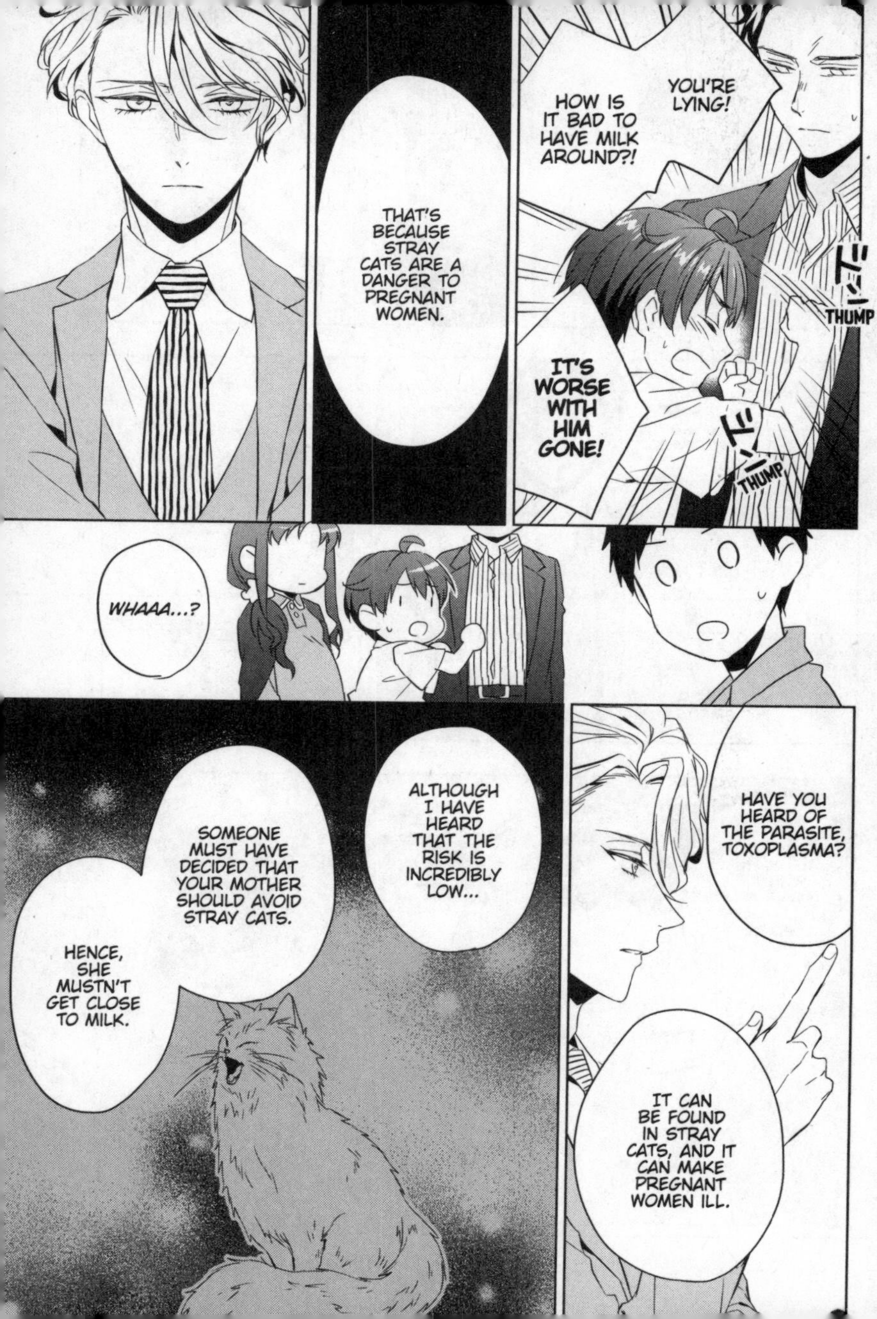
YOU'RE LYING!
HOW IS IT BAD TO HAVE MILK AROUND?!
THUMP
IT'S WORSE WITH HIM GONE!
THUMP
THAT'S BECAUSE STRAY CATS ARE A DANGER TO PREGNANT WOMEN.
WHAAA...?
HAVE YOU HEARD OF THE PARASITE, TOXOPLASMA?
IT CAN BE FOUND IN STRAY CATS, AND IT CAN MAKE PREGNANT WOMEN ILL.
ALTHOUGH I HAVE HEARD THAT THE RISK IS INCREDIBLY LOW...
SOMEONE MUST HAVE DECIDED THAT YOUR MOTHER SHOULD AVOID STRAY CATS.
HENCE, SHE MUSTN'T GET CLOSE TO MILK.

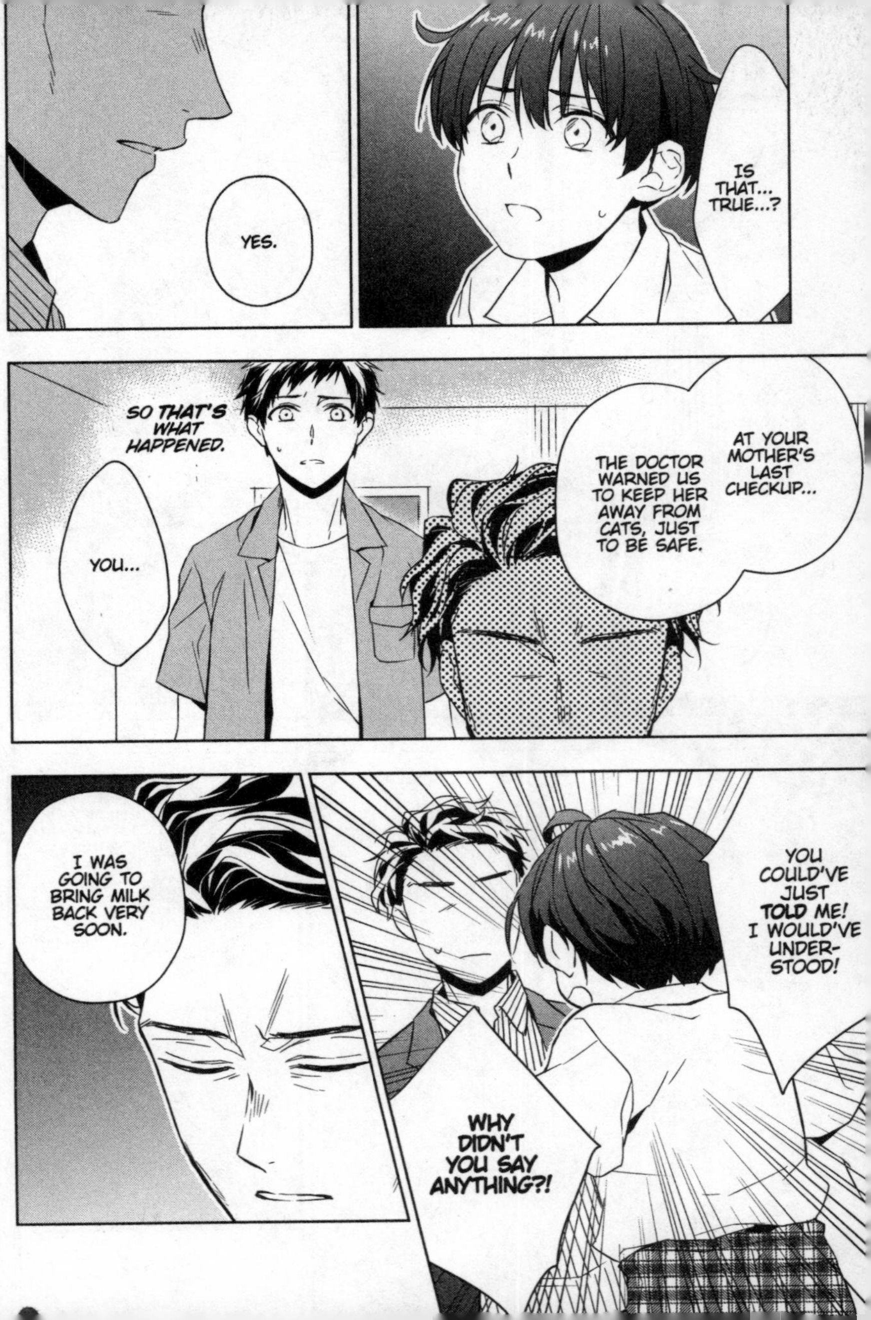
IS THAT... TRUE...?
YES.
AT YOUR MOTHER'S LAST CHECKUP...
THE DOCTOR WARNED US TO KEEP HER AWAY FROM CATS, JUST TO BE SAFE.
SO THAT'S WHAT HAPPENED.
YOU...
YOU COULD'VE JUST TOLD ME! I WOULD'VE UNDER-STOOD!
WHY DIDN'T YOU SAY ANYTHING?!
I WAS GOING TO BRING MILK BACK VERY SOON.

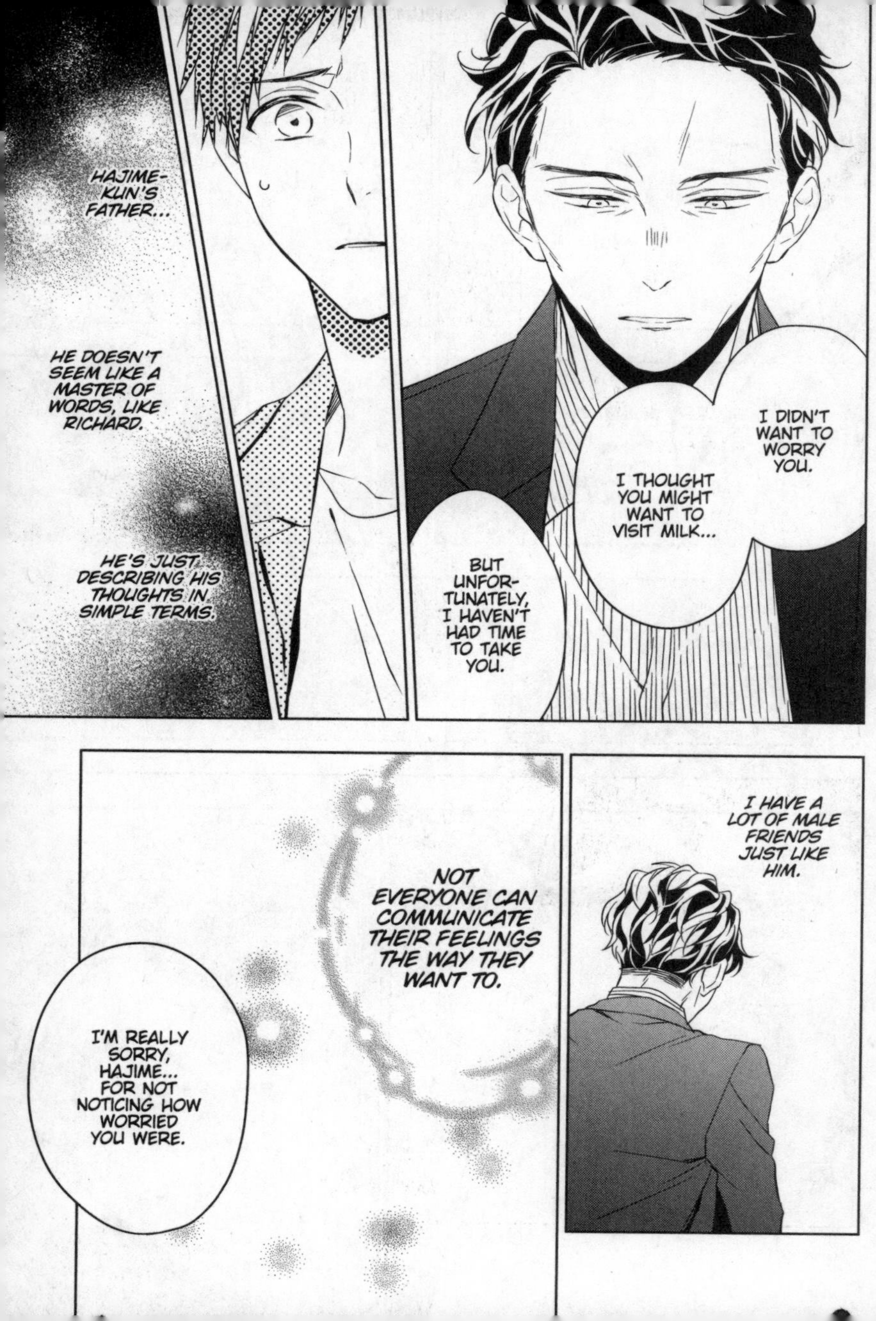
I DIDN'T WANT TO WORRY YOU.
I THOUGHT YOU MIGHT WANT TO VISIT MILK...
BUT UNFORTUNATELY, I HAVEN'T HAD TIME TO TAKE YOU.
HAJIME-KUN'S FATHER...
HE DOESN'T SEEM LIKE A MASTER OF WORDS, LIKE RICHARD.
HE'S JUST DESCRIBING HIS THOUGHTS IN SIMPLE TERMS.
I HAVE A LOT OF MALE FRIENDS JUST LIKE HIM.
NOT EVERYONE CAN COMMUNICATE THEIR FEELINGS THE WAY THEY WANT TO.
I'M REALLY SORRY, HAJIME... FOR NOT NOTICING HOW WORRIED YOU WERE.

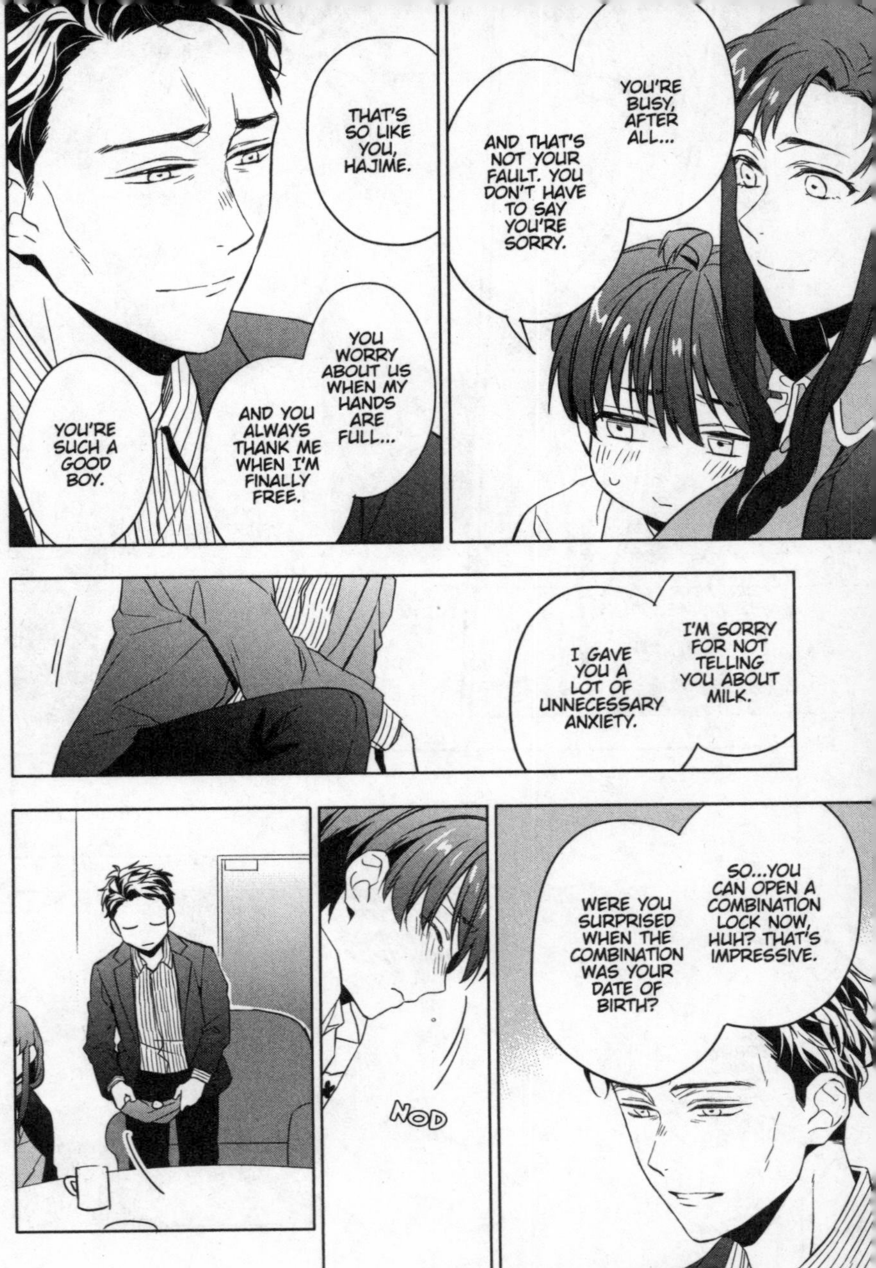
YOU'RE BUSY, AFTER ALL...
AND THAT'S NOT YOUR FAULT. YOU DON'T HAVE TO SAY YOU'RE SORRY.
THAT'S SO LIKE YOU, HAJIME.
YOU WORRY ABOUT US WHEN MY HANDS ARE FULL...
AND YOU ALWAYS THANK ME WHEN I'M FINALLY FREE.
YOU'RE SUCH A GOOD BOY.
I'M SORRY FOR NOT TELLING YOU ABOUT MILK.
I GAVE YOU A LOT OF UNNECESSARY ANXIETY.
SO...YOU CAN OPEN A COMBINATION LOCK NOW, HUH? THAT'S IMPRESSIVE.
WERE YOU SURPRISED WHEN THE COMBINATION WAS YOUR DATE OF BIRTH?
NOD

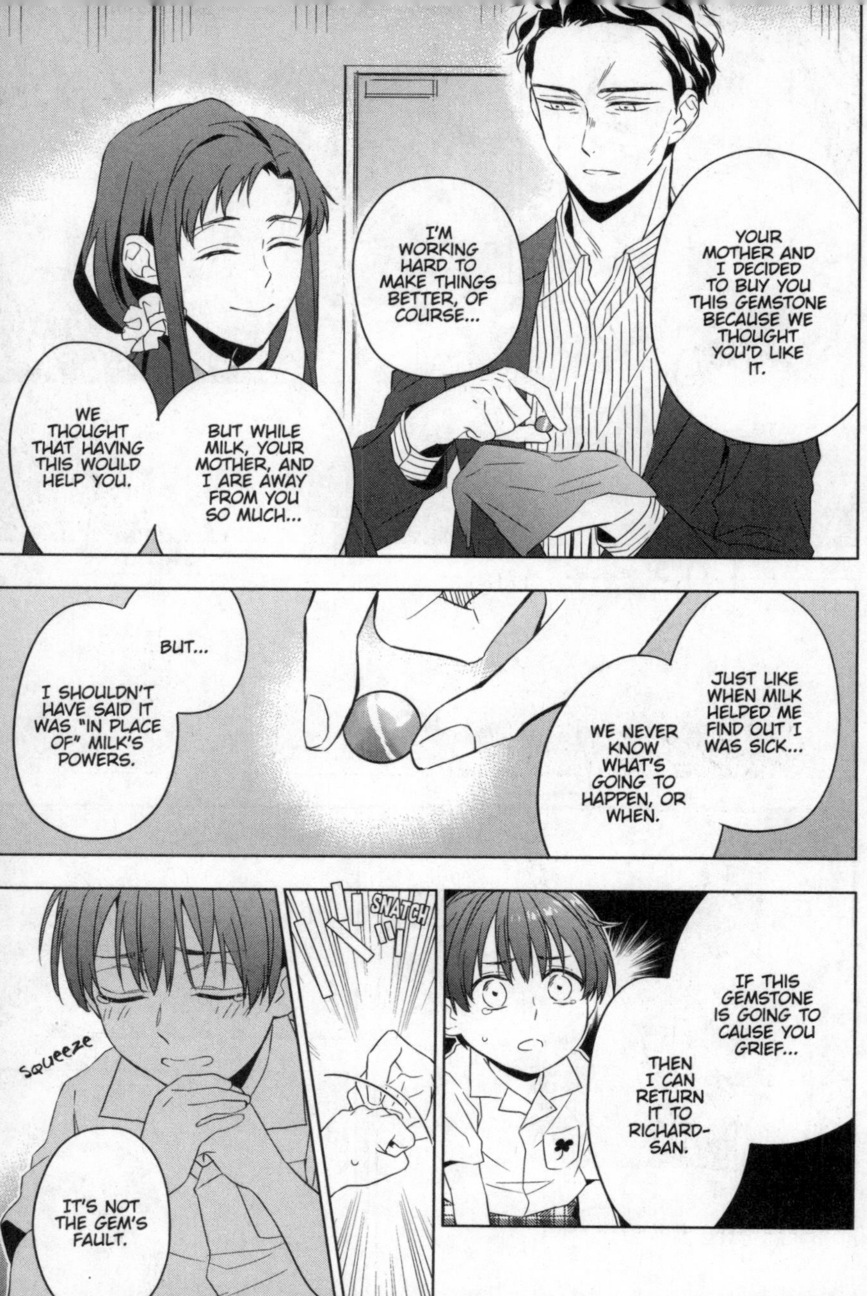
YOUR MOTHER AND I DECIDED TO BUY YOU THIS GEMSTONE BECAUSE WE THOUGHT YOU'D LIKE IT.
I'M WORKING HARD TO MAKE THINGS BETTER, OF COURSE...
BUT WHILE MILK, YOUR MOTHER, AND I ARE AWAY FROM YOU SO MUCH...
WE THOUGHT THAT HAVING THIS WOULD HELP YOU.
JUST LIKE WHEN MILK HELPED ME FIND OUT I WAS SICK...
WE NEVER KNOW WHAT'S GOING TO HAPPEN, OR WHEN.
BUT...
I SHOULDN'T HAVE SAID IT WAS "IN PLACE OF" MILK'S POWERS.
IF THIS GEMSTONE IS GOING TO CAUSE YOU GRIEF...
THEN I CAN RETURN IT TO RICHARD-SAN.
SNATCH
Squeeze
IT'S NOT THE GEM'S FAULT.

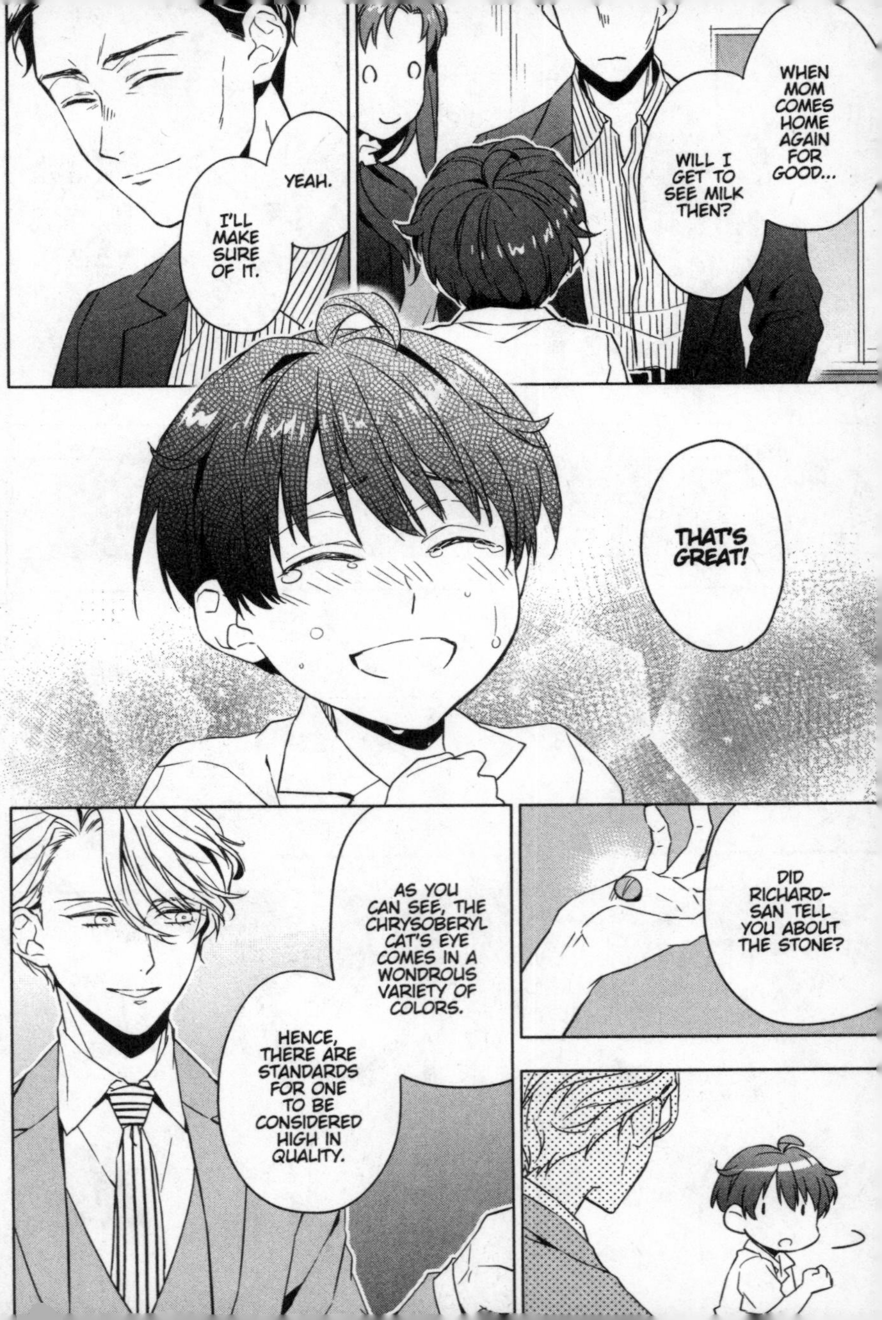
WHEN MOM COMES HOME AGAIN FOR GOOD...
WILL I GET TO SEE MILK THEN?
YEAH.
I'LL MAKE SURE OF IT.
THAT'S GREAT!
DID RICHARD-SAN TELL YOU ABOUT THE STONE?
AS YOU CAN SEE, THE CHRYSOBERYL CAT'S EYE COMES IN A WONDROUS VARIETY OF COLORS.
HENCE, THERE ARE STANDARDS FOR ONE TO BE CONSIDERED HIGH IN QUALITY.

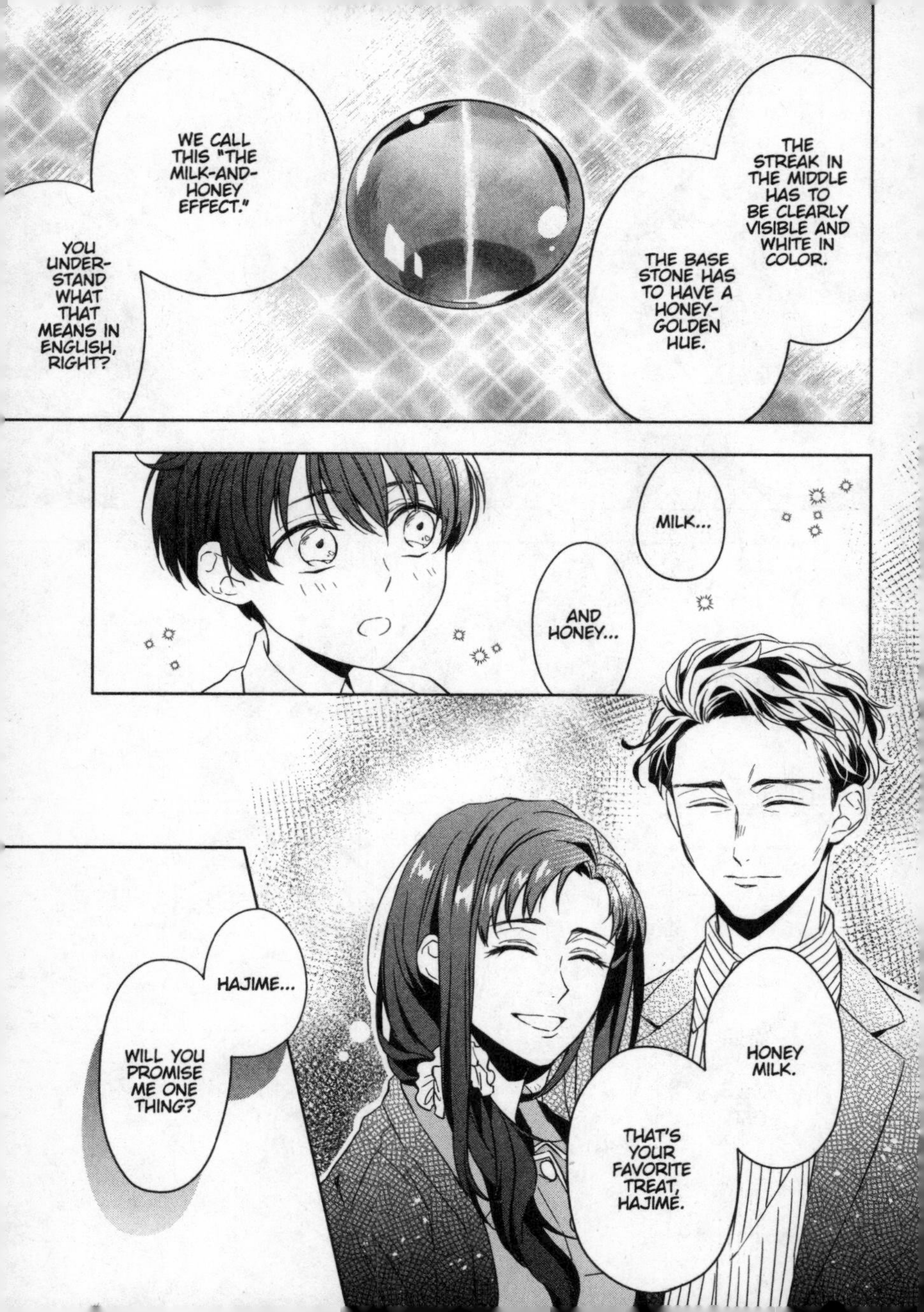
THE STREAK IN THE MIDDLE HAS TO BE CLEARLY VISIBLE AND WHITE IN COLOR.
THE BASE STONE HAS TO HAVE A HONEY-GOLDEN HUE.
WE CALL THIS "THE MILK-AND-HONEY EFFECT."
YOU UNDERSTAND WHAT THAT MEANS IN ENGLISH, RIGHT?
MILK...
AND HONEY...
HONEY MILK.
THAT'S YOUR FAVORITE TREAT, HAJIME.
HAJIME...
WILL YOU PROMISE ME ONE THING?

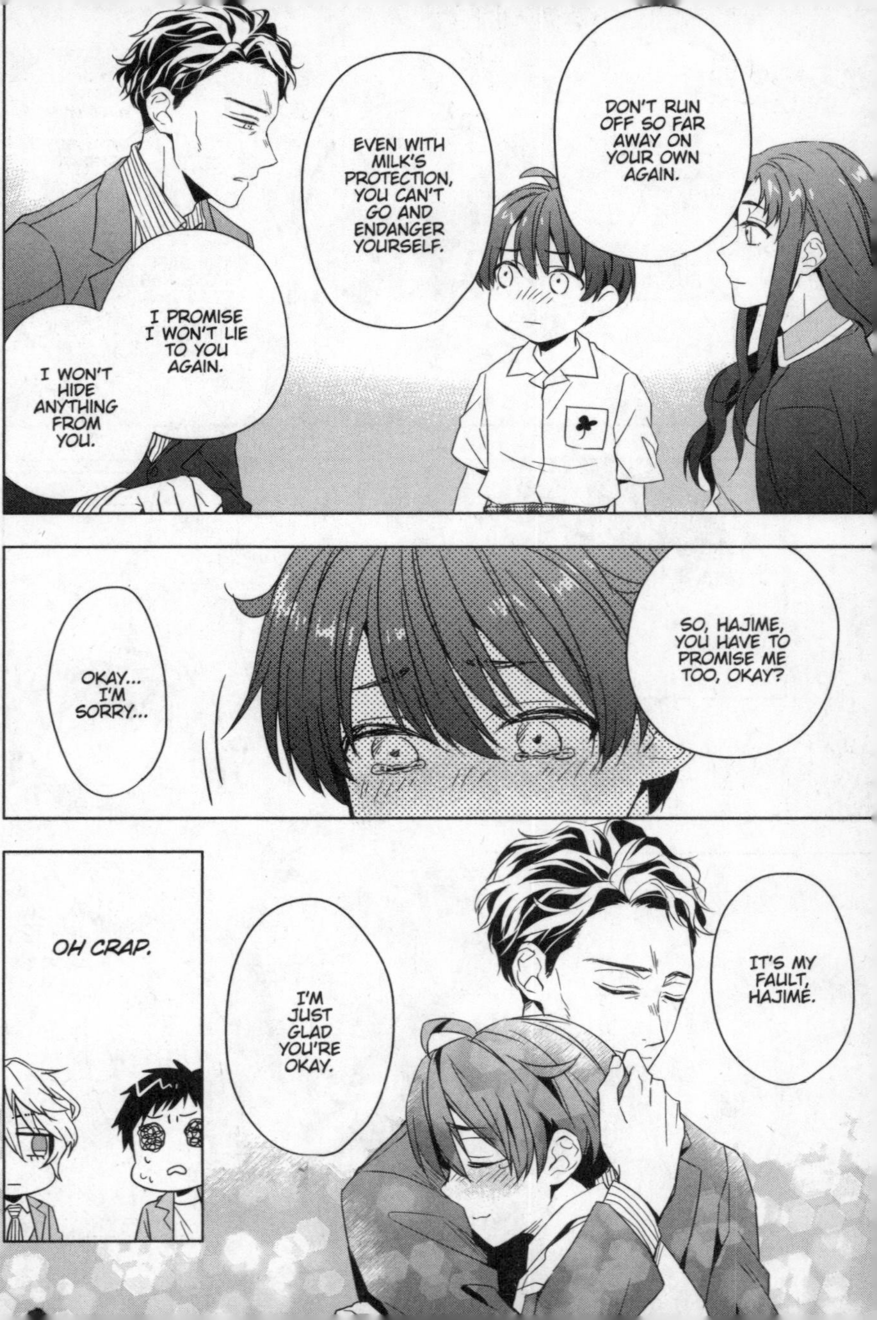
DON'T RUN OFF SO FAR AWAY ON YOUR OWN AGAIN.
EVEN WITH MILK'S PROTECTION, YOU CAN'T GO AND ENDANGER YOURSELF.
I PROMISE I WON'T LIE TO YOU AGAIN.
I WON'T HIDE ANYTHING FROM YOU.
SO, HAJIME, YOU HAVE TO PROMISE ME TOO, OKAY?
OKAY... I'M SORRY...
IT'S MY FAULT, HAJIME.
I'M JUST GLAD YOU'RE OKAY.
OH CRAP.

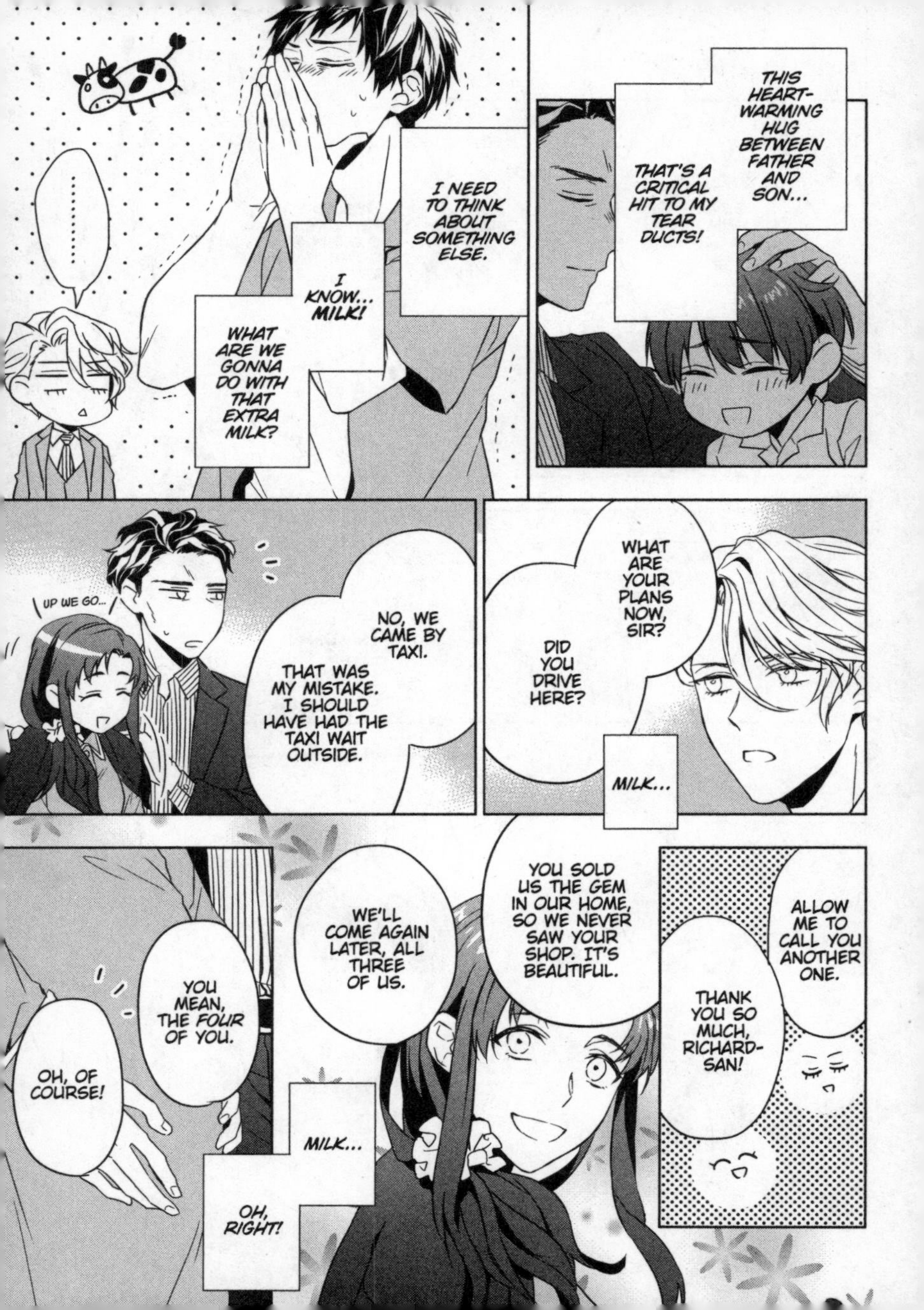
THIS HEART-WARMING HUG BETWEEN FATHER AND SON...
THAT'S A CRITICAL HIT TO MY TEAR DUCTS!
I NEED TO THINK ABOUT SOMETHING ELSE.
I KNOW... MILK!
WHAT ARE WE GONNA DO WITH THAT EXTRA MILK?
......
WHAT ARE YOUR PLANS NOW, SIR?
DID YOU DRIVE HERE?
MILK...
NO, WE CAME BY TAXI.
THAT WAS MY MISTAKE. I SHOULD HAVE HAD THE TAXI WAIT OUTSIDE.
UP WE GO...
ALLOW ME TO CALL YOU ANOTHER ONE.
THANK YOU SO MUCH, RICHARD-SAN!
YOU SOLD US THE GEM IN OUR HOME, SO WE NEVER SAW YOUR SHOP. IT'S BEAUTIFUL.
WE'LL COME AGAIN LATER, ALL THREE OF US.
YOU MEAN, THE FOUR OF YOU.
OH, OF COURSE!
MILK...
OH, RIGHT!

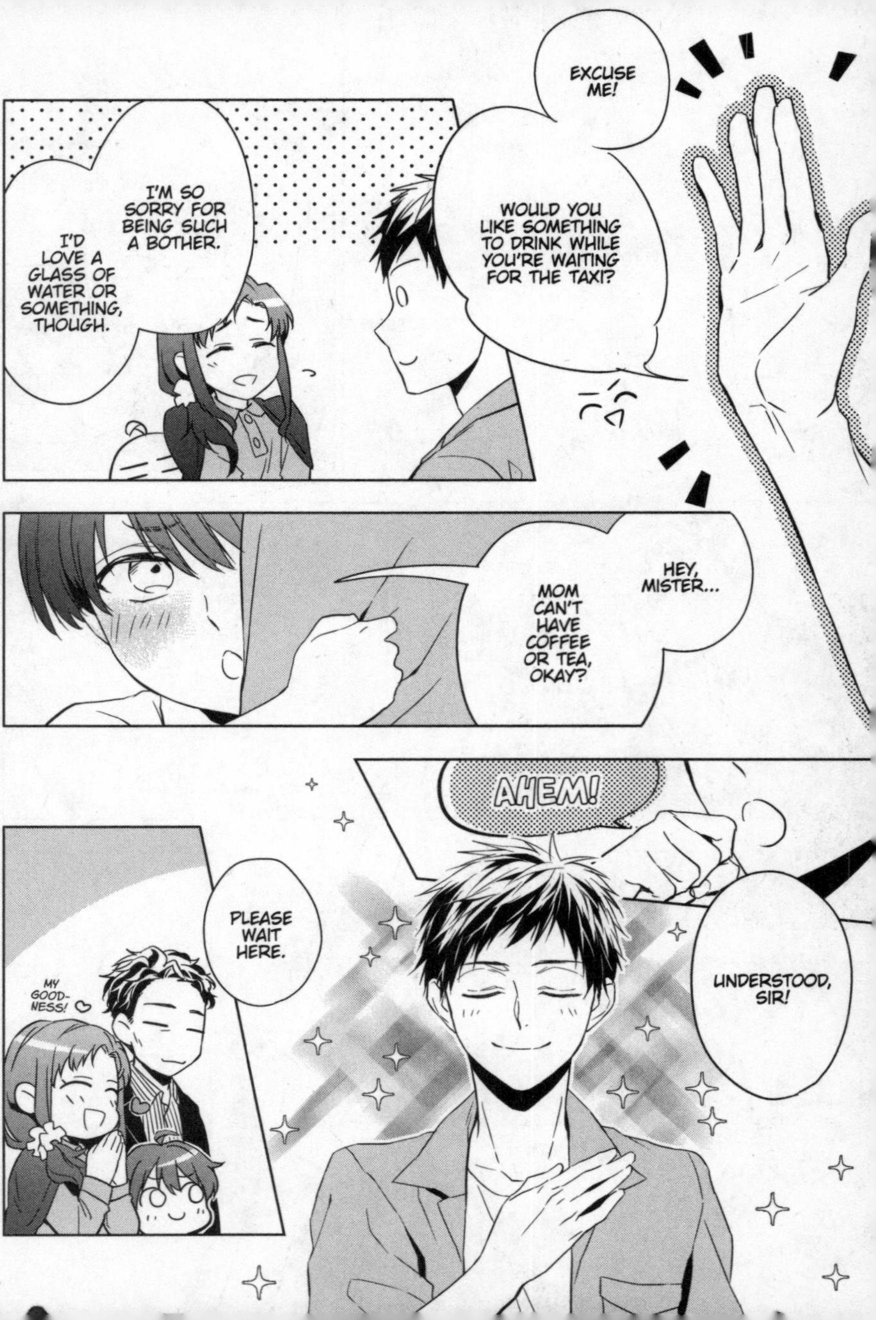
EXCUSE ME!
WOULD YOU LIKE SOMETHING TO DRINK WHILE YOU'RE WAITING FOR THE TAXI?
I'M SO SORRY FOR BEING SUCH A BOTHER.
I'D LOVE A GLASS OF WATER OR SOMETHING, THOUGH.
HEY, MISTER...
MOM CAN'T HAVE COFFEE OR TEA, OKAY?
AHEM!
UNDERSTOOD, SIR!
PLEASE WAIT HERE.
MY GOODNESS!

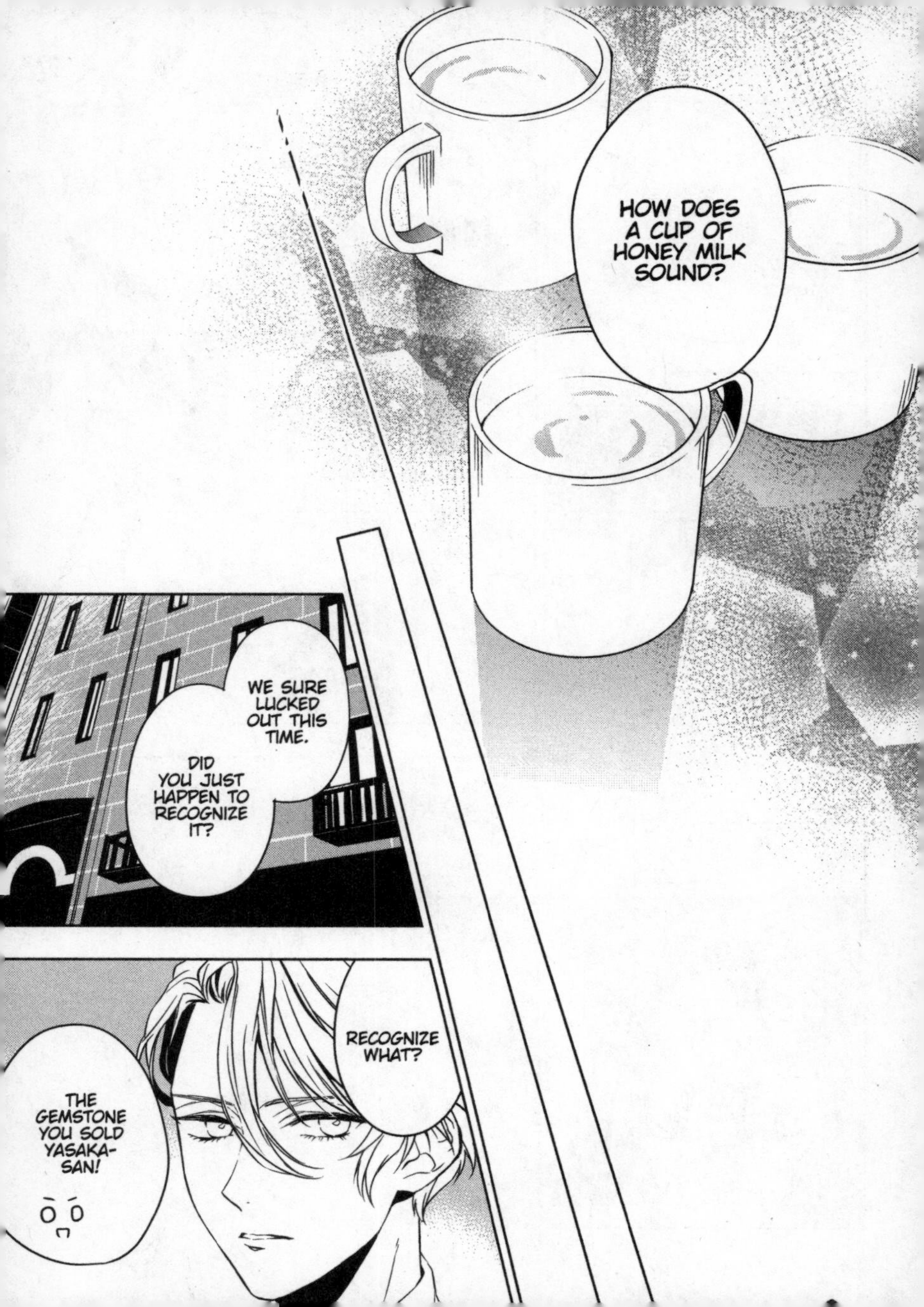
HOW DOES A CUP OF HONEY MILK SOUND?
WE SURE LUCKED OUT THIS TIME.
DID YOU JUST HAPPEN TO RECOGNIZE IT?
RECOGNIZE WHAT?
THE GEMSTONE YOU SOLD YASAKA-SAN!

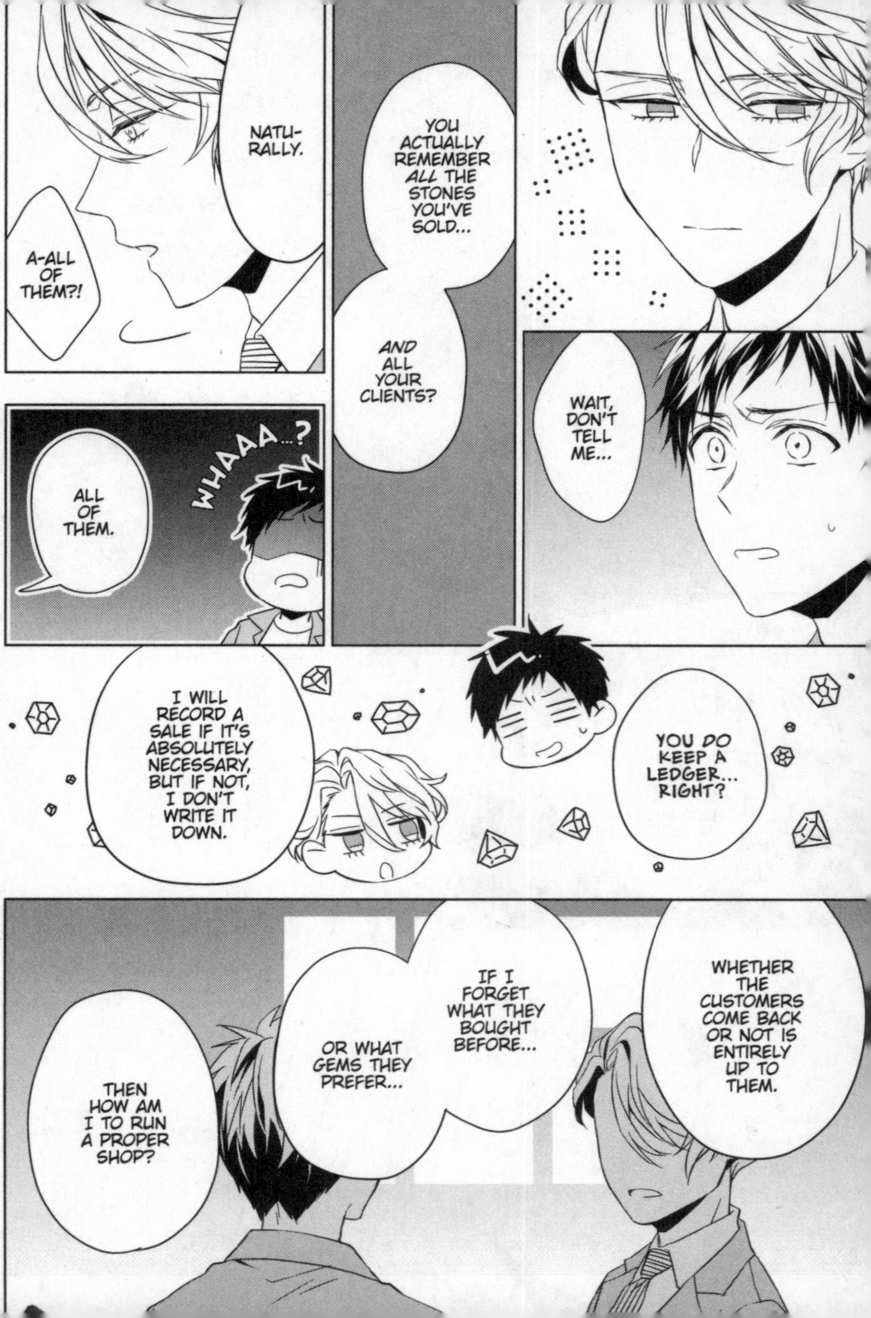
WAIT, DON'T TELL ME...
YOU ACTUALLY REMEMBER *ALL* THE STONES YOU'VE SOLD...
AND ALL YOUR CLIENTS?
NATU-RALLY.
A-ALL OF THEM?!
ALL OF THEM.
WHAAA...?
YOU *DO* KEEP A LEDGER... RIGHT?
I WILL RECORD A SALE IF IT'S ABSOLUTELY NECESSARY, BUT IF NOT, I DON'T WRITE IT DOWN.
WHETHER THE CUSTOMERS COME BACK OR NOT IS ENTIRELY UP TO THEM.
IF I FORGET WHAT THEY BOUGHT BEFORE...
OR WHAT GEMS THEY PREFER...
THEN HOW AM I TO RUN A PROPER SHOP?

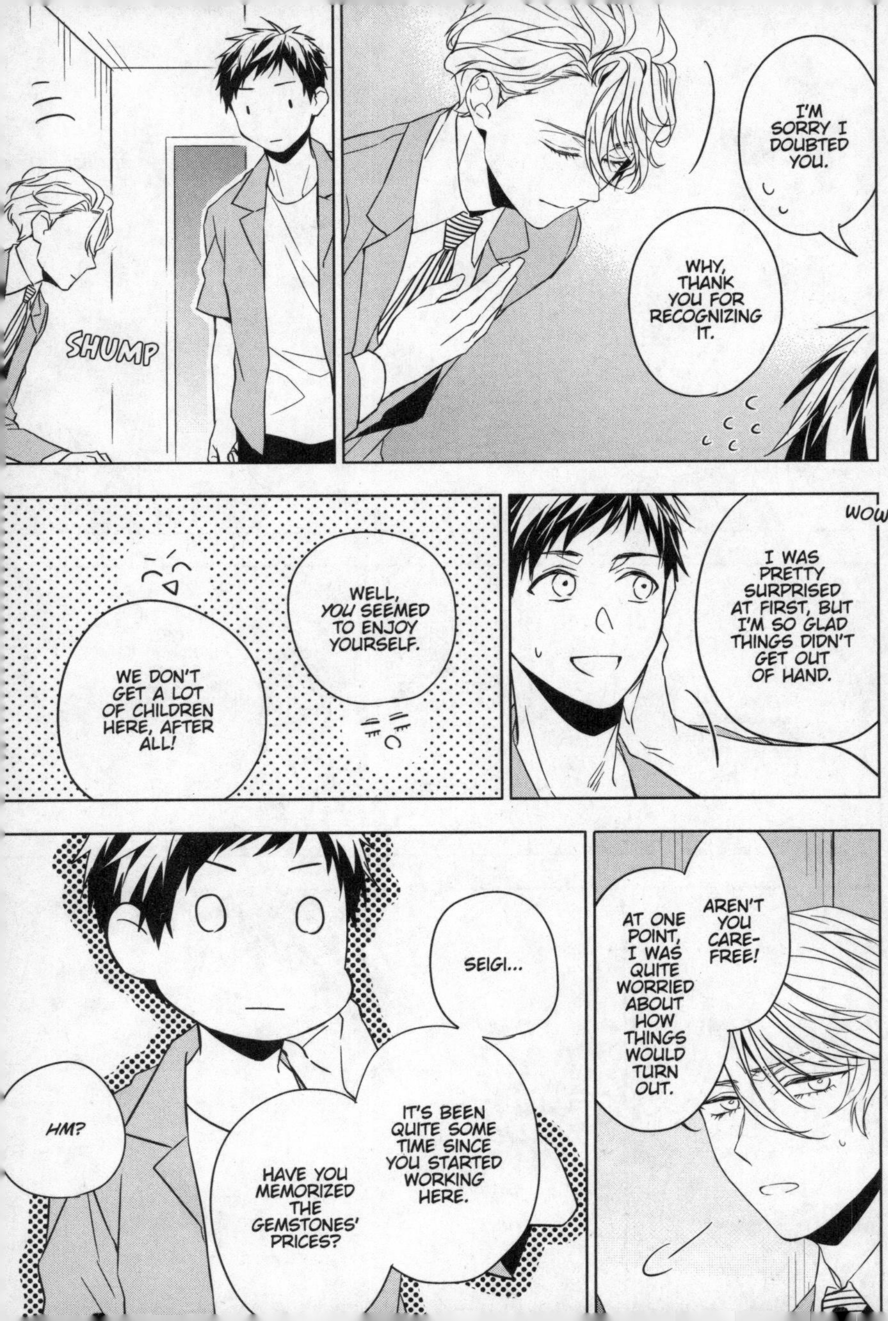
I'M SORRY I DOUBTED YOU.
WHY, THANK YOU FOR RECOGNIZING IT.
SHUMP
WOW!
I WAS PRETTY SURPRISED AT FIRST, BUT I'M SO GLAD THINGS DIDN'T GET OUT OF HAND.
WELL, *YOU* SEEMED TO ENJOY YOURSELF.
WE DON'T GET A LOT OF CHILDREN HERE, AFTER ALL!
AREN'T YOU CARE-FREE!
AT ONE POINT, I WAS QUITE WORRIED ABOUT HOW THINGS WOULD TURN OUT.
SEIGI...
IT'S BEEN QUITE SOME TIME SINCE YOU STARTED WORKING HERE.
HAVE YOU MEMORIZED THE GEMSTONES' PRICES?
HM?

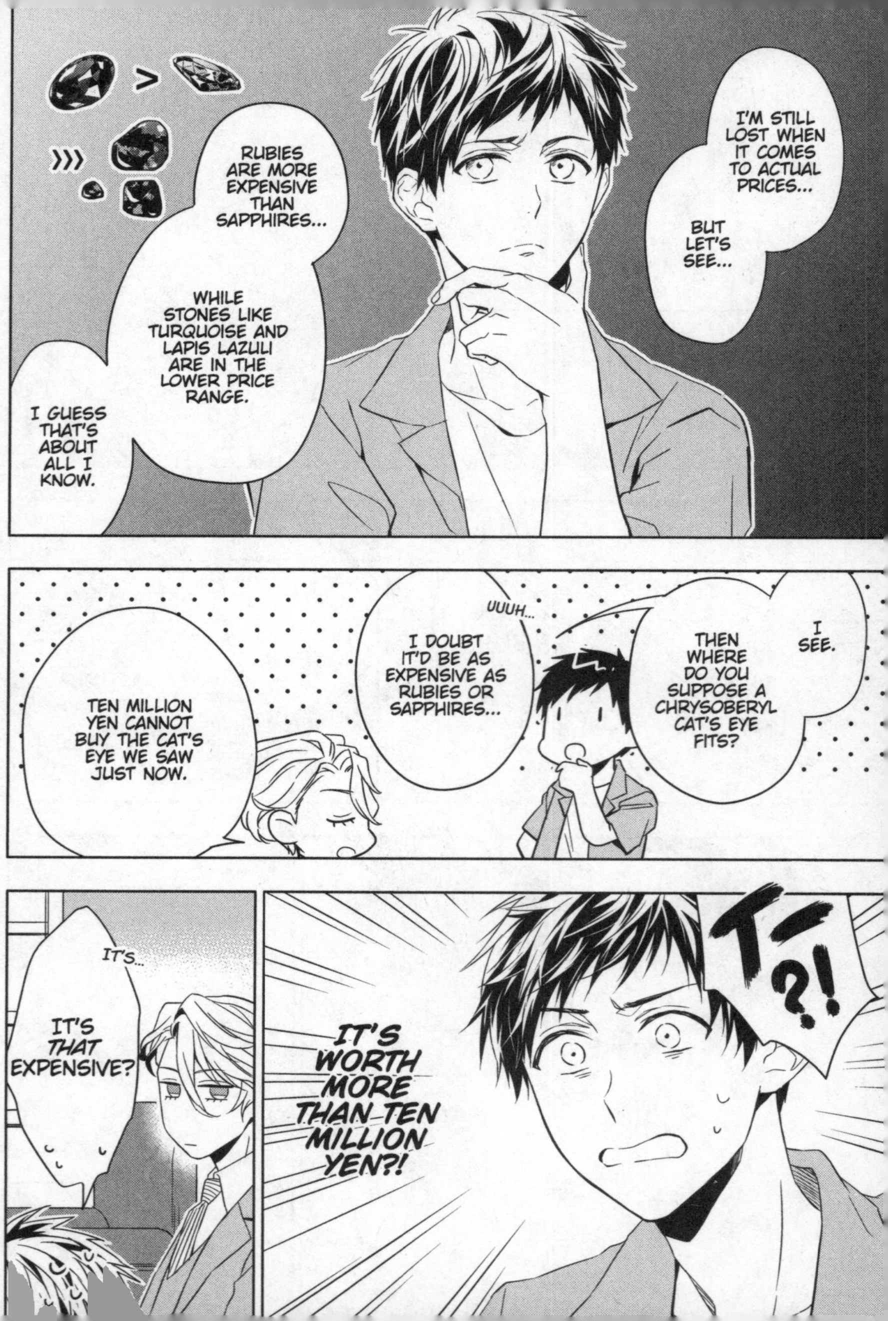
I'M STILL LOST WHEN IT COMES TO ACTUAL PRICES...
BUT LET'S SEE...
RUBIES ARE MORE EXPENSIVE THAN SAPPHIRES...
WHILE STONES LIKE TURQUOISE AND LAPIS LAZULI ARE IN THE LOWER PRICE RANGE.
I GUESS THAT'S ABOUT ALL I KNOW.
I SEE.
THEN WHERE DO YOU SUPPOSE A CHRYSOBERYL CAT'S EYE FITS?
UUUH...
I DOUBT IT'D BE AS EXPENSIVE AS RUBIES OR SAPPHIRES...
TEN MILLION YEN CANNOT BUY THE CAT'S EYE WE SAW JUST NOW.
T-?!
IT'S WORTH MORE THAN TEN MILLION YEN?!
IT'S...
IT'S *THAT* EXPENSIVE?

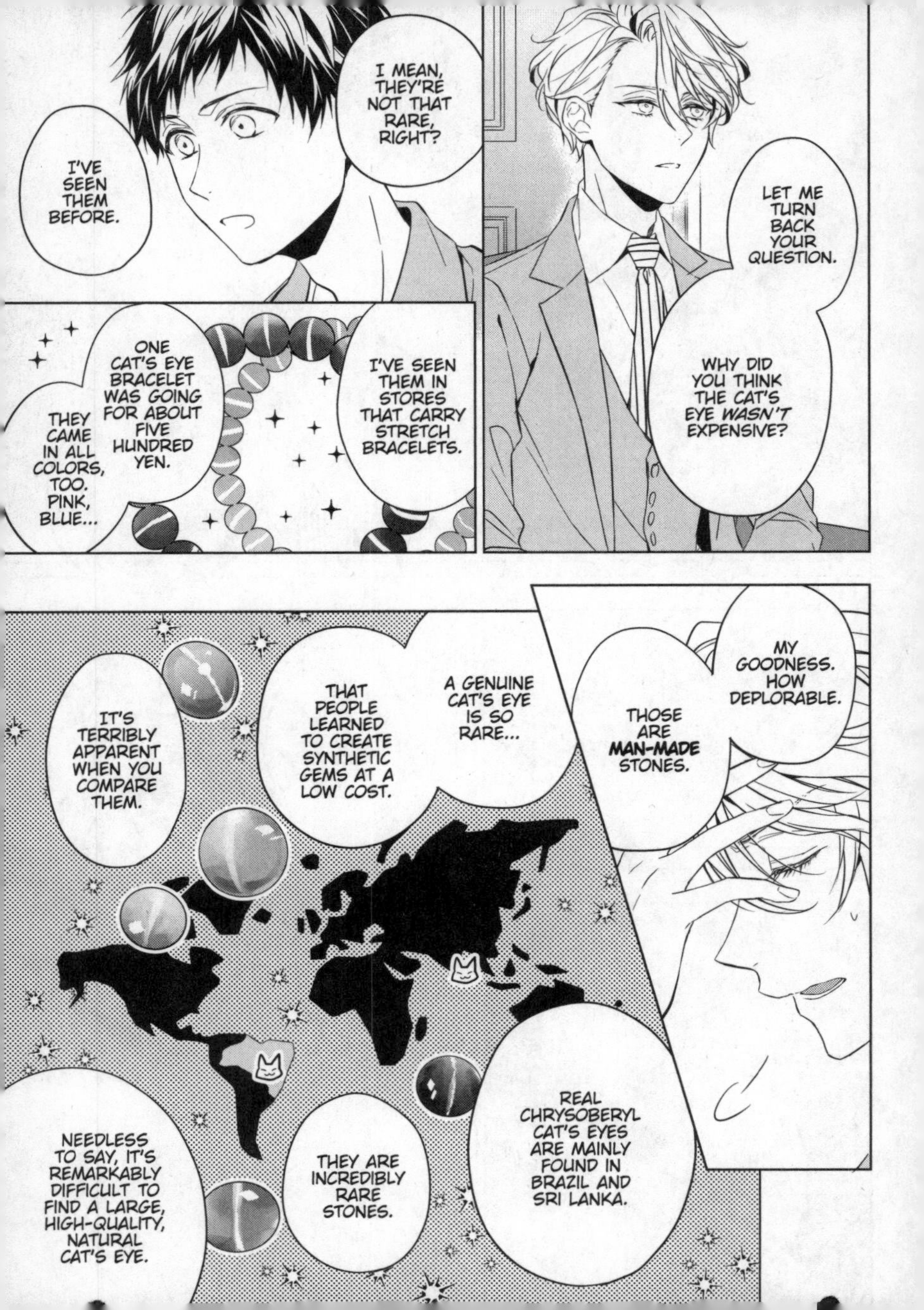
LET ME TURN BACK YOUR QUESTION.
WHY DID YOU THINK THE CAT'S EYE *WASN'T* EXPENSIVE?
I MEAN, THEY'RE NOT THAT RARE, RIGHT?
I'VE SEEN THEM BEFORE.
I'VE SEEN THEM IN STORES THAT CARRY STRETCH BRACELETS.
ONE CAT'S EYE BRACELET WAS GOING FOR ABOUT FIVE HUNDRED YEN.
THEY CAME IN ALL COLORS, TOO. PINK, BLUE...
MY GOODNESS. HOW DEPLORABLE.
THOSE ARE **MAN-MADE** STONES.
A GENUINE CAT'S EYE IS SO RARE...
THAT PEOPLE LEARNED TO CREATE SYNTHETIC GEMS AT A LOW COST.
IT'S TERRIBLY APPARENT WHEN YOU COMPARE THEM.
REAL CHRYSOBERYL CAT'S EYES ARE MAINLY FOUND IN BRAZIL AND SRI LANKA.
THEY ARE INCREDIBLY RARE STONES.
NEEDLESS TO SAY, IT'S REMARKABLY DIFFICULT TO FIND A LARGE, HIGH-QUALITY, NATURAL CAT'S EYE.

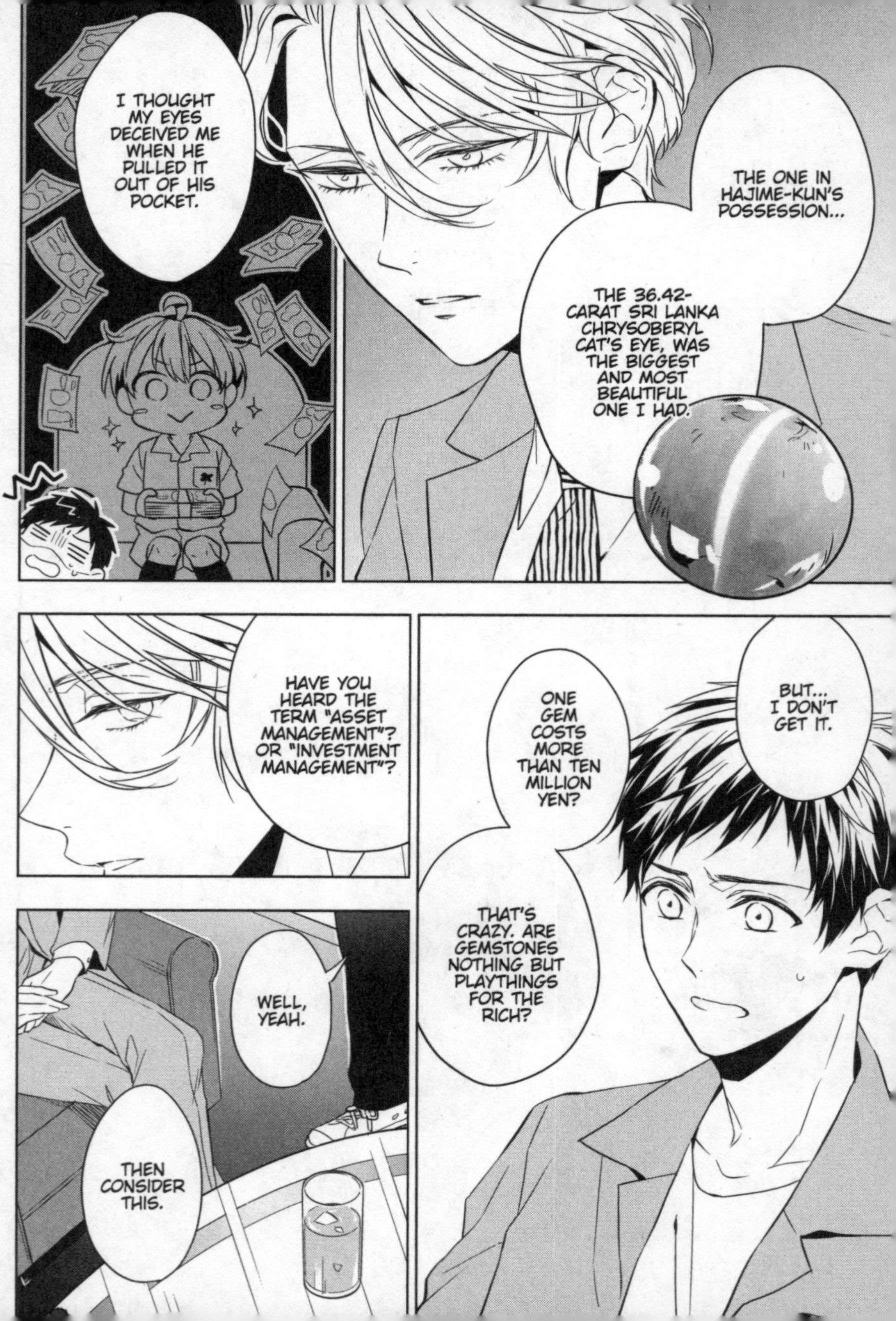
THE ONE IN HAJIME-KUN'S POSSESSION...
THE 36.42-CARAT SRI LANKA CHRYSOBERYL CAT'S EYE, WAS THE BIGGEST AND MOST BEAUTIFUL ONE I HAD.
I THOUGHT MY EYES DECEIVED ME WHEN HE PULLED IT OUT OF HIS POCKET.
BUT... I DON'T GET IT.
ONE GEM COSTS MORE THAN TEN MILLION YEN?
THAT'S CRAZY. ARE GEMSTONES NOTHING BUT PLAYTHINGS FOR THE RICH?
HAVE YOU HEARD THE TERM "ASSET MANAGEMENT"? OR "INVESTMENT MANAGEMENT"?
WELL, YEAH.
THEN CONSIDER THIS.

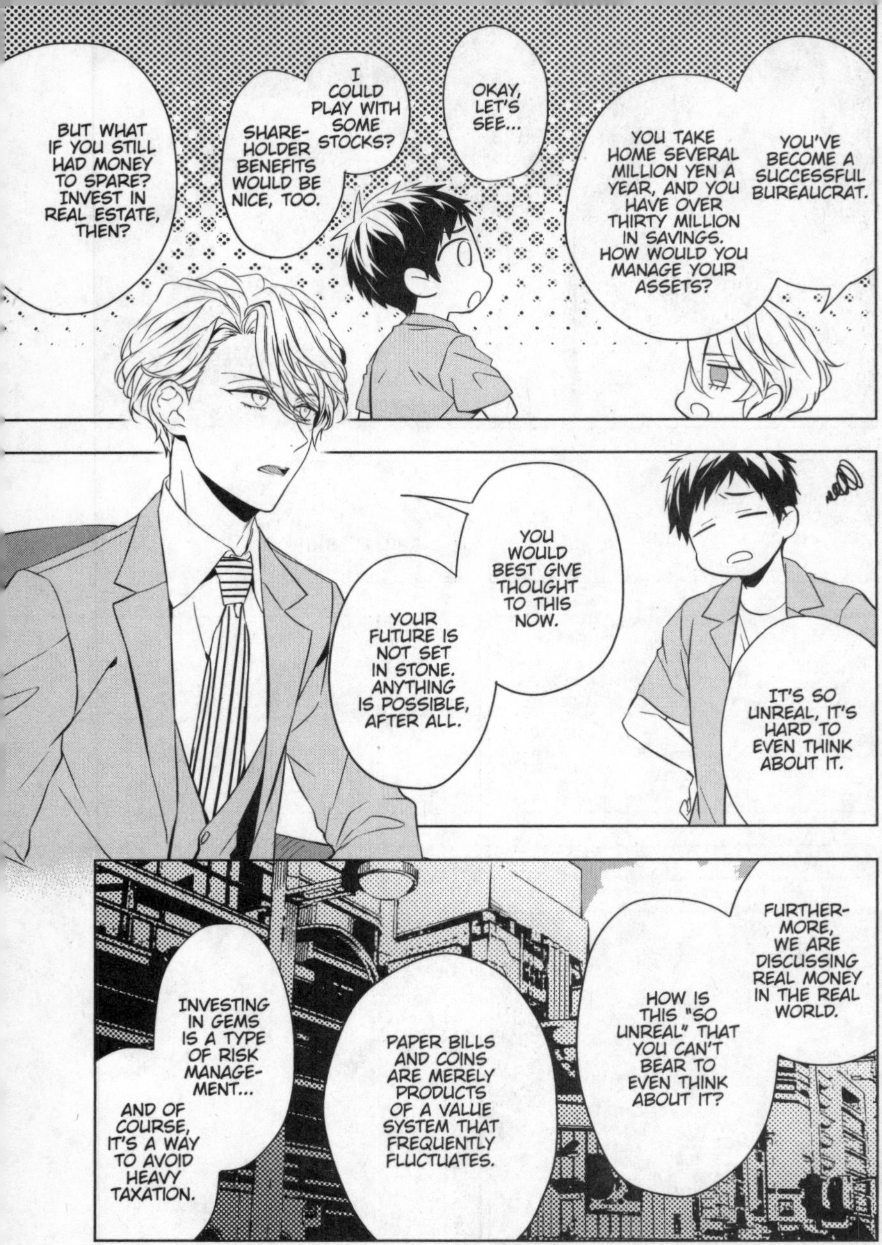
YOU'VE BECOME A SUCCESSFUL BUREAUCRAT.
YOU TAKE HOME SEVERAL MILLION YEN A YEAR, AND YOU HAVE OVER THIRTY MILLION IN SAVINGS. HOW WOULD YOU MANAGE YOUR ASSETS?
OKAY, LET'S SEE...
I COULD PLAY WITH SOME STOCKS?
SHAREHOLDER BENEFITS WOULD BE NICE, TOO.
BUT WHAT IF YOU STILL HAD MONEY TO SPARE? INVEST IN REAL ESTATE, THEN?
IT'S SO UNREAL, IT'S HARD TO EVEN THINK ABOUT IT.
YOU WOULD BEST GIVE THOUGHT TO THIS NOW.
YOUR FUTURE IS NOT SET IN STONE. ANYTHING IS POSSIBLE, AFTER ALL.
FURTHERMORE, WE ARE DISCUSSING REAL MONEY IN THE REAL WORLD.
HOW IS THIS "SO UNREAL" THAT YOU CAN'T BEAR TO EVEN THINK ABOUT IT?
PAPER BILLS AND COINS ARE MERELY PRODUCTS OF A VALUE SYSTEM THAT FREQUENTLY FLUCTUATES.
INVESTING IN GEMS IS A TYPE OF RISK MANAGEMENT...
AND OF COURSE, IT'S A WAY TO AVOID HEAVY TAXATION.

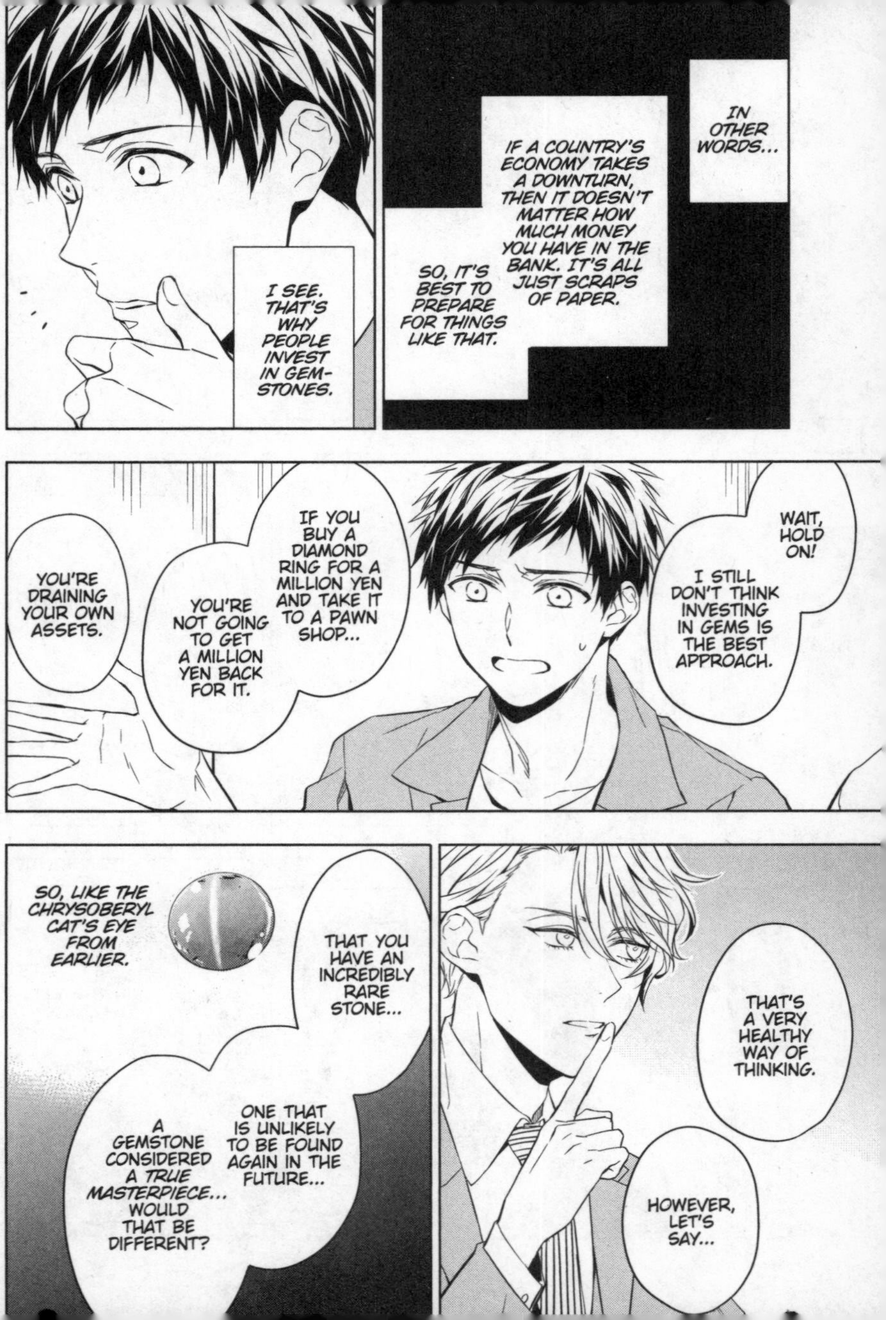
IN OTHER WORDS...
IF A COUNTRY'S ECONOMY TAKES A DOWNTURN, THEN IT DOESN'T MATTER HOW MUCH MONEY YOU HAVE IN THE BANK. IT'S ALL JUST SCRAPS OF PAPER.
SO, IT'S BEST TO PREPARE FOR THINGS LIKE THAT.
I SEE. THAT'S WHY PEOPLE INVEST IN GEMSTONES.
WAIT, HOLD ON!
I STILL DON'T THINK INVESTING IN GEMS IS THE BEST APPROACH.
IF YOU BUY A DIAMOND RING FOR A MILLION YEN AND TAKE IT TO A PAWN SHOP...
YOU'RE NOT GOING TO GET A MILLION YEN BACK FOR IT.
YOU'RE DRAINING YOUR OWN ASSETS.
THAT'S A VERY HEALTHY WAY OF THINKING.
HOWEVER, LET'S SAY...
THAT YOU HAVE AN INCREDIBLY RARE STONE...
SO, LIKE THE CHRYSOBERYL CAT'S EYE FROM EARLIER.
ONE THAT IS UNLIKELY TO BE FOUND AGAIN IN THE FUTURE...
A GEMSTONE CONSIDERED A *TRUE* MASTERPIECE... WOULD THAT BE DIFFERENT?

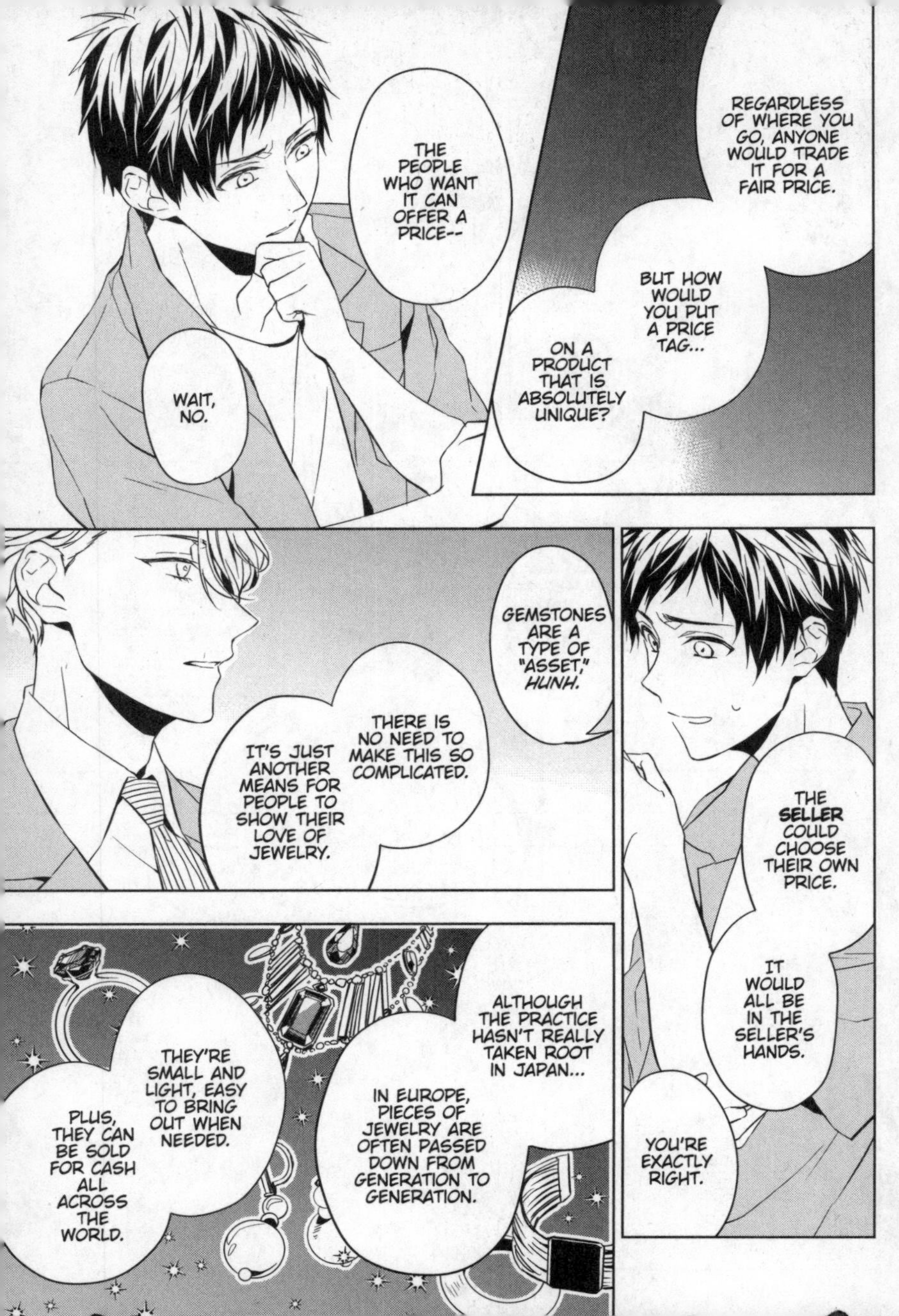
REGARDLESS OF WHERE YOU GO, ANYONE WOULD TRADE IT FOR A FAIR PRICE.
BUT HOW WOULD YOU PUT A PRICE TAG...
ON A PRODUCT THAT IS ABSOLUTELY UNIQUE?
THE PEOPLE WHO WANT IT CAN OFFER A PRICE--
WAIT, NO.
THE **SELLER** COULD CHOOSE THEIR OWN PRICE.
IT WOULD ALL BE IN THE SELLER'S HANDS.
YOU'RE EXACTLY RIGHT.
GEMSTONES ARE A TYPE OF "ASSET," *HUNH.*
THERE IS NO NEED TO MAKE THIS SO COMPLICATED.
IT'S JUST ANOTHER MEANS FOR PEOPLE TO SHOW THEIR LOVE OF JEWELRY.
ALTHOUGH THE PRACTICE HASN'T REALLY TAKEN ROOT IN JAPAN...
IN EUROPE, PIECES OF JEWELRY ARE OFTEN PASSED DOWN FROM GENERATION TO GENERATION.
THEY'RE SMALL AND LIGHT, EASY TO BRING OUT WHEN NEEDED.
PLUS, THEY CAN BE SOLD FOR CASH ALL ACROSS THE WORLD.

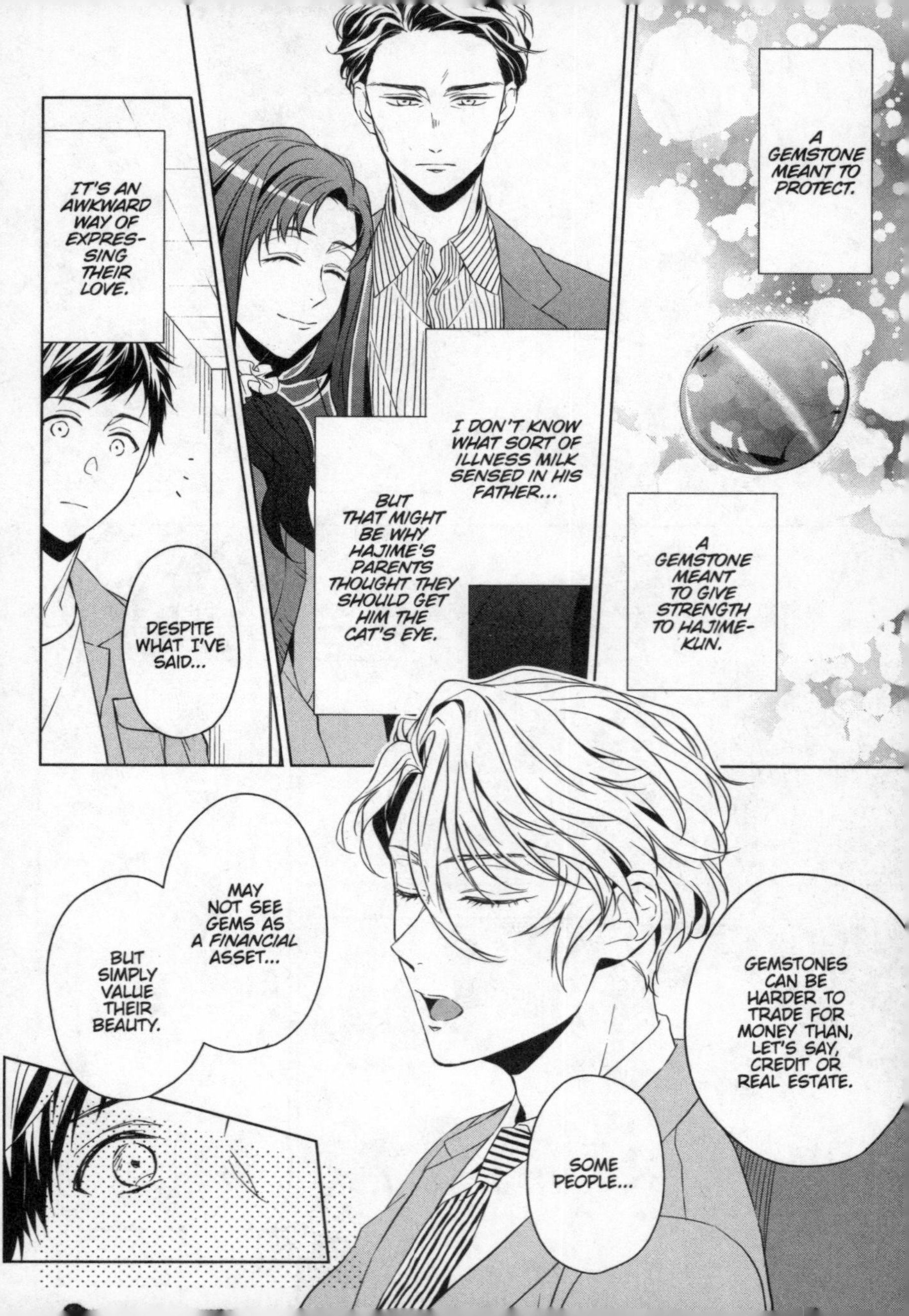
A GEMSTONE MEANT TO PROTECT.
A GEMSTONE MEANT TO GIVE STRENGTH TO HAJIME-KUN.
I DON'T KNOW WHAT SORT OF ILLNESS MILK SENSED IN HIS FATHER...
BUT THAT MIGHT BE WHY HAJIME'S PARENTS THOUGHT THEY SHOULD GET HIM THE CAT'S EYE.
IT'S AN AWKWARD WAY OF EXPRESSING THEIR LOVE.
DESPITE WHAT I'VE SAID...
GEMSTONES CAN BE HARDER TO TRADE FOR MONEY THAN, LET'S SAY, CREDIT OR REAL ESTATE.
SOME PEOPLE...
MAY NOT SEE GEMS AS A *FINANCIAL* ASSET...
BUT SIMPLY VALUE THEIR BEAUTY.

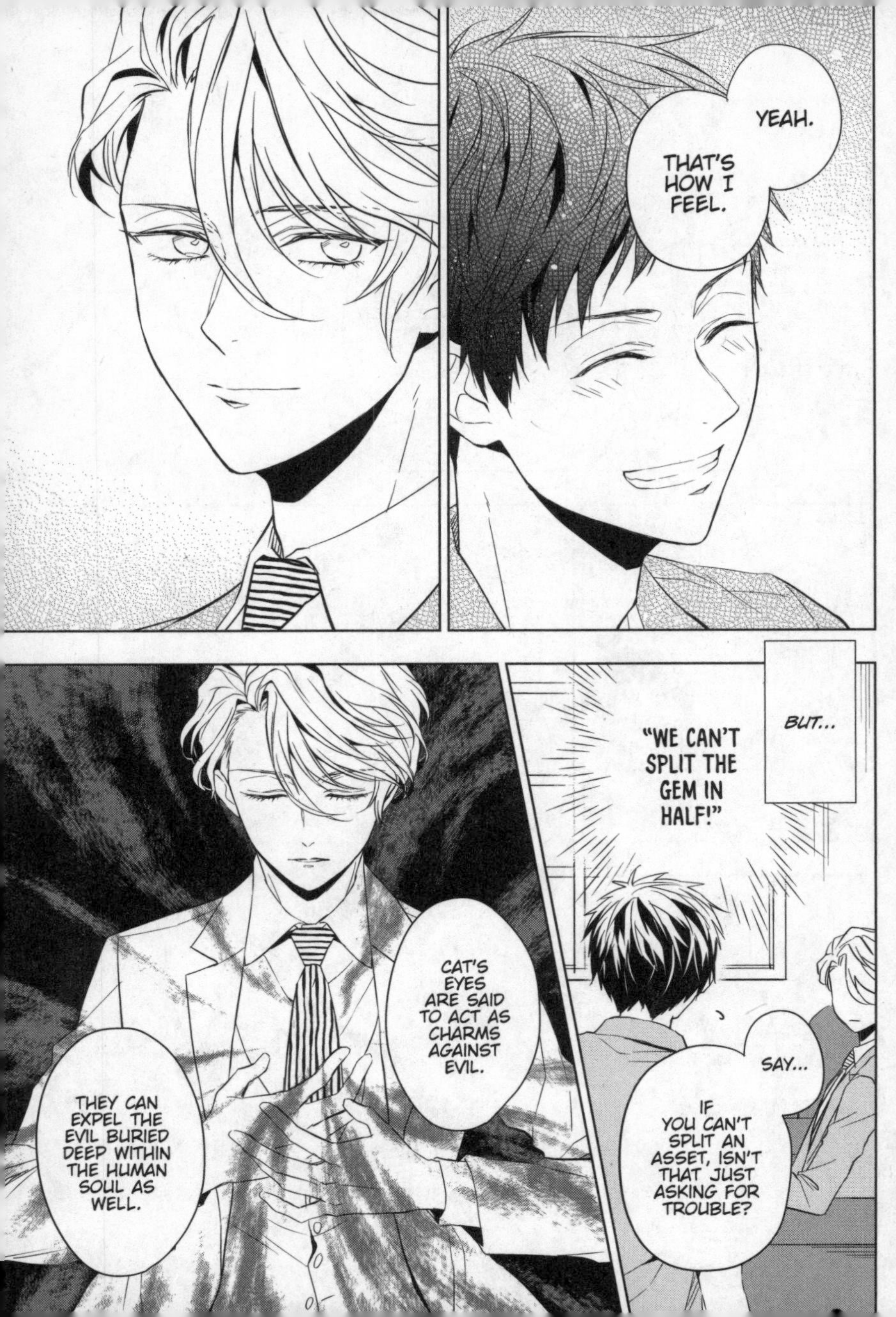
YEAH.
THAT'S HOW I FEEL.
BUT...
"WE CAN'T SPLIT THE GEM IN HALF!"
SAY...
IF YOU CAN'T SPLIT AN ASSET, ISN'T THAT JUST ASKING FOR TROUBLE?
CAT'S EYES ARE SAID TO ACT AS CHARMS AGAINST EVIL.
THEY CAN EXPEL THE EVIL BURIED DEEP WITHIN THE HUMAN SOUL AS WELL.

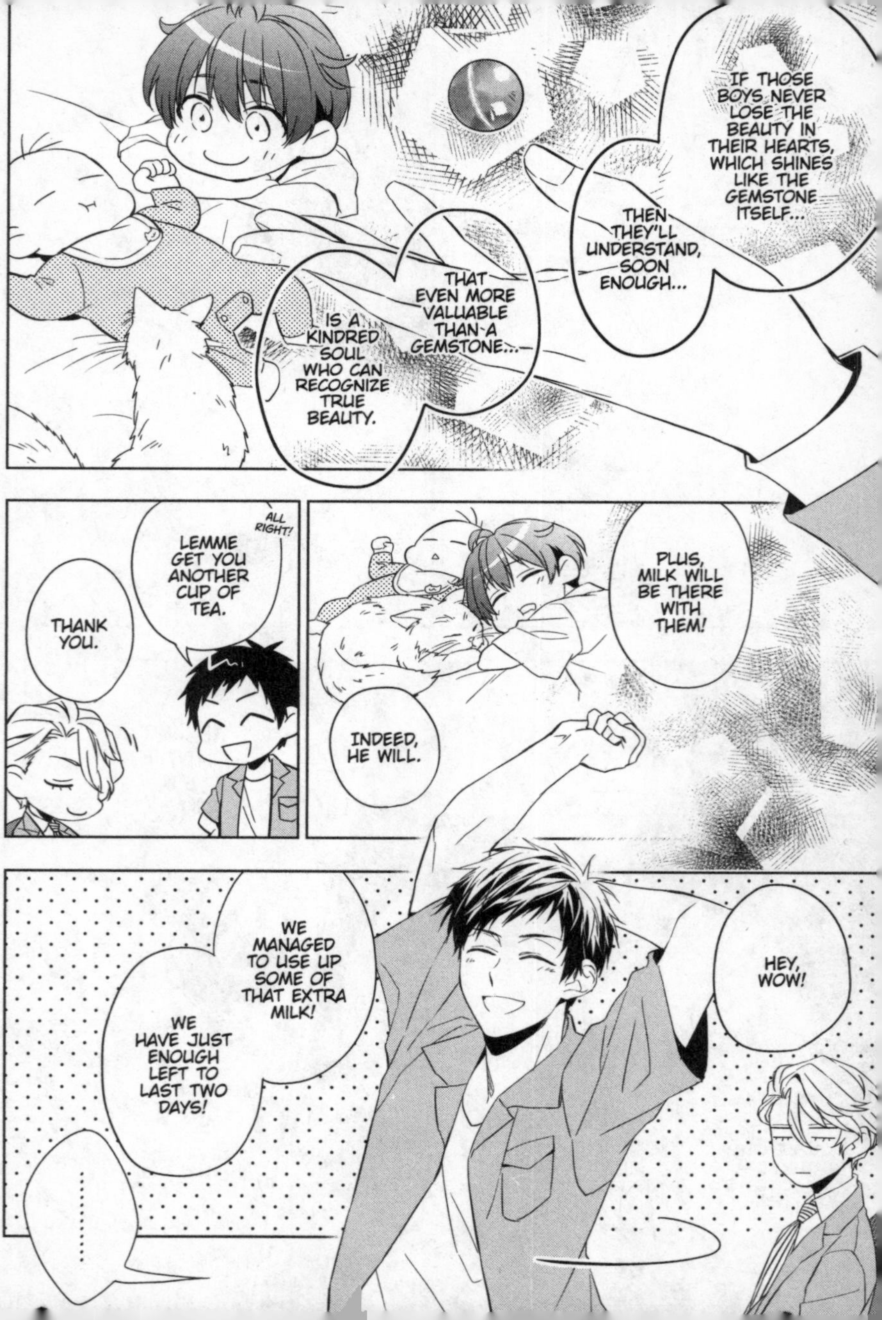
IF THOSE BOYS NEVER LOSE THE BEAUTY IN THEIR HEARTS, WHICH SHINES LIKE THE GEMSTONE ITSELF...
THEN THEY'LL UNDERSTAND, SOON ENOUGH...
THAT EVEN MORE VALUABLE THAN A GEMSTONE...
IS A KINDRED SOUL WHO CAN RECOGNIZE TRUE BEAUTY.
PLUS, MILK WILL BE THERE WITH THEM!
INDEED, HE WILL.
LEMME GET YOU ANOTHER CUP OF TEA.
ALL RIGHT!
THANK YOU.
HEY, WOW!
WE MANAGED TO USE UP SOME OF THAT EXTRA MILK!
WE HAVE JUST ENOUGH LEFT TO LAST TWO DAYS!
......

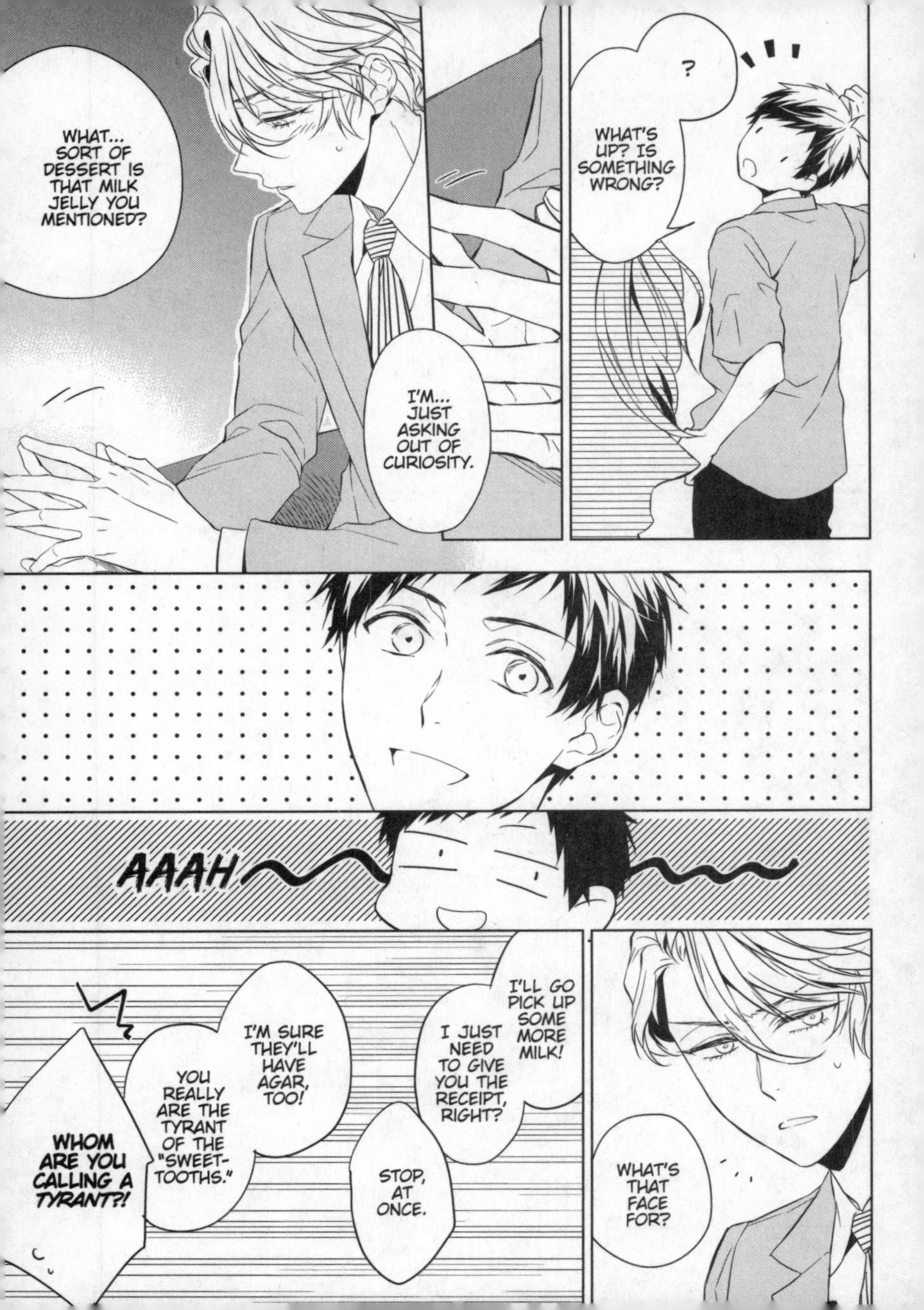
?
WHAT'S UP? IS SOMETHING WRONG?
WHAT... SORT OF DESSERT IS THAT MILK JELLY YOU MENTIONED?
I'M... JUST ASKING OUT OF CURIOSITY.
AAAH
WHAT'S THAT FACE FOR?
I'LL GO PICK UP SOME MORE MILK!
I JUST NEED TO GIVE YOU THE RECEIPT, RIGHT?
I'M SURE THEY'LL HAVE AGAR, TOO!
STOP, AT ONCE.
YOU REALLY ARE THE TYRANT OF THE "SWEET-TOOTHS."
WHOM ARE YOU CALLING A *TYRANT?!*

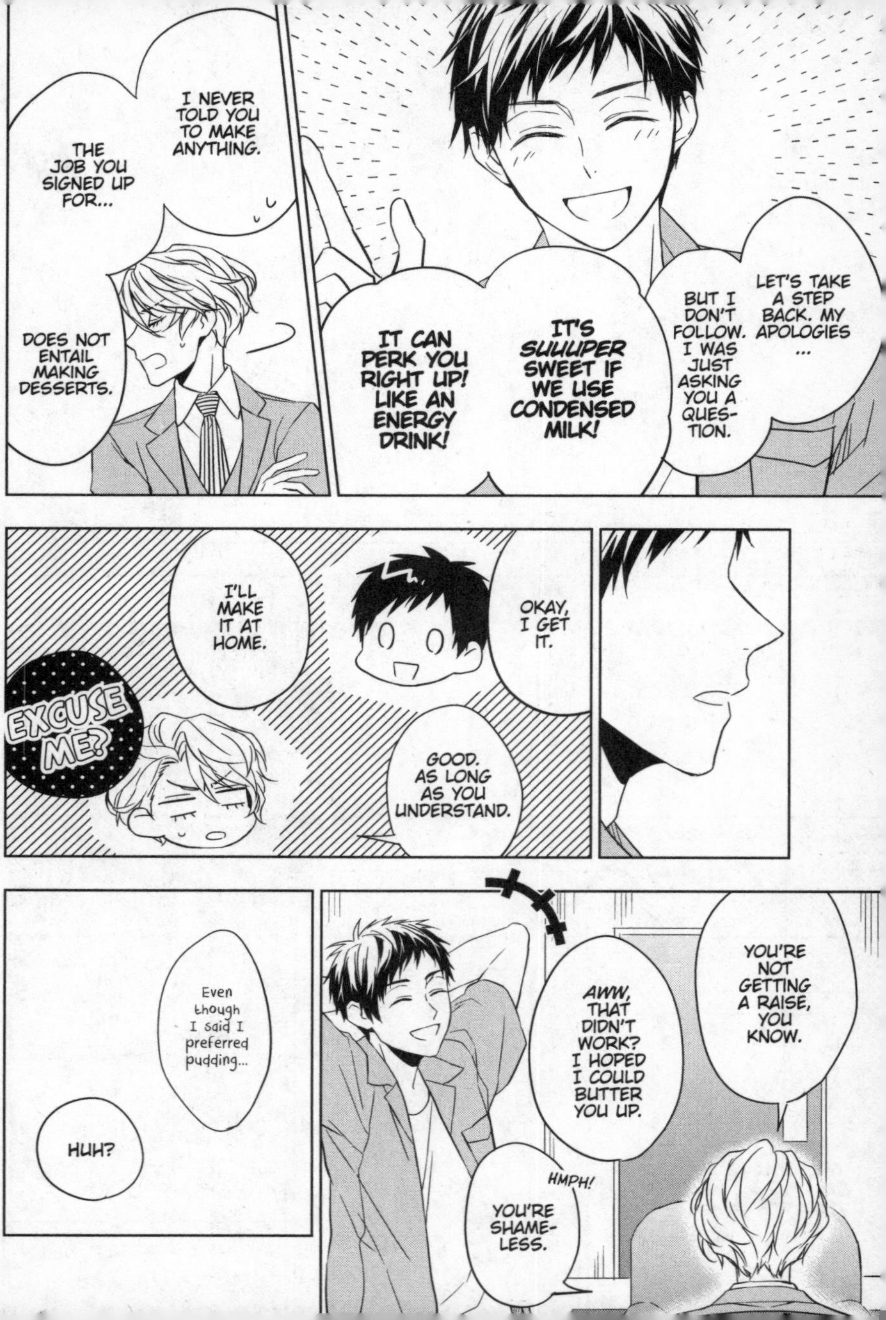

LET'S TAKE A STEP BACK. MY APOLOGIES ...
BUT I DON'T FOLLOW. I WAS JUST ASKING YOU A QUESTION.
IT'S SUUUPER SWEET IF WE USE CONDENSED MILK!
IT CAN PERK YOU RIGHT UP! LIKE AN ENERGY DRINK!
I NEVER TOLD YOU TO MAKE ANYTHING.
THE JOB YOU SIGNED UP FOR...
DOES NOT ENTAIL MAKING DESSERTS.
OKAY, I GET IT.
GOOD. AS LONG AS YOU UNDERSTAND.
I'LL MAKE IT AT HOME.
EXCUSE ME?
YOU'RE NOT GETTING A RAISE, YOU KNOW.
AWW, THAT DIDN'T WORK? I HOPED I COULD BUTTER YOU UP.
HMPH!
YOU'RE SHAME-LESS.
Even though I said I preferred pudding...
HUH?

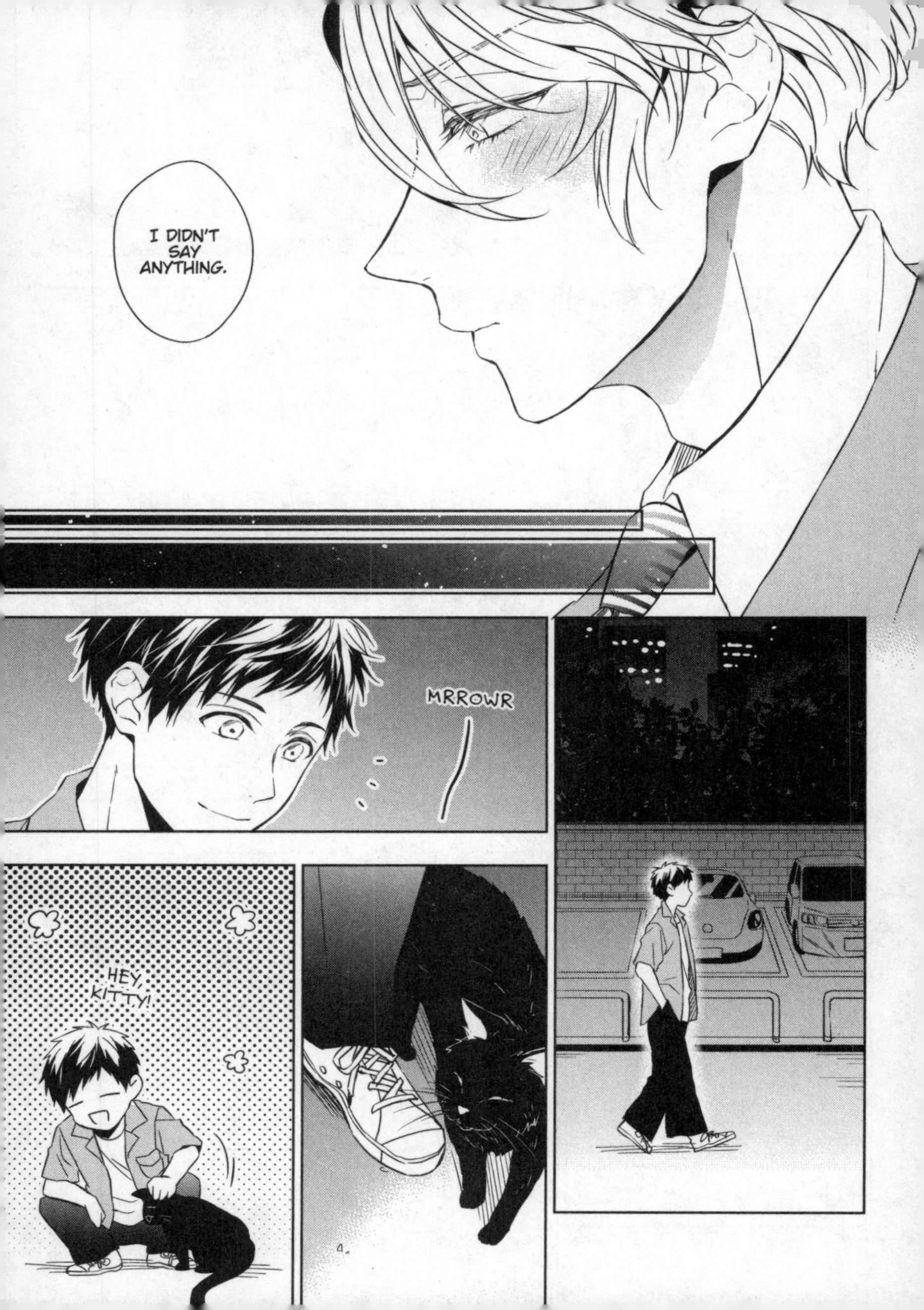
I DIDN'T SAY ANYTHING.
MRROWR
HEY, KITTY!

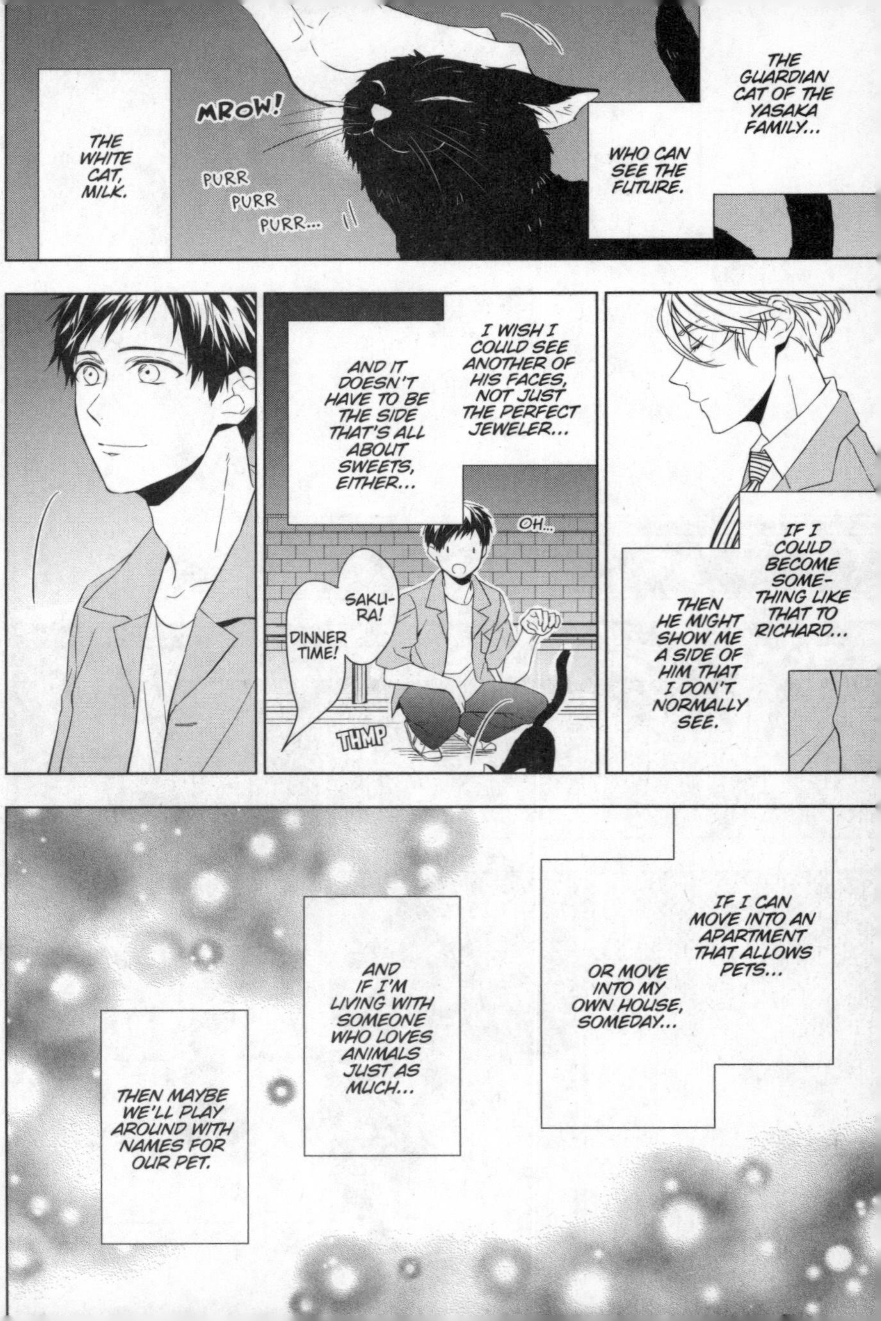
THE GUARDIAN CAT OF THE YASAKA FAMILY...
WHO CAN SEE THE FUTURE.
MROW!
PURR PURR PURR...
THE WHITE CAT, MILK.
IF I COULD BECOME SOME-THING LIKE THAT TO RICHARD...
THEN HE MIGHT SHOW ME A SIDE OF HIM THAT I DON'T NORMALLY SEE.
I WISH I COULD SEE ANOTHER OF HIS FACES, NOT JUST THE PERFECT JEWELER...
AND IT DOESN'T HAVE TO BE THE SIDE THAT'S ALL ABOUT SWEETS, EITHER...
OH...
SAKU-RA! DINNER TIME!
THMP
IF I CAN MOVE INTO AN APARTMENT THAT ALLOWS PETS...
OR MOVE INTO MY OWN HOUSE, SOMEDAY...
AND IF I'M LIVING WITH SOMEONE WHO LOVES ANIMALS JUST AS MUCH...
THEN MAYBE WE'LL PLAY AROUND WITH NAMES FOR OUR PET.

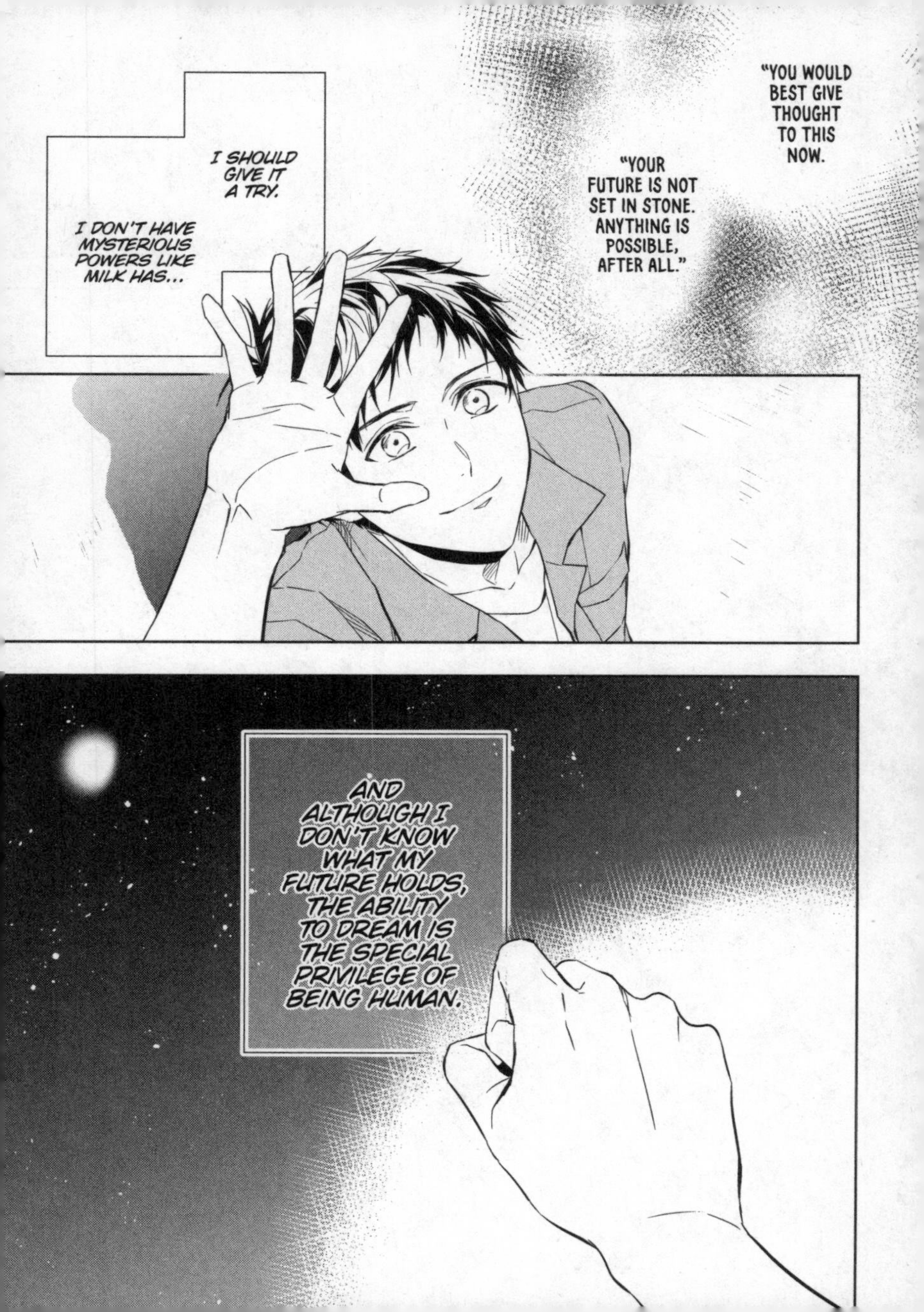
"YOU WOULD BEST GIVE THOUGHT TO THIS NOW.
"YOUR FUTURE IS NOT SET IN STONE. ANYTHING IS POSSIBLE, AFTER ALL."
I SHOULD GIVE IT A TRY.
I DON'T HAVE MYSTERIOUS POWERS LIKE MILK HAS...
AND ALTHOUGH I DON'T KNOW WHAT MY FUTURE HOLDS, THE ABILITY TO DREAM IS THE SPECIAL PRIVILEGE OF BEING HUMAN.

THE CASE FILES OF JEWELER RICHARD

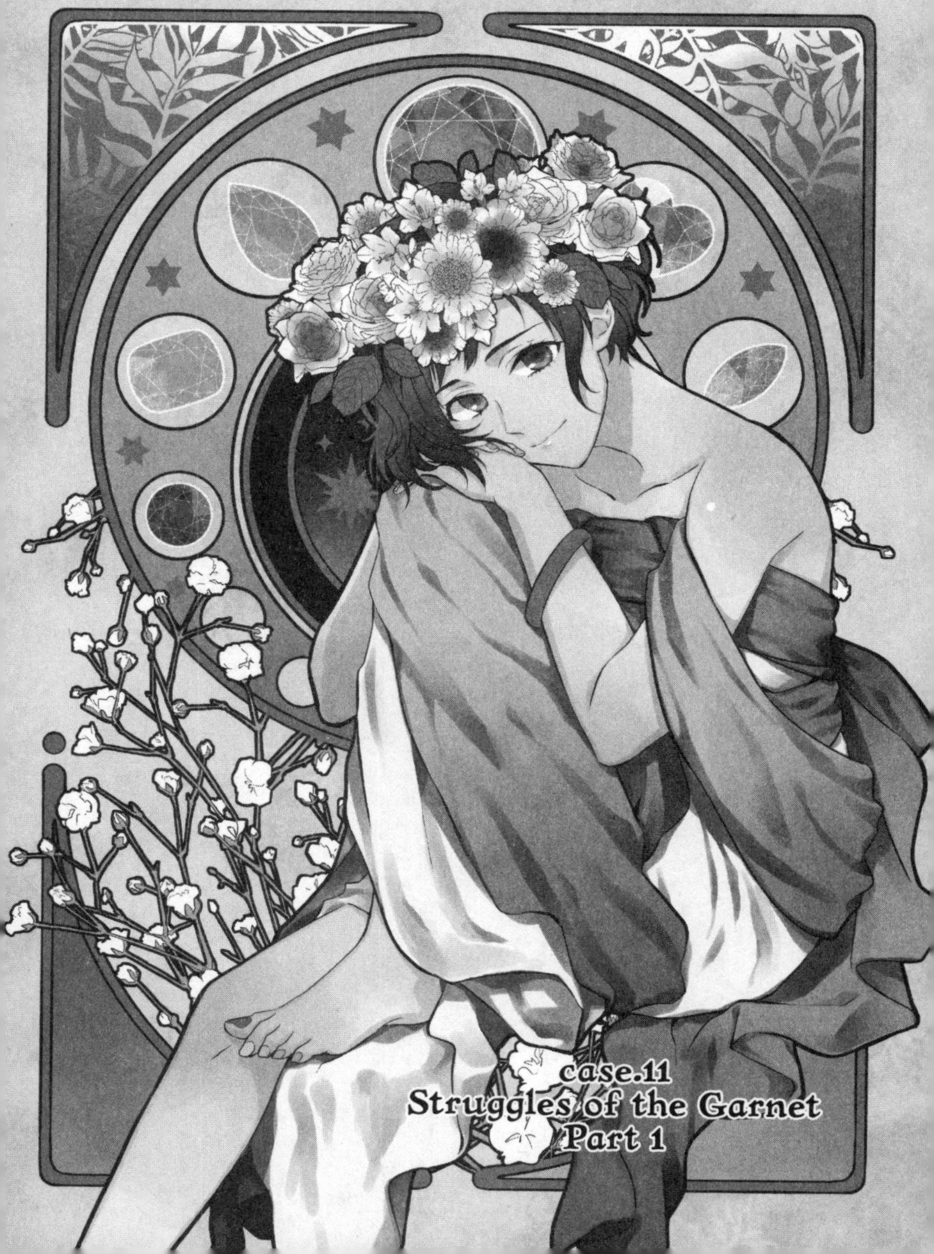
case.11
Struggles of the Garnet
Part 1

THE CASE FILES OF JEWELER RICHARD

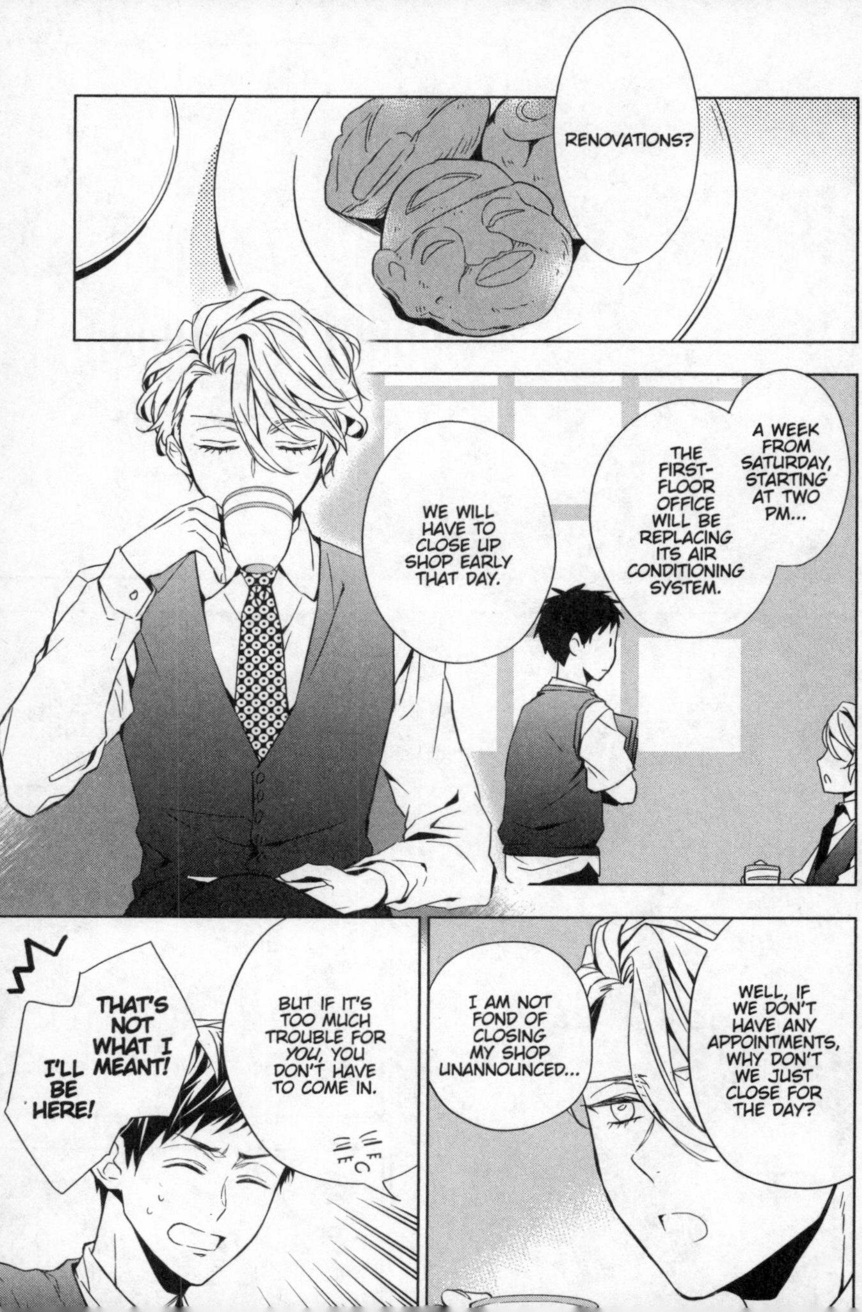
RENOVATIONS?
A WEEK FROM SATURDAY, STARTING AT TWO PM...
THE FIRST-FLOOR OFFICE WILL BE REPLACING ITS AIR CONDITIONING SYSTEM.
WE WILL HAVE TO CLOSE UP SHOP EARLY THAT DAY.
WELL, IF WE DON'T HAVE ANY APPOINTMENTS, WHY DON'T WE JUST CLOSE FOR THE DAY?
I AM NOT FOND OF CLOSING MY SHOP UNANNOUNCED...
BUT IF IT'S TOO MUCH TROUBLE FOR *YOU*, YOU DON'T HAVE TO COME IN.
THAT'S NOT WHAT I MEANT!
I'LL BE HERE!

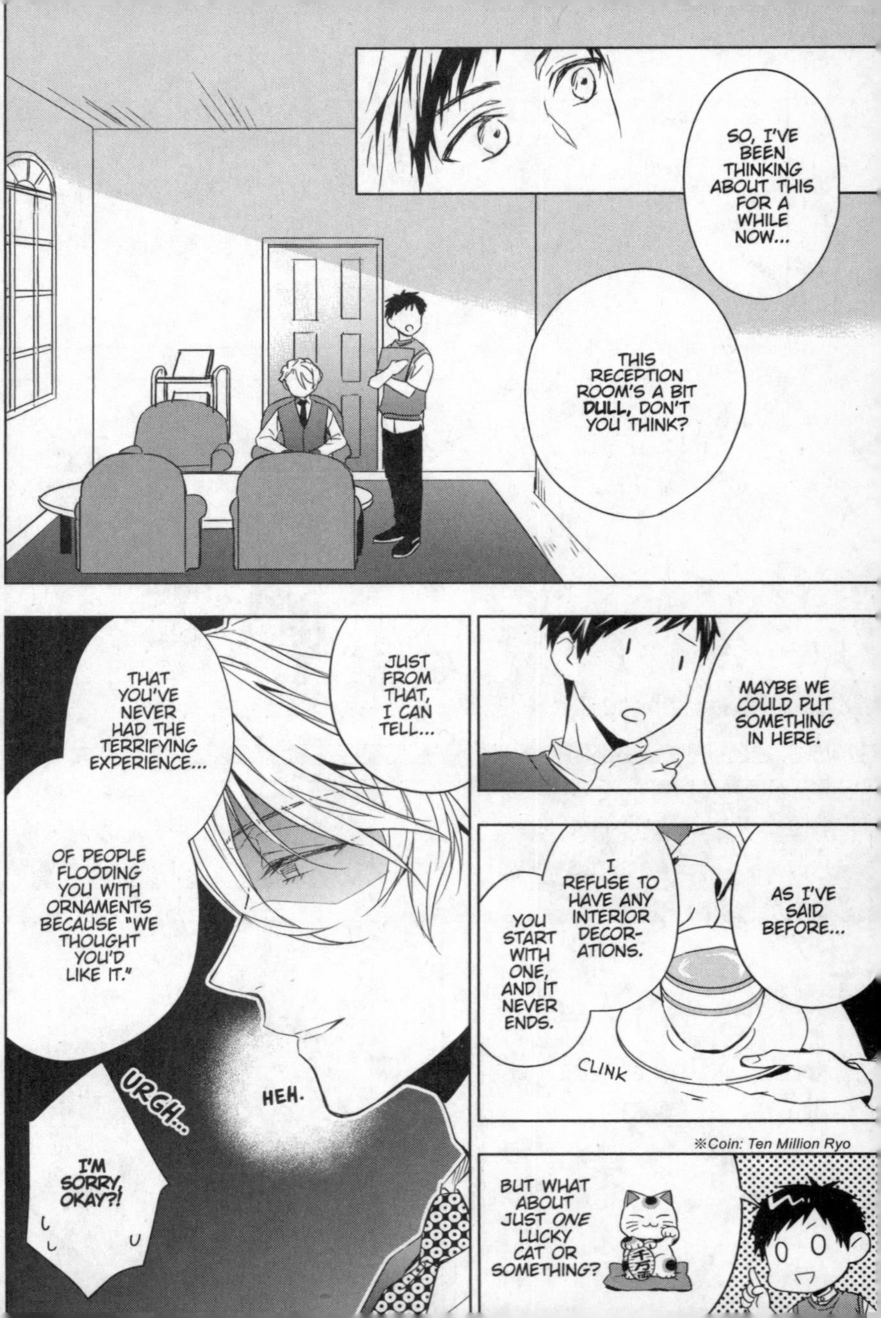
SO, I'VE BEEN THINKING ABOUT THIS FOR A WHILE NOW...
THIS RECEPTION ROOM'S A BIT **DULL,** DON'T YOU THINK?
MAYBE WE COULD PUT SOMETHING IN HERE.
AS I'VE SAID BEFORE...
I REFUSE TO HAVE ANY INTERIOR DECOR-ATIONS.
YOU START WITH ONE, AND IT NEVER ENDS.
CLINK
※Coin: Ten Million Ryo
BUT WHAT ABOUT JUST *ONE* LUCKY CAT OR SOMETHING?
JUST FROM THAT, I CAN TELL...
THAT YOU'VE NEVER HAD THE TERRIFYING EXPERIENCE...
OF PEOPLE FLOODING YOU WITH ORNAMENTS BECAUSE "WE THOUGHT YOU'D LIKE IT."
HEH.
URGH...
I'M SORRY, OKAY?!

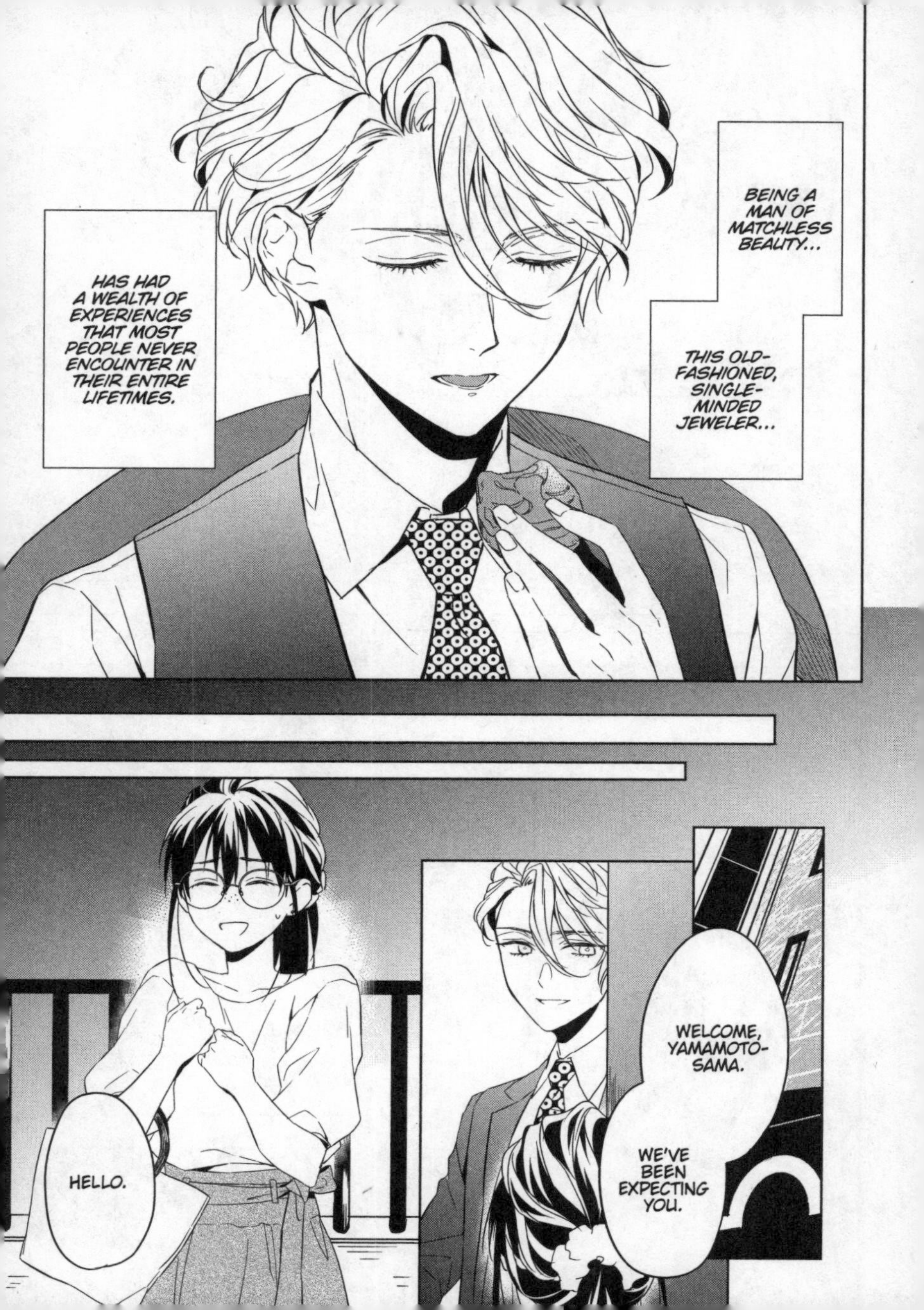
BEING A MAN OF MATCHLESS BEAUTY...
THIS OLD-FASHIONED, SINGLE-MINDED JEWELER...
HAS HAD A WEALTH OF EXPERIENCES THAT MOST PEOPLE NEVER ENCOUNTER IN THEIR ENTIRE LIFETIMES.
WELCOME, YAMAMOTO-SAMA.
WE'VE BEEN EXPECTING YOU.
HELLO.

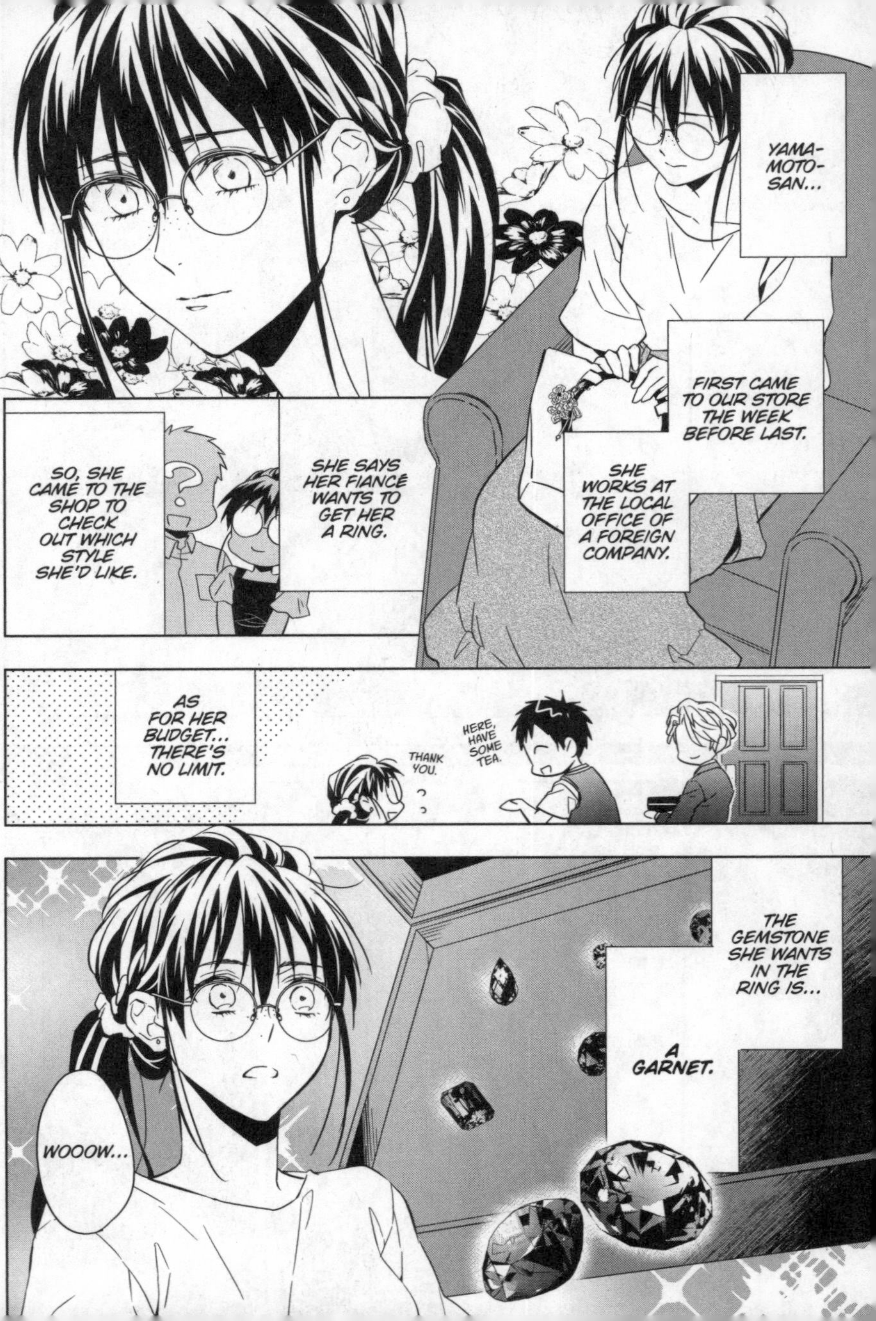
YAMA-MOTO-SAN...
FIRST CAME TO OUR STORE THE WEEK BEFORE LAST.
SHE WORKS AT THE LOCAL OFFICE OF A FOREIGN COMPANY.
SHE SAYS HER FIANCÉ WANTS TO GET HER A RING.
SO, SHE CAME TO THE SHOP TO CHECK OUT WHICH STYLE SHE'D LIKE.
HERE, HAVE SOME TEA.
THANK YOU.
AS FOR HER BUDGET... THERE'S NO LIMIT.
THE GEMSTONE SHE WANTS IN THE RING IS...
A GARNET.
WOOOW...

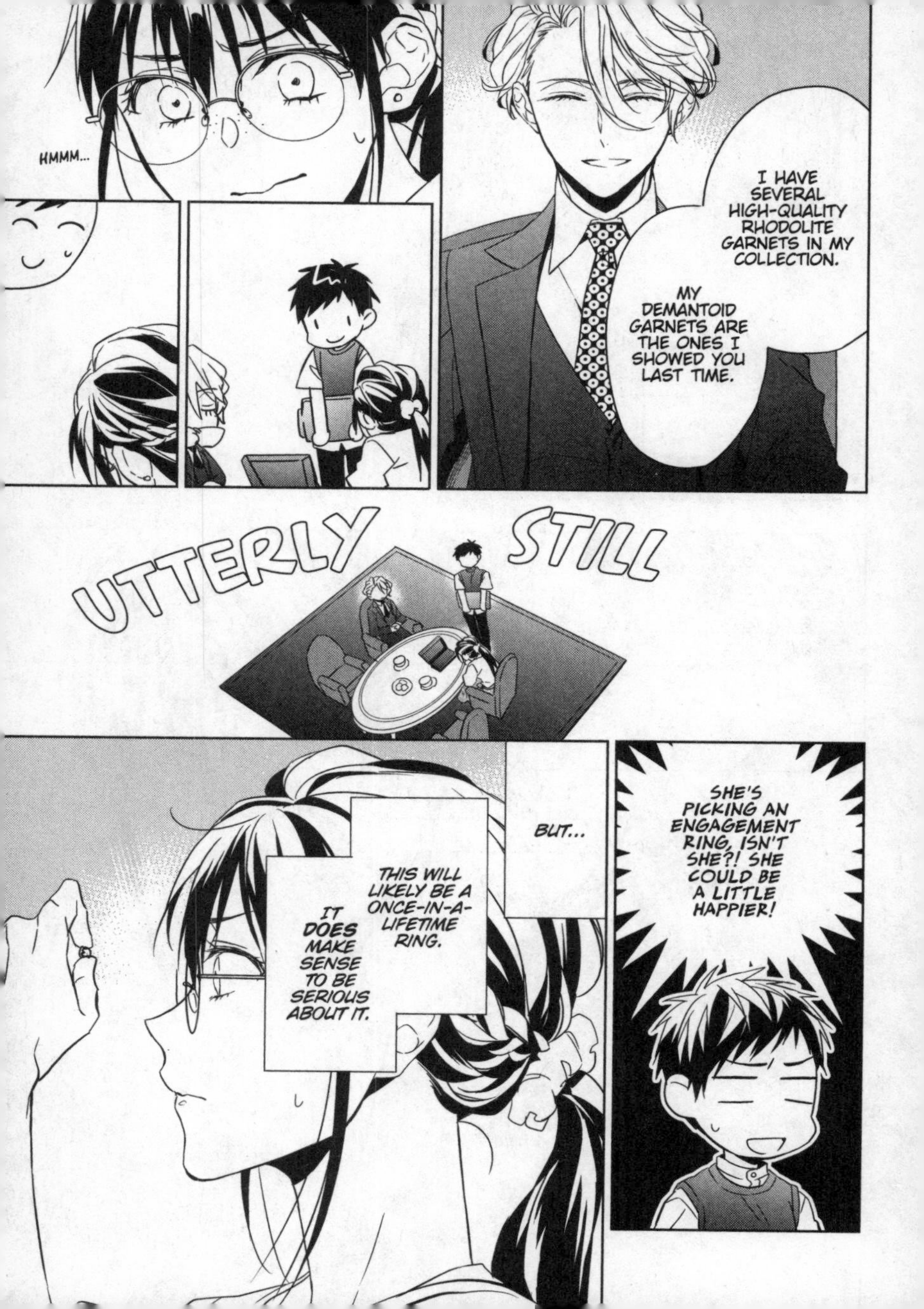
I HAVE SEVERAL HIGH-QUALITY RHODOLITE GARNETS IN MY COLLECTION.
MY DEMANTOID GARNETS ARE THE ONES I SHOWED YOU LAST TIME.
HMMM...
UTTERLY STILL
SHE'S PICKING AN ENGAGEMENT RING, ISN'T SHE?! SHE COULD BE A LITTLE HAPPIER!
BUT...
THIS WILL LIKELY BE A ONCE-IN-A-LIFETIME RING.
IT DOES MAKE SENSE TO BE SERIOUS ABOUT IT.

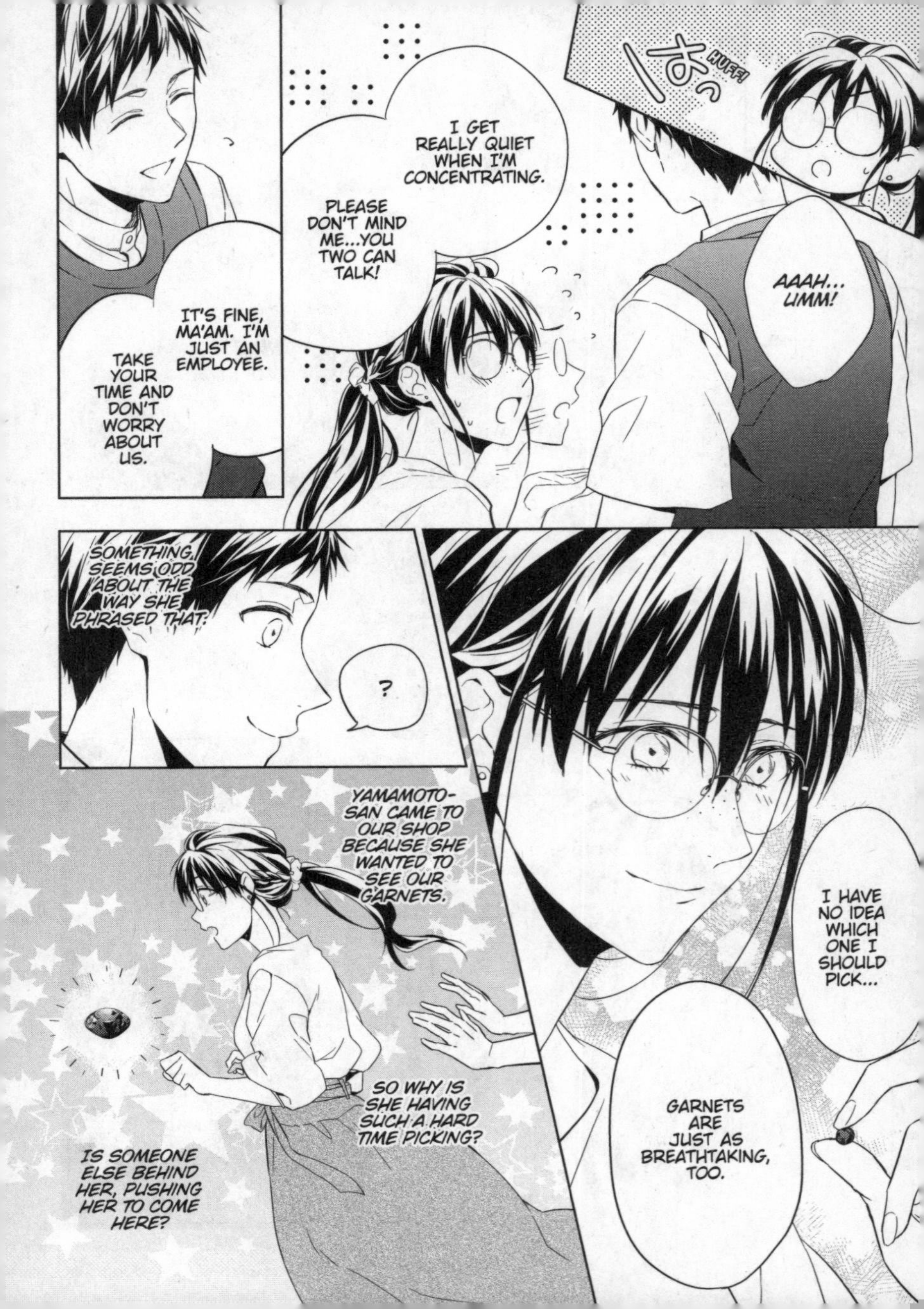
はっ
HUFF!
AAAH... UMM!
I GET REALLY QUIET WHEN I'M CONCENTRATING.
PLEASE DON'T MIND ME...YOU TWO CAN TALK!
IT'S FINE, MA'AM. I'M JUST AN EMPLOYEE.
TAKE YOUR TIME AND DON'T WORRY ABOUT US.
I HAVE NO IDEA WHICH ONE I SHOULD PICK...
GARNETS ARE JUST AS BREATHTAKING, TOO.
SOMETHING SEEMS ODD ABOUT THE WAY SHE PHRASED THAT.
?
YAMAMOTO-SAN CAME TO OUR SHOP BECAUSE SHE WANTED TO SEE OUR GARNETS.
SO WHY IS SHE HAVING SUCH A HARD TIME PICKING?
IS SOMEONE ELSE BEHIND HER, PUSHING HER TO COME HERE?

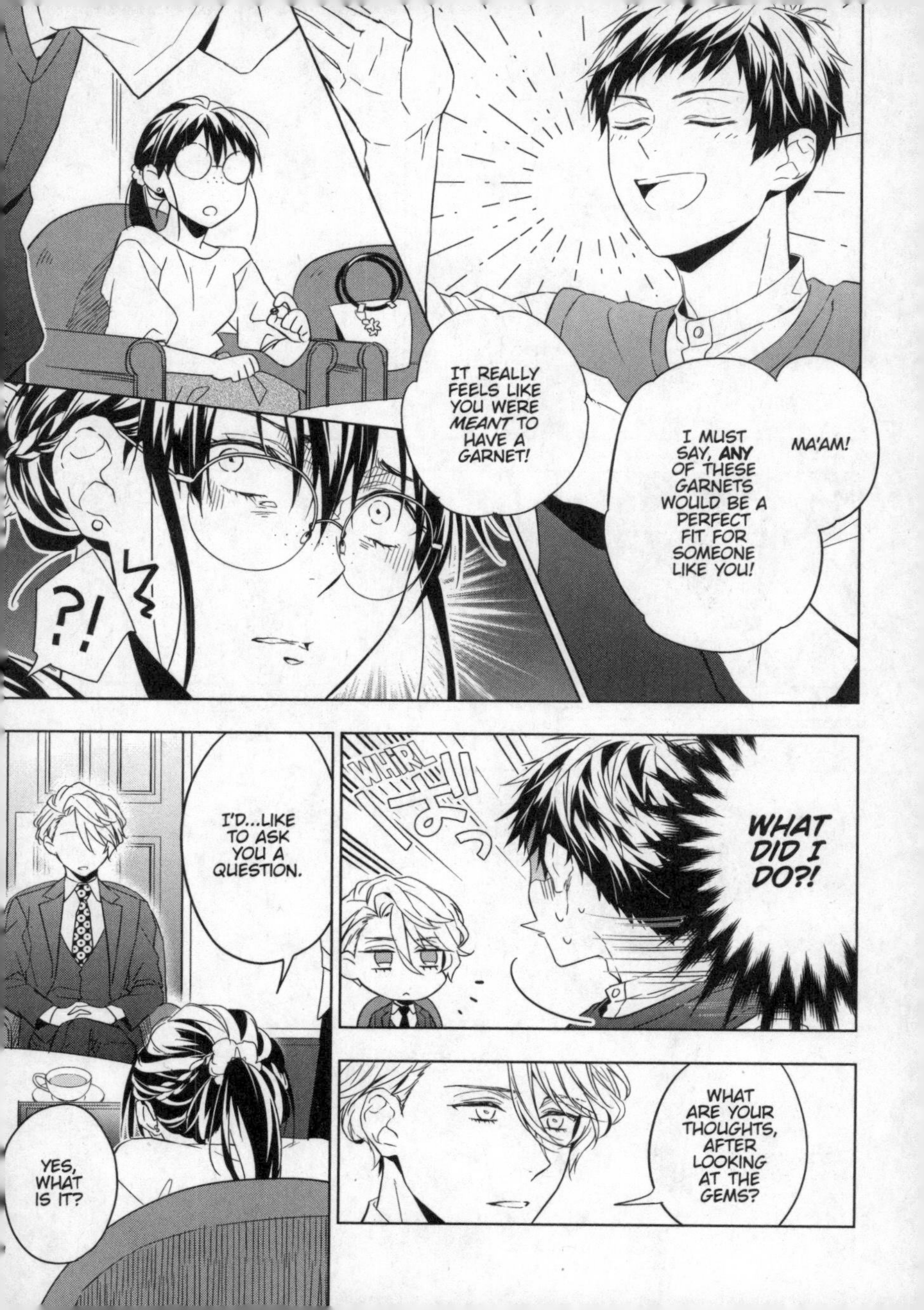
MA'AM!
I MUST SAY, ANY OF THESE GARNETS WOULD BE A PERFECT FIT FOR SOMEONE LIKE YOU!
IT REALLY FEELS LIKE YOU WERE *MEANT* TO HAVE A GARNET!
?!
WHIRL
WHAT DID I DO?!
WHAT ARE YOUR THOUGHTS, AFTER LOOKING AT THE GEMS?
I'D...LIKE TO ASK YOU A QUESTION.
YES, WHAT IS IT?

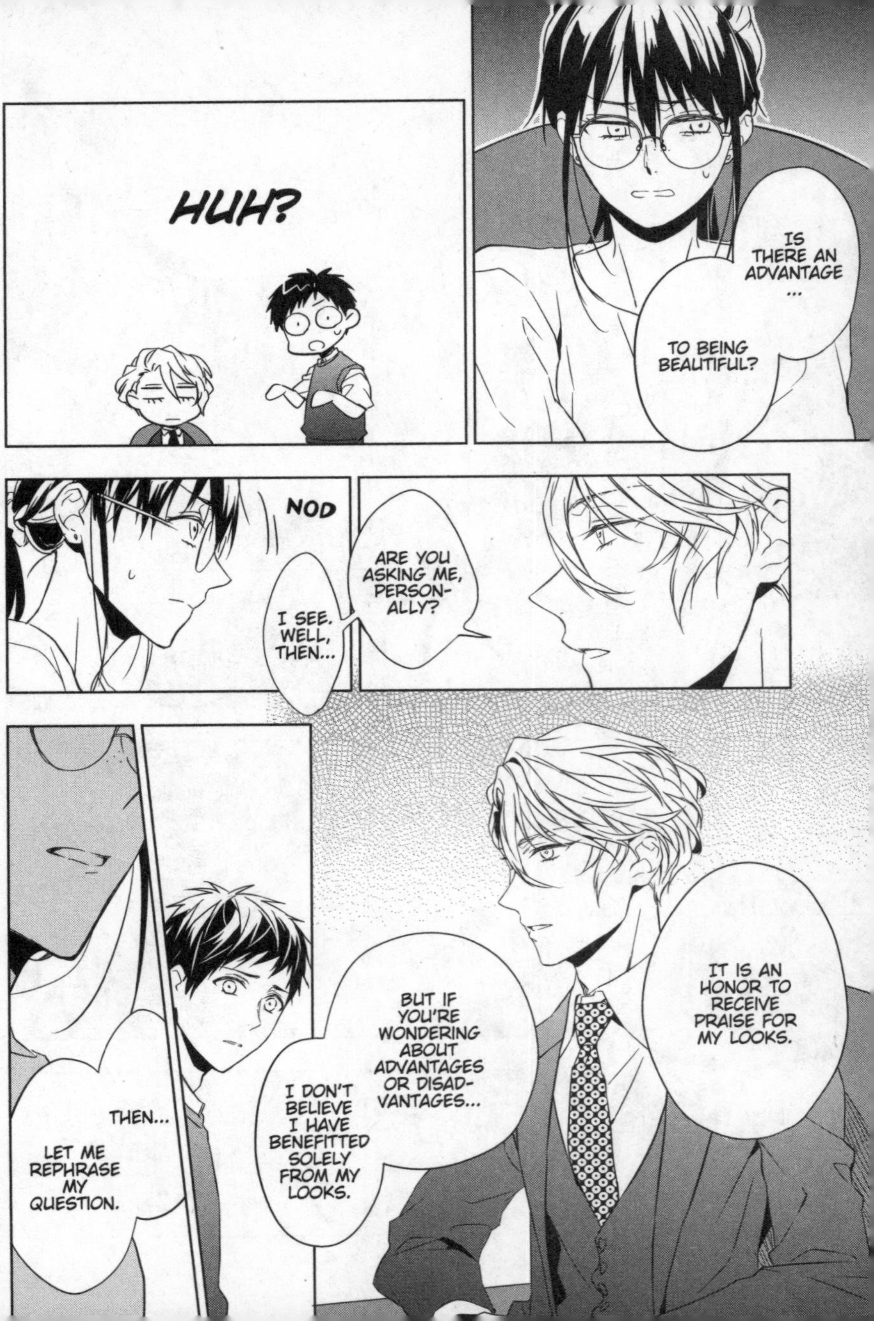
IS THERE AN ADVANTAGE ...
TO BEING BEAUTIFUL?
HUH?
ARE YOU ASKING ME, PERSONALLY?
NOD
I SEE. WELL, THEN...
IT IS AN HONOR TO RECEIVE PRAISE FOR MY LOOKS.
BUT IF YOU'RE WONDERING ABOUT ADVANTAGES OR DISADVANTAGES...
I DON'T BELIEVE I HAVE BENEFITTED SOLELY FROM MY LOOKS.
THEN...
LET ME REPHRASE MY QUESTION.

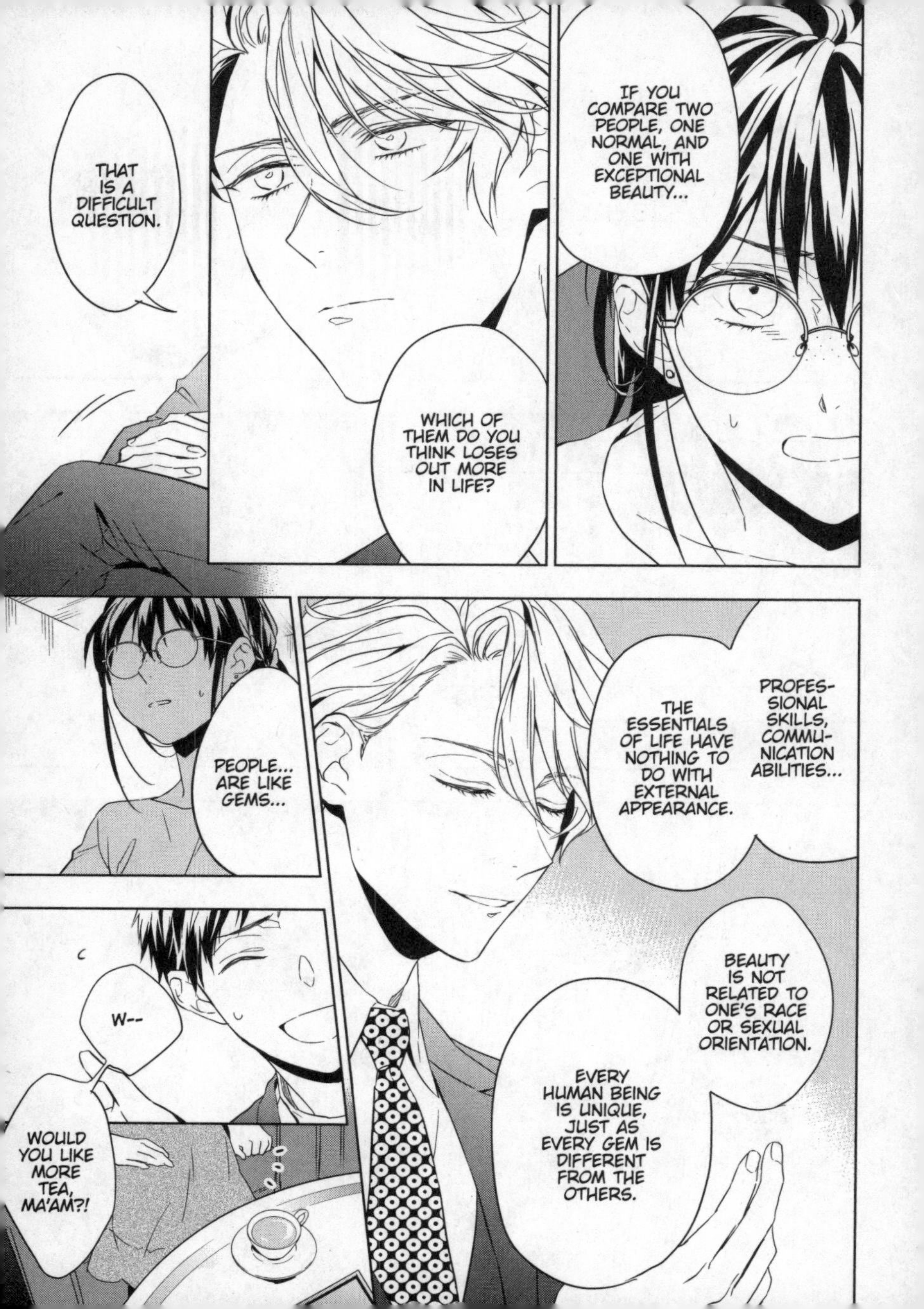
IF YOU COMPARE TWO PEOPLE, ONE NORMAL, AND ONE WITH EXCEPTIONAL BEAUTY...
WHICH OF THEM DO YOU THINK LOSES OUT MORE IN LIFE?
THAT IS A DIFFICULT QUESTION.
PROFESSIONAL SKILLS, COMMUNICATION ABILITIES...
THE ESSENTIALS OF LIFE HAVE NOTHING TO DO WITH EXTERNAL APPEARANCE.
BEAUTY IS NOT RELATED TO ONE'S RACE OR SEXUAL ORIENTATION.
EVERY HUMAN BEING IS UNIQUE, JUST AS EVERY GEM IS DIFFERENT FROM THE OTHERS.
PEOPLE... ARE LIKE GEMS...
W--
WOULD YOU LIKE MORE TEA, MA'AM?!

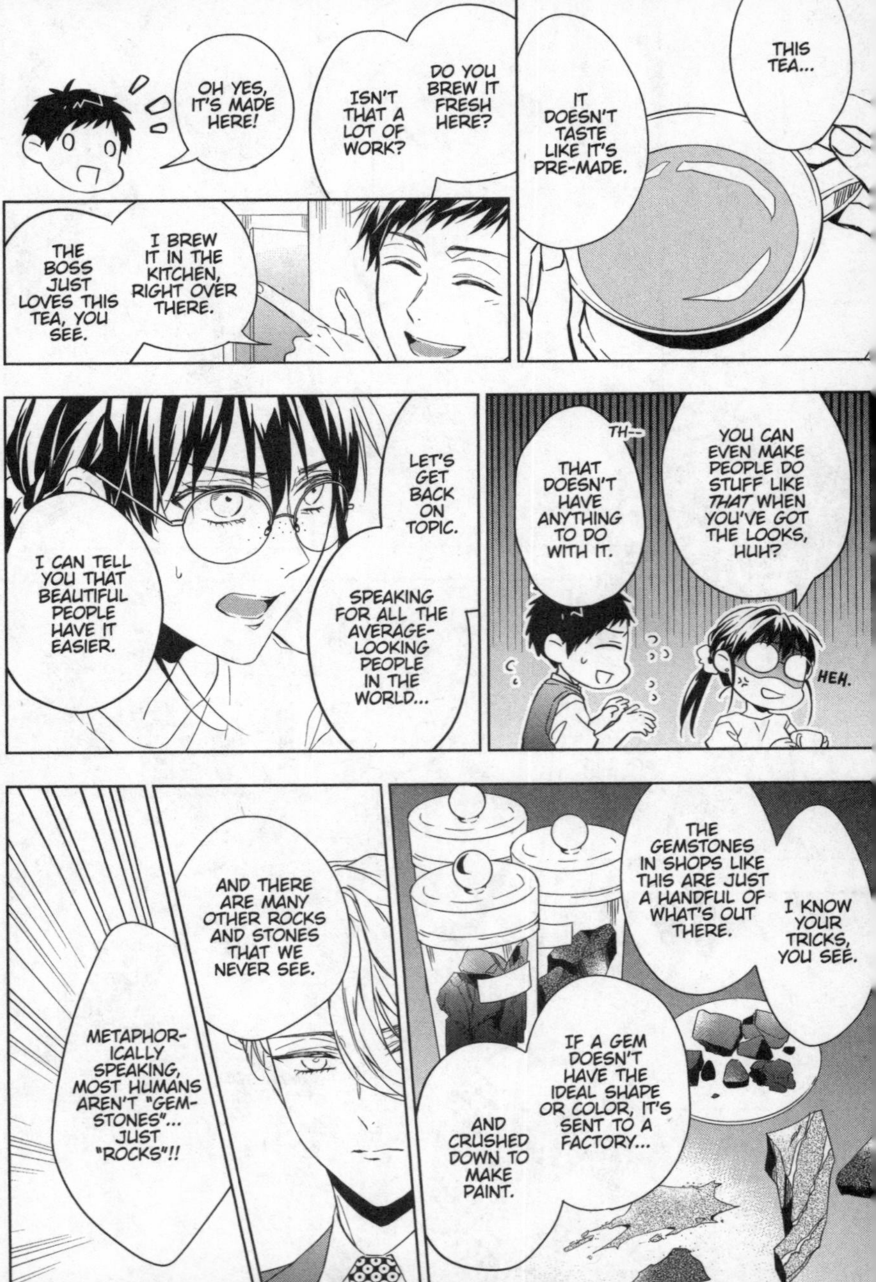
THIS TEA...
IT DOESN'T TASTE LIKE IT'S PRE-MADE.
DO YOU BREW IT FRESH HERE?
ISN'T THAT A LOT OF WORK?
OH YES, IT'S MADE HERE!
I BREW IT IN THE KITCHEN, RIGHT OVER THERE.
THE BOSS JUST LOVES THIS TEA, YOU SEE.
YOU CAN EVEN MAKE PEOPLE DO STUFF LIKE *THAT* WHEN YOU'VE GOT THE LOOKS, HUH?
HEH.
TH--
THAT DOESN'T HAVE ANYTHING TO DO WITH IT.
LET'S GET BACK ON TOPIC.
SPEAKING FOR ALL THE AVERAGE-LOOKING PEOPLE IN THE WORLD...
I CAN TELL YOU THAT BEAUTIFUL PEOPLE HAVE IT EASIER.
I KNOW YOUR TRICKS, YOU SEE.
THE GEMSTONES IN SHOPS LIKE THIS ARE JUST A HANDFUL OF WHAT'S OUT THERE.
IF A GEM DOESN'T HAVE THE IDEAL SHAPE OR COLOR, IT'S SENT TO A FACTORY...
AND CRUSHED DOWN TO MAKE PAINT.
AND THERE ARE MANY OTHER ROCKS AND STONES THAT WE NEVER SEE.
METAPHOR-ICALLY SPEAKING, MOST HUMANS AREN'T "GEM-STONES"... JUST "ROCKS"!!

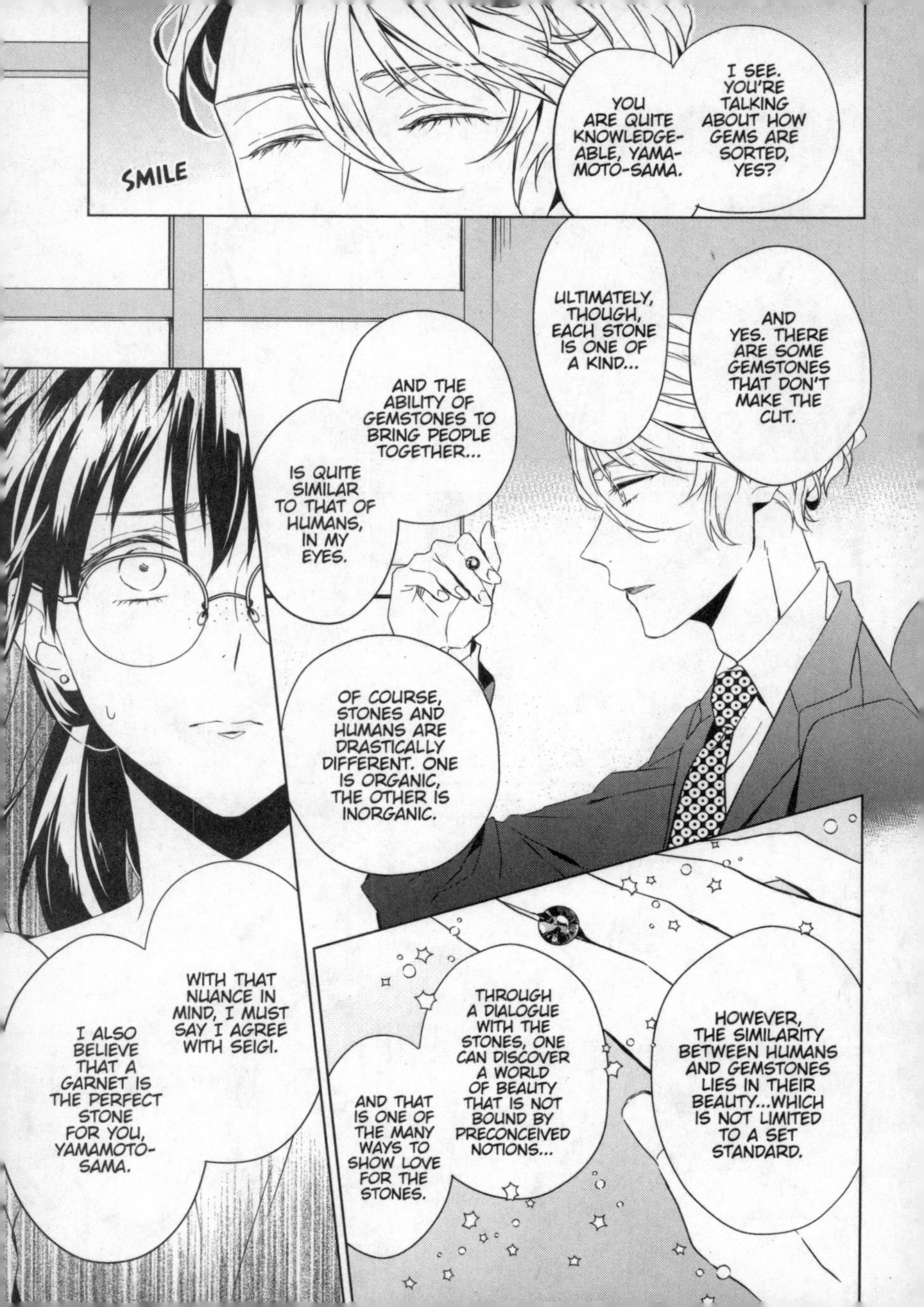
I SEE. YOU'RE TALKING ABOUT HOW GEMS ARE SORTED, YES?
YOU ARE QUITE KNOWLEDGE-ABLE, YAMA-MOTO-SAMA.
SMILE
AND YES. THERE ARE SOME GEMSTONES THAT DON'T MAKE THE CUT.
ULTIMATELY, THOUGH, EACH STONE IS ONE OF A KIND...
AND THE ABILITY OF GEMSTONES TO BRING PEOPLE TOGETHER...
IS QUITE SIMILAR TO THAT OF HUMANS, IN MY EYES.
OF COURSE, STONES AND HUMANS ARE DRASTICALLY DIFFERENT. ONE IS ORGANIC, THE OTHER IS INORGANIC.
HOWEVER, THE SIMILARITY BETWEEN HUMANS AND GEMSTONES LIES IN THEIR BEAUTY...WHICH IS NOT LIMITED TO A SET STANDARD.
THROUGH A DIALOGUE WITH THE STONES, ONE CAN DISCOVER A WORLD OF BEAUTY THAT IS NOT BOUND BY PRECONCEIVED NOTIONS...
AND THAT IS ONE OF THE MANY WAYS TO SHOW LOVE FOR THE STONES.
WITH THAT NUANCE IN MIND, I MUST SAY I AGREE WITH SEIGI.
I ALSO BELIEVE THAT A GARNET IS THE PERFECT STONE FOR YOU, YAMAMOTO-SAMA.

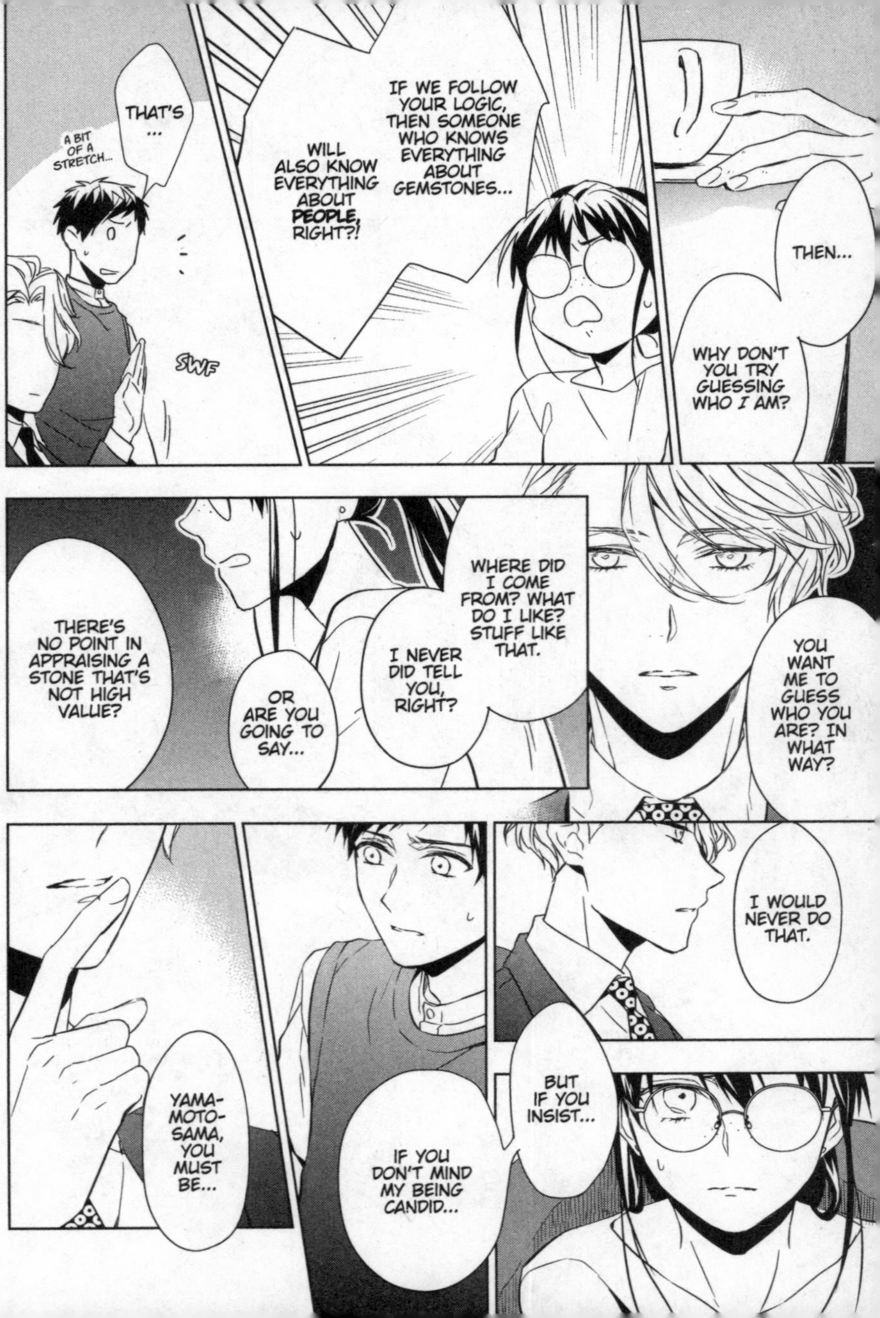
THEN...
WHY DON'T YOU TRY GUESSING WHO I AM?
IF WE FOLLOW YOUR LOGIC, THEN SOMEONE WHO KNOWS EVERYTHING ABOUT GEMSTONES...
WILL ALSO KNOW EVERYTHING ABOUT PEOPLE, RIGHT?!
THAT'S...
A BIT OF A STRETCH...
SWF
YOU WANT ME TO GUESS WHO YOU ARE? IN WHAT WAY?
WHERE DID I COME FROM? WHAT DO I LIKE? STUFF LIKE THAT.
I NEVER DID TELL YOU, RIGHT?
OR ARE YOU GOING TO SAY...
THERE'S NO POINT IN APPRAISING A STONE THAT'S NOT HIGH VALUE?
I WOULD NEVER DO THAT.
BUT IF YOU INSIST...
IF YOU DON'T MIND MY BEING CANDID...
YAMA-MOTO-SAMA, YOU MUST BE...

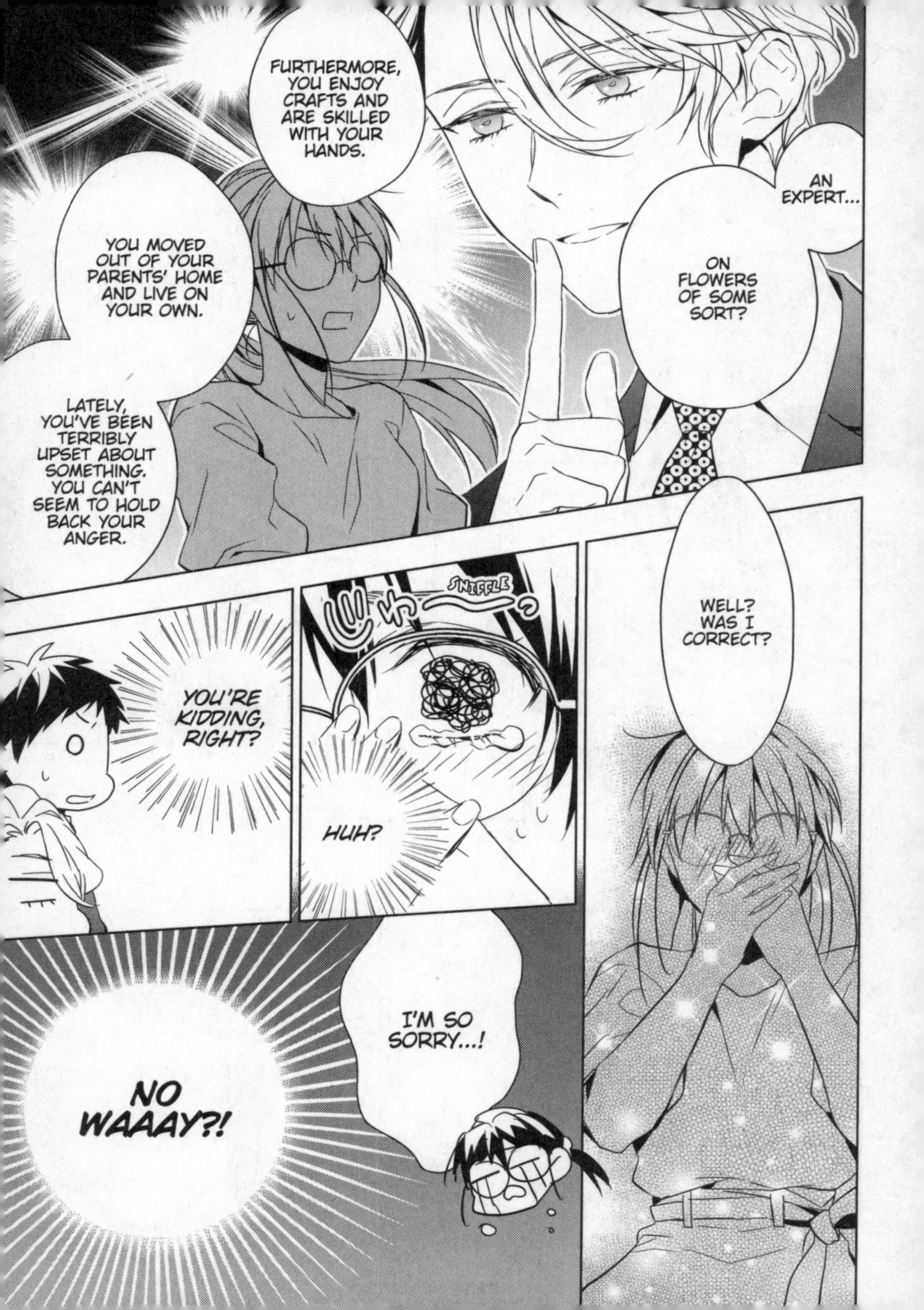
FURTHERMORE, YOU ENJOY CRAFTS AND ARE SKILLED WITH YOUR HANDS.
AN EXPERT...
ON FLOWERS OF SOME SORT?
YOU MOVED OUT OF YOUR PARENTS' HOME AND LIVE ON YOUR OWN.
LATELY, YOU'VE BEEN TERRIBLY UPSET ABOUT SOMETHING. YOU CAN'T SEEM TO HOLD BACK YOUR ANGER.
WELL? WAS I CORRECT?
SNIFFLE
HUH?
YOU'RE KIDDING, RIGHT?
I'M SO SORRY...!
NO WAAAY?!

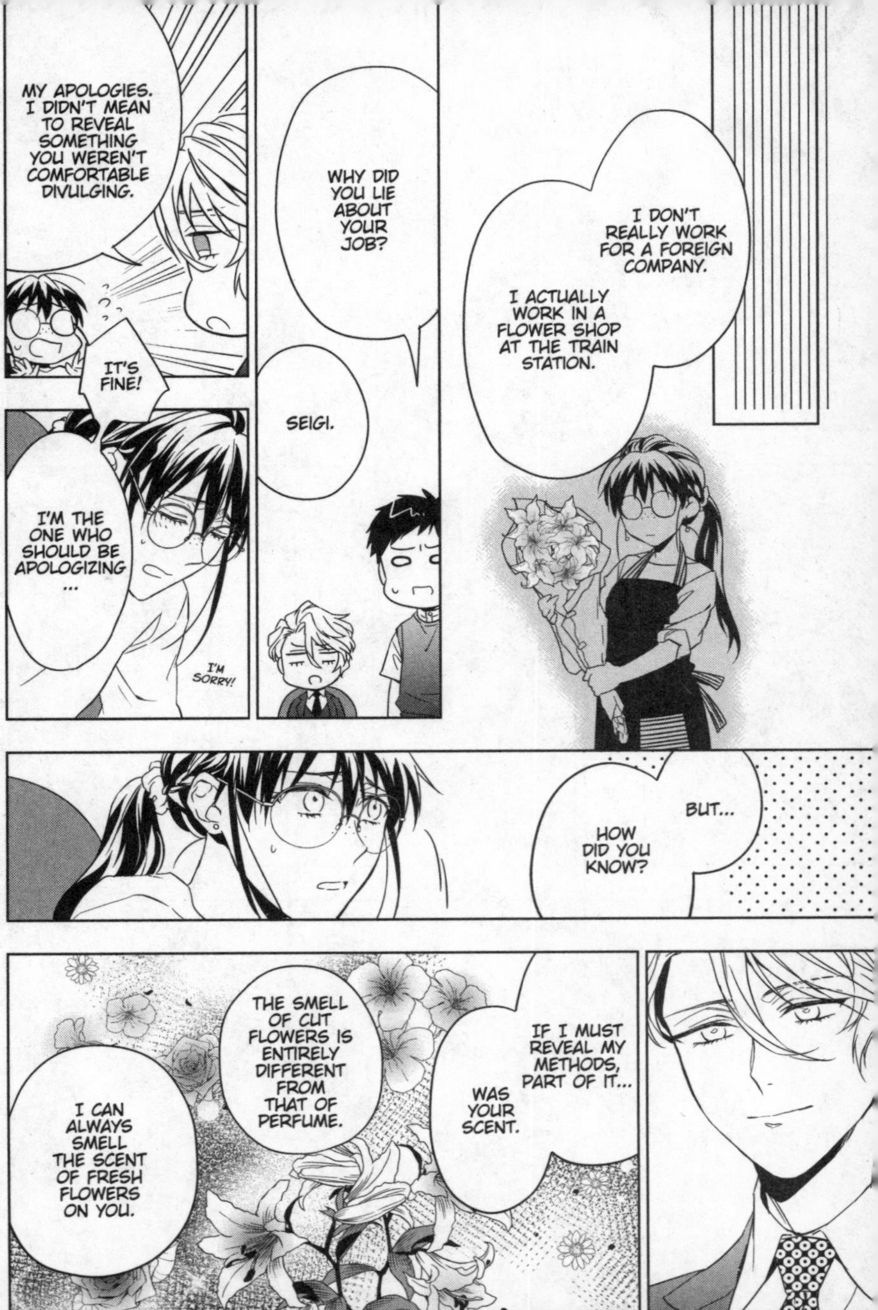
I DON'T REALLY WORK FOR A FOREIGN COMPANY.
I ACTUALLY WORK IN A FLOWER SHOP AT THE TRAIN STATION.
WHY DID YOU LIE ABOUT YOUR JOB?
SEIGI.
MY APOLOGIES. I DIDN'T MEAN TO REVEAL SOMETHING YOU WEREN'T COMFORTABLE DIVULGING.
IT'S FINE!
I'M THE ONE WHO SHOULD BE APOLOGIZING ...
I'M SORRY!
BUT...
HOW DID YOU KNOW?
IF I MUST REVEAL MY METHODS, PART OF IT...
WAS YOUR SCENT.
THE SMELL OF CUT FLOWERS IS ENTIRELY DIFFERENT FROM THAT OF PERFUME.
I CAN ALWAYS SMELL THE SCENT OF FRESH FLOWERS ON YOU.

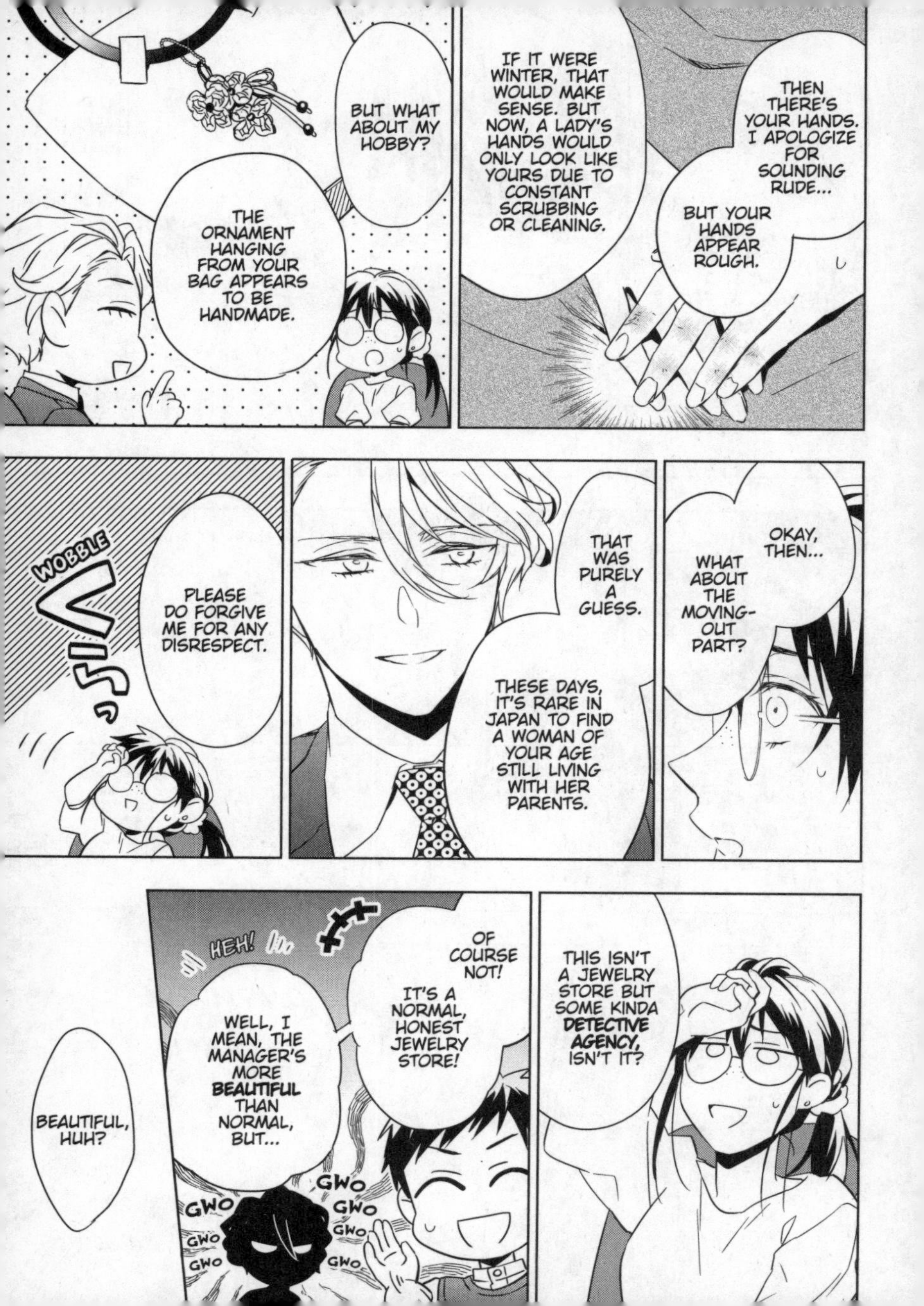
THEN THERE'S YOUR HANDS. I APOLOGIZE FOR SOUNDING RUDE...
BUT YOUR HANDS APPEAR ROUGH.
IF IT WERE WINTER, THAT WOULD MAKE SENSE. BUT NOW, A LADY'S HANDS WOULD ONLY LOOK LIKE YOURS DUE TO CONSTANT SCRUBBING OR CLEANING.
BUT WHAT ABOUT MY HOBBY?
THE ORNAMENT HANGING FROM YOUR BAG APPEARS TO BE HANDMADE.
OKAY, THEN...
WHAT ABOUT THE MOVING-OUT PART?
THAT WAS PURELY A GUESS.
THESE DAYS, IT'S RARE IN JAPAN TO FIND A WOMAN OF YOUR AGE STILL LIVING WITH HER PARENTS.
PLEASE DO FORGIVE ME FOR ANY DISRESPECT.
WOBBLE
THIS ISN'T A JEWELRY STORE BUT SOME KINDA **DETECTIVE AGENCY,** ISN'T IT?
OF COURSE NOT!
IT'S A NORMAL, HONEST JEWELRY STORE!
HEH!
WELL, I MEAN, THE MANAGER'S MORE **BEAUTIFUL** THAN NORMAL, BUT...
BEAUTIFUL, HUH?
GWO GWO GWO GWO GWO GWO GWO GWO

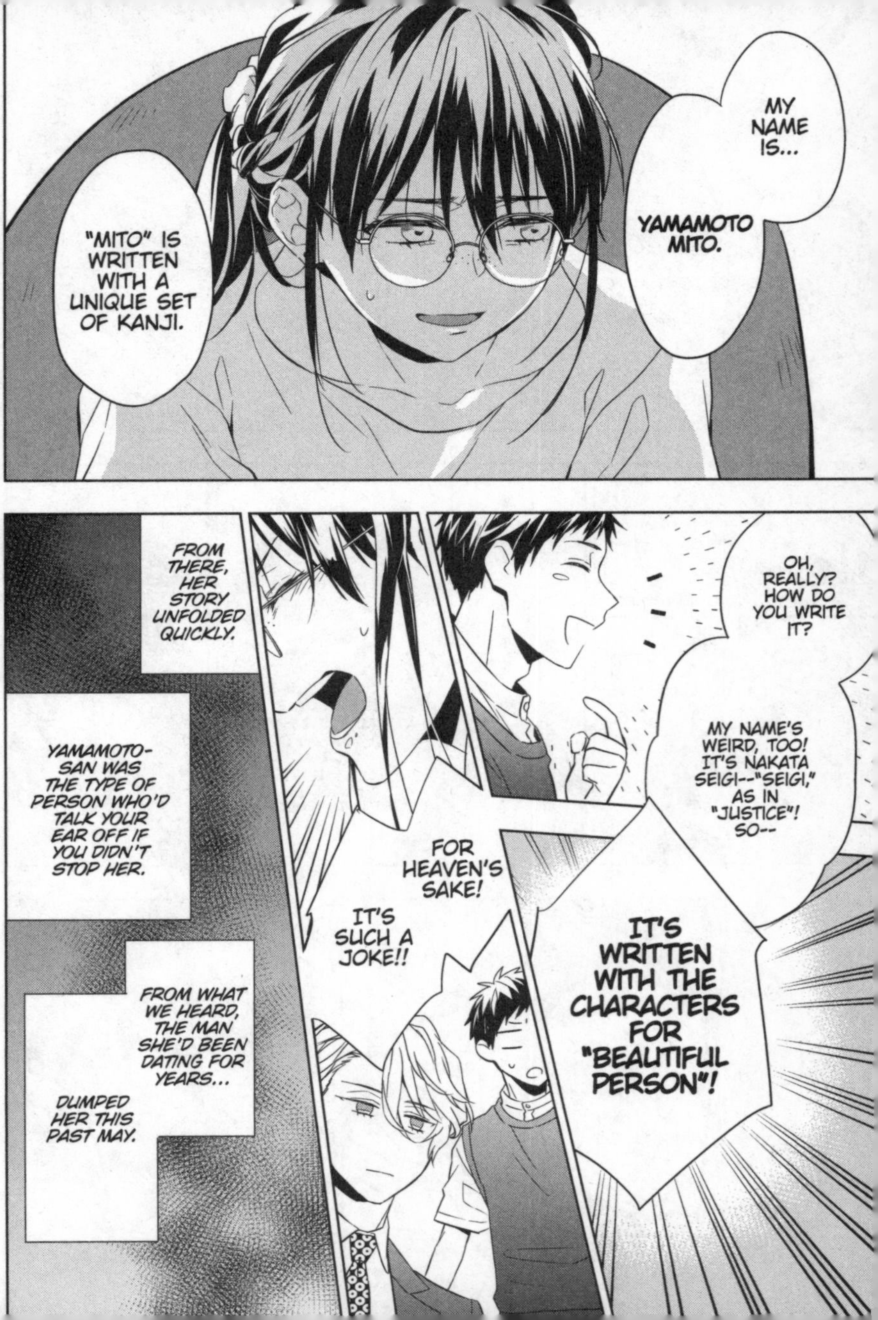
MY NAME IS...
YAMAMOTO MITO.
"MITO" IS WRITTEN WITH A UNIQUE SET OF KANJI.
OH, REALLY? HOW DO YOU WRITE IT?
MY NAME'S WEIRD, TOO! IT'S NAKATA SEIGI--"SEIGI," AS IN "JUSTICE"! SO--
FROM THERE, HER STORY UNFOLDED QUICKLY.
IT'S WRITTEN WITH THE CHARACTERS FOR "BEAUTIFUL PERSON"!
FOR HEAVEN'S SAKE!
IT'S SUCH A JOKE!!
YAMAMOTO-SAN WAS THE TYPE OF PERSON WHO'D TALK YOUR EAR OFF IF YOU DIDN'T STOP HER.
FROM WHAT WE HEARD, THE MAN SHE'D BEEN DATING FOR YEARS...
DUMPED HER THIS PAST MAY.

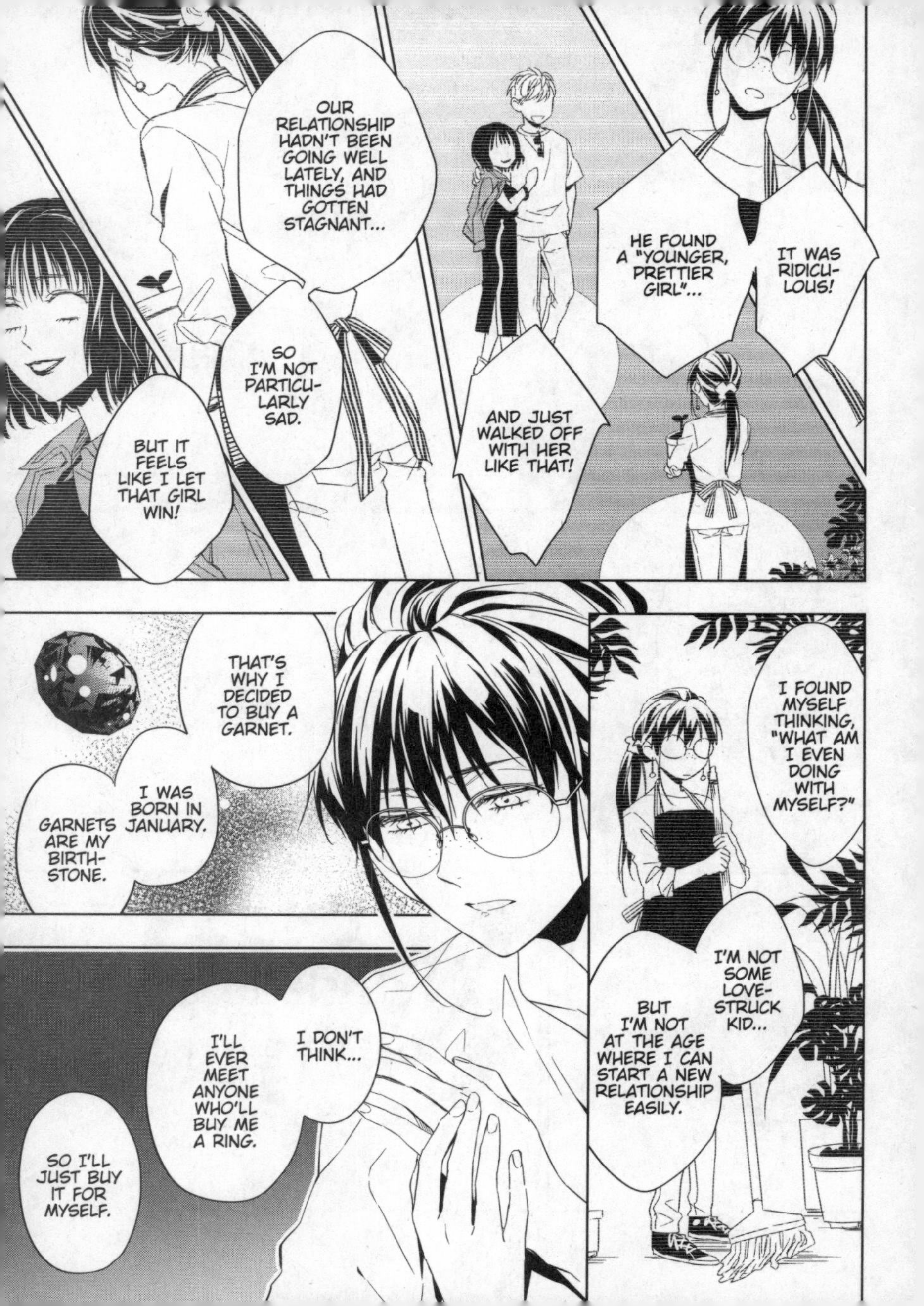
OUR RELATIONSHIP HADN'T BEEN GOING WELL LATELY, AND THINGS HAD GOTTEN STAGNANT...
HE FOUND A "YOUNGER, PRETTIER GIRL"...
IT WAS RIDICULOUS!
AND JUST WALKED OFF WITH HER LIKE THAT!
SO I'M NOT PARTICULARLY SAD.
BUT IT FEELS LIKE I LET THAT GIRL WIN!
I FOUND MYSELF THINKING, "WHAT AM I EVEN DOING WITH MYSELF?"
I'M NOT SOME LOVE-STRUCK KID...
BUT I'M NOT AT THE AGE WHERE I CAN START A NEW RELATIONSHIP EASILY.
THAT'S WHY I DECIDED TO BUY A GARNET.
I WAS BORN IN JANUARY.
GARNETS ARE MY BIRTHSTONE.
I DON'T THINK...
I'LL EVER MEET ANYONE WHO'LL BUY ME A RING.
SO I'LL JUST BUY IT FOR MYSELF.

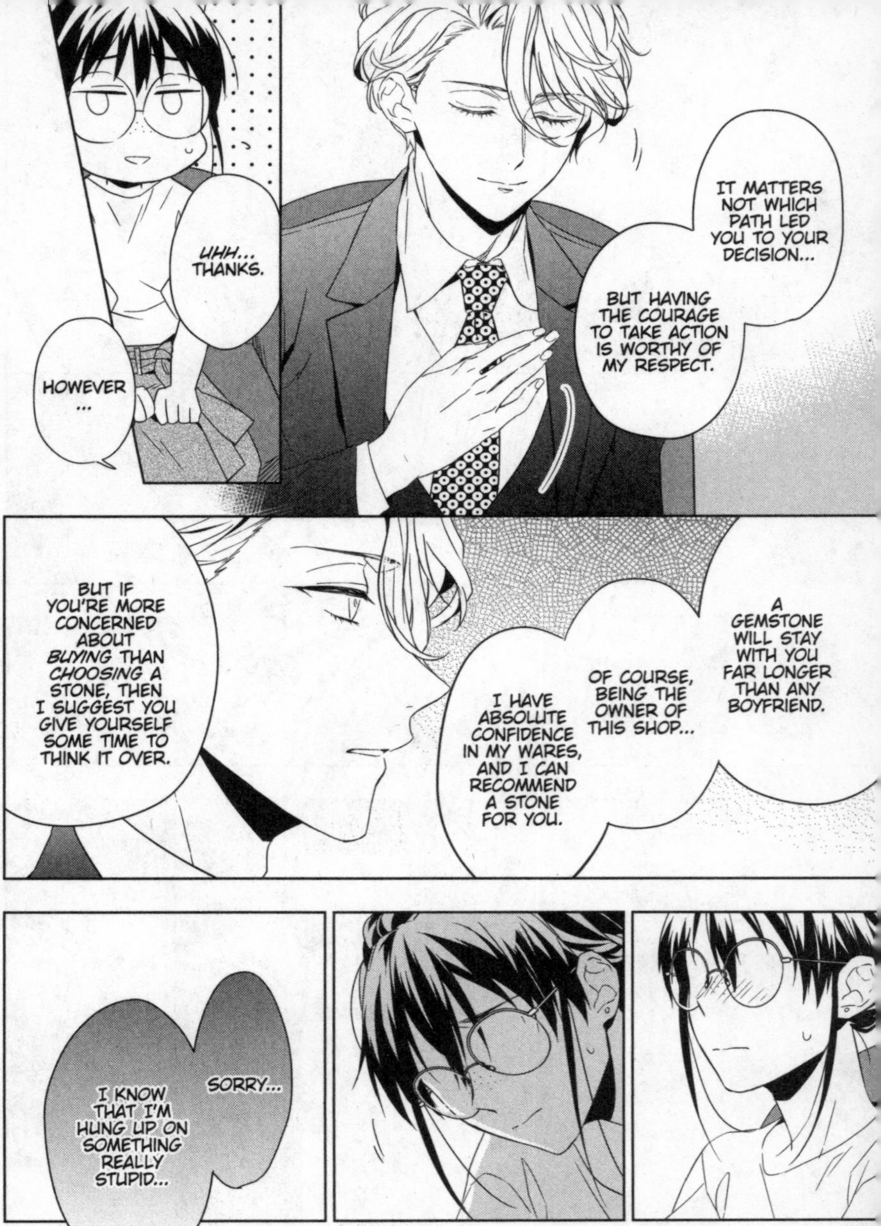
IT MATTERS NOT WHICH PATH LED YOU TO YOUR DECISION...
BUT HAVING THE COURAGE TO TAKE ACTION IS WORTHY OF MY RESPECT.
UHH... THANKS.
HOWEVER ...
A GEMSTONE WILL STAY WITH YOU FAR LONGER THAN ANY BOYFRIEND.
OF COURSE, BEING THE OWNER OF THIS SHOP...
I HAVE ABSOLUTE CONFIDENCE IN MY WARES, AND I CAN RECOMMEND A STONE FOR YOU.
BUT IF YOU'RE MORE CONCERNED ABOUT *BUYING* THAN *CHOOSING* A STONE, THEN I SUGGEST YOU GIVE YOURSELF SOME TIME TO THINK IT OVER.
SORRY...
I KNOW THAT I'M HUNG UP ON SOMETHING REALLY STUPID...

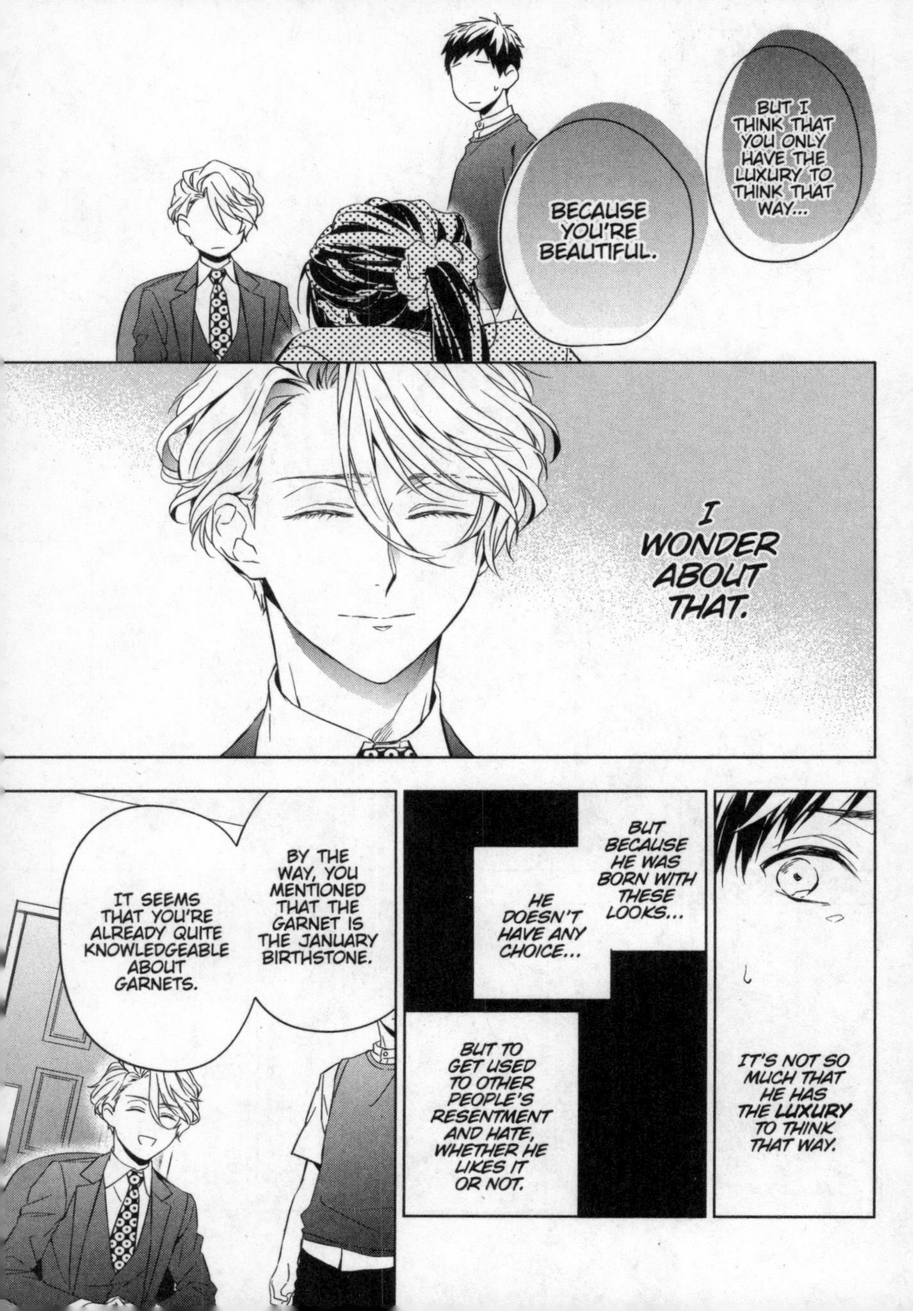
BUT I THINK THAT YOU ONLY HAVE THE LUXURY TO THINK THAT WAY...
BECAUSE YOU'RE BEAUTIFUL.
I WONDER ABOUT THAT.
IT'S NOT SO MUCH THAT HE HAS THE LUXURY TO THINK THAT WAY.
BUT BECAUSE HE WAS BORN WITH THESE LOOKS...
HE DOESN'T HAVE ANY CHOICE...
BUT TO GET USED TO OTHER PEOPLE'S RESENTMENT AND HATE, WHETHER HE LIKES IT OR NOT.
BY THE WAY, YOU MENTIONED THAT THE GARNET IS THE JANUARY BIRTHSTONE.
IT SEEMS THAT YOU'RE ALREADY QUITE KNOWLEDGEABLE ABOUT GARNETS.

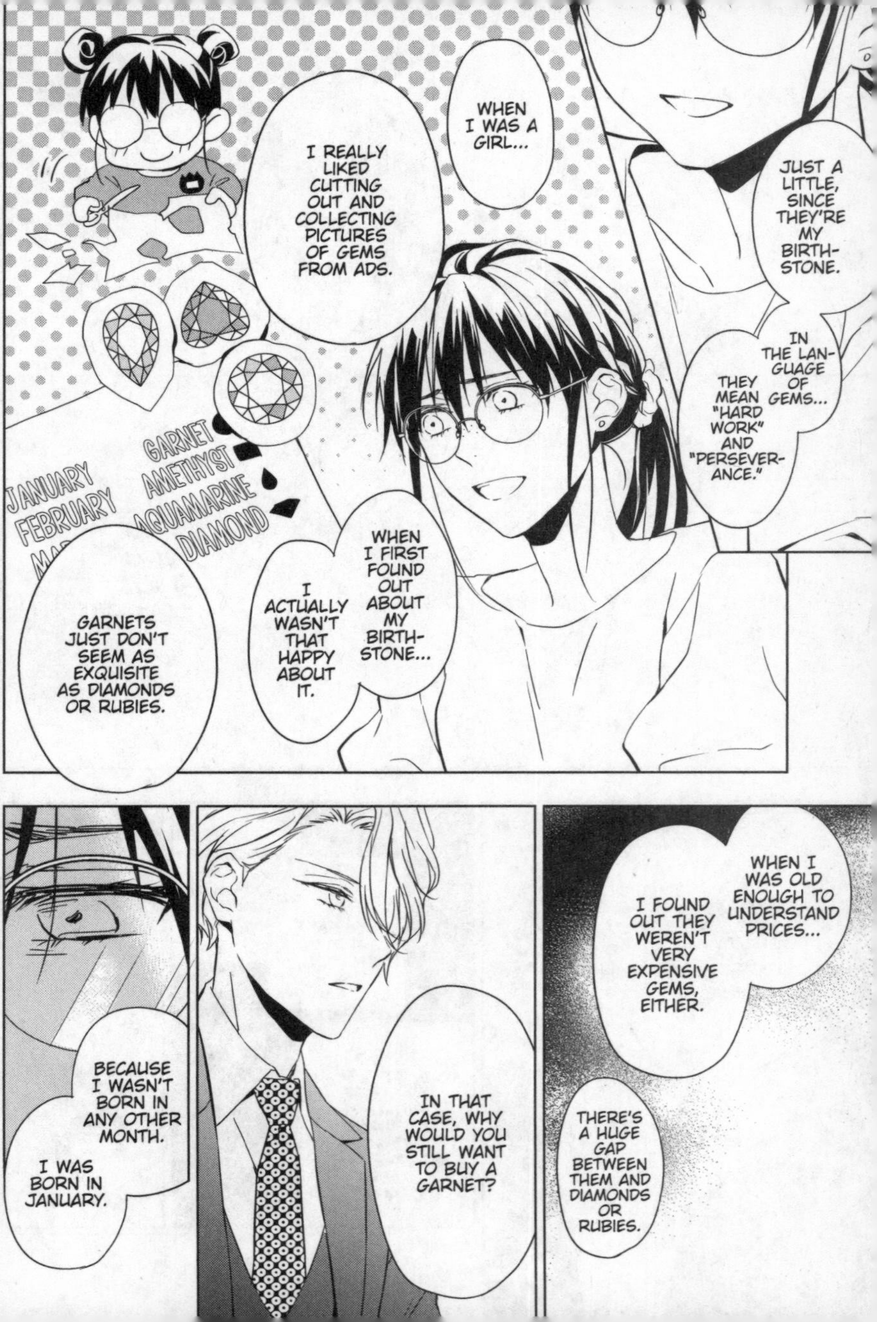
JUST A LITTLE, SINCE THEY'RE MY BIRTHSTONE.
IN THE LANGUAGE OF GEMS... THEY MEAN "HARD WORK" AND "PERSEVERANCE."
WHEN I WAS A GIRL...
I REALLY LIKED CUTTING OUT AND COLLECTING PICTURES OF GEMS FROM ADS.
JANUARY GARNET
FEBRUARY AMETHYST
AQUAMARINE
DIAMOND
WHEN I FIRST FOUND OUT ABOUT MY BIRTHSTONE...
I ACTUALLY WASN'T THAT HAPPY ABOUT IT.
GARNETS JUST DON'T SEEM AS EXQUISITE AS DIAMONDS OR RUBIES.
WHEN I WAS OLD ENOUGH TO UNDERSTAND PRICES...
I FOUND OUT THEY WEREN'T VERY EXPENSIVE GEMS, EITHER.
THERE'S A HUGE GAP BETWEEN THEM AND DIAMONDS OR RUBIES.
IN THAT CASE, WHY WOULD YOU STILL WANT TO BUY A GARNET?
BECAUSE I WASN'T BORN IN ANY OTHER MONTH.
I WAS BORN IN JANUARY.

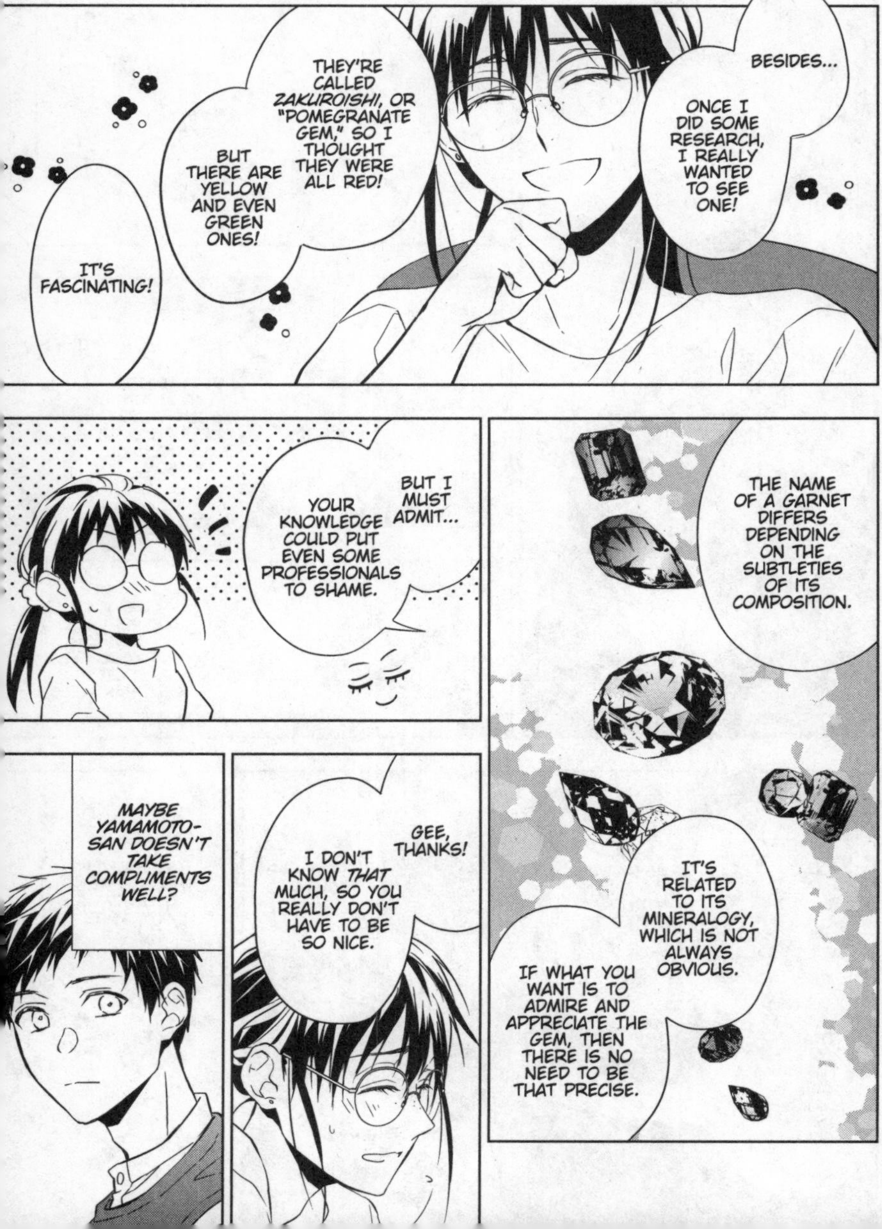
BESIDES...
ONCE I DID SOME RESEARCH, I REALLY WANTED TO SEE ONE!
THEY'RE CALLED *ZAKUROISHI*, OR "POMEGRANATE GEM," SO I THOUGHT THEY WERE ALL RED!
BUT THERE ARE YELLOW AND EVEN GREEN ONES!
IT'S FASCINATING!
THE NAME OF A GARNET DIFFERS DEPENDING ON THE SUBTLETIES OF ITS COMPOSITION.
IT'S RELATED TO ITS MINERALOGY, WHICH IS NOT ALWAYS OBVIOUS.
IF WHAT YOU WANT IS TO ADMIRE AND APPRECIATE THE GEM, THEN THERE IS NO NEED TO BE THAT PRECISE.
BUT I MUST ADMIT...
YOUR KNOWLEDGE COULD PUT EVEN SOME PROFESSIONALS TO SHAME.
GEE, THANKS!
I DON'T KNOW *THAT* MUCH, SO YOU REALLY DON'T HAVE TO BE SO NICE.
MAYBE YAMAMOTO-SAN DOESN'T TAKE COMPLIMENTS WELL?

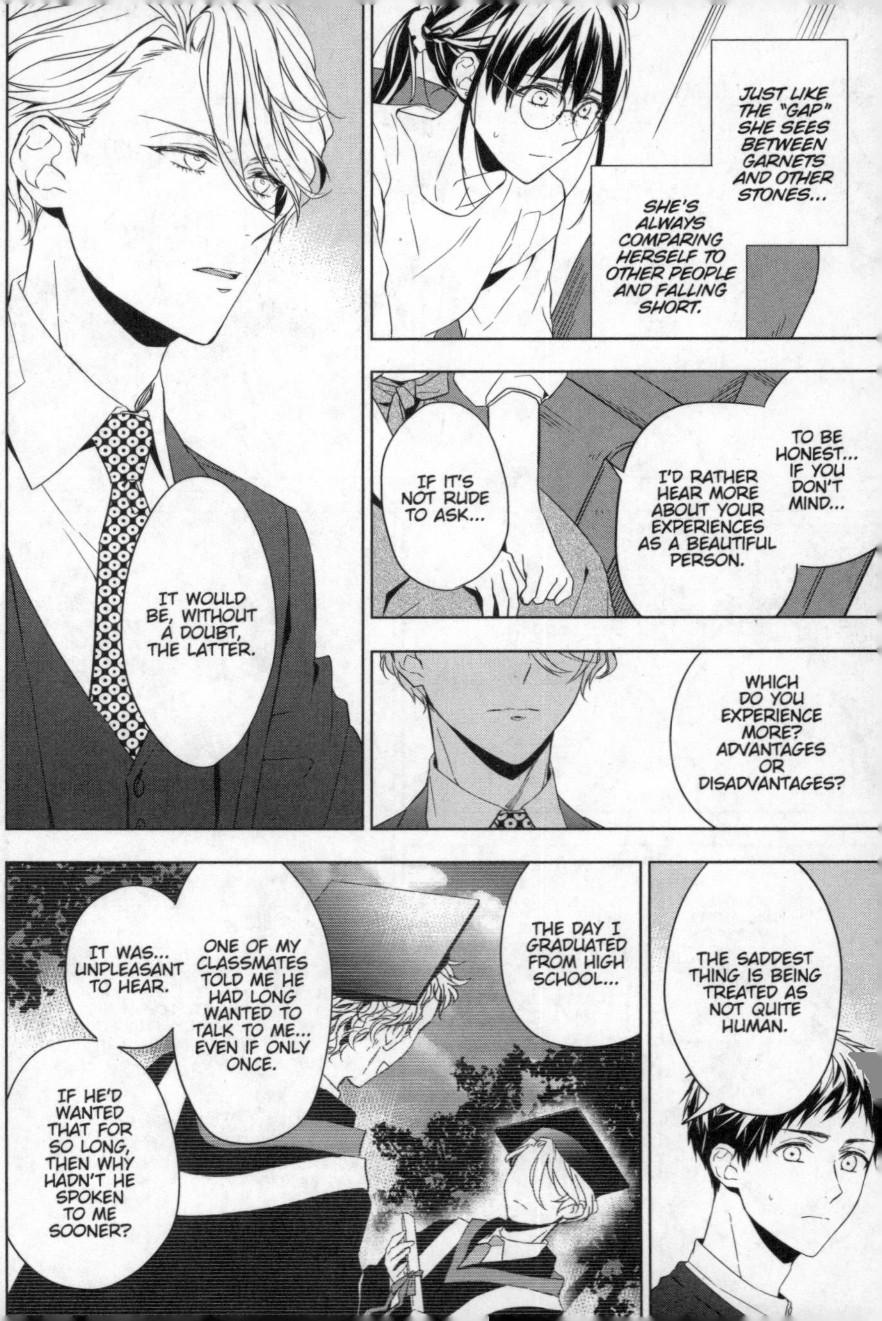
JUST LIKE THE "GAP" SHE SEES BETWEEN GARNETS AND OTHER STONES...
SHE'S ALWAYS COMPARING HERSELF TO OTHER PEOPLE AND FALLING SHORT.
TO BE HONEST... IF YOU DON'T MIND...
I'D RATHER HEAR MORE ABOUT YOUR EXPERIENCES AS A BEAUTIFUL PERSON.
IF IT'S NOT RUDE TO ASK...
WHICH DO YOU EXPERIENCE MORE? ADVANTAGES OR DISADVANTAGES?
IT WOULD BE, WITHOUT A DOUBT, THE LATTER.
THE SADDEST THING IS BEING TREATED AS NOT QUITE HUMAN.
THE DAY I GRADUATED FROM HIGH SCHOOL...
ONE OF MY CLASSMATES TOLD ME HE HAD LONG WANTED TO TALK TO ME... EVEN IF ONLY ONCE.
IT WAS... UNPLEASANT TO HEAR.
IF HE'D WANTED THAT FOR SO LONG, THEN WHY HADN'T HE SPOKEN TO ME SOONER?

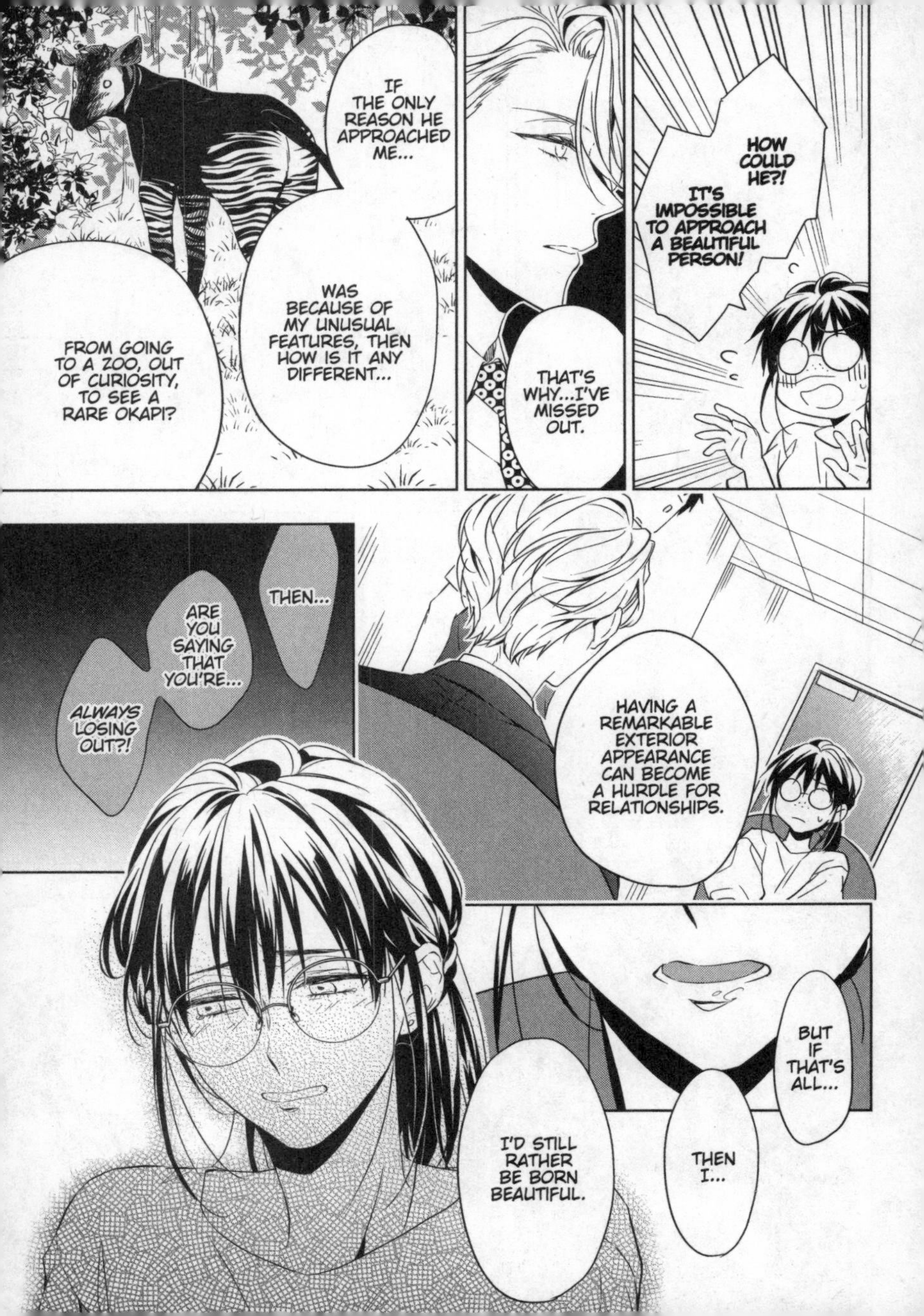
HOW COULD HE?!
IT'S IMPOSSIBLE TO APPROACH A BEAUTIFUL PERSON!
THAT'S WHY...I'VE MISSED OUT.
IF THE ONLY REASON HE APPROACHED ME...
WAS BECAUSE OF MY UNUSUAL FEATURES, THEN HOW IS IT ANY DIFFERENT...
FROM GOING TO A ZOO, OUT OF CURIOSITY, TO SEE A RARE OKAPI?
HAVING A REMARKABLE EXTERIOR APPEARANCE CAN BECOME A HURDLE FOR RELATIONSHIPS.
THEN...
ARE YOU SAYING THAT YOU'RE...
ALWAYS LOSING OUT?!
BUT IF THAT'S ALL...
THEN I...
I'D STILL RATHER BE BORN BEAUTIFUL.

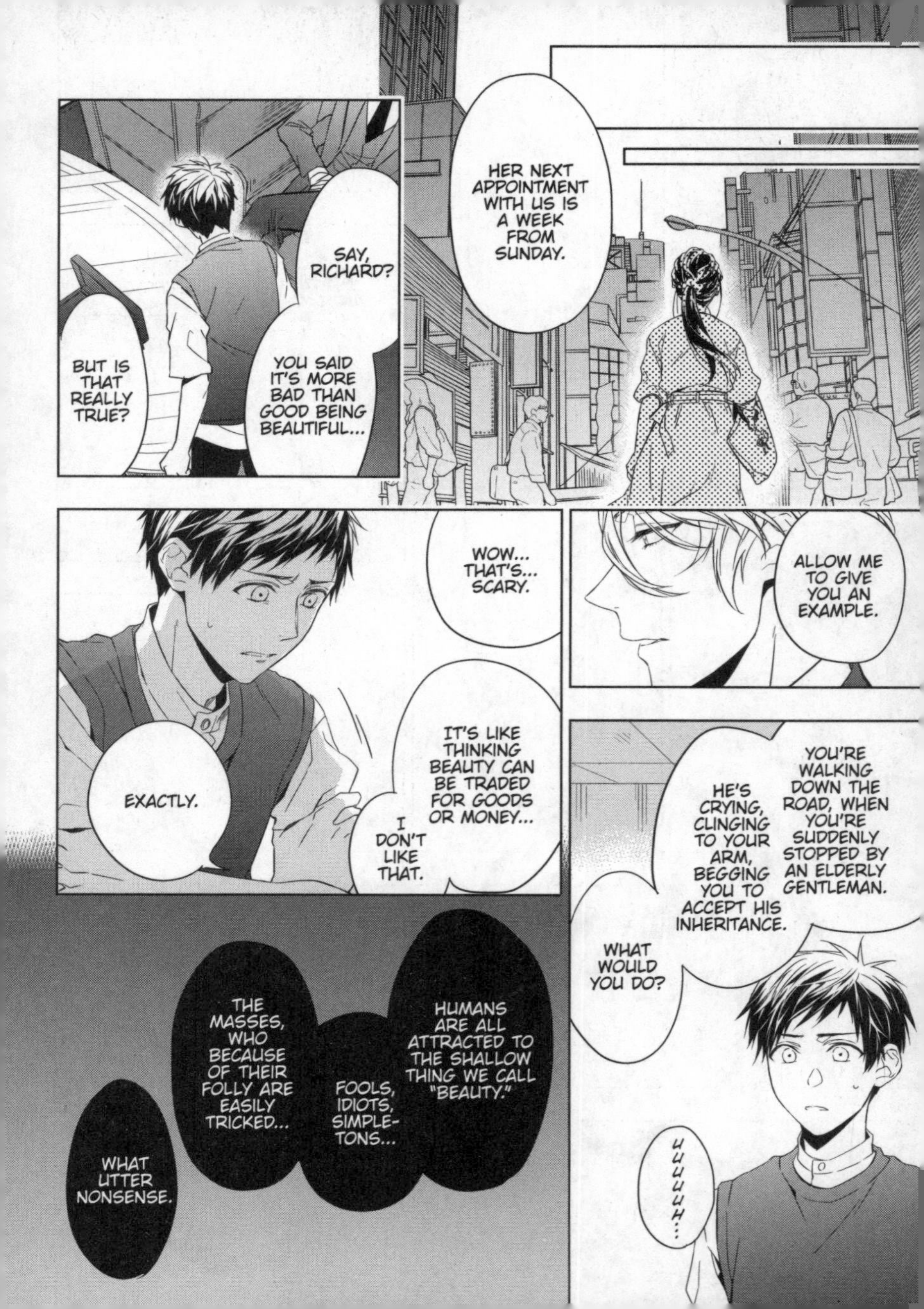
HER NEXT APPOINTMENT WITH US IS A WEEK FROM SUNDAY.
SAY, RICHARD?
YOU SAID IT'S MORE BAD THAN GOOD BEING BEAUTIFUL...
BUT IS THAT REALLY TRUE?
ALLOW ME TO GIVE YOU AN EXAMPLE.
YOU'RE WALKING DOWN THE ROAD, WHEN YOU'RE SUDDENLY STOPPED BY AN ELDERLY GENTLEMAN.
HE'S CRYING, CLINGING TO YOUR ARM, BEGGING YOU TO ACCEPT HIS INHERITANCE.
WHAT WOULD YOU DO?
UUUUUH...
WOW... THAT'S... SCARY.
IT'S LIKE THINKING BEAUTY CAN BE TRADED FOR GOODS OR MONEY...
I DON'T LIKE THAT.
EXACTLY.
HUMANS ARE ALL ATTRACTED TO THE SHALLOW THING WE CALL "BEAUTY."
FOOLS, IDIOTS, SIMPLETONS...
THE MASSES, WHO BECAUSE OF THEIR FOLLY ARE EASILY TRICKED...
WHAT UTTER NONSENSE.

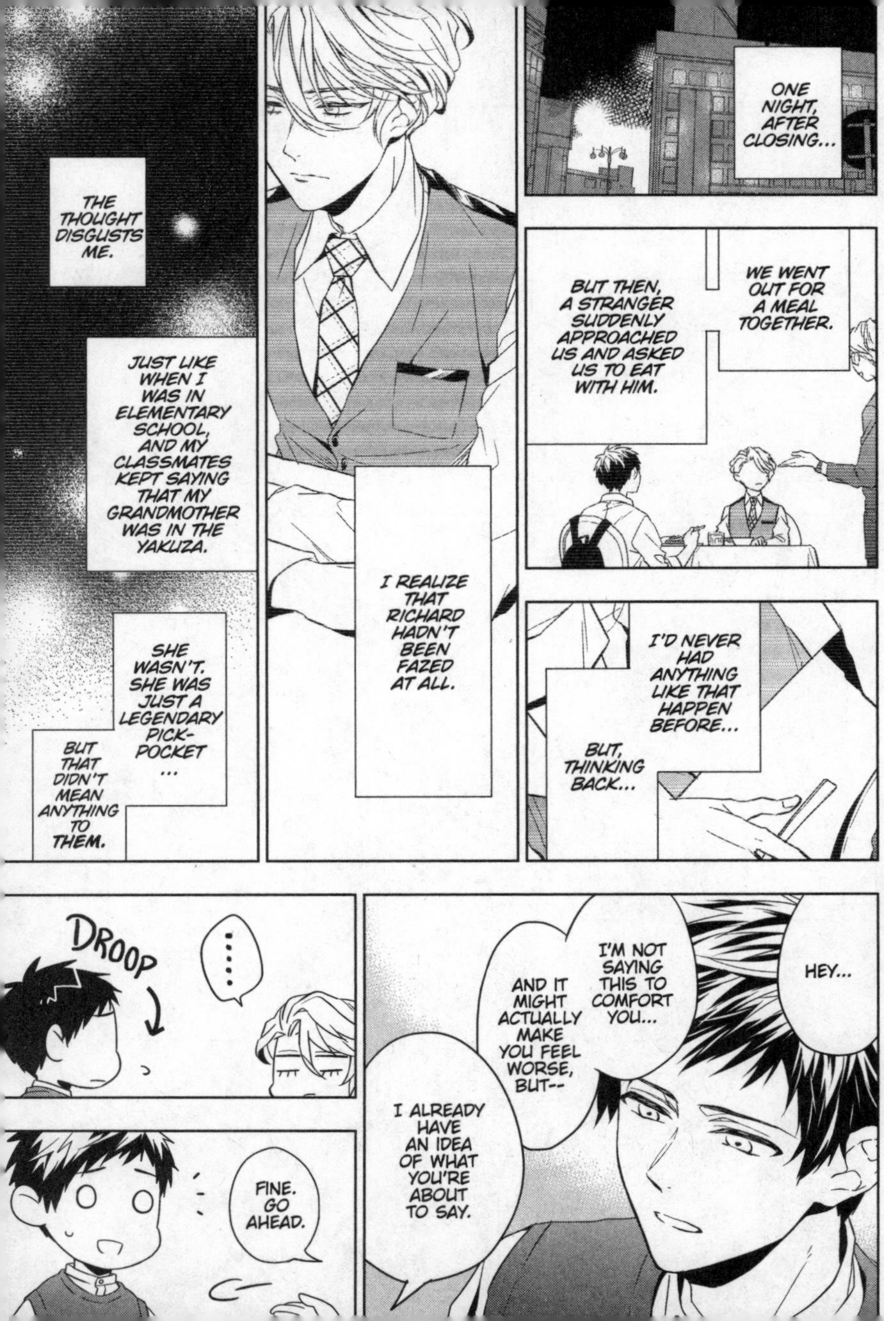
ONE NIGHT, AFTER CLOSING...
WE WENT OUT FOR A MEAL TOGETHER.
BUT THEN, A STRANGER SUDDENLY APPROACHED US AND ASKED US TO EAT WITH HIM.
I'D NEVER HAD ANYTHING LIKE THAT HAPPEN BEFORE...
BUT, THINKING BACK...
I REALIZE THAT RICHARD HADN'T BEEN FAZED AT ALL.
THE THOUGHT DISGUSTS ME.
JUST LIKE WHEN I WAS IN ELEMENTARY SCHOOL, AND MY CLASSMATES KEPT SAYING THAT MY GRANDMOTHER WAS IN THE YAKUZA.
SHE WASN'T. SHE WAS JUST A LEGENDARY PICK-POCKET...
BUT THAT DIDN'T MEAN ANYTHING TO THEM.
HEY...
I'M NOT SAYING THIS TO COMFORT YOU...
AND IT MIGHT ACTUALLY MAKE YOU FEEL WORSE, BUT--
I ALREADY HAVE AN IDEA OF WHAT YOU'RE ABOUT TO SAY.
DROOP
.....
FINE. GO AHEAD.

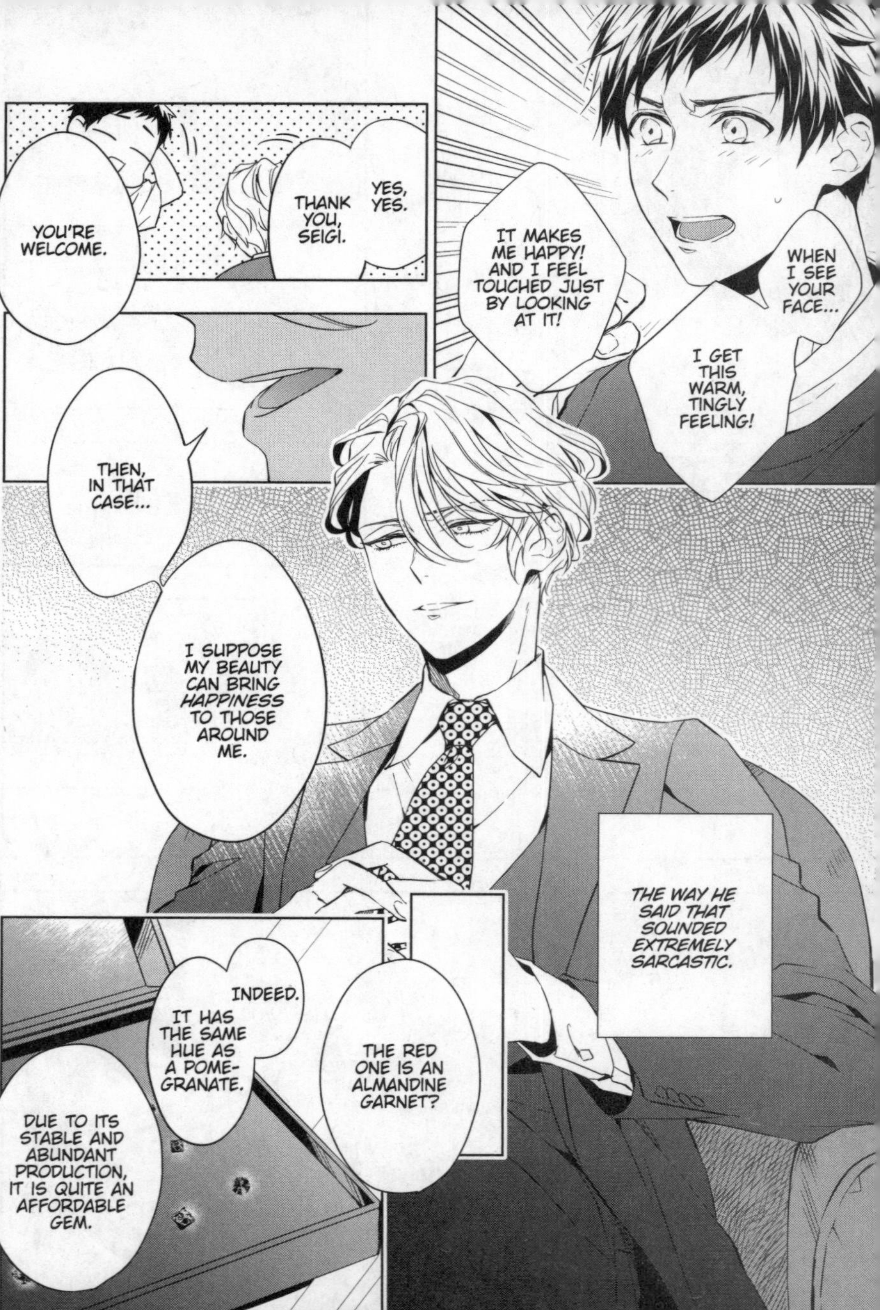
WHEN I SEE YOUR FACE...
I GET THIS WARM, TINGLY FEELING!
IT MAKES ME HAPPY! AND I FEEL TOUCHED JUST BY LOOKING AT IT!
YES, YES.
THANK YOU, SEIGI.
YOU'RE WELCOME.
THEN, IN THAT CASE...
I SUPPOSE MY BEAUTY CAN BRING *HAPPINESS* TO THOSE AROUND ME.
THE WAY HE SAID THAT SOUNDED EXTREMELY SARCASTIC.
THE RED ONE IS AN ALMANDINE GARNET?
INDEED.
IT HAS THE SAME HUE AS A POMEGRANATE.
DUE TO ITS STABLE AND ABUNDANT PRODUCTION, IT IS QUITE AN AFFORDABLE GEM.

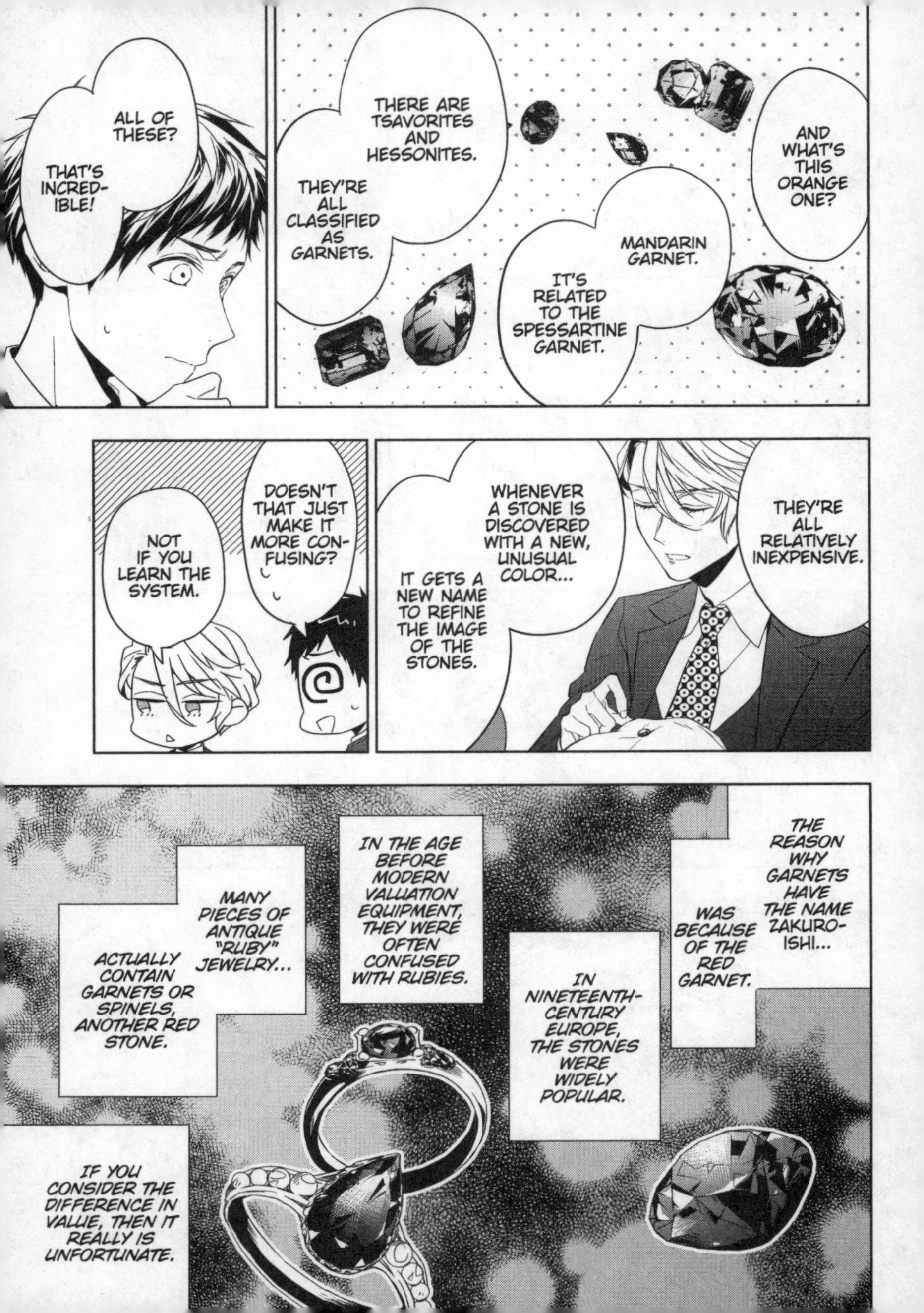
THERE ARE TSAVORITES AND HESSONITES.
THEY'RE ALL CLASSIFIED AS GARNETS.
AND WHAT'S THIS ORANGE ONE?
MANDARIN GARNET.
IT'S RELATED TO THE SPESSARTINE GARNET.
ALL OF THESE?
THAT'S INCREDIBLE!
THEY'RE ALL RELATIVELY INEXPENSIVE.
WHENEVER A STONE IS DISCOVERED WITH A NEW, UNUSUAL COLOR...
IT GETS A NEW NAME TO REFINE THE IMAGE OF THE STONES.
DOESN'T THAT JUST MAKE IT MORE CON-FUSING?
NOT IF YOU LEARN THE SYSTEM.
THE REASON WHY GARNETS HAVE THE NAME ZAKURO-ISHI...
WAS BECAUSE OF THE RED GARNET.
IN NINETEENTH-CENTURY EUROPE, THE STONES WERE WIDELY POPULAR.
IN THE AGE BEFORE MODERN VALUATION EQUIPMENT, THEY WERE OFTEN CONFUSED WITH RUBIES.
MANY PIECES OF ANTIQUE "RUBY" JEWELRY...
ACTUALLY CONTAIN GARNETS OR SPINELS, ANOTHER RED STONE.
IF YOU CONSIDER THE DIFFERENCE IN VALUE, THEN IT REALLY IS UNFORTUNATE.

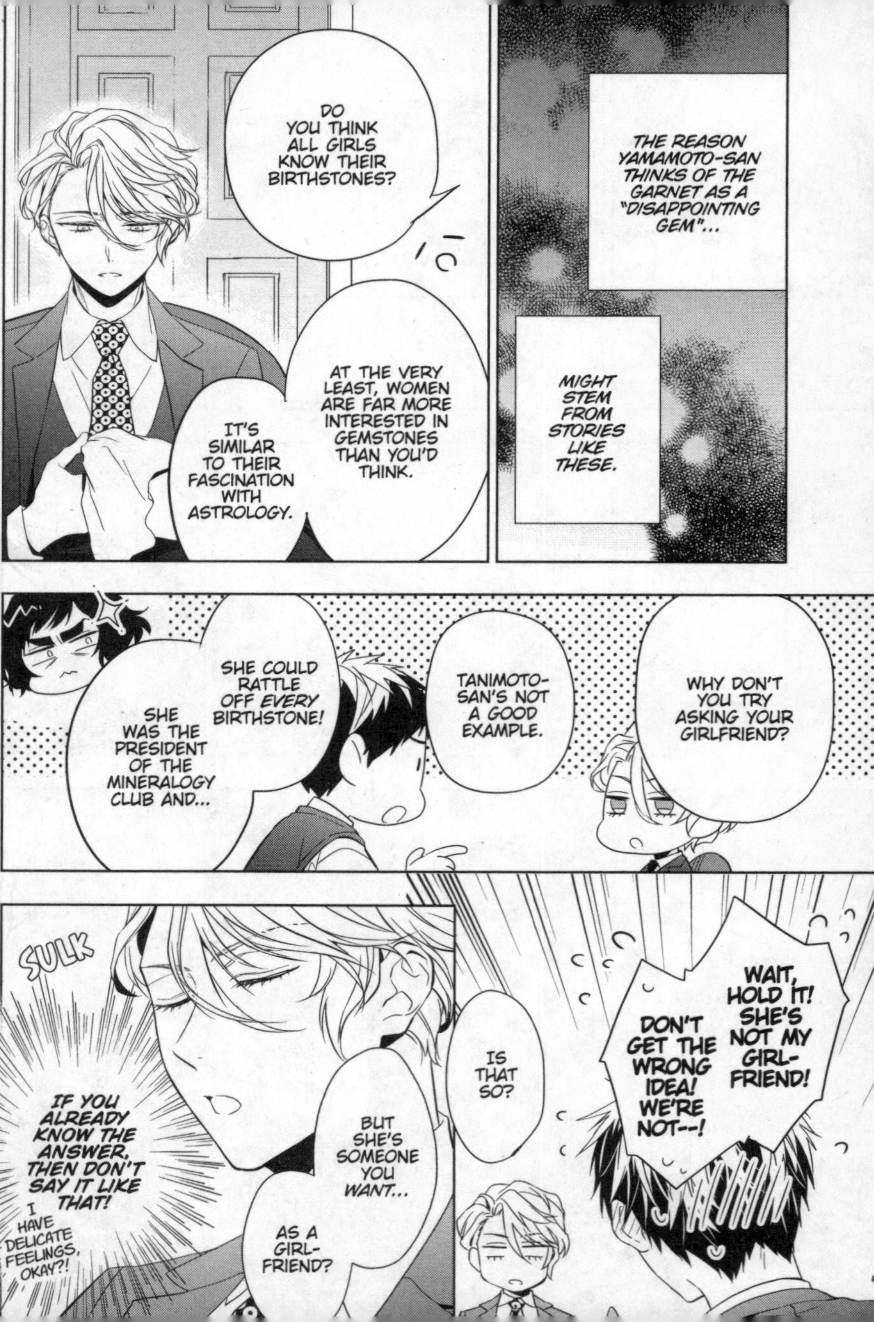
THE REASON YAMAMOTO-SAN THINKS OF THE GARNET AS A "DISAPPOINTING GEM"...
MIGHT STEM FROM STORIES LIKE THESE.
DO YOU THINK ALL GIRLS KNOW THEIR BIRTHSTONES?
AT THE VERY LEAST, WOMEN ARE FAR MORE INTERESTED IN GEMSTONES THAN YOU'D THINK.
IT'S SIMILAR TO THEIR FASCINATION WITH ASTROLOGY.
WHY DON'T YOU TRY ASKING YOUR GIRLFRIEND?
TANIMOTO-SAN'S NOT A GOOD EXAMPLE.
SHE WAS THE PRESIDENT OF THE MINERALOGY CLUB AND...
SHE COULD RATTLE OFF *EVERY* BIRTHSTONE!
WAIT, HOLD IT! SHE'S NOT MY GIRL-FRIEND!
DON'T GET THE WRONG IDEA! WE'RE NOT--!
IS THAT SO?
BUT SHE'S SOMEONE YOU WANT...
AS A GIRL-FRIEND?
SULK
IF YOU ALREADY KNOW THE ANSWER, THEN DON'T SAY IT LIKE THAT!
I HAVE DELICATE FEELINGS, OKAY?!

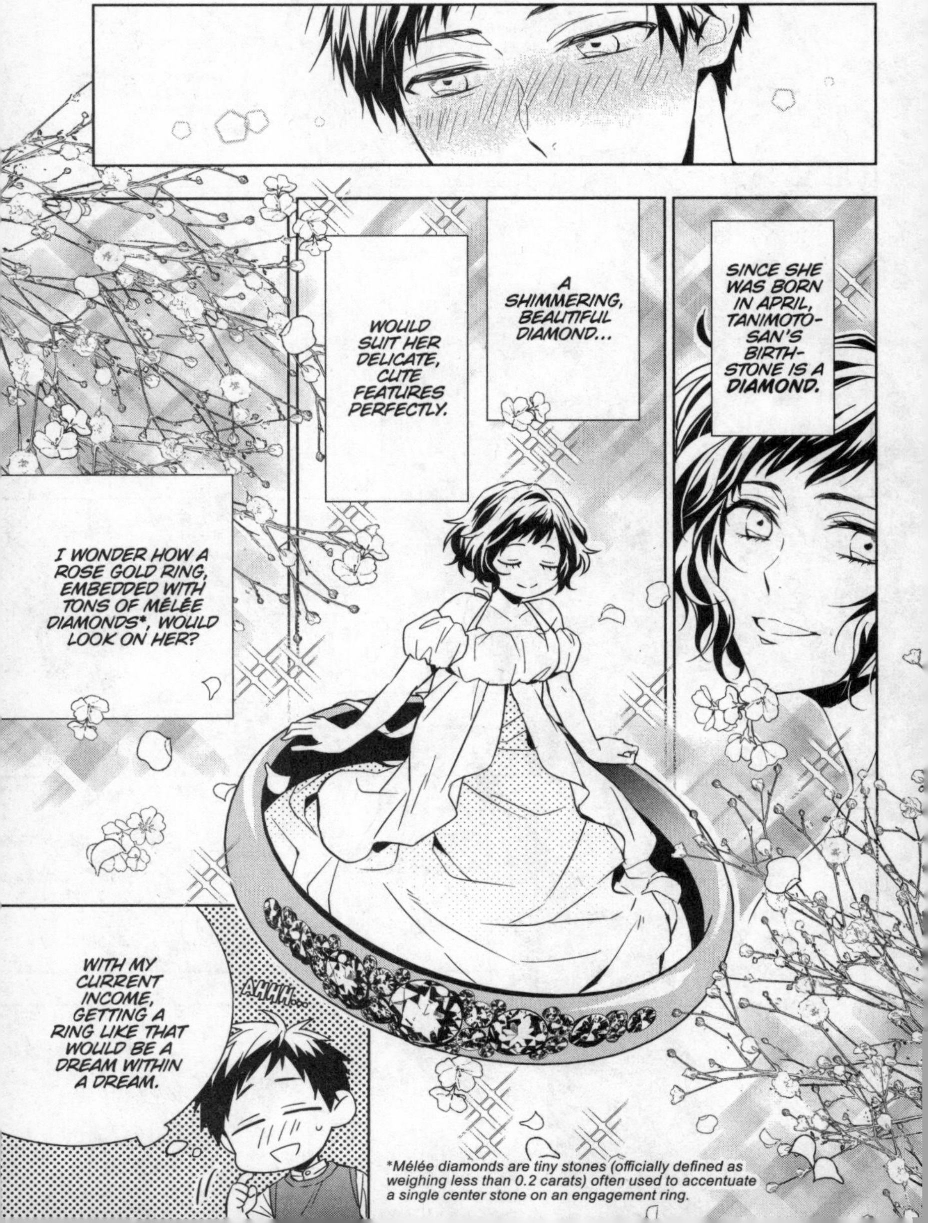
SINCE SHE WAS BORN IN APRIL, TANIMOTO-SAN'S BIRTH-STONE IS A DIAMOND.
A SHIMMERING, BEAUTIFUL DIAMOND...
WOULD SUIT HER DELICATE, CUTE FEATURES PERFECTLY.
I WONDER HOW A ROSE GOLD RING, EMBEDDED WITH TONS OF MÉLÉE DIAMONDS*, WOULD LOOK ON HER?
AHHH...
WITH MY CURRENT INCOME, GETTING A RING LIKE THAT WOULD BE A DREAM WITHIN A DREAM.

*Mélée diamonds are tiny stones (officially defined as weighing less than 0.2 carats) often used to accentuate a single center stone on an engagement ring.

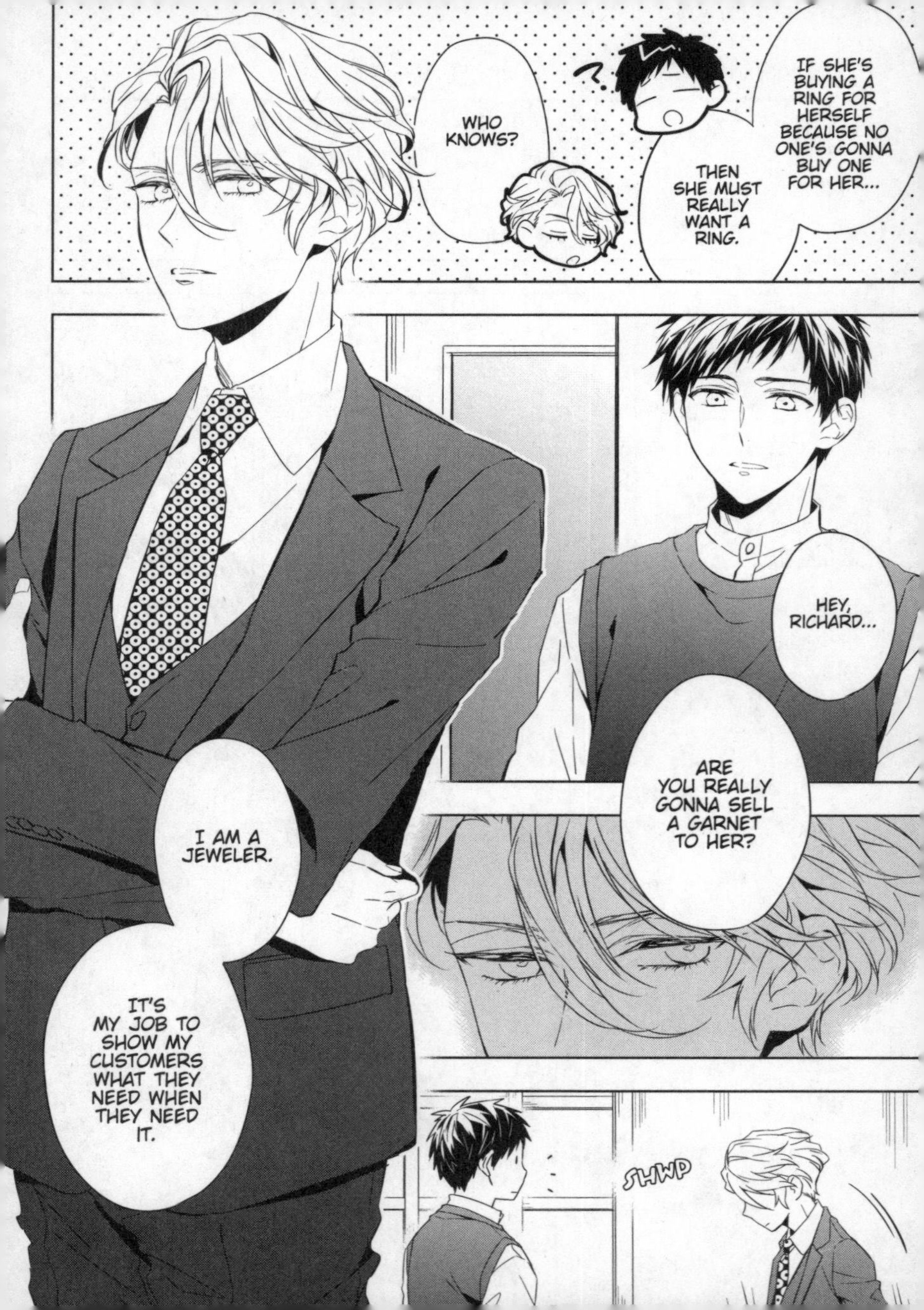
IF SHE'S BUYING A RING FOR HERSELF BECAUSE NO ONE'S GONNA BUY ONE FOR HER...
THEN SHE MUST REALLY WANT A RING.
?
WHO KNOWS?
HEY, RICHARD...
ARE YOU REALLY GONNA SELL A GARNET TO HER?
SHWP
I AM A JEWELER.
IT'S MY JOB TO SHOW MY CUSTOMERS WHAT THEY NEED WHEN THEY NEED IT.

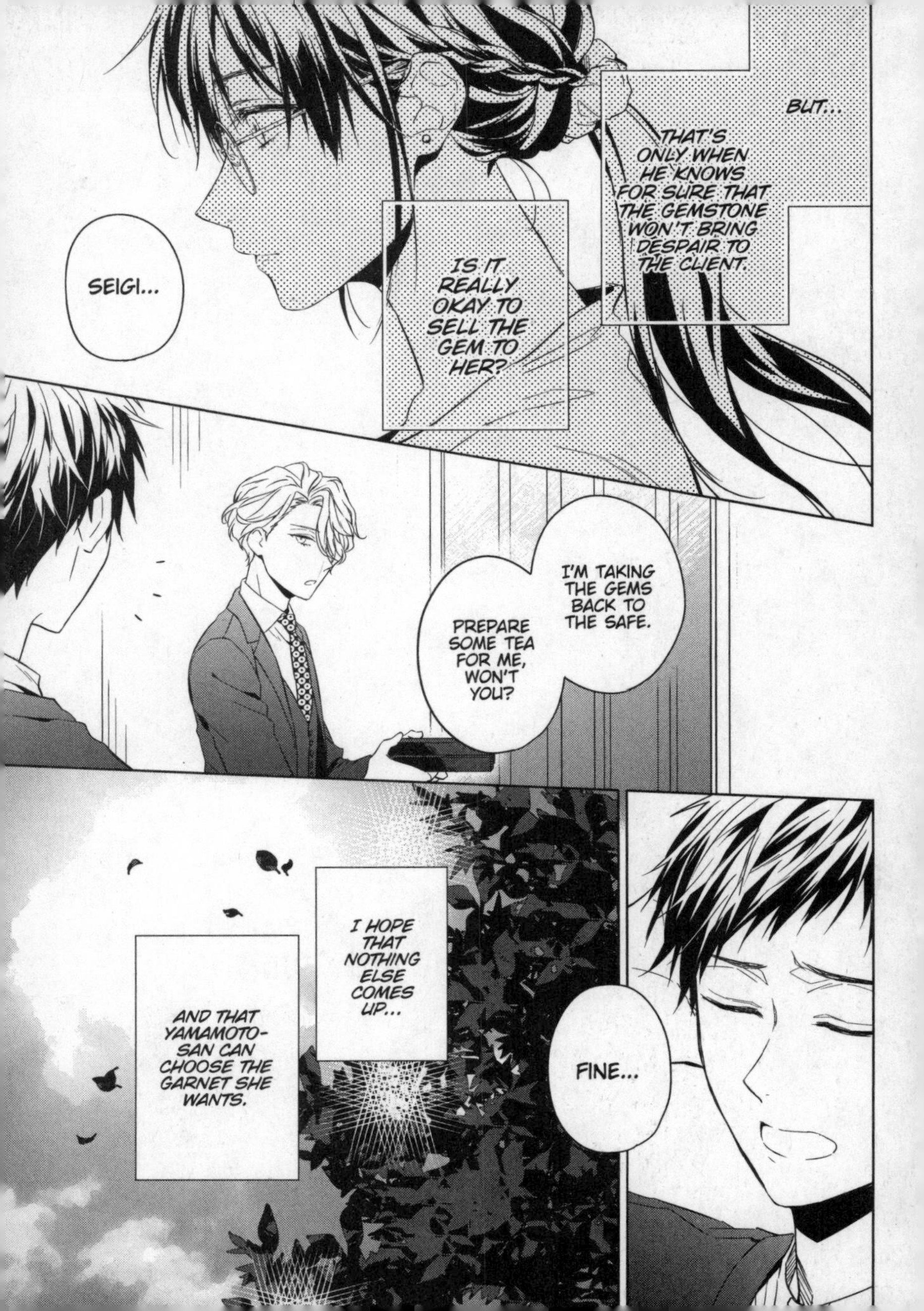
BUT...
THAT'S ONLY WHEN HE KNOWS FOR SURE THAT THE GEMSTONE WON'T BRING DESPAIR TO THE CLIENT.
IS IT REALLY OKAY TO SELL THE GEM TO HER?
SEIGI...
I'M TAKING THE GEMS BACK TO THE SAFE.
PREPARE SOME TEA FOR ME, WON'T YOU?
FINE...
I HOPE THAT NOTHING ELSE COMES UP...
AND THAT YAMAMOTO-SAN CAN CHOOSE THE GARNET SHE WANTS.

THE CASE FILES OF JEWELER RICHARD

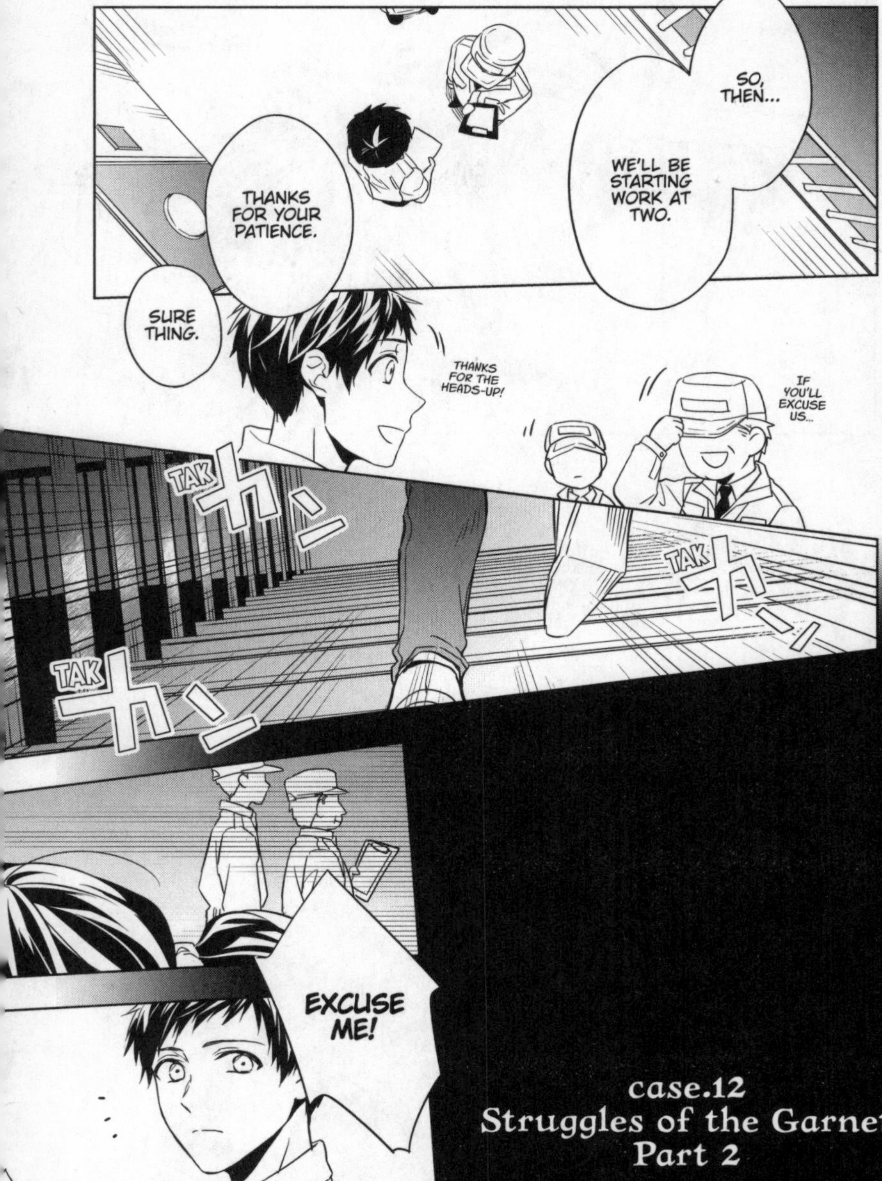
SO, THEN...
WE'LL BE STARTING WORK AT TWO.
THANKS FOR YOUR PATIENCE.
SURE THING.
IF YOU'LL EXCUSE US...
THANKS FOR THE HEADS-UP!
TAK
TAK
TAK
EXCUSE ME!
case.12
Struggles of the Garnet
Part 2

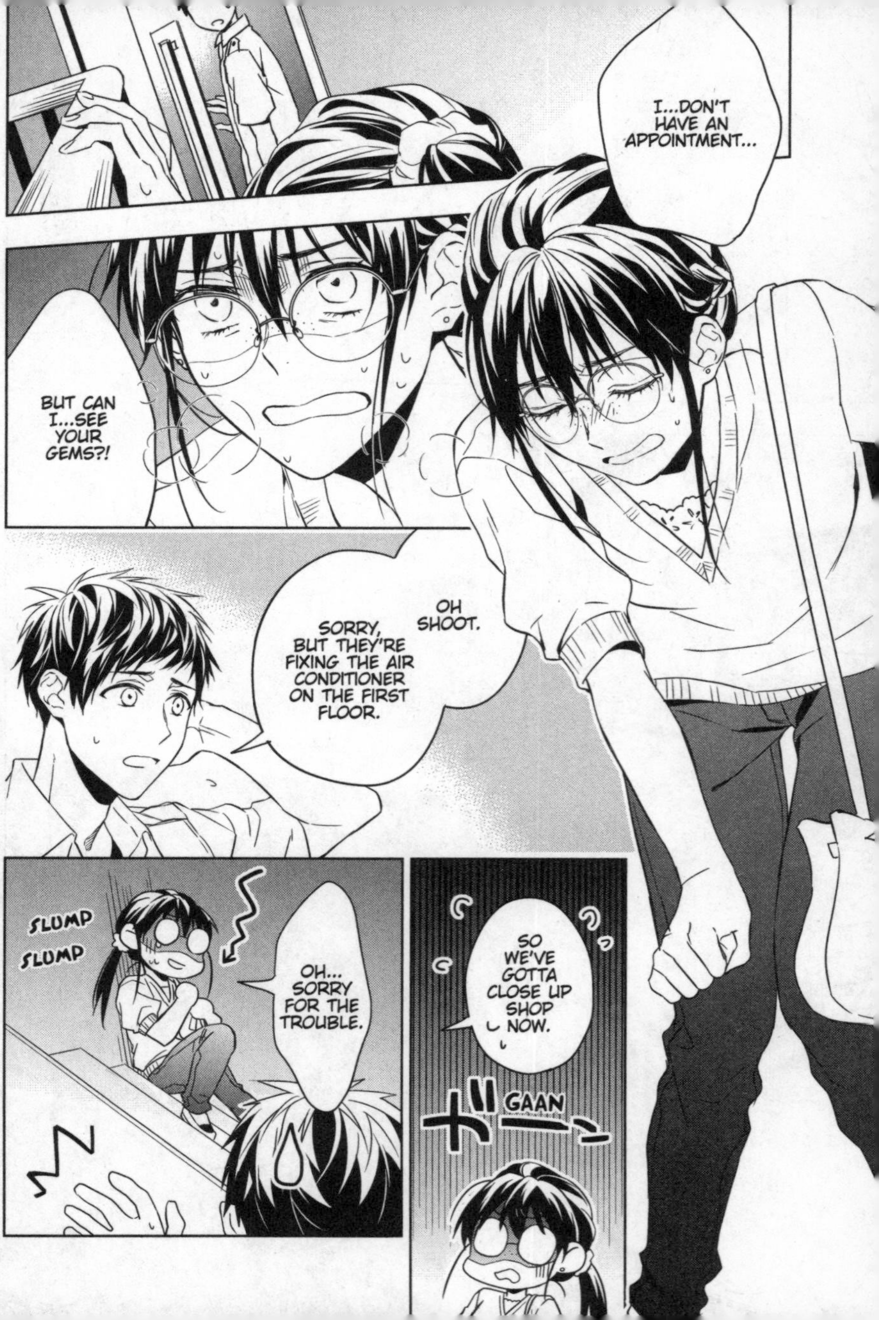
I...DON'T HAVE AN APPOINTMENT...
BUT CAN I...SEE YOUR GEMS?!
OH SHOOT.
SORRY, BUT THEY'RE FIXING THE AIR CONDITIONER ON THE FIRST FLOOR.
SO WE'VE GOTTA CLOSE UP SHOP NOW.
GAAN
OH... SORRY FOR THE TROUBLE.
SLUMP
SLUMP

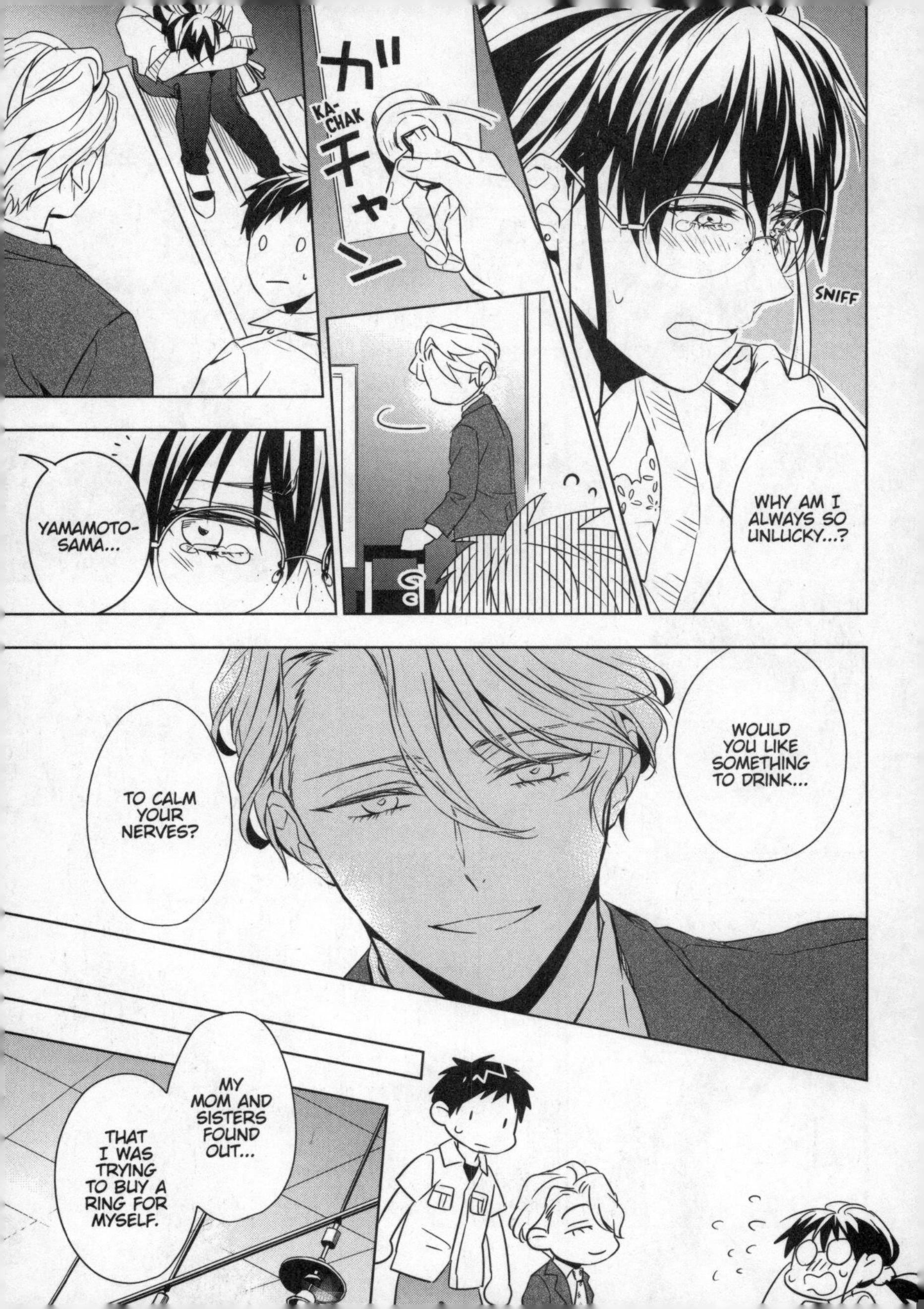
SNIFF
WHY AM I ALWAYS SO UNLUCKY...?
ガチャン
KA-CHAK
YAMAMOTO-SAMA...
WOULD YOU LIKE SOMETHING TO DRINK...
TO CALM YOUR NERVES?
MY MOM AND SISTERS FOUND OUT...
THAT I WAS TRYING TO BUY A RING FOR MYSELF.

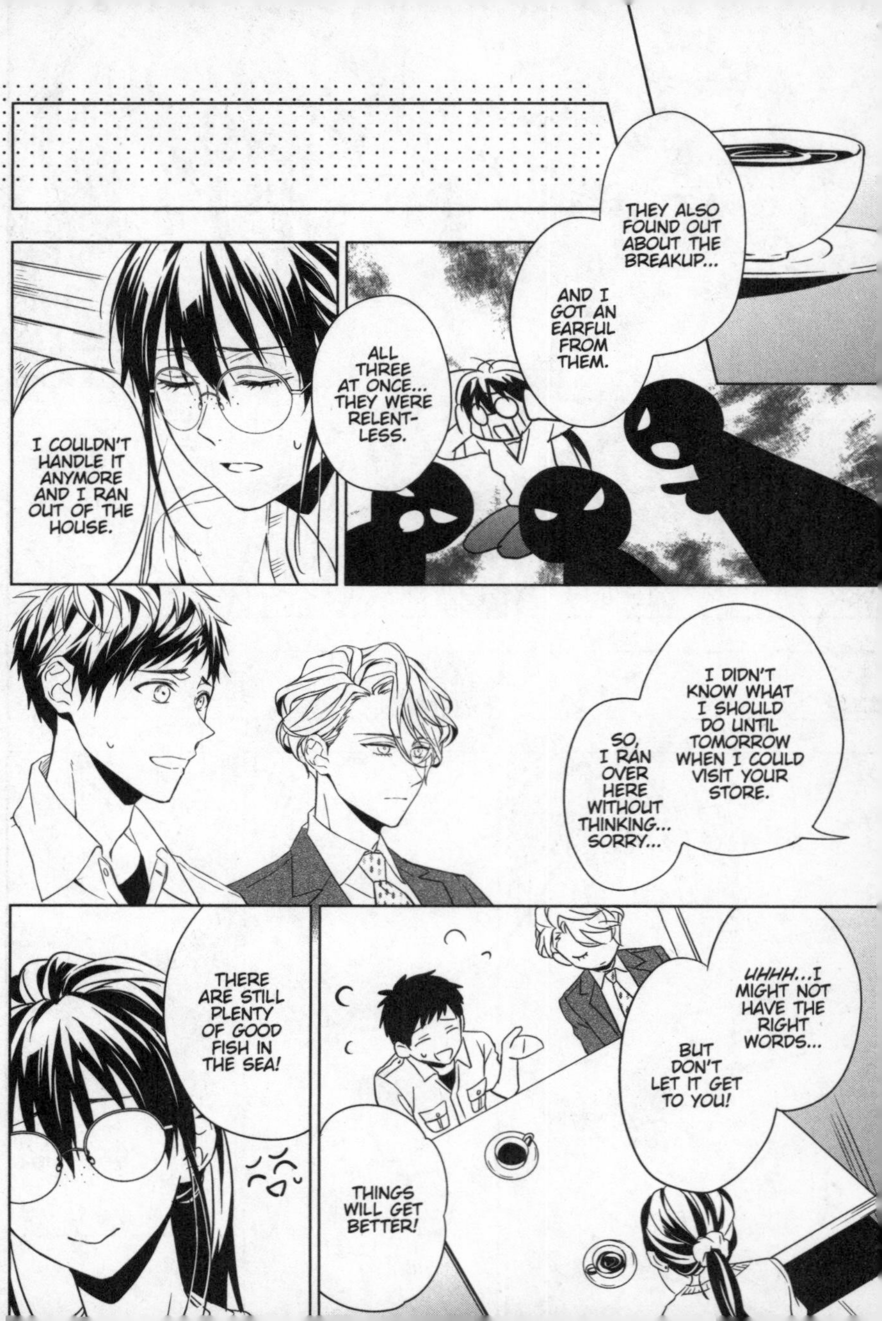

THEY ALSO FOUND OUT ABOUT THE BREAKUP...
AND I GOT AN EARFUL FROM THEM.
ALL THREE AT ONCE... THEY WERE RELENTLESS.
I COULDN'T HANDLE IT ANYMORE AND I RAN OUT OF THE HOUSE.
I DIDN'T KNOW WHAT I SHOULD DO UNTIL TOMORROW WHEN I COULD VISIT YOUR STORE.
SO, I RAN OVER HERE WITHOUT THINKING... SORRY...
UHHH...I MIGHT NOT HAVE THE RIGHT WORDS...
BUT DON'T LET IT GET TO YOU!
THINGS WILL GET BETTER!
THERE ARE STILL PLENTY OF GOOD FISH IN THE SEA!

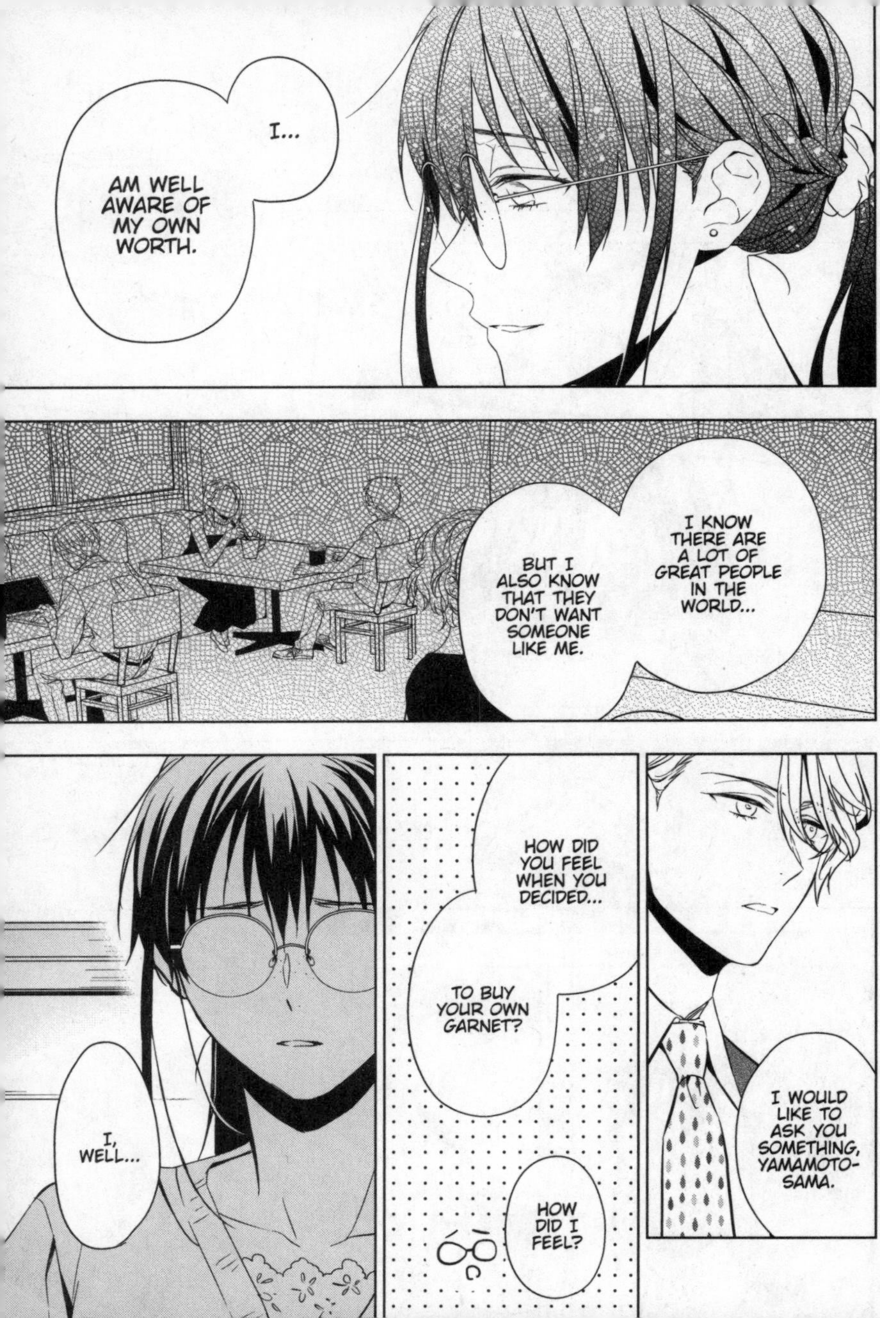
I...
AM WELL AWARE OF MY OWN WORTH.
I KNOW THERE ARE A LOT OF GREAT PEOPLE IN THE WORLD...
BUT I ALSO KNOW THAT THEY DON'T WANT SOMEONE LIKE ME.
I WOULD LIKE TO ASK YOU SOMETHING, YAMAMOTO-SAMA.
HOW DID YOU FEEL WHEN YOU DECIDED...
TO BUY YOUR OWN GARNET?
HOW DID I FEEL?
I, WELL...

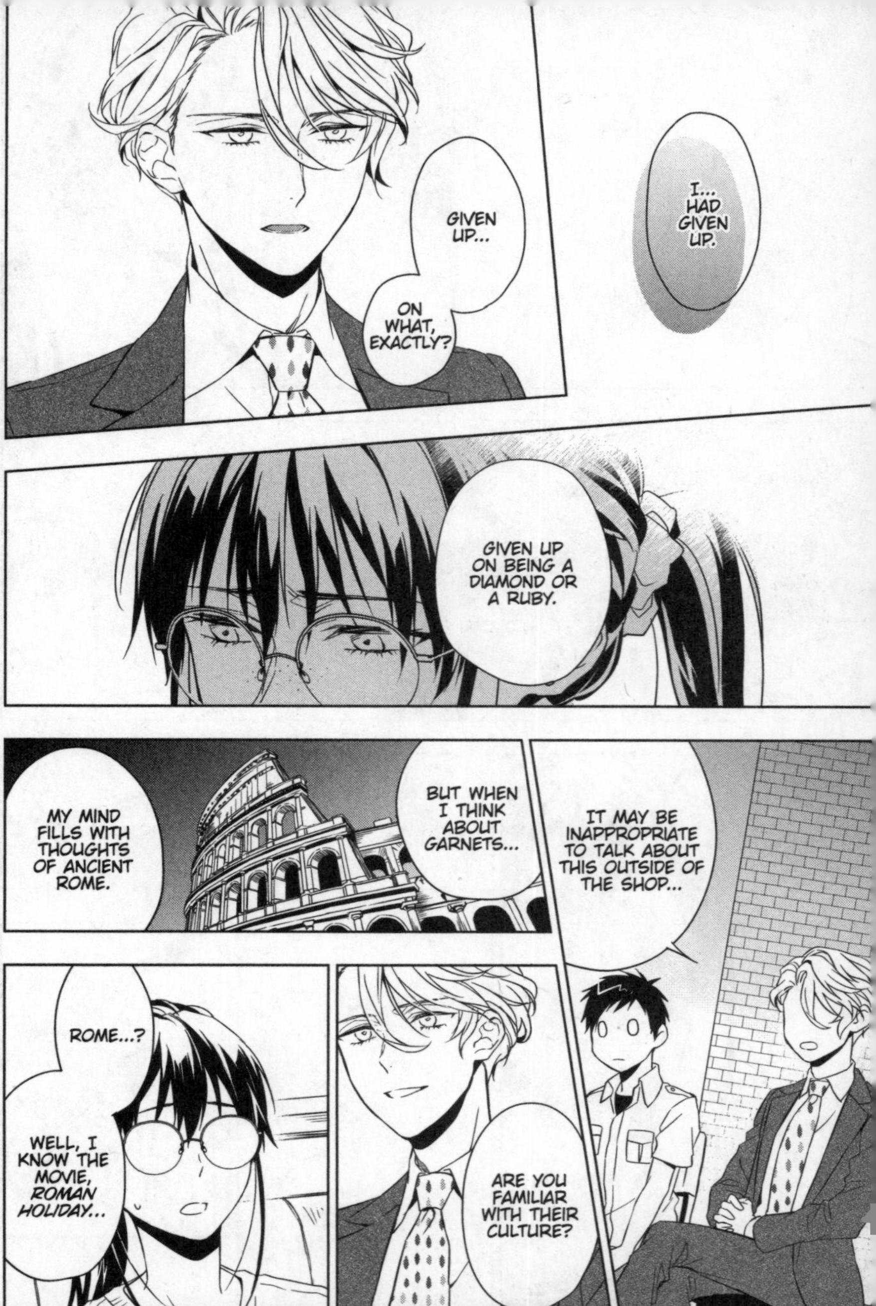
I... HAD GIVEN UP.
GIVEN UP...
ON WHAT, EXACTLY?
GIVEN UP ON BEING A DIAMOND OR A RUBY.
IT MAY BE INAPPROPRIATE TO TALK ABOUT THIS OUTSIDE OF THE SHOP...
BUT WHEN I THINK ABOUT GARNETS...
MY MIND FILLS WITH THOUGHTS OF ANCIENT ROME.
ARE YOU FAMILIAR WITH THEIR CULTURE?
ROME...?
WELL, I KNOW THE MOVIE, *ROMAN HOLIDAY*...

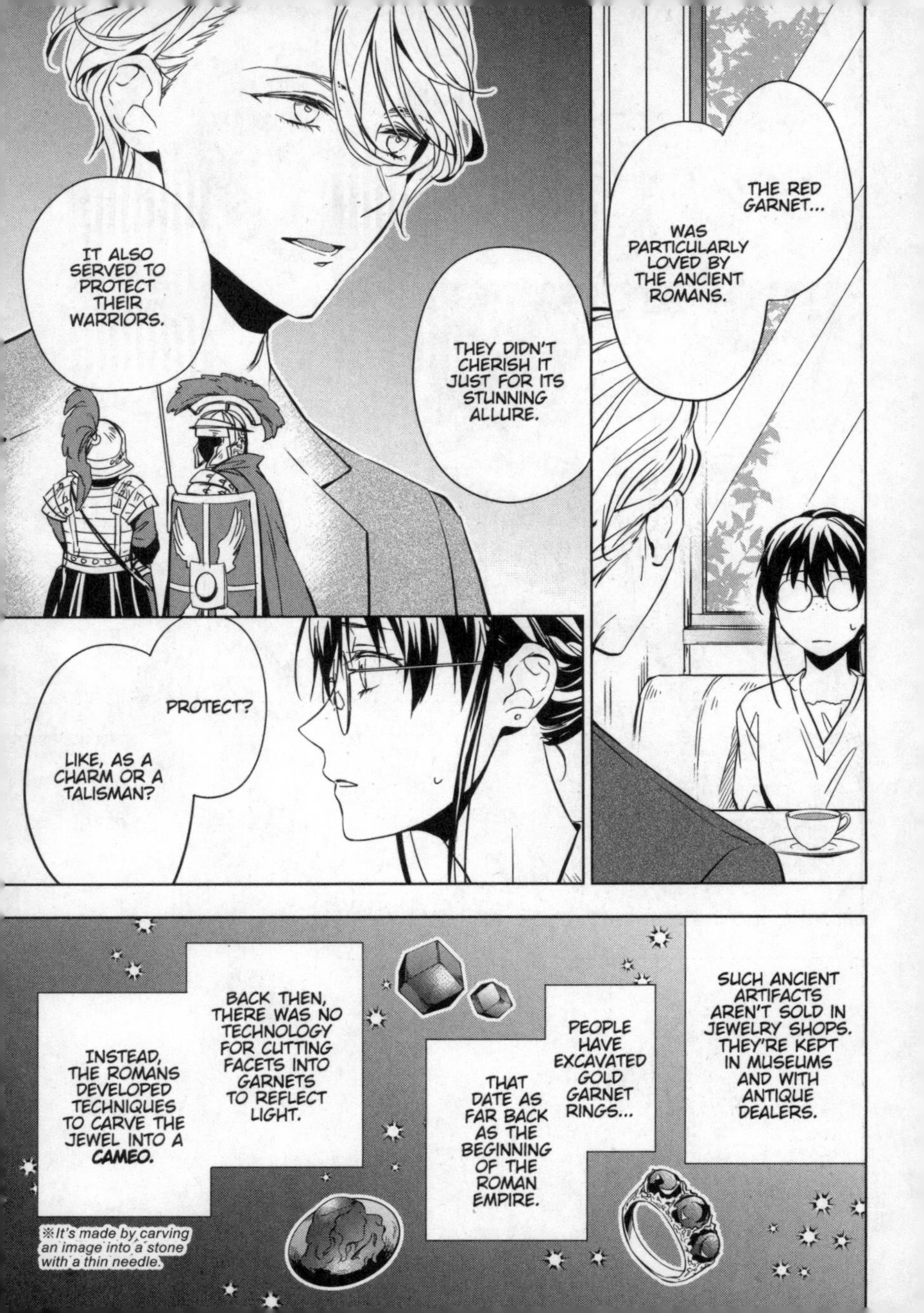
THE RED GARNET...
WAS PARTICULARLY LOVED BY THE ANCIENT ROMANS.
THEY DIDN'T CHERISH IT JUST FOR ITS STUNNING ALLURE.
IT ALSO SERVED TO PROTECT THEIR WARRIORS.
PROTECT?
LIKE, AS A CHARM OR A TALISMAN?
SUCH ANCIENT ARTIFACTS AREN'T SOLD IN JEWELRY SHOPS. THEY'RE KEPT IN MUSEUMS AND WITH ANTIQUE DEALERS.
PEOPLE HAVE EXCAVATED GOLD GARNET RINGS...
THAT DATE AS FAR BACK AS THE BEGINNING OF THE ROMAN EMPIRE.
BACK THEN, THERE WAS NO TECHNOLOGY FOR CUTTING FACETS INTO GARNETS TO REFLECT LIGHT.
INSTEAD, THE ROMANS DEVELOPED TECHNIQUES TO CARVE THE JEWEL INTO A **CAMEO.**
※It's made by carving an image into a stone with a thin needle.

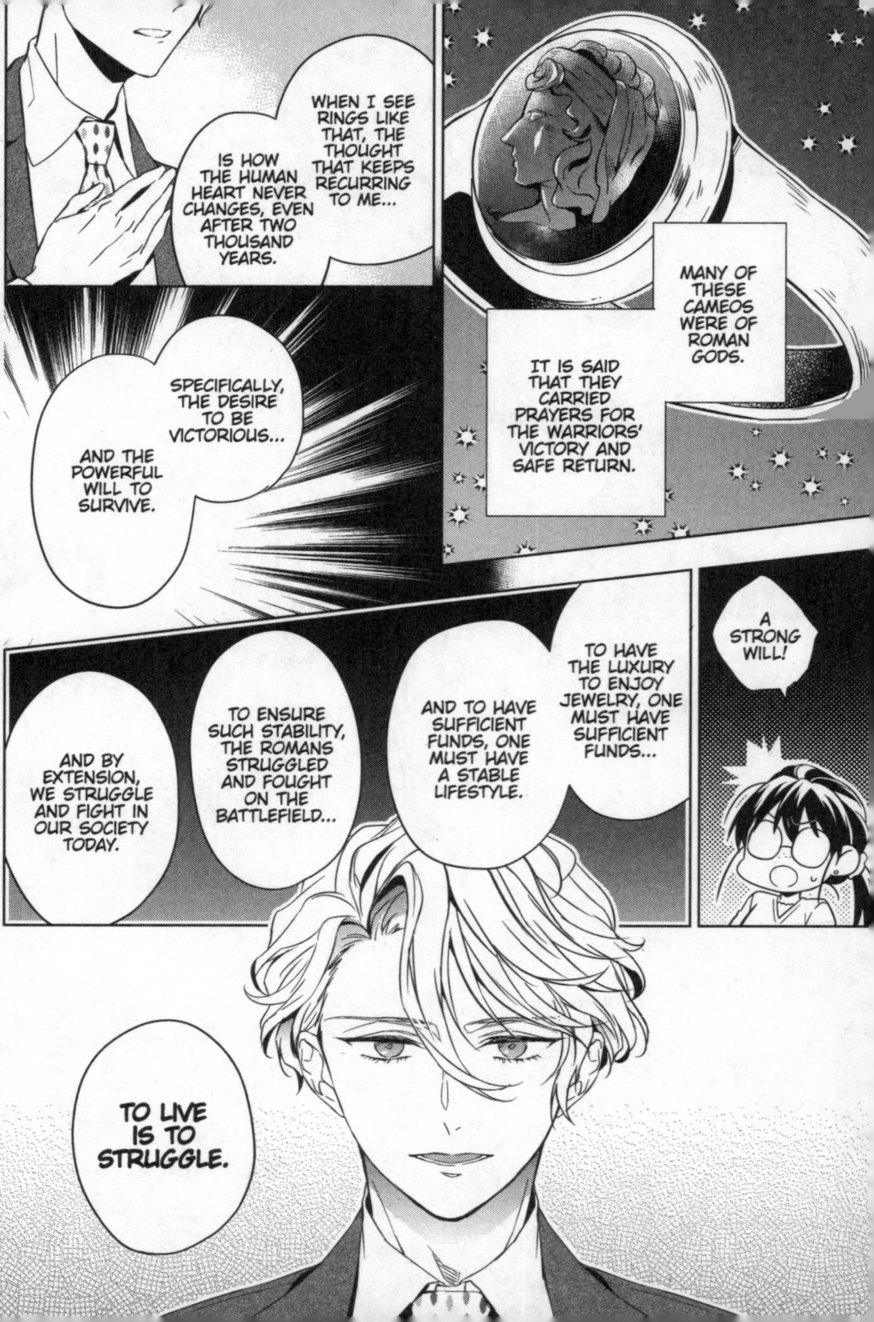
MANY OF THESE CAMEOS WERE OF ROMAN GODS.
IT IS SAID THAT THEY CARRIED PRAYERS FOR THE WARRIORS' VICTORY AND SAFE RETURN.
WHEN I SEE RINGS LIKE THAT, THE THOUGHT THAT KEEPS RECURRING TO ME...
IS HOW THE HUMAN HEART NEVER CHANGES, EVEN AFTER TWO THOUSAND YEARS.
SPECIFICALLY, THE DESIRE TO BE VICTORIOUS...
AND THE POWERFUL WILL TO SURVIVE.
A STRONG WILL!
TO HAVE THE LUXURY TO ENJOY JEWELRY, ONE MUST HAVE SUFFICIENT FUNDS...
AND TO HAVE SUFFICIENT FUNDS, ONE MUST HAVE A STABLE LIFESTYLE.
TO ENSURE SUCH STABILITY, THE ROMANS STRUGGLED AND FOUGHT ON THE BATTLEFIELD...
AND BY EXTENSION, WE STRUGGLE AND FIGHT IN OUR SOCIETY TODAY.
TO LIVE IS TO STRUGGLE.

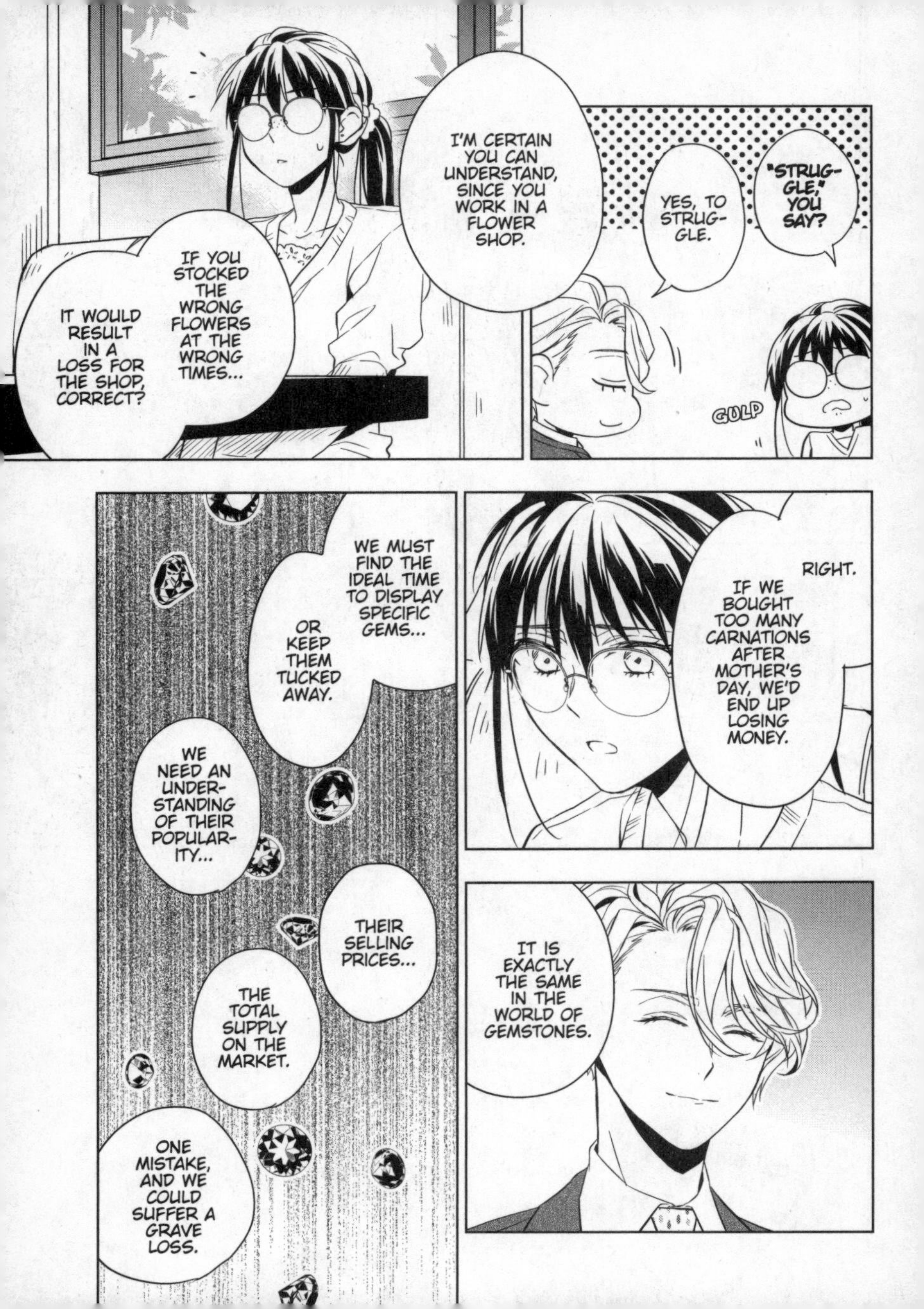
"STRUG-GLE," YOU SAY?
YES, TO STRUG-GLE.
GULP
I'M CERTAIN YOU CAN UNDERSTAND, SINCE YOU WORK IN A FLOWER SHOP.
IF YOU STOCKED THE WRONG FLOWERS AT THE WRONG TIMES...
IT WOULD RESULT IN A LOSS FOR THE SHOP, CORRECT?
RIGHT.
IF WE BOUGHT TOO MANY CARNATIONS AFTER MOTHER'S DAY, WE'D END UP LOSING MONEY.
IT IS EXACTLY THE SAME IN THE WORLD OF GEMSTONES.
WE MUST FIND THE IDEAL TIME TO DISPLAY SPECIFIC GEMS...
OR KEEP THEM TUCKED AWAY.
WE NEED AN UNDER-STANDING OF THEIR POPULAR-ITY...
THEIR SELLING PRICES...
THE TOTAL SUPPLY ON THE MARKET.
ONE MISTAKE, AND WE COULD SUFFER A GRAVE LOSS.

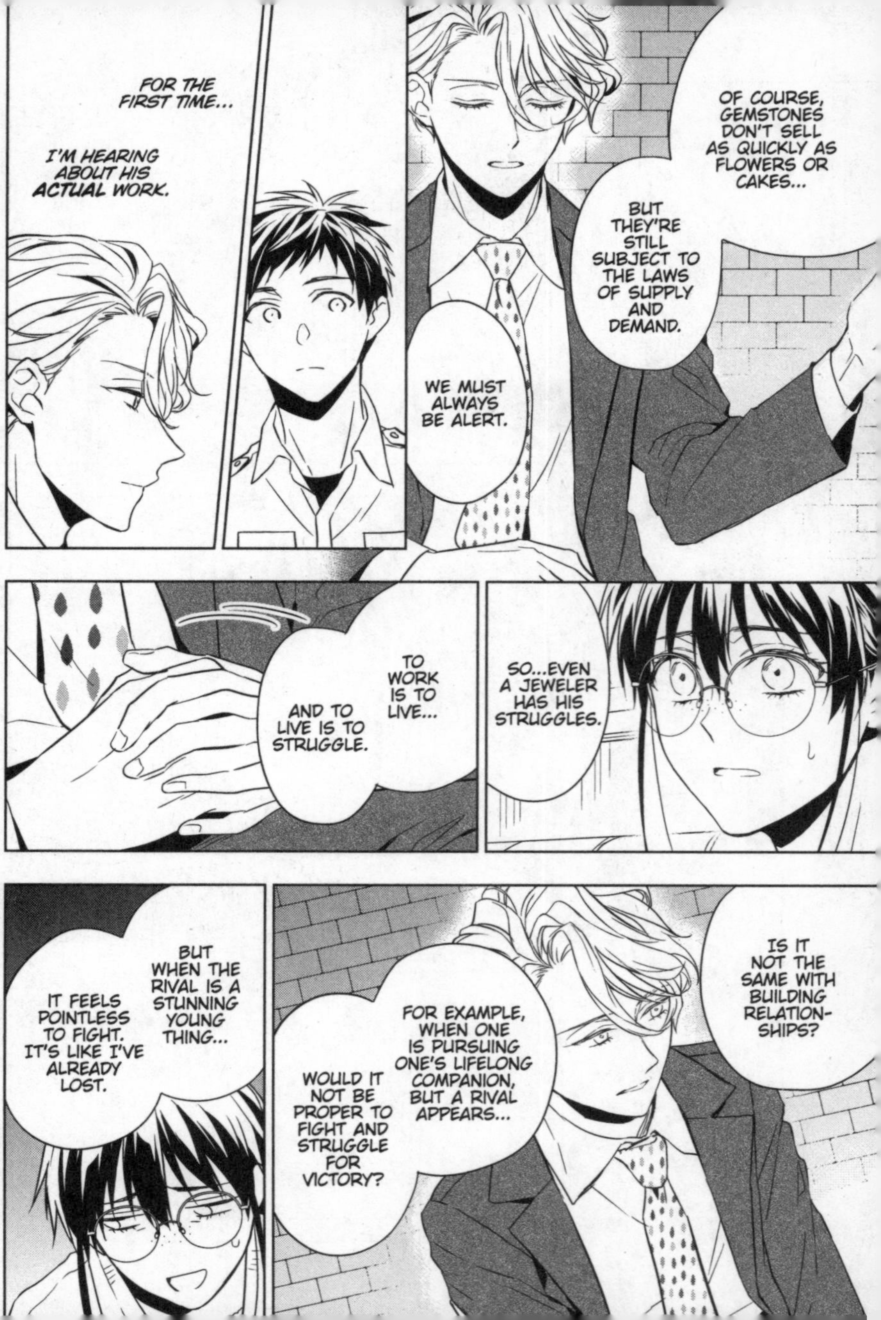
OF COURSE, GEMSTONES DON'T SELL AS QUICKLY AS FLOWERS OR CAKES...
BUT THEY'RE STILL SUBJECT TO THE LAWS OF SUPPLY AND DEMAND.
WE MUST ALWAYS BE ALERT.
FOR THE FIRST TIME...
I'M HEARING ABOUT HIS ACTUAL WORK.
SO...EVEN A JEWELER HAS HIS STRUGGLES.
TO WORK IS TO LIVE...
AND TO LIVE IS TO STRUGGLE.
IS IT NOT THE SAME WITH BUILDING RELATION-SHIPS?
FOR EXAMPLE, WHEN ONE IS PURSUING ONE'S LIFELONG COMPANION, BUT A RIVAL APPEARS...
WOULD IT NOT BE PROPER TO FIGHT AND STRUGGLE FOR VICTORY?
BUT WHEN THE RIVAL IS A STUNNING YOUNG THING...
IT FEELS POINTLESS TO FIGHT. IT'S LIKE I'VE ALREADY LOST.

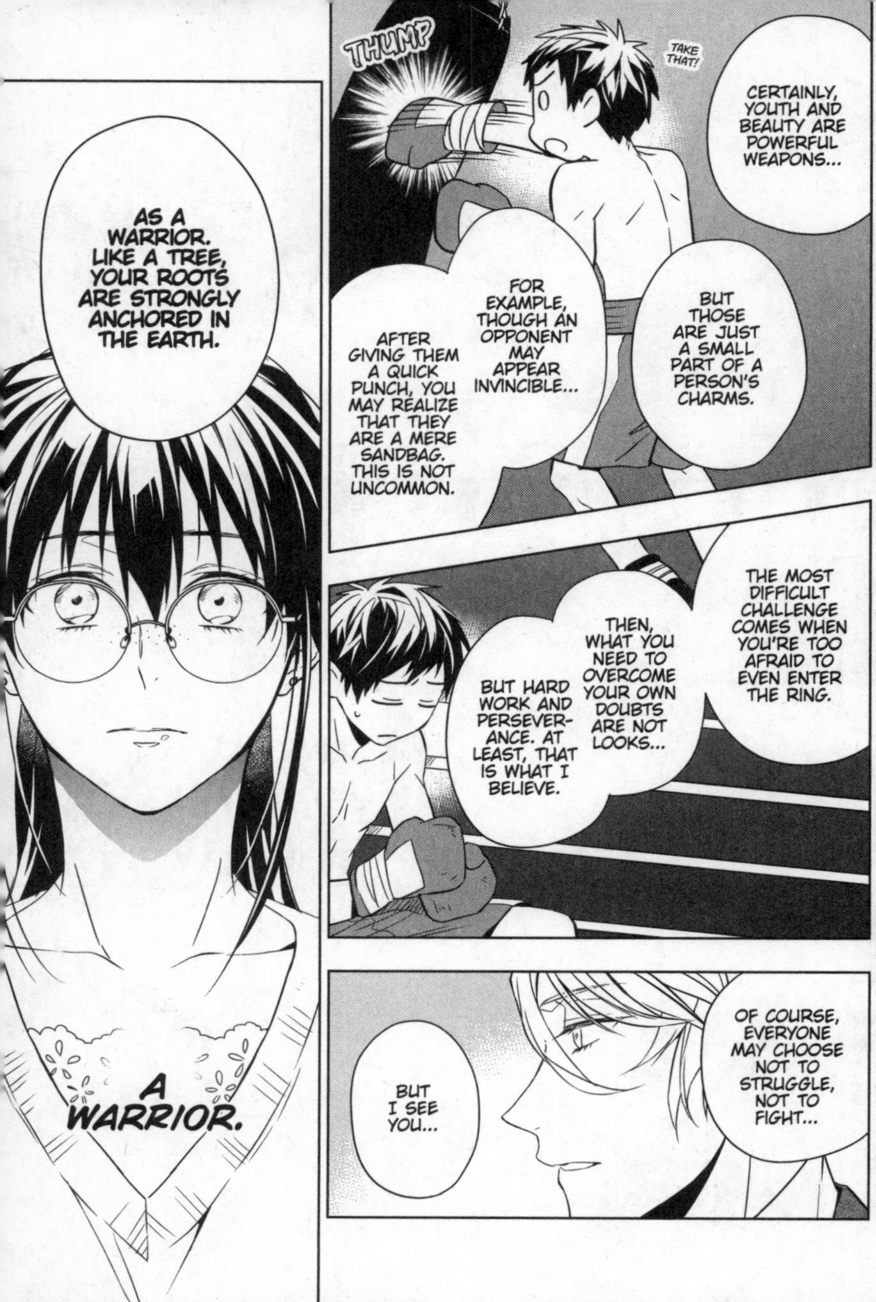
CERTAINLY, YOUTH AND BEAUTY ARE POWERFUL WEAPONS...
TAKE THAT!
THUMP
BUT THOSE ARE JUST A SMALL PART OF A PERSON'S CHARMS.
FOR EXAMPLE, THOUGH AN OPPONENT MAY APPEAR INVINCIBLE...
AFTER GIVING THEM A QUICK PUNCH, YOU MAY REALIZE THAT THEY ARE A MERE SANDBAG. THIS IS NOT UNCOMMON.
THE MOST DIFFICULT CHALLENGE COMES WHEN YOU'RE TOO AFRAID TO EVEN ENTER THE RING.
THEN, WHAT YOU NEED TO OVERCOME YOUR OWN DOUBTS ARE NOT LOOKS...
BUT HARD WORK AND PERSEVER-ANCE. AT LEAST, THAT IS WHAT I BELIEVE.
OF COURSE, EVERYONE MAY CHOOSE NOT TO STRUGGLE, NOT TO FIGHT...
BUT I SEE YOU...
AS A WARRIOR. LIKE A TREE, YOUR ROOTS ARE STRONGLY ANCHORED IN THE EARTH.
A WARRIOR.

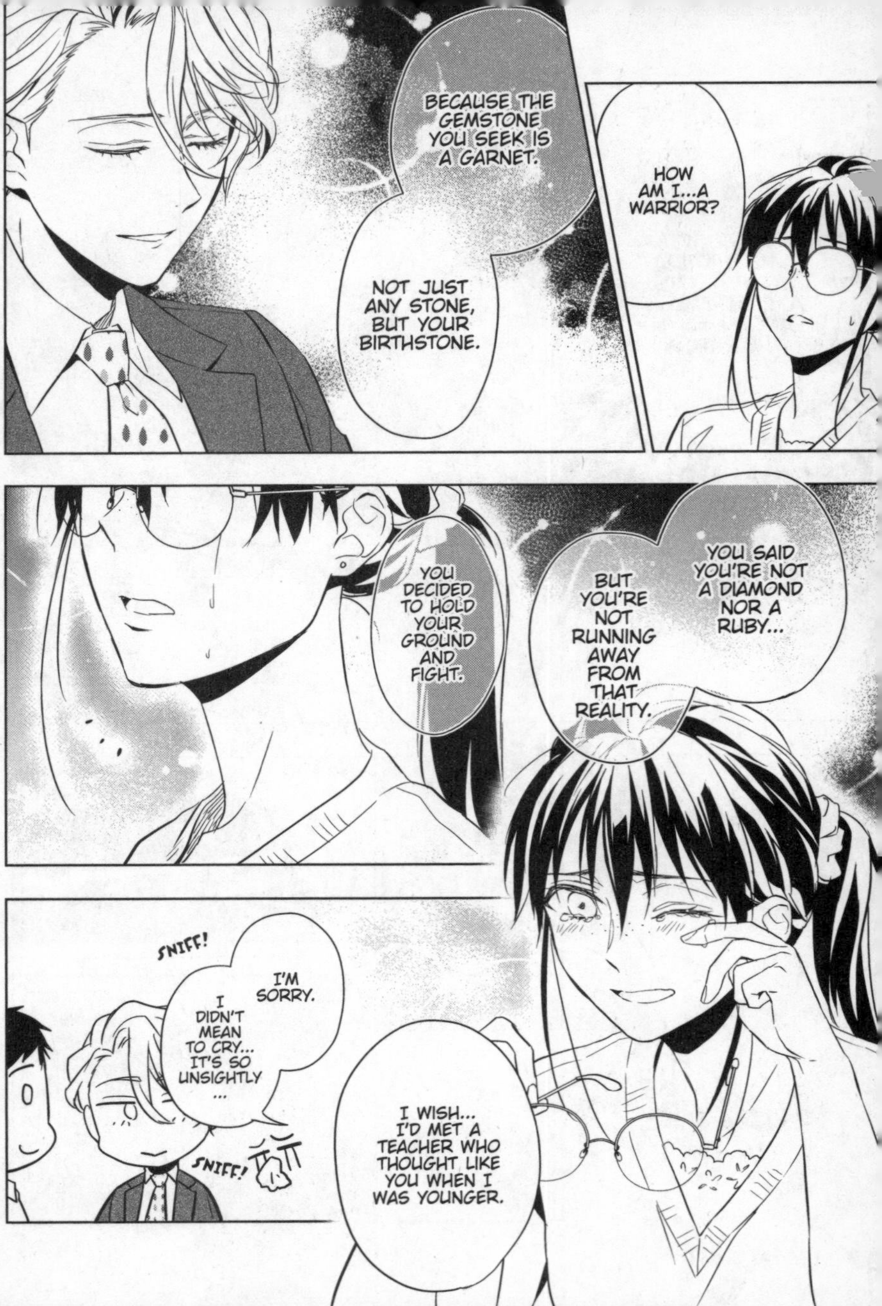
HOW AM I...A WARRIOR?
BECAUSE THE GEMSTONE YOU SEEK IS A GARNET.
NOT JUST ANY STONE, BUT YOUR BIRTHSTONE.
YOU SAID YOU'RE NOT A DIAMOND NOR A RUBY...
BUT YOU'RE NOT RUNNING AWAY FROM THAT REALITY.
YOU DECIDED TO HOLD YOUR GROUND AND FIGHT.
I WISH... I'D MET A TEACHER WHO THOUGHT LIKE YOU WHEN I WAS YOUNGER.
SNIFF!
I'M SORRY.
I DIDN'T MEAN TO CRY... IT'S SO UNSIGHTLY ...
SNIFF!

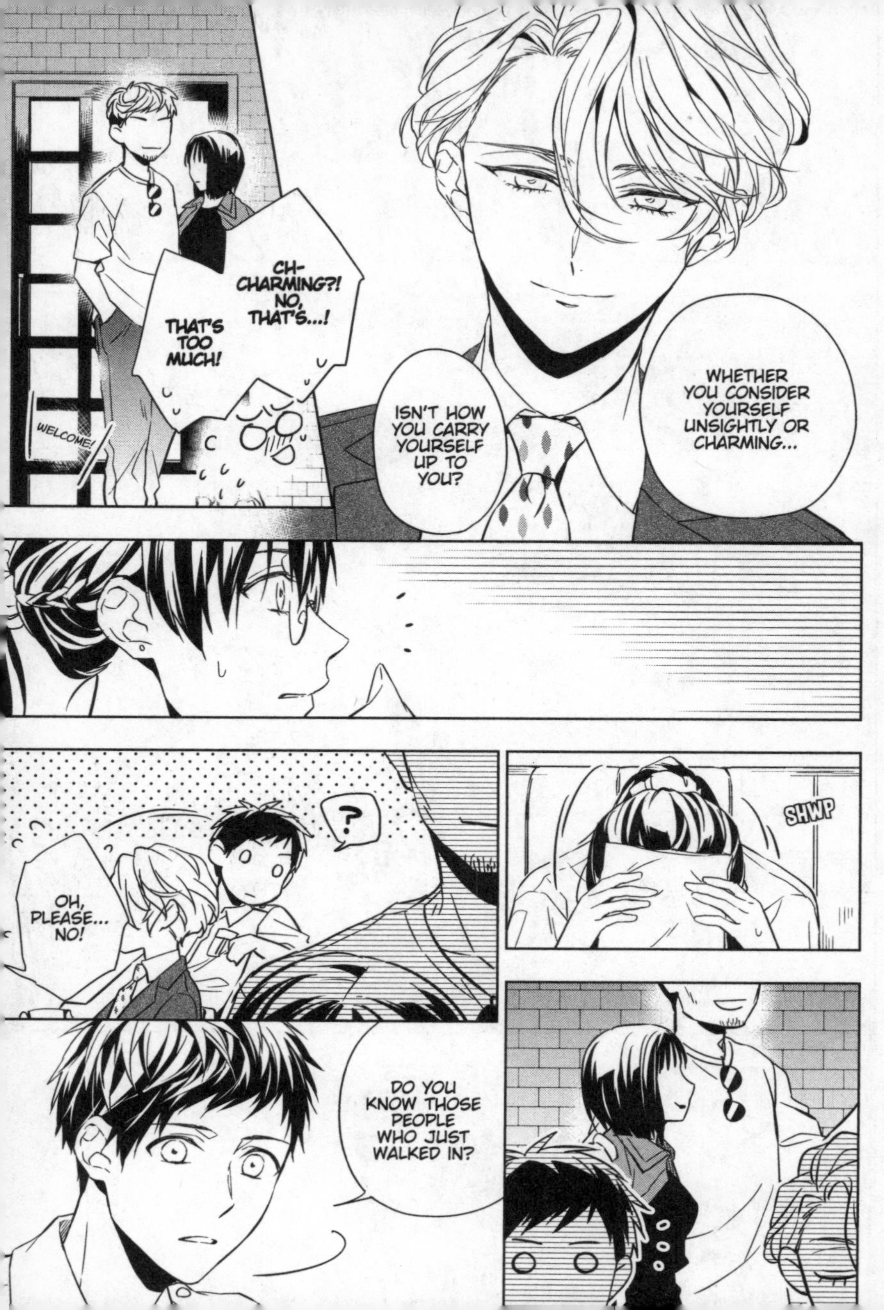
WHETHER YOU CONSIDER YOURSELF UNSIGHTLY OR CHARMING...
ISN'T HOW YOU CARRY YOURSELF UP TO YOU?
CH-CHARMING?! NO, THAT'S...!
THAT'S TOO MUCH!
WELCOME!
...
SHWP
?
OH, PLEASE... NO!
DO YOU KNOW THOSE PEOPLE WHO JUST WALKED IN?

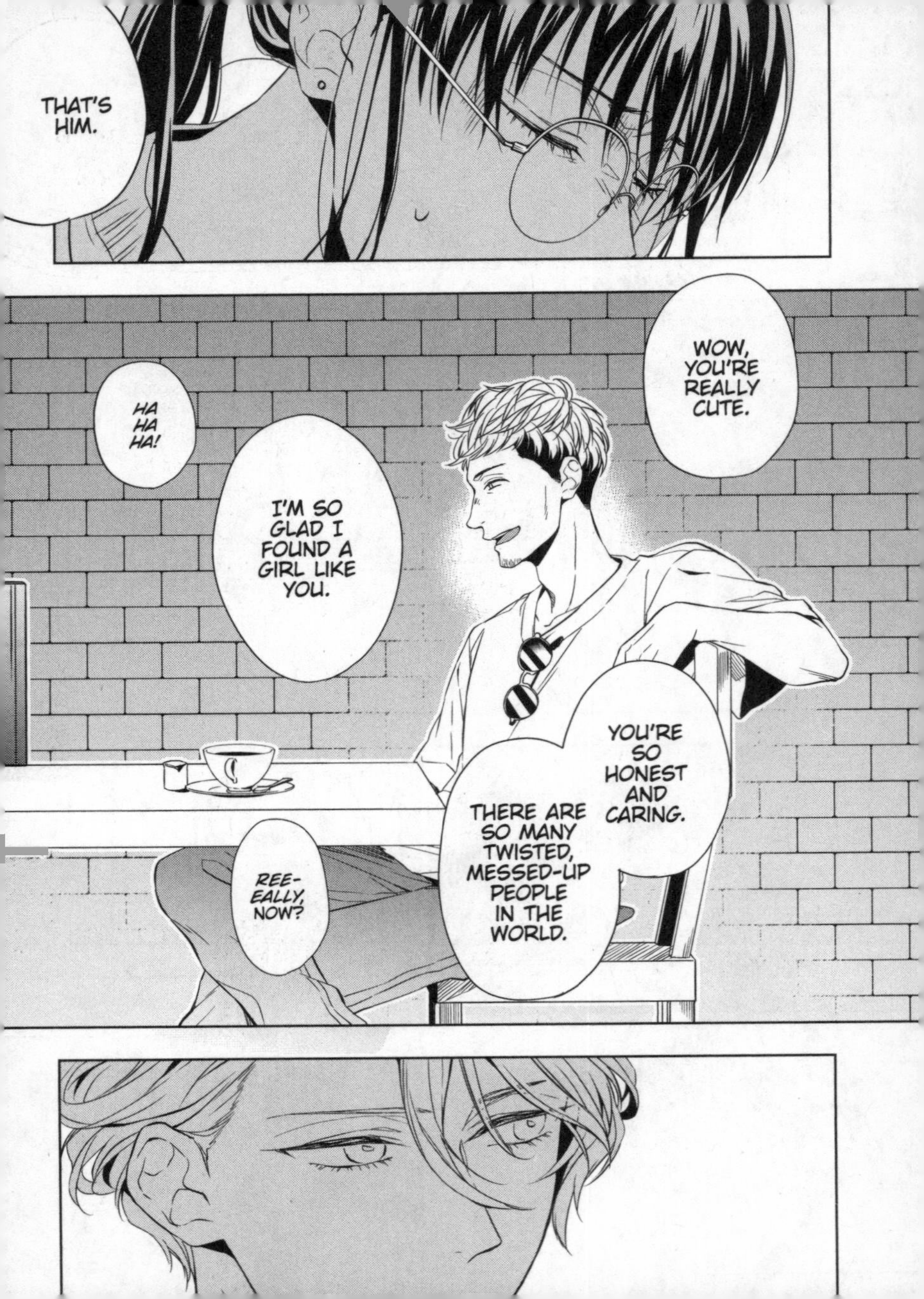
THAT'S HIM.
WOW, YOU'RE REALLY CUTE.
HA HA HA!
I'M SO GLAD I FOUND A GIRL LIKE YOU.
YOU'RE SO HONEST AND CARING.
THERE ARE SO MANY TWISTED, MESSED-UP PEOPLE IN THE WORLD.
REE-EALLY, NOW?

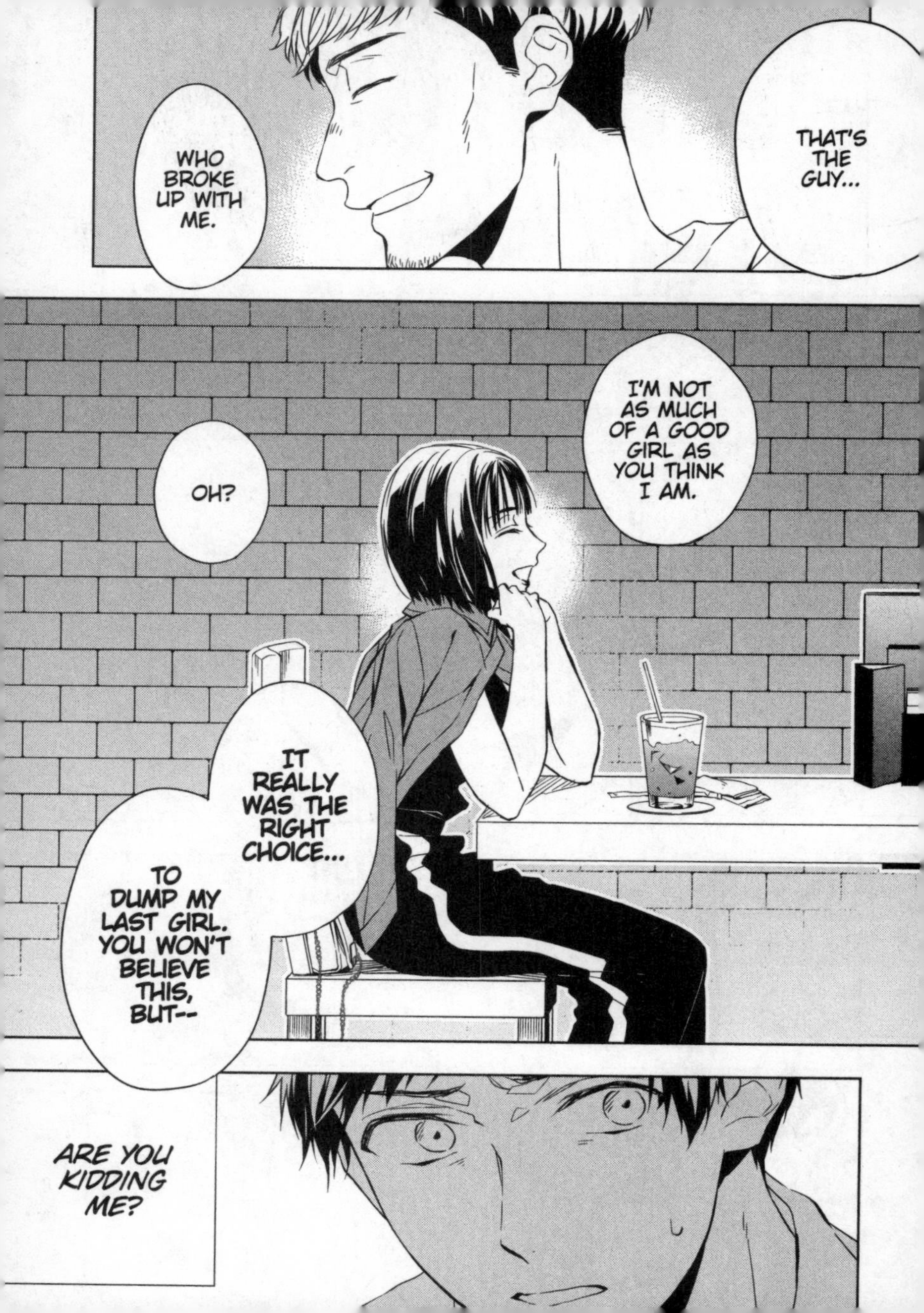
THAT'S THE GUY...
WHO BROKE UP WITH ME.
I'M NOT AS MUCH OF A GOOD GIRL AS YOU THINK I AM.
OH?
IT REALLY WAS THE RIGHT CHOICE...
TO DUMP MY LAST GIRL. YOU WON'T BELIEVE THIS, BUT--
ARE YOU KIDDING ME?

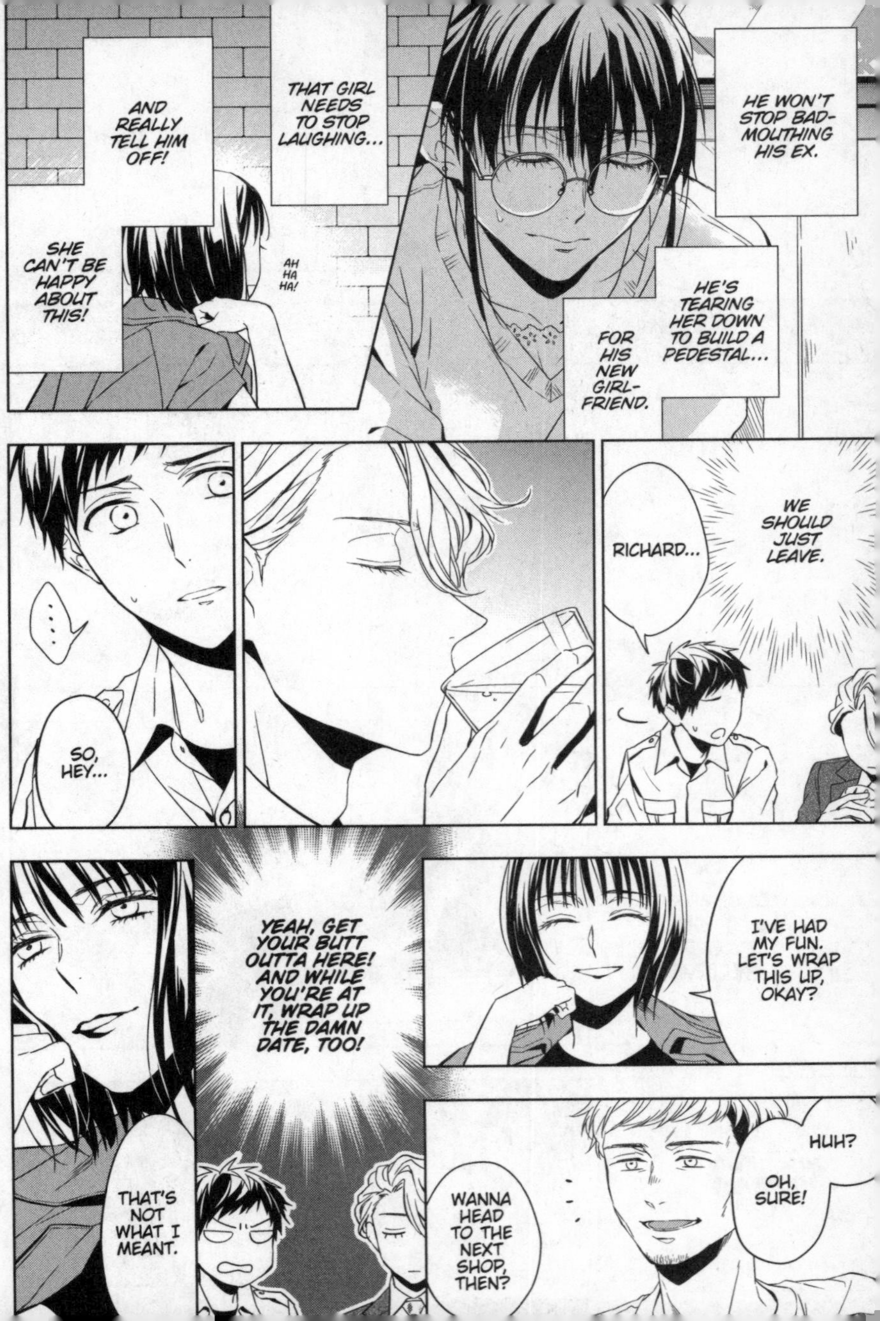
HE WON'T STOP BAD-MOUTHING HIS EX.
HE'S TEARING HER DOWN TO BUILD A PEDESTAL...
FOR HIS NEW GIRL-FRIEND.
THAT GIRL NEEDS TO STOP LAUGHING...
AND REALLY TELL HIM OFF!
AH HA HA!
SHE CAN'T BE HAPPY ABOUT THIS!
WE SHOULD JUST LEAVE.
RICHARD...
...
SO, HEY...
I'VE HAD MY FUN. LET'S WRAP THIS UP, OKAY?
HUH?
OH, SURE!
WANNA HEAD TO THE NEXT SHOP, THEN?
YEAH, GET YOUR BUTT OUTTA HERE! AND WHILE YOU'RE AT IT, WRAP UP THE DAMN DATE, TOO!
THAT'S NOT WHAT I MEANT.

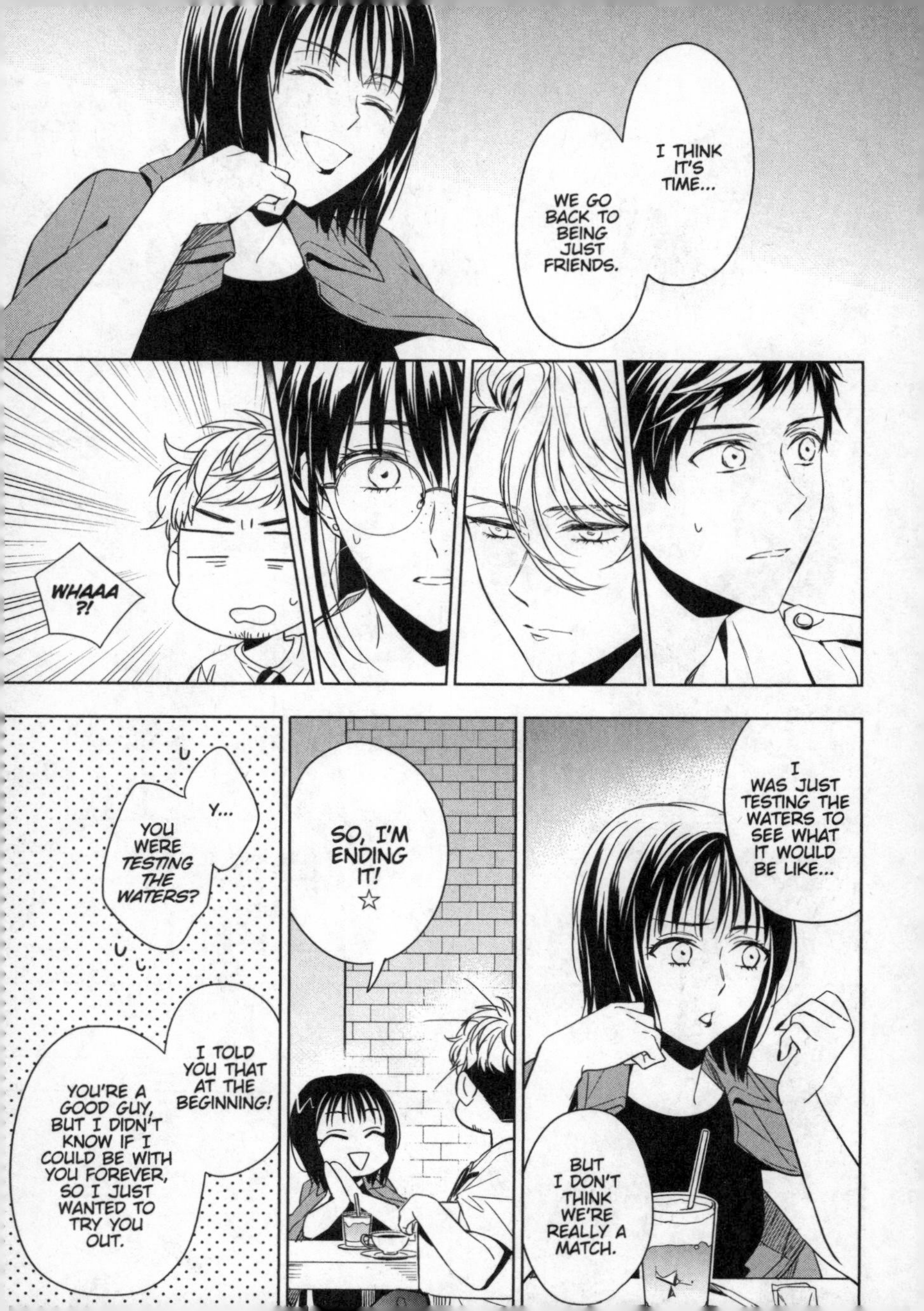
I THINK IT'S TIME...
WE GO BACK TO BEING JUST FRIENDS.
WHAAA ?!
I WAS JUST TESTING THE WATERS TO SEE WHAT IT WOULD BE LIKE...
BUT I DON'T THINK WE'RE REALLY A MATCH.
SO, I'M ENDING IT! ☆
Y... YOU WERE TESTING THE WATERS?
I TOLD YOU THAT AT THE BEGINNING!
YOU'RE A GOOD GUY, BUT I DIDN'T KNOW IF I COULD BE WITH YOU FOREVER, SO I JUST WANTED TO TRY YOU OUT.

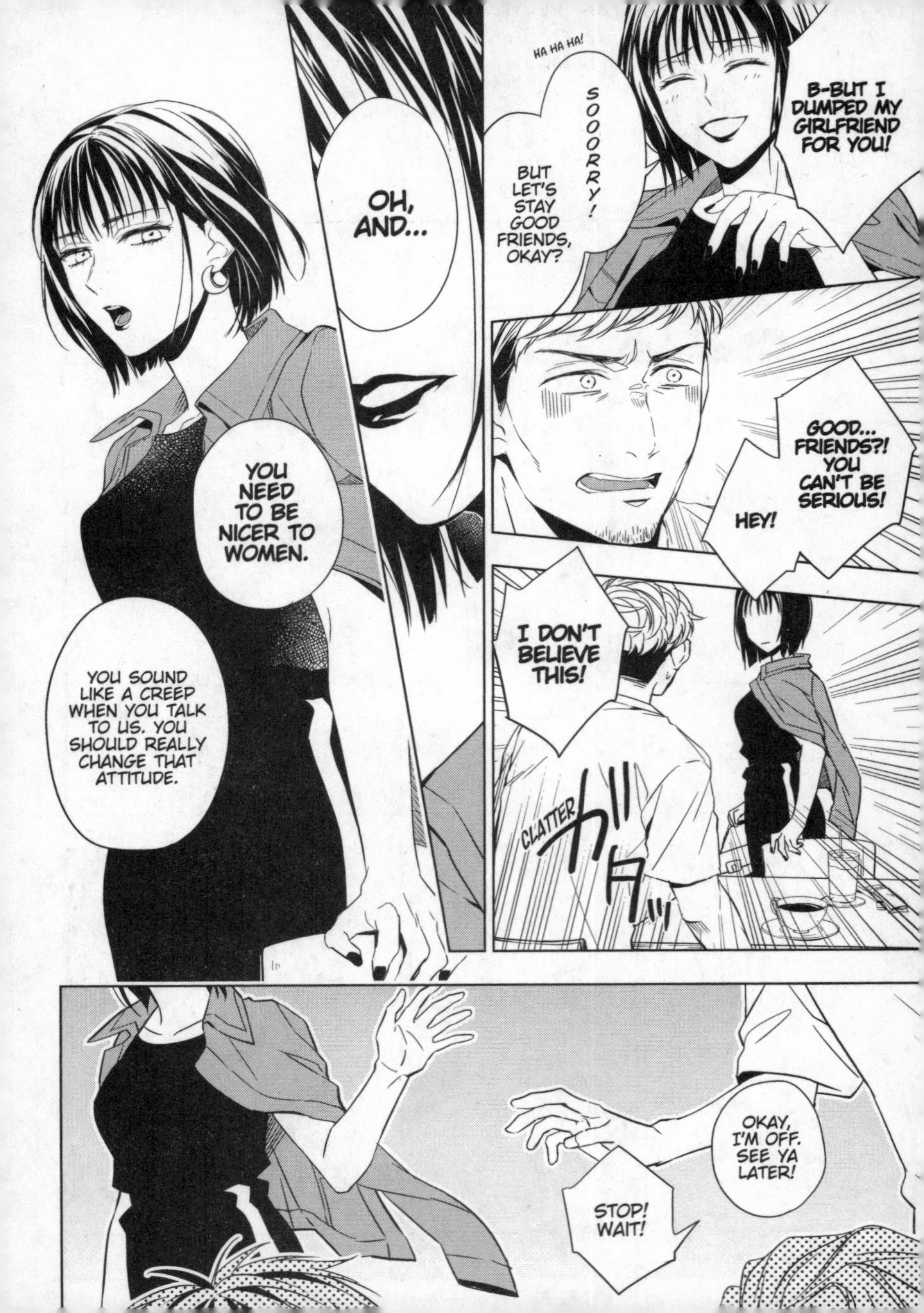
B-BUT I DUMPED MY GIRLFRIEND FOR YOU!
HA HA HA!
SOOOORRY!
BUT LET'S STAY GOOD FRIENDS, OKAY?
GOOD... FRIENDS?! YOU CAN'T BE SERIOUS!
HEY!
I DON'T BELIEVE THIS!
CLATTER
OH, AND...
YOU NEED TO BE NICER TO WOMEN.
YOU SOUND LIKE A CREEP WHEN YOU TALK TO US. YOU SHOULD REALLY CHANGE THAT ATTITUDE.
OKAY, I'M OFF. SEE YA LATER!
STOP! WAIT!

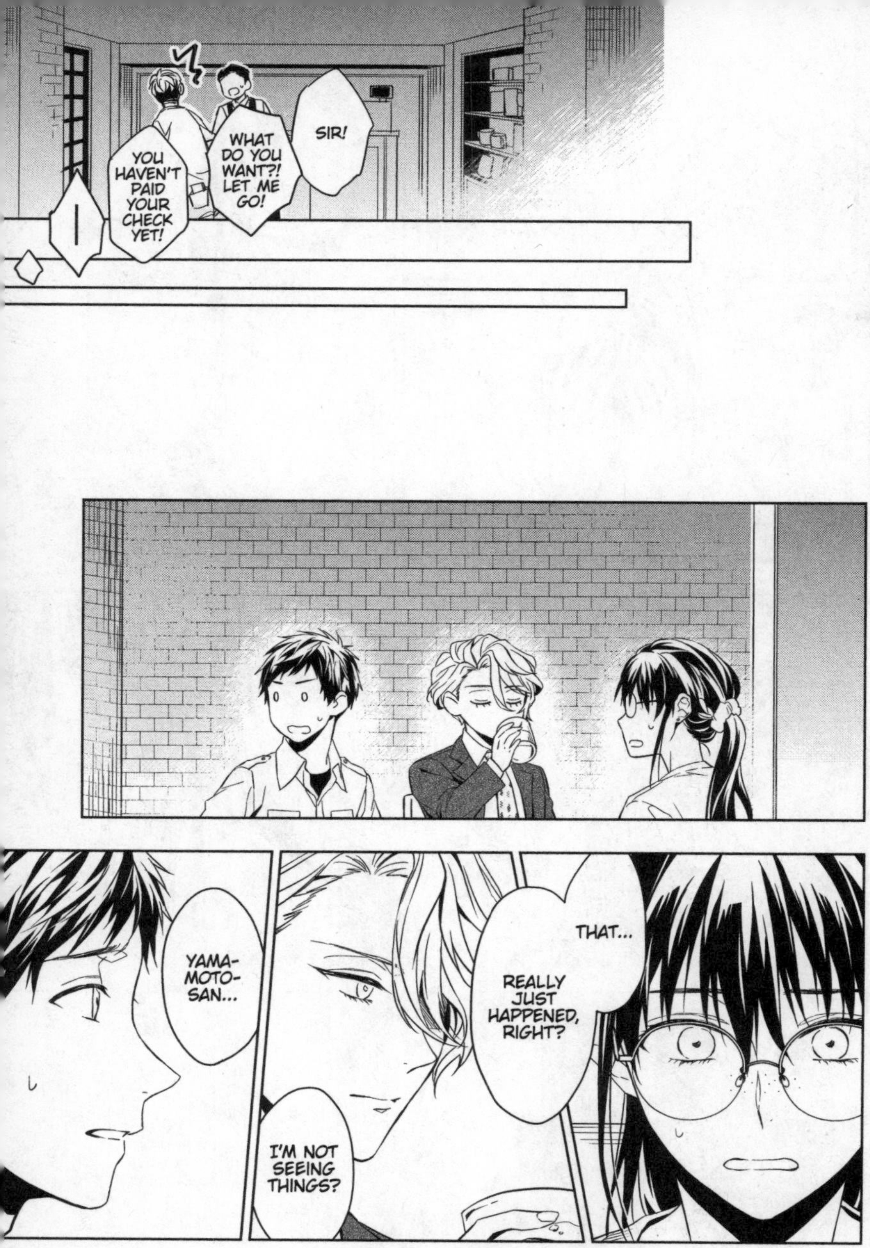
SIR!
WHAT DO YOU WANT?! LET ME GO!
YOU HAVEN'T PAID YOUR CHECK YET!
THAT...
REALLY JUST HAPPENED, RIGHT?
I'M NOT SEEING THINGS?
YAMA-MOTO-SAN...

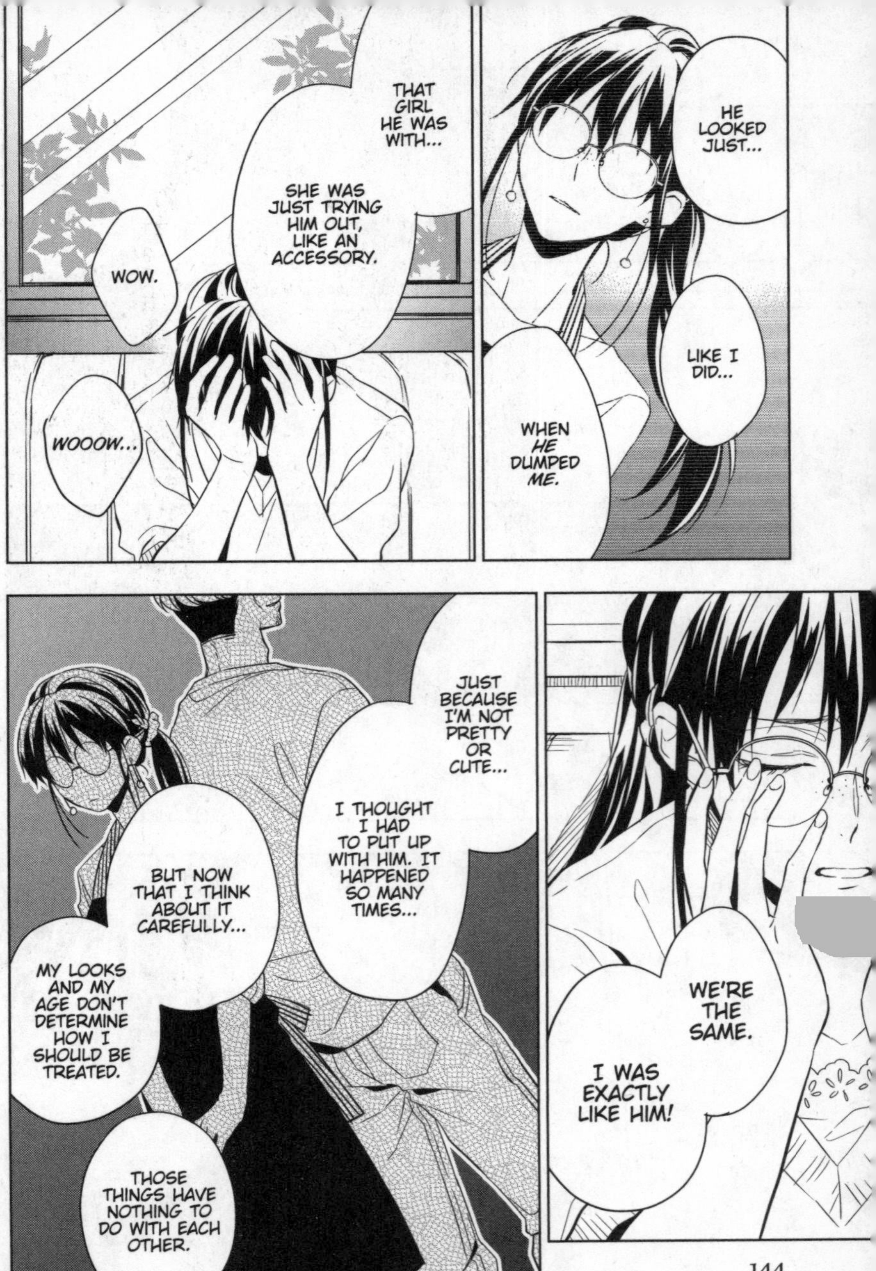
HE LOOKED JUST...
LIKE I DID...
WHEN *HE* DUMPED *ME*.
THAT GIRL HE WAS WITH...
SHE WAS JUST TRYING HIM OUT, LIKE AN ACCESSORY.
WOW.
WOOOW...
WE'RE THE SAME.
I WAS EXACTLY LIKE HIM!
JUST BECAUSE I'M NOT PRETTY OR CUTE...
I THOUGHT I HAD TO PUT UP WITH HIM. IT HAPPENED SO MANY TIMES...
BUT NOW THAT I THINK ABOUT IT CAREFULLY...
MY LOOKS AND MY AGE DON'T DETERMINE HOW I SHOULD BE TREATED.
THOSE THINGS HAVE NOTHING TO DO WITH EACH OTHER.

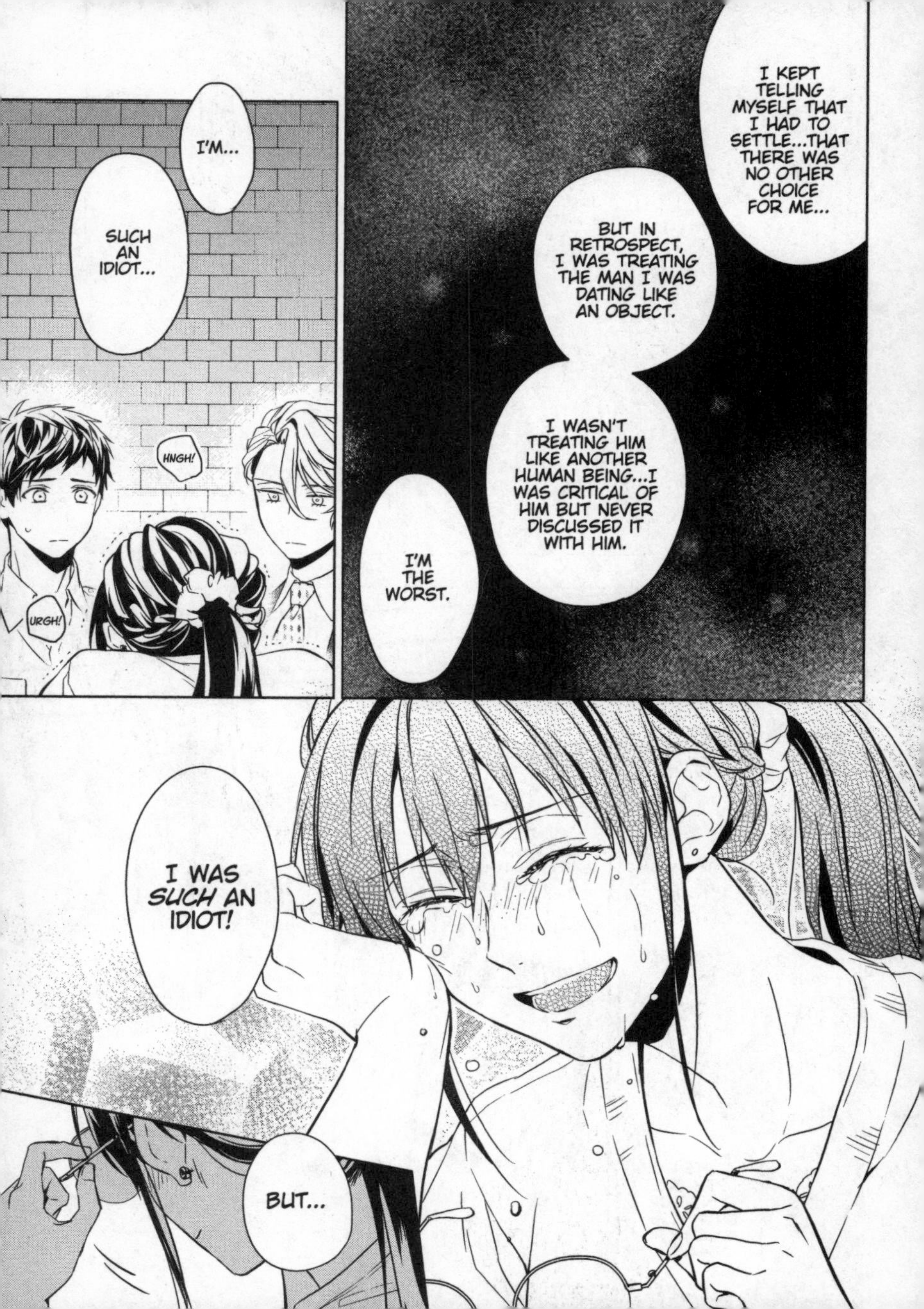
I KEPT TELLING MYSELF THAT I HAD TO SETTLE...THAT THERE WAS NO OTHER CHOICE FOR ME...
BUT IN RETROSPECT, I WAS TREATING THE MAN I WAS DATING LIKE AN OBJECT.
I WASN'T TREATING HIM LIKE ANOTHER HUMAN BEING...I WAS CRITICAL OF HIM BUT NEVER DISCUSSED IT WITH HIM.
I'M THE WORST.
I'M...
SUCH AN IDIOT...
HNGH!
URGH!
I WAS SUCH AN IDIOT!
BUT...

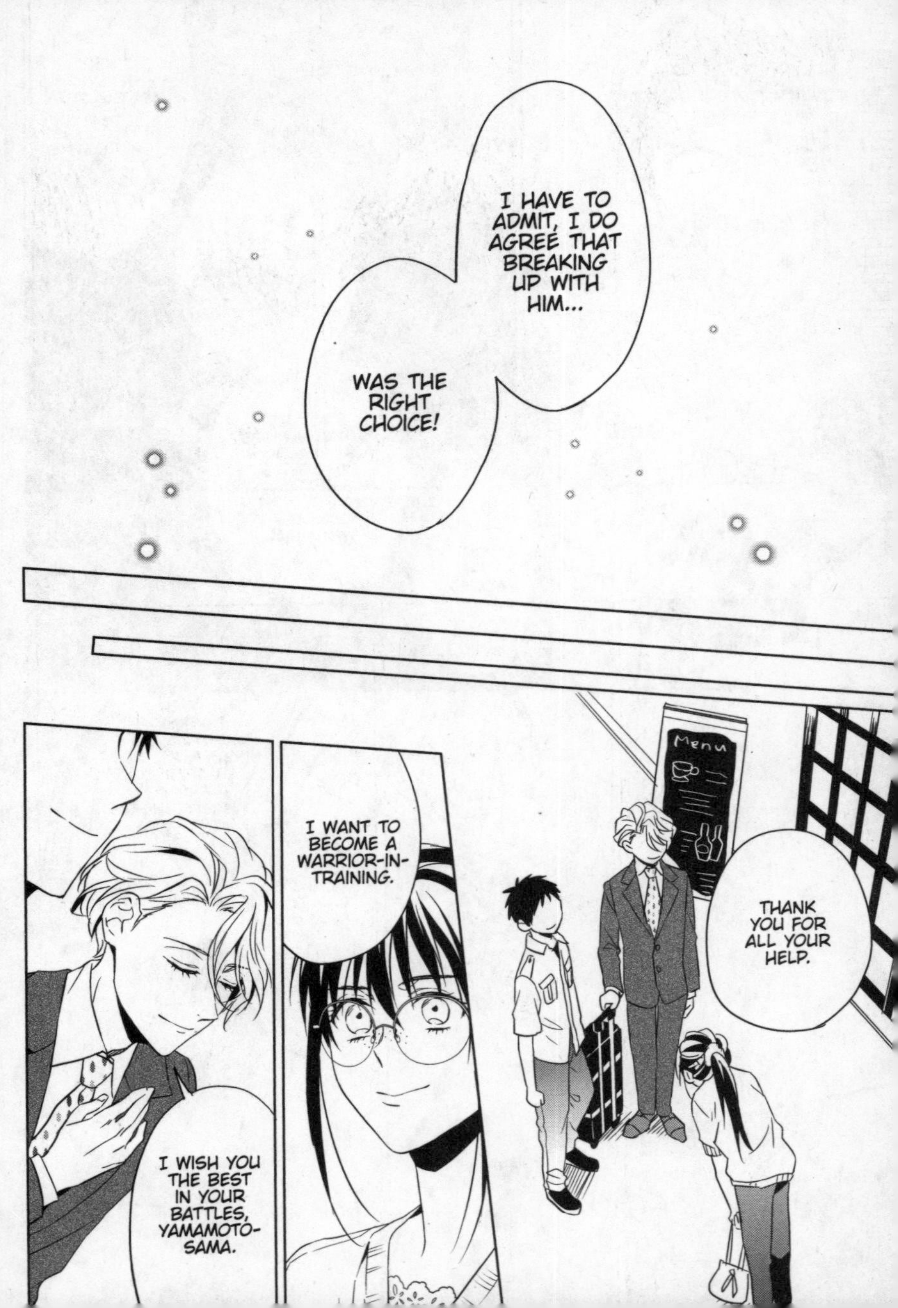
I HAVE TO ADMIT, I DO AGREE THAT BREAKING UP WITH HIM...
WAS THE RIGHT CHOICE!
THANK YOU FOR ALL YOUR HELP.
I WANT TO BECOME A WARRIOR-IN-TRAINING.
I WISH YOU THE BEST IN YOUR BATTLES, YAMAMOTO-SAMA.

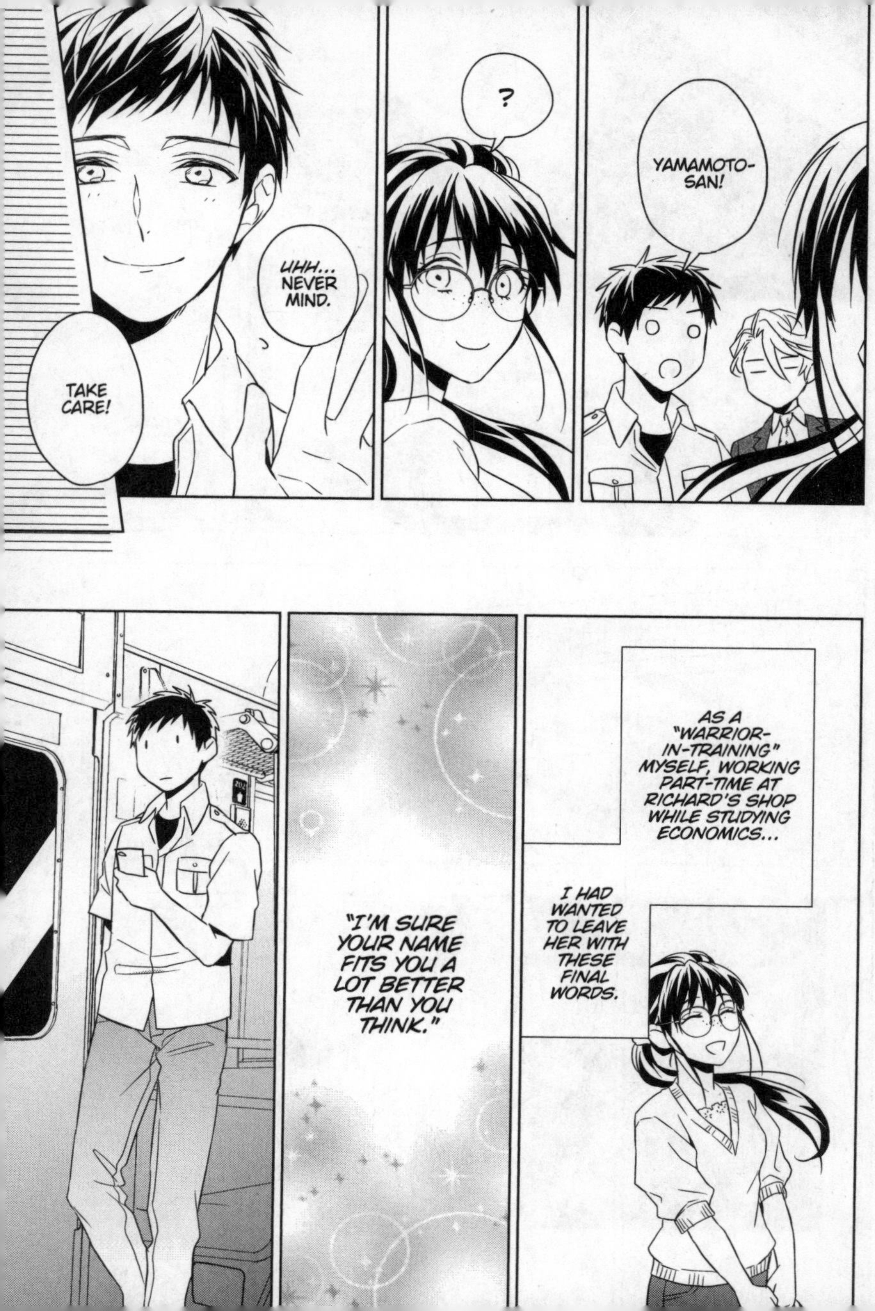
YAMAMOTO-SAN!
?
UHH... NEVER MIND.
TAKE CARE!
AS A "WARRIOR-IN-TRAINING" MYSELF, WORKING PART-TIME AT RICHARD'S SHOP WHILE STUDYING ECONOMICS...
I HAD WANTED TO LEAVE HER WITH THESE FINAL WORDS.
"I'M SURE YOUR NAME FITS YOU A LOT BETTER THAN YOU THINK."

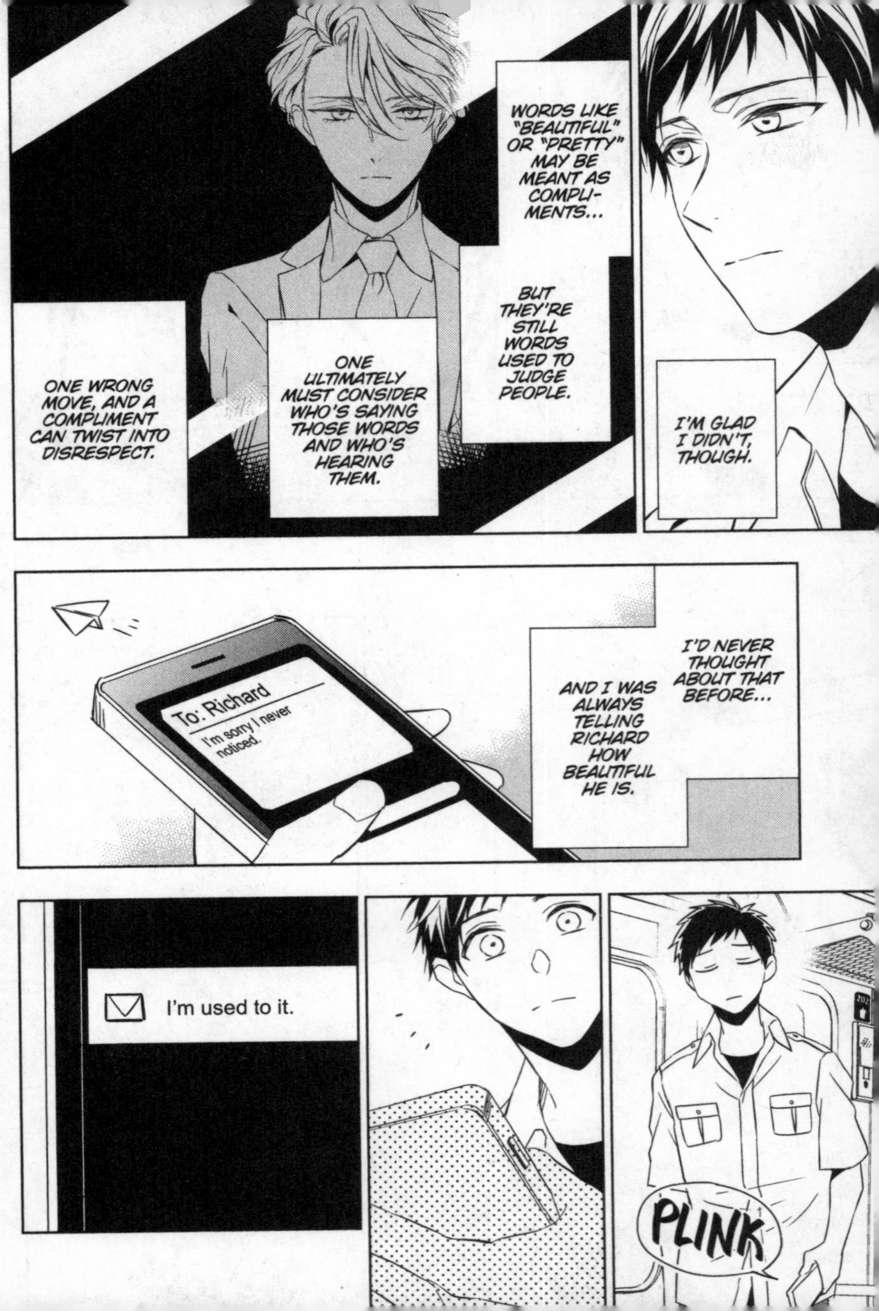
WORDS LIKE "BEAUTIFUL" OR "PRETTY" MAY BE MEANT AS COMPLI-MENTS...
BUT THEY'RE STILL WORDS USED TO JUDGE PEOPLE.
ONE ULTIMATELY MUST CONSIDER WHO'S SAYING THOSE WORDS AND WHO'S HEARING THEM.
ONE WRONG MOVE, AND A COMPLIMENT CAN TWIST INTO DISRESPECT.
I'M GLAD I DIDN'T, THOUGH.
I'D NEVER THOUGHT ABOUT THAT BEFORE...
AND I WAS ALWAYS TELLING RICHARD HOW BEAUTIFUL HE IS.
To: Richard
I'm sorry I never noticed.
PLINK
I'm used to it.

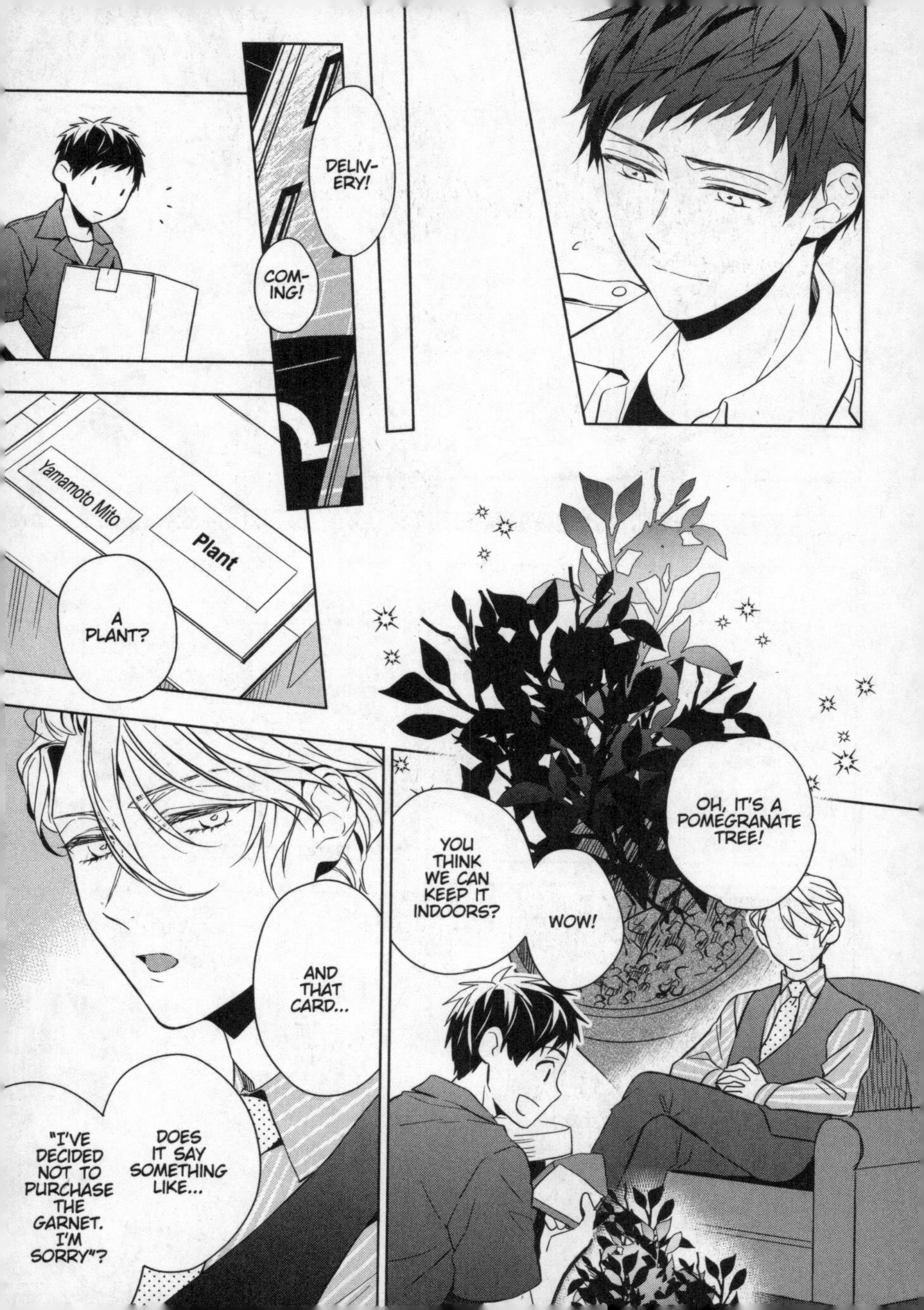
DELIV-ERY!
COM-ING!
OH, IT'S A POMEGRANATE TREE!
WOW!
YOU THINK WE CAN KEEP IT INDOORS?
Yamamoto Mito
Plant
A PLANT?
AND THAT CARD...
DOES IT SAY SOMETHING LIKE...
"I'VE DECIDED NOT TO PURCHASE THE GARNET. I'M SORRY"?

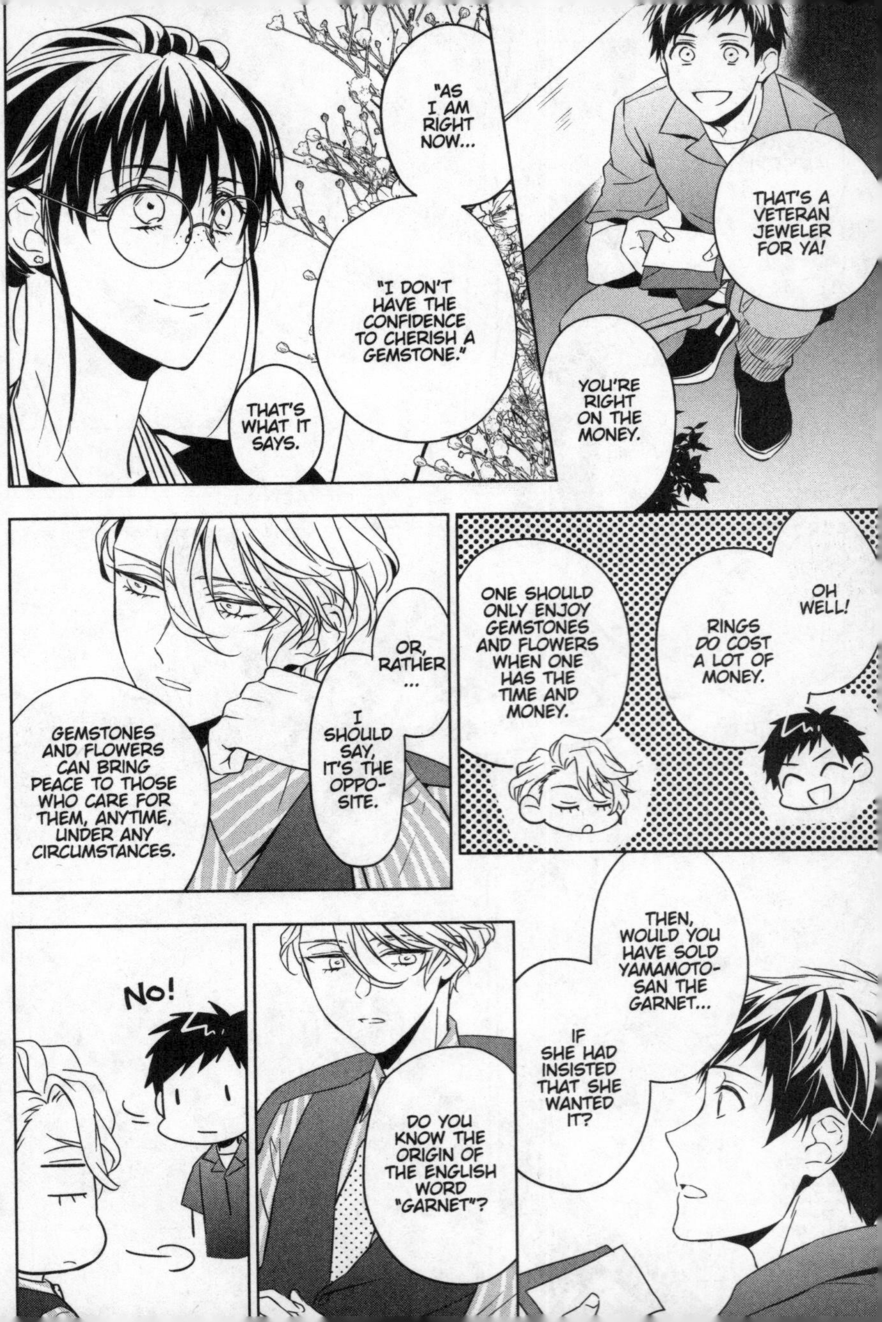
THAT'S A VETERAN JEWELER FOR YA!
YOU'RE RIGHT ON THE MONEY.
"AS I AM RIGHT NOW...
"I DON'T HAVE THE CONFIDENCE TO CHERISH A GEMSTONE."
THAT'S WHAT IT SAYS.
OH WELL!
RINGS DO COST A LOT OF MONEY.
ONE SHOULD ONLY ENJOY GEMSTONES AND FLOWERS WHEN ONE HAS THE TIME AND MONEY.
OR, RATHER...
I SHOULD SAY, IT'S THE OPPO-SITE.
GEMSTONES AND FLOWERS CAN BRING PEACE TO THOSE WHO CARE FOR THEM, ANYTIME, UNDER ANY CIRCUMSTANCES.
THEN, WOULD YOU HAVE SOLD YAMAMOTO-SAN THE GARNET...
IF SHE HAD INSISTED THAT SHE WANTED IT?
DO YOU KNOW THE ORIGIN OF THE ENGLISH WORD "GARNET"?
No!

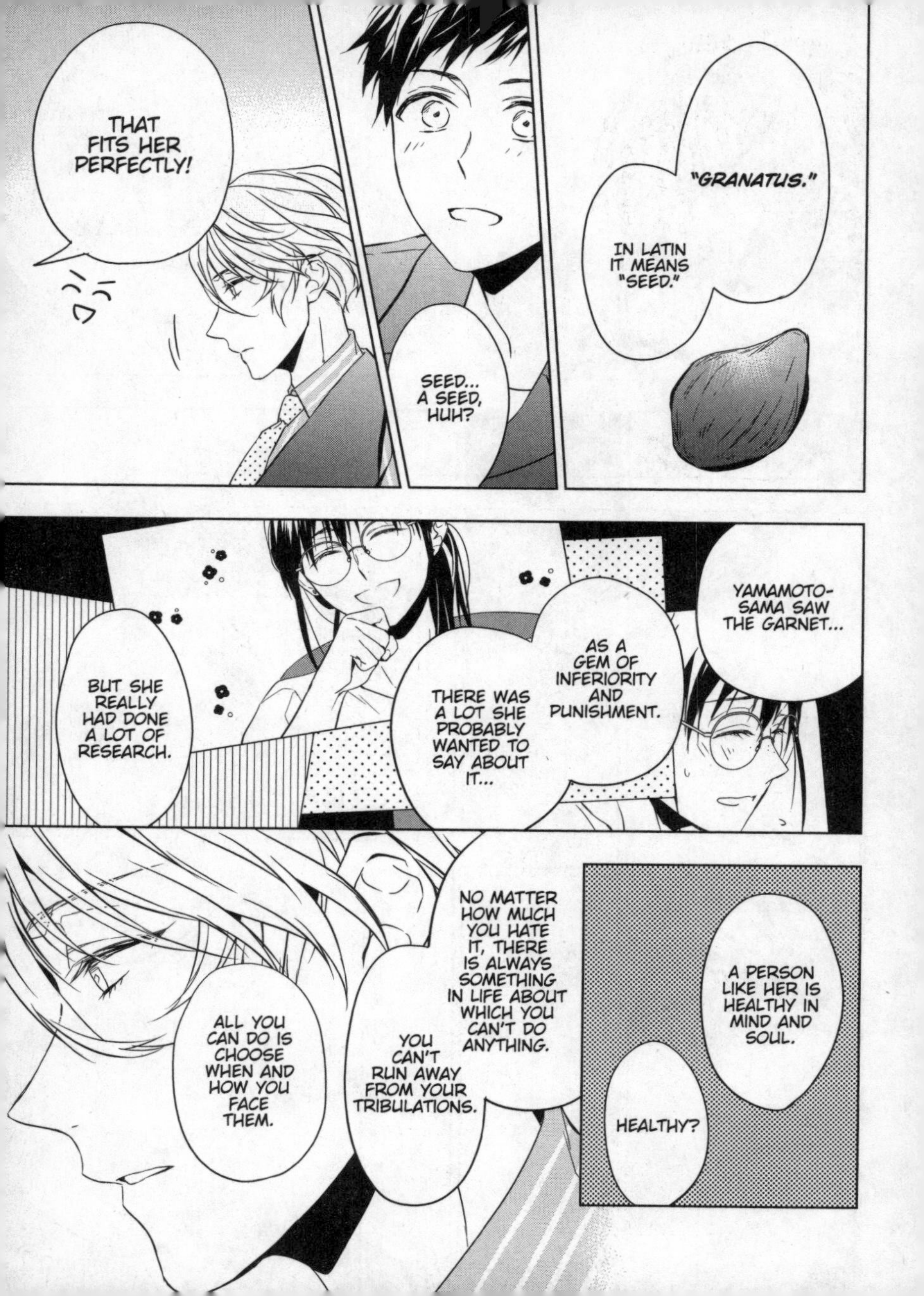
"GRANATUS."
IN LATIN IT MEANS "SEED."
SEED... A SEED, HUH?
THAT FITS HER PERFECTLY!
YAMAMOTO-SAMA SAW THE GARNET...
AS A GEM OF INFERIORITY AND PUNISHMENT.
THERE WAS A LOT SHE PROBABLY WANTED TO SAY ABOUT IT...
BUT SHE REALLY HAD DONE A LOT OF RESEARCH.
A PERSON LIKE HER IS HEALTHY IN MIND AND SOUL.
HEALTHY?
NO MATTER HOW MUCH YOU HATE IT, THERE IS ALWAYS SOMETHING IN LIFE ABOUT WHICH YOU CAN'T DO ANYTHING.
YOU CAN'T RUN AWAY FROM YOUR TRIBULATIONS.
ALL YOU CAN DO IS CHOOSE WHEN AND HOW YOU FACE THEM.

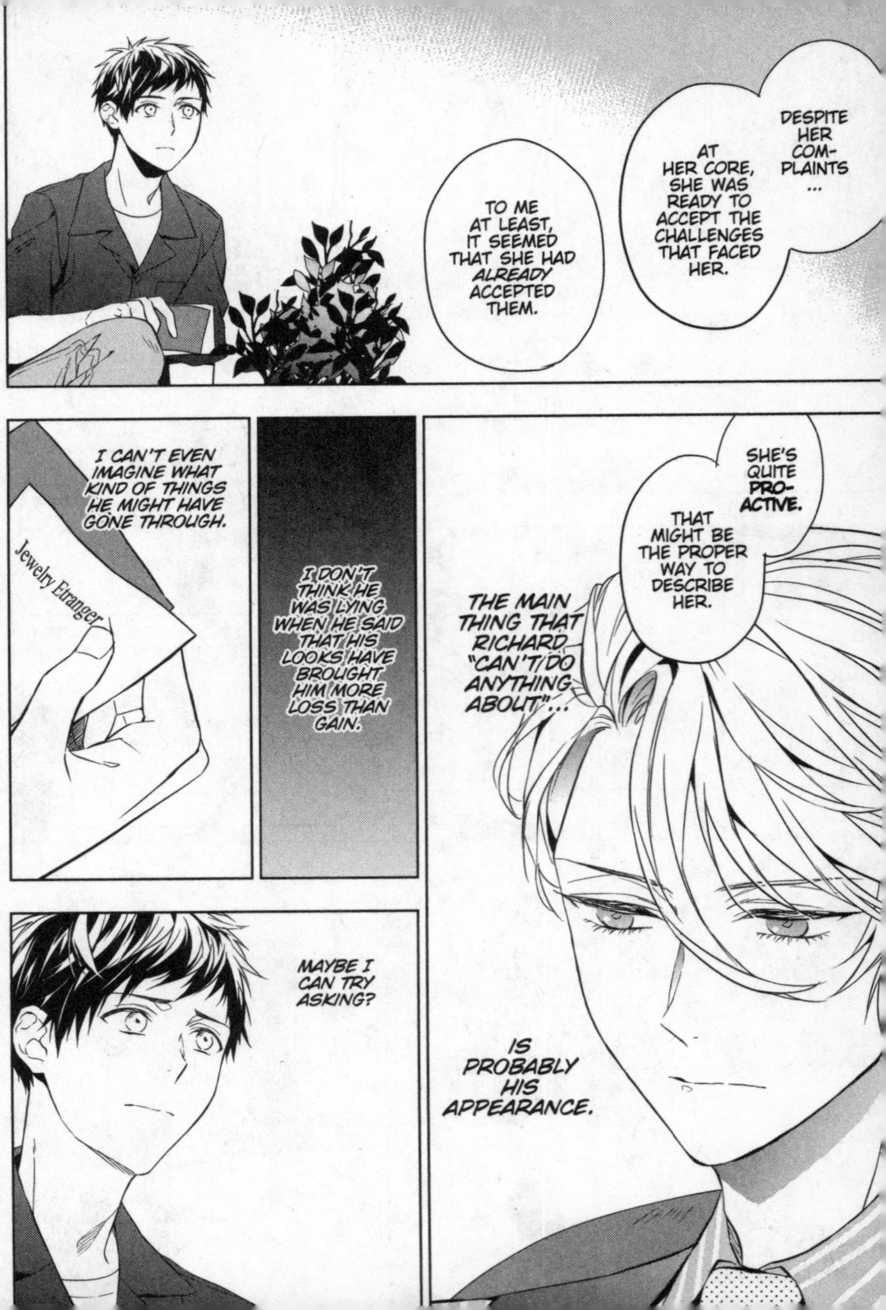
DESPITE HER COM-PLAINTS...
AT HER CORE, SHE WAS READY TO ACCEPT THE CHALLENGES THAT FACED HER.
TO ME AT LEAST, IT SEEMED THAT SHE HAD ALREADY ACCEPTED THEM.
SHE'S QUITE PRO-ACTIVE.
THAT MIGHT BE THE PROPER WAY TO DESCRIBE HER.
THE MAIN THING THAT RICHARD "CAN'T DO ANYTHING ABOUT"...
IS PROBABLY HIS APPEARANCE.
I DON'T THINK HE WAS LYING WHEN HE SAID THAT HIS LOOKS HAVE BROUGHT HIM MORE LOSS THAN GAIN.
I CAN'T EVEN IMAGINE WHAT KIND OF THINGS HE MIGHT HAVE GONE THROUGH.
Jewelry Etranger
MAYBE I CAN TRY ASKING?

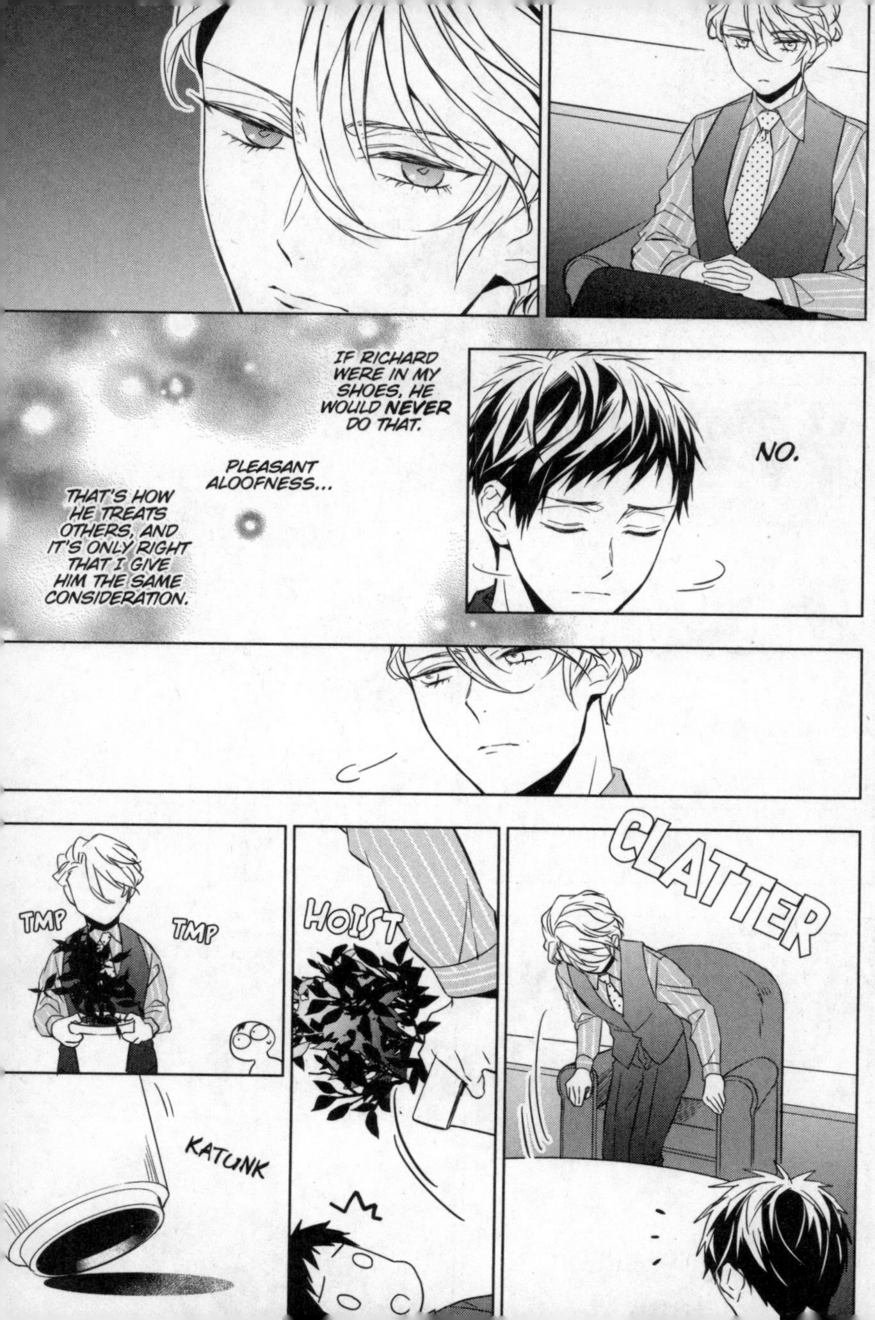
NO.
IF RICHARD WERE IN MY SHOES, HE WOULD **NEVER** DO THAT.
PLEASANT ALOOFNESS...
THAT'S HOW HE TREATS OTHERS, AND IT'S ONLY RIGHT THAT I GIVE HIM THE SAME CONSIDERATION.
CLATTER
HOIST
TMP
TMP
KATUNK

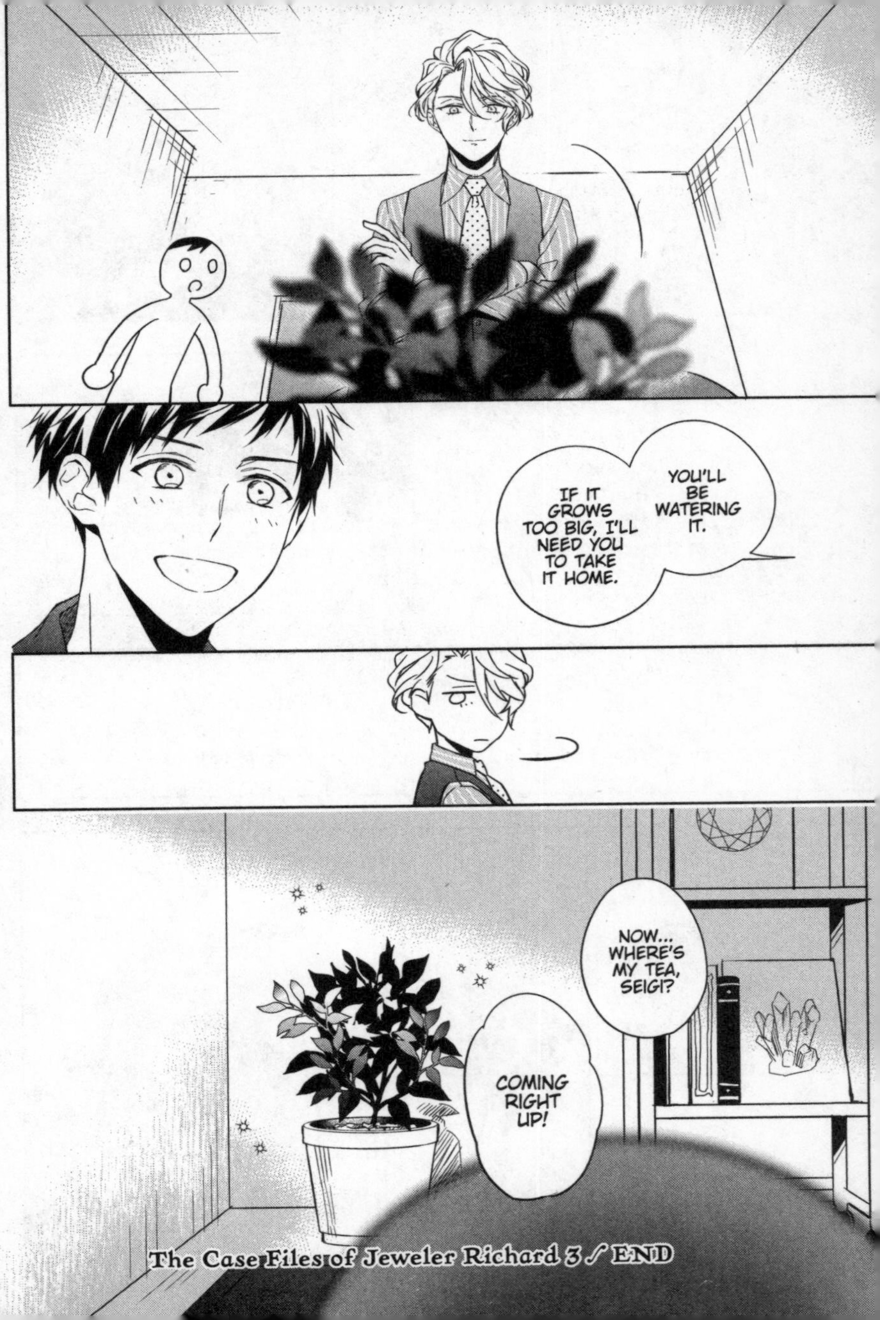
YOU'LL BE WATERING IT.
IF IT GROWS TOO BIG, I'LL NEED YOU TO TAKE IT HOME.
NOW... WHERE'S MY TEA, SEIGI?
COMING RIGHT UP!
The Case Files of Jeweler Richard 3 / END

Hello! **Akatsuki** here.
Welcome to Jewelry Etranger!

Thank you very much for picking up *The Case Files of Jeweler Richard* Volume 3!

The two members of Etranger have finally gotten past being strangers. Their desire to know each other and to be understood is finally blooming! (I think?)

A lot of people have been visiting the jewelry shop, so the conversations there became the main focus of these two episodes. I was particularly worried about how to create the visuals of the characters and the composition of the scenes in order to tell the story most effectively.

How do you think it went? There were countless moments when I thought my skills were lacking, but I hope I was able to bring out the passion and depth of the original work in manga form, if only a little bit.

I will be forever grateful for the opportunity to draw the manga, and to all of you for reading our work. I will keep putting everything I have into my pen as we continue forward!

I hope to see all of you again in another book.

Special Thanks:
Editor I-san
Tsujimura-sensei
Yukihiro-sensei
Designer, Dan-san
My Family, My Friends
and you

THERE ARE SOME EXTRAS, BEGINNING ON THE NEXT PAGE!

MEOW!

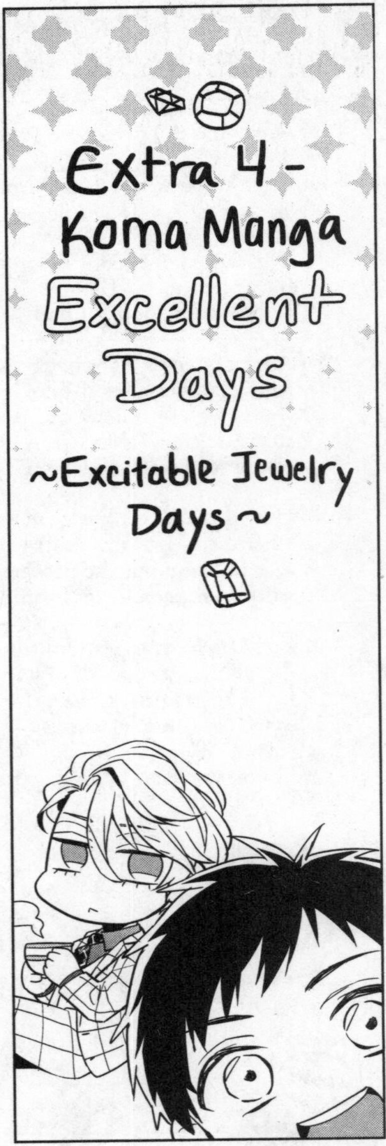
Extra 4-Koma Manga
Excellent Days
~Excitable Jewelry Days~

A Hapless Hero

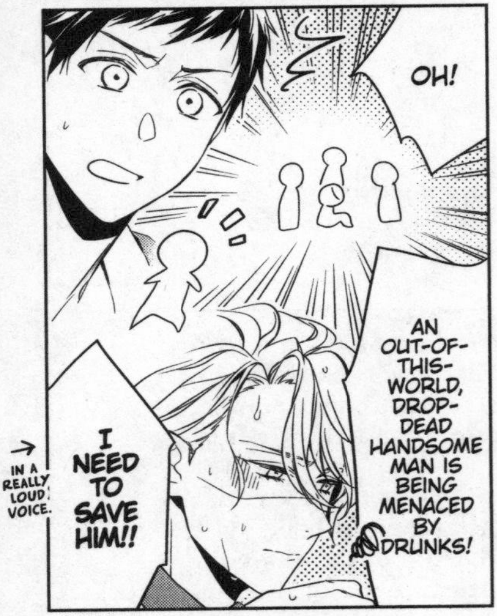
OH!
AN OUT-OF-THIS-WORLD, DROP-DEAD HANDSOME MAN IS BEING MENACED BY DRUNKS!
I NEED TO SAVE HIM!!
IN A REALLY LOUD VOICE.

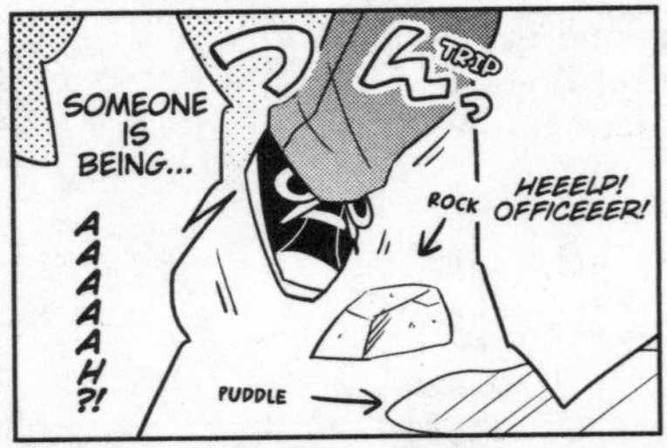
TRIP
HEEELP! OFFICEEER!
ROCK
SOMEONE IS BEING...
AAAAAAH?!
PUDDLE

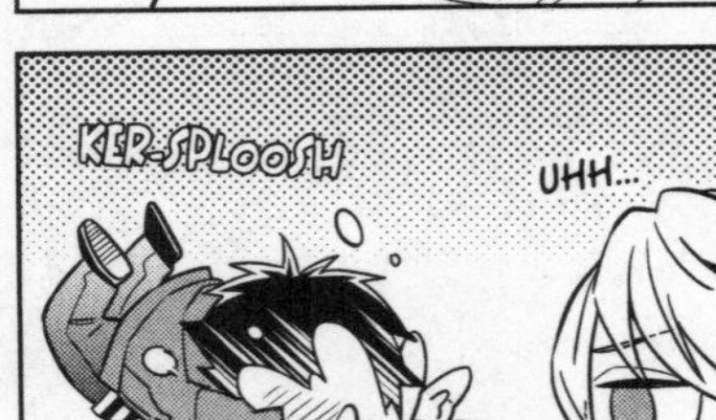
UHH...
KER-SPLOOSH

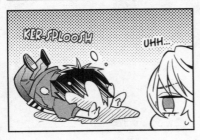

An Overly Thoughtful Man ①

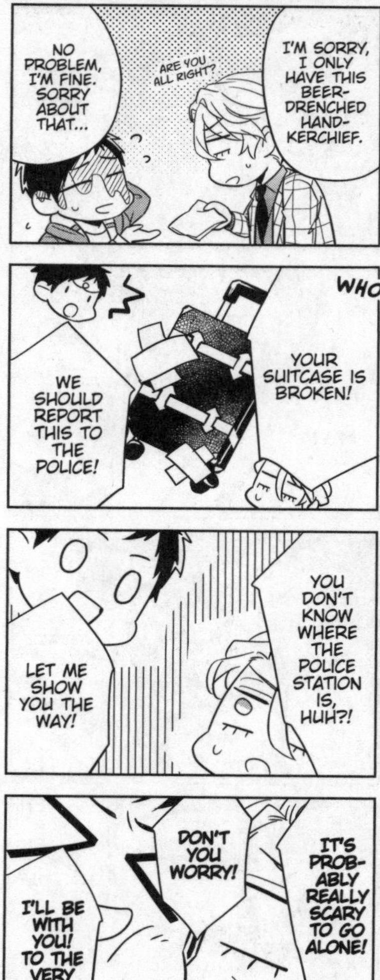
I'M SORRY, I ONLY HAVE THIS BEER-DRENCHED HANDKERCHIEF.
ARE YOU ALL RIGHT?
NO PROBLEM, I'M FINE. SORRY ABOUT THAT...
WHOA!
YOUR SUITCASE IS BROKEN!
WE SHOULD REPORT THIS TO THE POLICE!
YOU DON'T KNOW WHERE THE POLICE STATION IS, HUH?!
LET ME SHOW YOU THE WAY!
IT'S PROBABLY REALLY SCARY TO GO ALONE!
DON'T YOU WORRY!
I'LL BE WITH YOU! TO THE VERY END!

An Overly Thoughtful Man ②

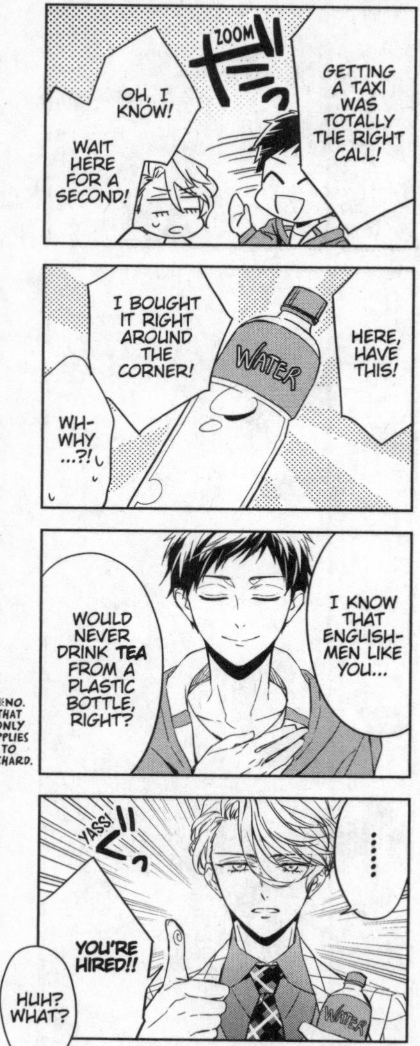
GETTING A TAXI WAS TOTALLY THE RIGHT CALL!
ZOOM
OH, I KNOW!
WAIT HERE FOR A SECOND!
HERE, HAVE THIS!
I BOUGHT IT RIGHT AROUND THE CORNER!
WATER
WH-WHY ...?!
I KNOW THAT ENGLISHMEN LIKE YOU...
WOULD NEVER DRINK TEA FROM A PLASTIC BOTTLE, RIGHT?
......
YASS!
YOU'RE HIRED!!
WATER
HUH? WHAT?

※NO. THAT ONLY APPLIES TO RICHARD.

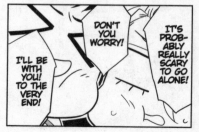

Beef Bun? Pork Bun!

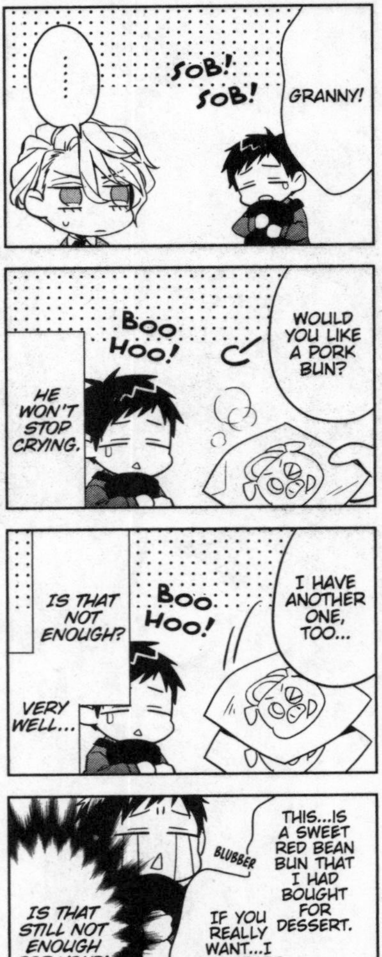
GRANNY!
SOB! SOB!
......
WOULD YOU LIKE A PORK BUN?
BOO HOO!
HE WON'T STOP CRYING.
I HAVE ANOTHER ONE, TOO...
BOO HOO!
IS THAT NOT ENOUGH?
VERY WELL...
THIS...IS A SWEET RED BEAN BUN THAT I HAD BOUGHT FOR DESSERT.
BLUBBER
IF YOU REALLY WANT...I CAN SPARE HALF...FOR YOU...
IS THAT STILL NOT ENOUGH FOR YOU?!
HOW GREEDY!!

Tired of Talking

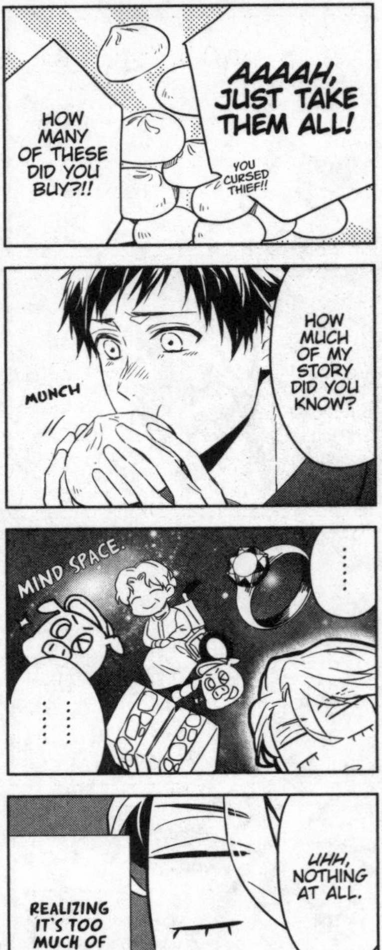
AAAAH, JUST TAKE THEM ALL!
YOU CURSED THIEF!!
HOW MANY OF THESE DID YOU BUY?!!
HOW MUCH OF MY STORY DID YOU KNOW?
MUNCH
......
MIND SPACE.
......
UHH, NOTHING AT ALL.
REALIZING IT'S TOO MUCH OF A PAIN TO EXPLAIN.

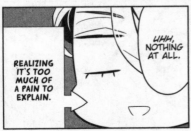

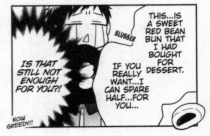

Grounds for Instant Employment

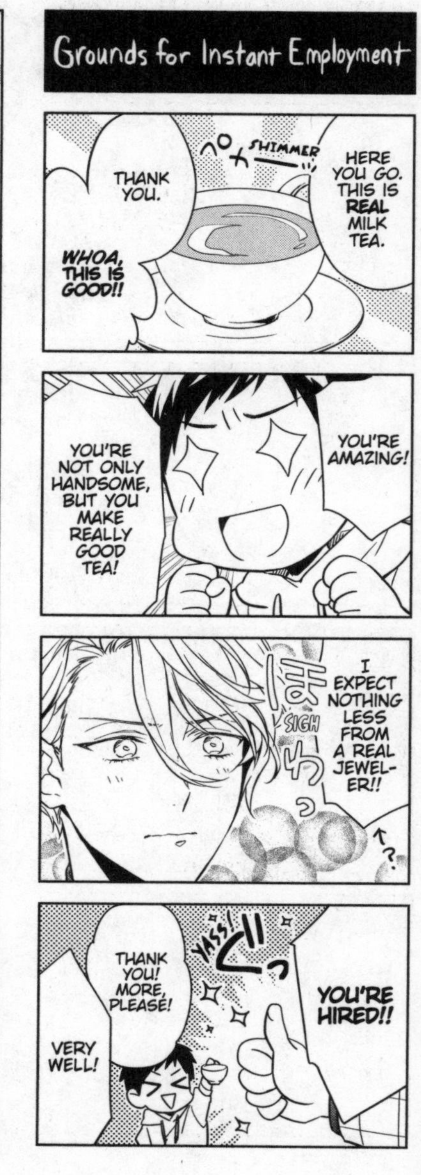
HERE YOU GO. THIS IS REAL MILK TEA.
SHIMMER
THANK YOU.
WHOA, THIS IS GOOD!!
YOU'RE AMAZING!
YOU'RE NOT ONLY HANDSOME, BUT YOU MAKE REALLY GOOD TEA!
I EXPECT NOTHING LESS FROM A REAL JEWELER!!
ほわっ
SIGH
?
YOU'RE HIRED!!
ぐっ
YASS!
THANK YOU! MORE, PLEASE!
VERY WELL!

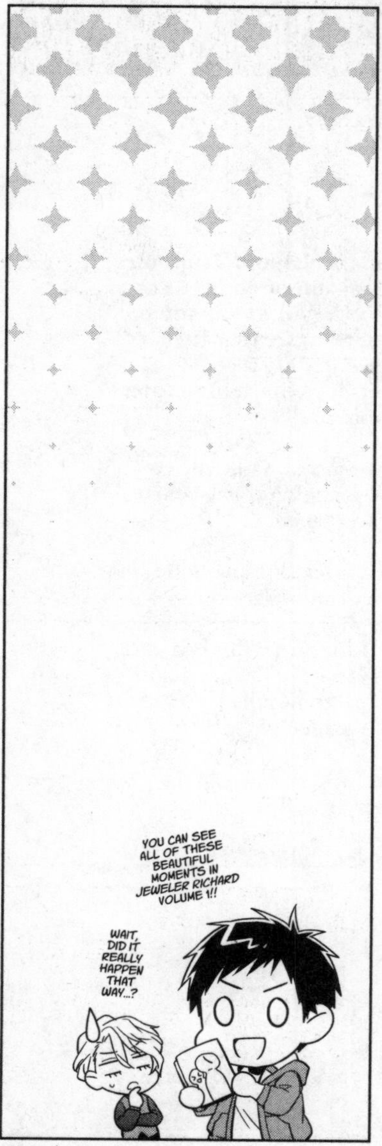
YOU CAN SEE ALL OF THESE BEAUTIFUL MOMENTS IN JEWELER RICHARD VOLUME 1!!
WAIT, DID IT REALLY HAPPEN THAT WAY...?

End

Hello, this is **Nanako Tsujimura**, the original author of *The Case Files of Jeweler Richard*. I am more than thrilled to see that Richard's and Seigi-kun's life together has already been compiled into three manga volumes!

Akatsuki-sensei, thank you so much for bringing this beautiful world into existence.

Just like a river, our characters' experiences and relationship will continue to flow as time goes by. Their relationship will bend and change, and I can't express how happy I feel to be able to watch them as a reader.

I hope all of you take care of yourselves as well.

Nanako Tsujimura

THE CASE FILES
OF
JEWELER
RICHARD

THE CASE FILES
OF
JEWELER
RICHARD

The Case Files of **Jeweler Richard**

Art: Mika Akatsuki Story: Nanako Tsujimura
Character Design: Utako Yukihiro

Volumes 1 and 2 are currently on sale!

MANGA
I
ART BY
Mika Akatsuki
STORY BY
Nanako Tsujimura
CHARACTER DESIGN BY
Utako Yukihiro
THE CASE FILES
OF
JEWELER
RICHARD

MANGA
II
ART BY
Mika
Akatsuki
STORY BY
Nanako
Tsujimura
CHARACTER DESIGN BY
Utako
Yukihiro
THE CASE FILES
OF
JEWELER
RICHARD

Justice of the Pink Sapphire

I'M HOPING YOU CAN APPRAISE IT FOR ME.

Blessings of the Amethyst

WHAT'S WRONG, KID? GIRL PROB-LEMS?

Truth of the Ruby

WOULDN'T BE ASKING THAT IF I WERE A GUY, WOULD YOU?

Recollection of the Diamond

The mysteries that lie hidden in each beautiful, shining, gem-like heart will come to light before your eyes!!

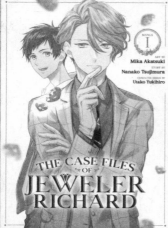

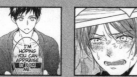

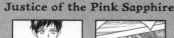

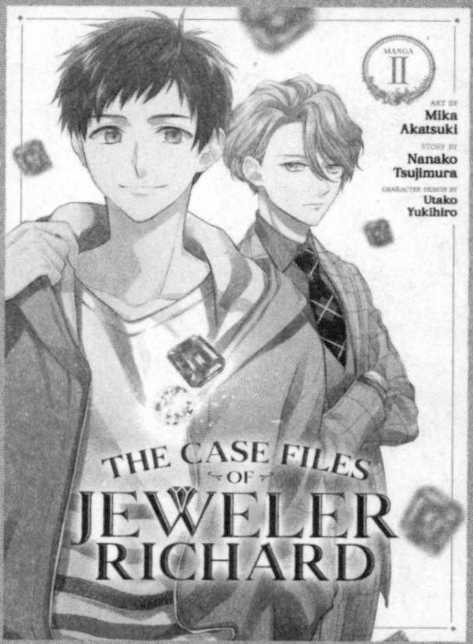

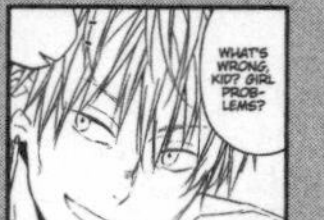

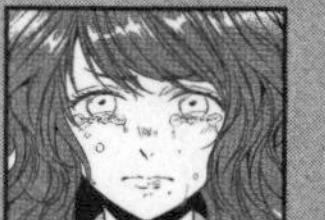

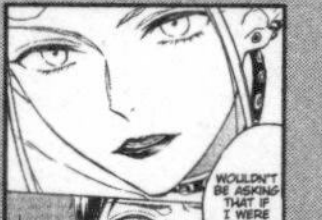

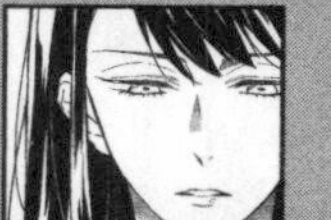

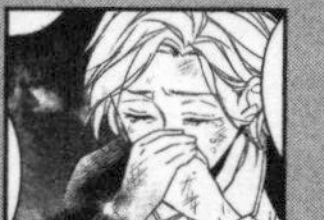

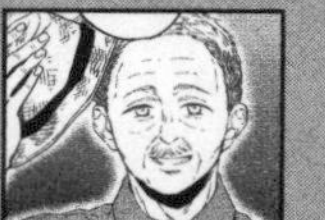

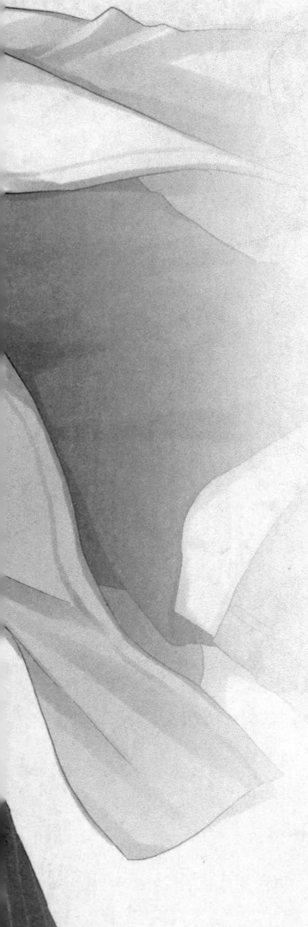

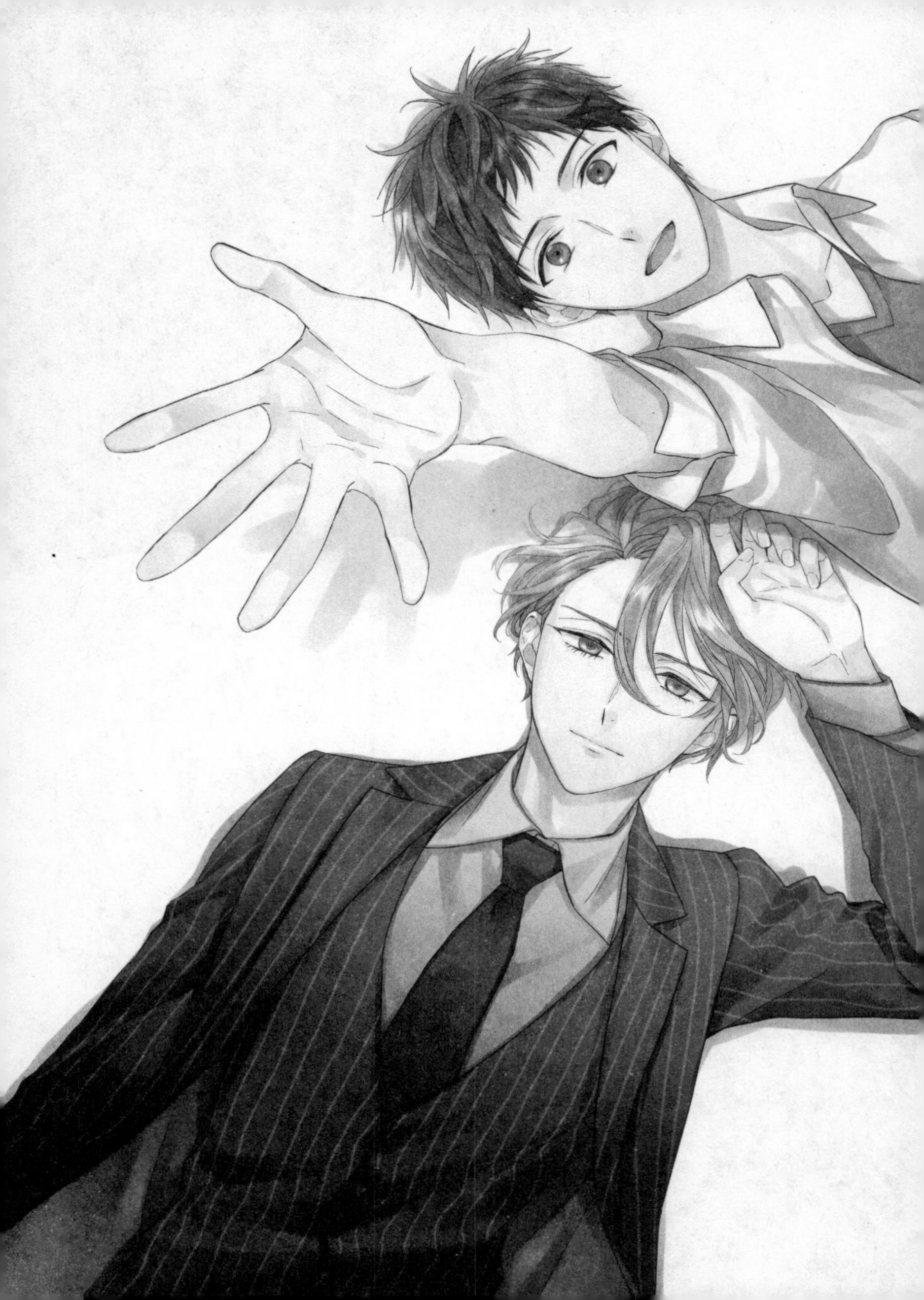

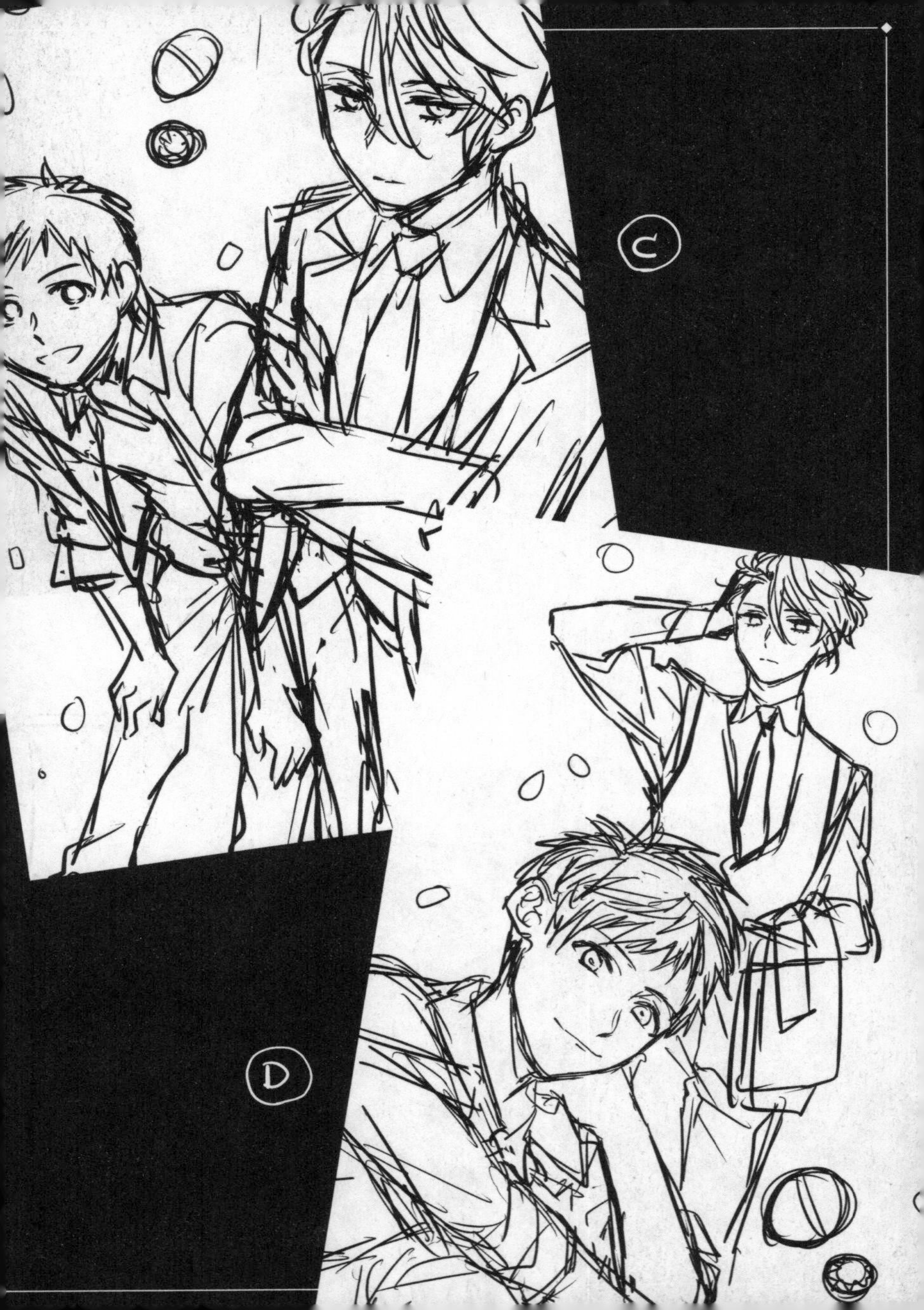
C
D

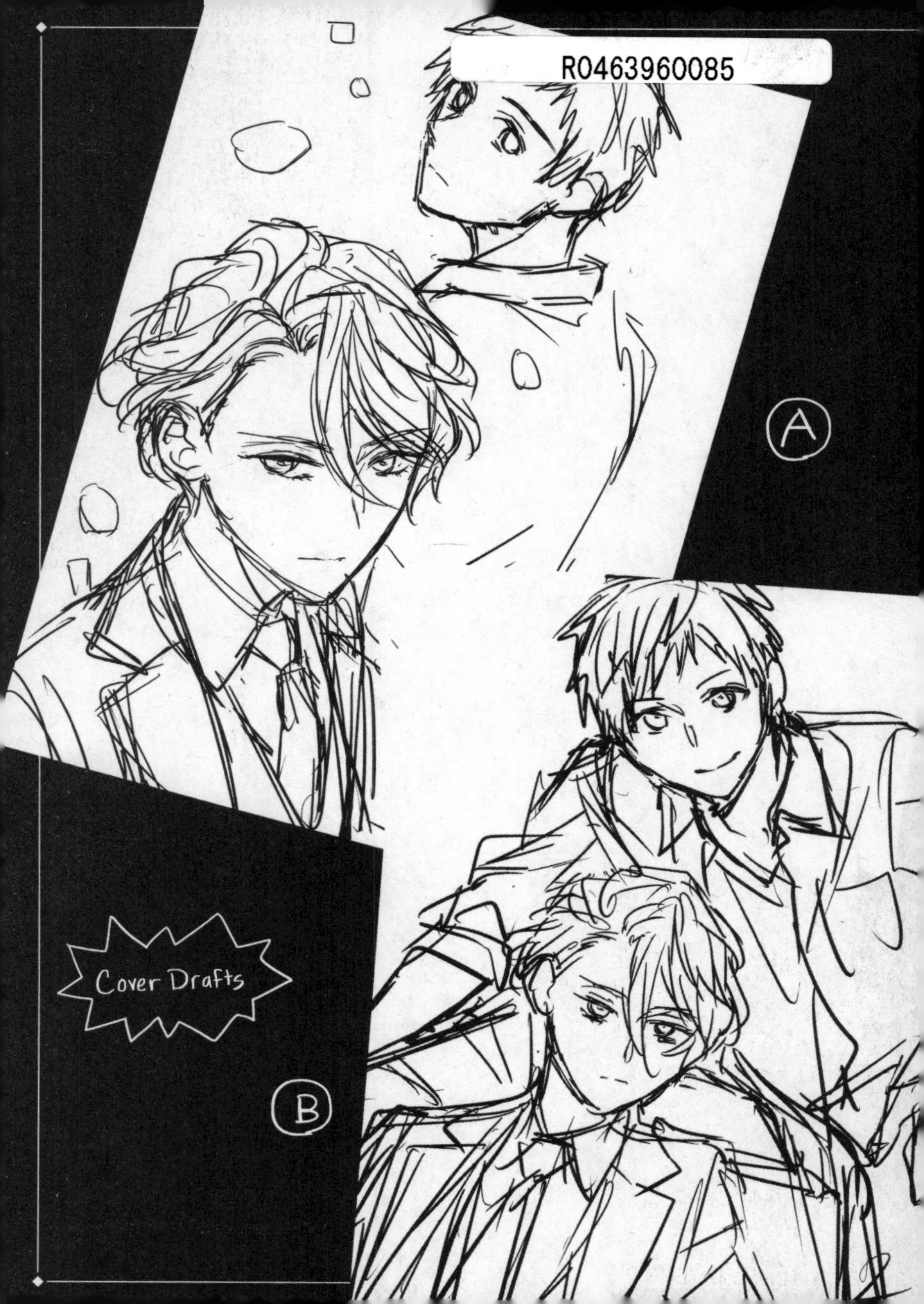
A
Cover Drafts
B

THE CASE FILES OF JEWELER RICHARD

SEVEN SEAS ENTERTAINMENT PRESENTS

The Case Files of Jeweler Richard

Vol. 3

art by MIKA AKATSUKI story by NANAKO TSUJIMURA character design by UTAKO YUKIHIRO

TRANSLATION
Jacqueline Fung

ADAPTATION
Kim Kindya

LETTERING
Danya Shevchenko

COVER DESIGN
H. Qi

PROOFREADER
Kurestin Armada

SENIOR EDITOR
Shanti Whitesides

PRODUCTION MANAGER
Lissa Pattillo

PREPRESS TECHNICIAN
Jules Valera

PRINT MANAGER
Rhiannon Rasmussen-Silverstein

EDITOR-IN-CHIEF
Julie Davis

ASSOCIATE PUBLISHER
Adam Arnold

PUBLISHER
Jason DeAngelis

First published in Japan in 2021 by Ichijinsha Inc., Tokyo.
Publication rights for this English edition arranged through Kodansha Ltd., Tokyo.

Seven Seas press and purchase enquiries can be sent to Marketing Manager Lianne Sentar at press@gomanga.com. Information regarding the distribution and purchase of digital editions is available from Digital Manager CK Russell at digital@gomanga.com.

ISBN: 978-1-63858-617-3
Printed in Canada
First Printing: August 2022
10 9 8 7 6 5 4 3 2 1

READING DIRECTIONS

This book reads from ***right to left***, Japanese style. If this is your first time reading manga, you start reading from the top right panel on each page and take it from there. If you get lost, just follow the numbered diagram here. It may seem backwards at first, but you'll get the hang of it! Have fun!!

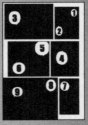

1
2
3
4
5
6
7
8
9